C EDITION

THE HAL LEONARD

REAL JAZZ BOOK

OVER **500** SONGS

HAL LEONARD
REAL
JAZZ
BOOK

ISBN 0-7935-6230-9

HAL•LEONARD®
CORPORATION

7777 W. BLUEMOUND RD. P.O. BOX 13819 MILWAUKEE, WI 53213

For all works contained herein:
Unauthorized copying, arranging, adapting, recording or public performance is an infringement of copyright.
Infringers are liable under the law.

Visit Hal Leonard Online at
www.halleonard.com

THE HAL LEONARD REAL JAZZ BOOK

CONTENTS

17 Adios	47 Blue Flame	92 Cross My Heart
19 Affirmation	53 Blue Prelude	94 Crystal Silence
18 After All	54 The Blue Room	95 Cupcake
22 After the Rain	53 Blue Star	98 Curves Ahead
23 Aftermath (Part II)	52 Blue Train (Blue Trane)	88 Dahomey Dance
22 Agua De Beber (Water to Drink)	55 Blueport	91 Dancing on the Ceiling
20 Aguas De Marco (Waters of March)	54 Blues for Alice	91 Darling, Je Vous Aime Beaucoup
23 Ain't She Sweet	56 Blues for D.P.	96 Dat Dere
24 Air Dancing	57 Blues for Junior (Pyramid)	90 The Dawn of Time
24 Aisha	58 Blues for Rosalinda	226 Days of Wine and Roses
25 Aja	55 Blues in Time	93 Deceptacon
26 Alabama	56 Blues March	100 Detour Ahead
26 Alfie	63 Blues on Time	100 Diminishing
27 Alice in Wonderland	63 Bluish Grey	103 Dindi
28 All Alone	64 Booze Brothers	104 Dippermouth Blues
28 Alone Too Long	59 Born to Be Bad	94 Doctor Jazz
29 And I Think About It All the Time	57 Bossa Antigua	106 Dolphin Dance
30 Anthropology	60 Both Sides of the Coin	102 Dolphin Dreams
30 Antigua	61 Brazil	101 Don't Smoke in Bed
31 April in Paris	62 Breakin' Away	97 Don't Worry 'Bout Me
32 Are You Havin' Any Fun?	58 Broadway	98 Don't You Know I Care (Or Don't You Care to Know)
32 Armando's Rhumba	65 Bullet Train	105 Down Hearted Blues
33 As Long as I Live	64 Buster's Last Stand	106 Down Under
34 Ashes to Ashes	66 Byrd Like	108 Down with Love
34 At Long Last Love	78 C'est Si Bon (It's So Good)	99 Dream a Little Dream of Me
35 Aunt Hagar's Blues	71 Cake Walking Babies from Home	109 Dream Dancing
36 Autumn in New York	66 Call Me Irresponsible	111 Drop Me Off in Harlem
37 Baja Bajo	67 Can't Take You Nowhere	110 East St. Louis Toodle-oo
36 Bark for Barksdale	72 Cannonball	112 Easy Does It
38 Bass Desires	69 Cantelope Island	107 Easy Living
40 Beautiful Love	68 Captain Fingers	112 Easy Rider (I Wonder Where My Easy Rider's Gone)
40 Before You Go	73 Caravan	113 Easy Street
41 Besame Mucho (Kiss Me Much)	72 Careful	109 Eight
42 Bessie's Blues	74 Carolina Shout	114 El Prince
42 The Best Thing for You	76 Cast Your Fate to the Wind	115 Eleven Four
43 Better Luck Next Time	70 Catching the Sun	116 Emancipation Blues
44 Between the Devil and the Deep Blue Sea	73 Cecilia Is Love	117 The End of Innocence
43 Big Nick	77 Chameleon	116 Epistrophy
44 Bijou	80 Change of Season	118 Equinox
45 Bill	77 Change Partners	119 Estate
46 Birk's Works	80 Chasin' the Trane	118 Ev'rything I Love
46 (What Did I Do to Be So) Black and Blue	81 A Child Is Born	120 The Face I Love
47 Black and Tan Fantasy	79 Christina	120 Falling Grace
48 Black Coffee	82 Chromozone	121 Falling in Love
50 Black Market	81 Cocktails for Two	124 Feels So Good
49 Black Orpheus	83 Come Back to Me	122 Filthy McNasty
51 Blackberry Winter	84 Con Alma	121 First Trip
52 Blame It on My Youth	84 Conception	123 500 Miles High
45 A Blossom Fell	85 Continental Blues	125 Flanagan
	89 Copenhagen	123 (Meet) The Flintstones
	85 Cousin Mary	126 Fly with the Wind
	86 The Crave	126 The Folks Who Live on the Hill
	89 Crazyology	
	90 The Creole Love Call	

127	For Heaven's Sake	172	I'm All Smiles	213	Like a Lover (O Cantador)
128	Forever in Love	175	I'm Gonna Go Fishin'	202	Lines and Spaces
124	Four on Six	173	I'm Just a Lucky So and So	214	Listen Here
128	Freckle Face	174	I'm Yours	216	Little Shoes
129	Freedom Jazz Dance	187	I've Found a New Baby (I Found a New Baby)	217	Little Sunflower
130	Freetime			218	Little Waltz
131	Frenesi	189	I've Got My Love to Keep Me Warm	203	Little White Lies
132	Friends			200	Lively Up Yourself
132	Full House	190	I've Got the World on a String	209	Livin'
133	Georgia on My Mind	165	If I Should Lose You	210	Lonely Girl
134	Gettin' Over the Blues	170	If We Meet Again, Part One	204	Look to the Sky
130	Giant Steps	169	If You Go	203	Love Is Just Around the Corner
136	Girl Talk	170	If You Never Come to Me (Inutil paisagem)	205	Love Is the Sweetest Thing
136	Glad to Be Unhappy			204	Love Letters
135	Godchild	175	Impressions	217	Love Lies
138	Going Home	176	In a Sentimental Mood	206	Love Me or Leave Me
139	Good Morning Heartache	176	In Love in Vain	219	Love You Madly
137	Good-Bye	177	In the Cool, Cool, Cool of the Evening	205	A Lovely Way to Spend an Evening
140	Gravy Waltz			206	Lover
141	Green Eyes (Aquellos Ojos Verdes)	177	In the Land of Ephesus	246	Lullaby of Birdland
140	Greens	178	In the Wee Small Hours of the Morning	218	Lydia
142	Growing			242	Mack the Knife
142	Guess I'll Hang My Tears out to Dry	178	In Walked Bud	228	Maiden Voyage
144	Happy Hunting Horn	179	Inside	221	Make a List (Make a Wish)
143	Happy with the Blues	180	Inside Out	220	Make Believe
144	The Hawk Talks	179	The Intrepid Fox	220	Makin' Whoopee!
146	Heebie Jeebies	180	Invitation	232	Mambo a La Savoy
145	Helen's Song	182	Is It You?	236	Mandy Make Up Your Mind
146	Here's to My Lady	183	Isn't It Romantic?	234	Manoir De Mes Reves (Django's Castle)
148	Here's to Your Illusions	181	Israel		
147	Hideaway	184	It Could Happen to You	221	Manteca
148	Honest I Do	181	It Don't Mean a Thing (If It Ain't Got That Swing)	223	Maputo
150	Hot Toddy			233	Mas Que Nada
149	How About Me?	185	It Only Happens When I Dance with You	229	(I'm Afraid) The Masquerade Is Over
150	How Are Things in Glocca Morra				
151	How Deep Is the Ocean (How High Is the Sky)	184	It's a Lovely Day Today	222	Me and My Baby
		185	It's Easy to Remember	235	Mimosa
152	How My Heart Sings	186	It's You	219	Mission: Impossible Theme
152	The Hucklebuck	186	It's You or No One	231	Moment's Notice
153	A Hundred Years from Today	188	Jazzmania	222	Mona Lisa
154	Hypnosis	191	Jitterbug Waltz	240	The Mooch
154	I Ain't Got Nothin' but the Blues	190	Josie and Rosie	225	Mood Indigo
156	I Am in Love	192	July	244	Moon Over Miami
155	I Can't Believe That You're in Love with Me	194	June Bug	241	Moon River
		195	June in January	244	Moonlight Becomes You
158	I Didn't Know About You	191	Just a Gigolo	245	(There Ought to Be A) Moonlight Saving Time
159	I Get Along Without You Very Well (Except Sometimes)	194	Just One More Chance		
		195	Just the Way We Planned It	243	More I Cannot Wish You
157	I Got It Bad and That Ain't Good	196	Keepin' out of Mischief Now	230	Mornin'
160	I Got You (I Feel Good)	197	Kogun	246	Morning Dance
161	I Gotta Right to Sing the Blues	212	La Fiesta	224	Morocco
158	I Hear Music	210	Lady Bird	248	Most Gentlemen Don't Like Love
162	I Keep Going Back to Joe's	196	Lady of the Evening	249	Mountain Greenery
162	I Left This Space for You	197	Lady Sings the Blues	226	Mr. Big Falls His J.G. Hand
160	I Let a Song Go out of My Heart	198	The Lady's in Love with You	228	Mr. Gone
163	I Mean You	211	Lament	238	Mr. Jelly-Lord
164	I Remember Bird	199	Last Night When We Were Young	237	Mr. Lucky
164	I Remember You	208	Last Resort	239	Mr. Wonderful
165	I Thought About You	208	Late Lament	227	My Attorney Bernie
166	I Told Ya I Love Ya Now Get Out	234	Laura	247	My Baby Just Cares for Me
167	I Watched Her Walk Away	211	Laurie	250	My Girl
168	I Wish I Were in Love Again	198	Lazy	248	My Heart Stood Still
168	I Wished on the Moon	214	Lazy River	252	My Ideal
171	I'll Build a Stairway to Paradise	215	Lemon Drop	251	My Old Flame
172	I'll Close My Eyes	201	Let's Face the Music and Dance	252	My Silent Love
174	I'm a Dreamer Aren't We All	199	Let's Get Lost	253	Naima (Niema)
171	I'm a Fool to Want You	207	Ligia	253	Nature Boy

Page	Title
255	Nearly
254	The Nearness of You
255	Never Let Me Go
256	New Orleans Blues
258	The Next Time It Happens
260	Nice Pants
260	The Night Has a Thousand Eyes
259	Night Train
261	Nobody Knows You When You're Down and Out
262	Nobody's Heart
262	Norwegian Wood (This Bird Has Flown)
263	Now It Can Be Told
264	Nuages
264	O Morro Nao Tem Vez (Favela) (Somewhere in the Hills)
265	Off Minor
265	On Broadway
268	On Green Dolphin Street
268	On the Border
266	Once I Loved (Amor Em Paz) (Love in Peace)
266	One Finger Snap
267	One for My Baby (And One More for the Road)
269	The One I Love (Belongs to Somebody Else)
270	Original Rays
271	Out of Nowhere
271	Parking Lot Blues
270	Passion Dance
272	Passion Flower
272	Peace
273	Penthouse Serenade
274	People in Me
275	Perfidia
276	Peri's Scope
276	Phoebe's Samba
277	The Place to Be
278	Please
279	Please Send Me Someone to Love
282	Poor Butterfly
280	Potato Head Blues
282	Prelude to a Kiss
284	Pretend
285	P.S. I Love You
281	Pure Imagination
283	Purple Orchids
286	The Rainbow Connection
287	Re: Person I Knew
287	Red Clay
288	A Remark You Made
290	Remember
289	Remind Me
290	Resemblance
291	Ridin' High
292	Rifftide
294	Right as the Rain
294	Ring Dem Bells
293	Ritmo De La Noche
295	Riverboat Shuffle
298	Rocker (Rock Salt)
296	Rockin' in Rhythm
297	St. Louis Blues
298	Samba Cantina
299	Say It Isn't So
300	Searching, Finding
302	Seems Like Old Times
300	Segment
301	Senor Carlos
303	Senor Mouse
302	Serengeti Walk (Slippin' in the Back Door)
305	The Shadow of Your Smile
304	Shaker Song
306	A Ship Without a Sail
307	Silhouette
306	Silver Hollow
308	Simple Samba
310	The Single Petal of a Rose
311	Sippin' at Bells
312	Slaughter on Tenth Avenue
309	A Sleepin' Bee
314	Smile from a Stranger
311	So Easy
313	So in Love
315	So You Say
316	Soft Lights and Sweet Music
316	Softly as in a Morning Sunrise
318	Solea
317	Some Skunk Funk
318	Somebody Loves Me
326	Someone to Light Up My Life (Se Todos Fossem Iguais a Voce)
319	Something I Dreamed Last Night
320	Somewhere Along the Way
320	Song for Lorraine
322	Song for Strayhorn
322	Song from M*A*S*H (Suicide Is Painless)
321	The Song Is Ended (But the Melody Lingers On)
323	Songbird
324	Sophisticated Lady
324	Stablemates
325	Stairway to the Stars
328	Star Dust
327	Stardreams
327	Stella by Starlight
329	Steppin' Out with My Baby
331	Stereophonic
330	Still Warm
330	Stolen Moments
331	Story of My Father
332	Straight Life
332	Straphangin'
333	Strollin'
334	Suddenly It's Spring
334	Sun
336	Sunday in New York
336	Surf Ride
335	Sway (Quien Sera)
338	Swing 41
337	Take a Walk
340	Take Five
340	Take Ten
341	Tanga
338	Tangerine
339	Teach Me Tonight
342	Tell Me a Bedtime Story
344	Thanks for the Memory
345	That Old Black Magic
346	That's Right
342	There's a Mingus Amonk Us
343	Things Ain't What They Used to Be
347	Things to Come
347	The Third Plane
348	This Is All I Ask (Beautiful Girls Walk a Little Slower)
350	This Masquerade
349	This Year's Kisses
349	Three Little Words
351	Till the Clouds Roll By
350	Time Was
352	To Each His Own
352	Toku-Do
353	Too Close for Comfort
358	Too Late Now
353	Topsy
354	Tourist in Paradise
356	Triste
364	Two Degrees East, Three Degrees West
355	Two of a Mind
356	Ultrafox
359	Unless It's You
357	The Very Thought of You
358	Visa
357	Walk Don't Run
360	Waltz New
359	Watermelon Man
360	Wave
362	We Three Blues
361	We'll Be Together Again
362	Wendy
363	West Coast Blues
366	What Do You See
364	What Is There to Say
366	What Will I Tell My Heart
370	What'll I Do?
365	When Sunny Gets Blue
367	When the Sun Comes Out
369	(There'll Be Bluebirds Over) The White Cliffs of Dover
368	Wholey Earth
369	Why Don't You Do Right (Get Me Some Money, Too!)
368	Why Was I Born?
370	The Wind
371	Windows
372	Wintersong
372	Without a Song
375	Wives and Lovers (Hey, Little Girl)
376	Woodyn' You
378	You Are Too Beautiful
379	You Brought a New Kind of Love to Me
378	You Couldn't Be Cuter
380	You Don't Know What Love Is
257	You Gotta Pay the Band
381	You Leave Me Breathless
382	You Took Advantage of Me
373	You're Blase
377	You're Driving Me Crazy! (What Did I Do?)
374	You're Everything
377	You're Mine You
376	You're Nearer
382	You've Changed
380	You've Made Me So Very Happy

COMPOSER/LYRICIST INDEX

Ewart G. Abner, Jr.
148 Honest I Do

Kurt Adams
320 Somewhere Along the Way

Harold Adamson
205 A Lovely Way to Spend an Evening

Walter Afanasieff
138 Going Home

Milton Ager
23 Ain't She Sweet

Eden Ahbez
253 Nature Boy

Toshiko Akiyoshi
197 Kogun

Roy Alfred
152 The Hucklebuck

Steve Allen
140 Gravy Waltz

Mike Altman
322 Song from M*A*S*H (Suicide Is Painless)

Morgan Ames
359 Unless It's You

Fabian Andree
99 Dream a Little Dream of Me

Harold Arlen
33 As Long as I Live
44 Between the Devil and the Deep Blue Sea
108 Down with Love
143 Happy with the Blues
161 I Gotta Right to Sing the Blues
190 I've Got the World on a String
199 Last Night When We Were Young
267 One for My Baby (And One More for the Road)
294 Right as the Rain
309 A Sleepin' Bee
345 That Old Black Magic
367 When the Sun Comes Out

Louis Armstrong
280 Potato Head Blues

Sidney Arodin
214 Lazy River

Kenneth L. Ascher
286 The Rainbow Connection

Boyd Atkins
146 Heebie Jeebies

Lovie Austin
105 Down Hearted Blues

Burt Bacharach
26 Alfie
375 Wives and Lovers (Hey, Little Girl)

Joseph Barbera
123 (Meet) The Flintstones

Howard Barnes
45 A Blossom Fell

Ary Barroso
61 Brazil

Edgar Battle
353 Topsy

Jay Beckenstein
70 Catching the Sun
246 Morning Dance
304 Shaker Song
320 Song for Lorraine

Walter Becker
25 Aja

Louis Bellson
144 The Hawk Talks

Jorge Ben
233 Mas Que Nada

George Benson
235 Mimosa

Alan Bergman
213 Like a Lover (O Cantador)

Marilyn Bergman
213 Like a Lover (O Cantador)

Irving Berlin
28 All Alone
42 The Best Thing for You
43 Better Luck Next Time
77 Change Partners
149 How About Me?
151 How Deep Is the Ocean (How High Is the Sky)
189 I've Got My Love to Keep Me Warm
185 It Only Happens When I Dance with You
184 It's a Lovely Day Today
196 Lady of the Evening
198 Lazy
201 Let's Face the Music and Dance
263 Now It Can Be Told
290 Remember
299 Say It Isn't So
316 Soft Lights and Sweet Music
321 The Song Is Ended (But the Melody Lingers On)
329 Steppin' Out with My Baby
349 This Year's Kisses
370 What'll I Do?

Buddy Bernier
260 The Night Has a Thousand Eyes

Henri Betti
78 C'est Si Bon (It's So Good)

Albany Bigard
225 Mood Indigo

Joe Bishop
47 Blue Flame
53 Blue Prelude

Marc Blitzstein
242 Mack the Knife

Rube Bloom
97 Don't Worry 'Bout Me
146 Here's to My Lady

Jerry Bock
239 Mr. Wonderful
353 Too Close for Comfort

Luiz Bonfa
49 Black Orpheus

Jerry Brainin
260 The Night Has a Thousand Eyes

Julius Brammer
191 Just a Gigolo

Michael Brecker
60 Both Sides of the Coin
270 Original Rays
332 Straphangin'
337 Take a Walk

Randy Brecker
180 Inside Out
317 Some Skunk Funk
342 There's a Mingus Amonk Us

Elise Bretton
127 For Heaven's Sake

Leslie Bricusse
281 Pure Imagination

Bruno Brighetti
119 Estate

Harry Brooks
46 (What Did I Do to Be So) Black and Blue

Shelton Brooks
112 Easy Rider (I Wonder Where My Easy Rider's Gone)

James Brown
160 I Got You (I Feel Good)

Lew Brown
174 I'm a Dreamer Aren't We All

Oscar Brown, Jr.
96 Dat Dere

Ray Brown
57 Blues for Junior (Pyramid)
140 Gravy Waltz
271 Parking Lot Blues

J. Tim Brymn
35 Aunt Hagar's Blues

Joe Burke
244 Moon Over Miami

Johnny Burke
184 It Could Happen to You
244 Moonlight Becomes You
334 Suddenly It's Spring

Sonny Burke
48 Black Coffee
327 Stardreams

Ralph Burns
44 Bijou

Nat Burton
369 (There'll Be Bluebirds Over) The White Cliffs of Dover

Val Burton
273 Penthouse Serenade

Bill Byrd
58 Broadway

George Cables
145 Helen's Song

Irving Caesar
191 Just a Gigolo

Sammy Cahn
66 Call Me Irresponsible
142 Guess I'll Hang My Tears out to Dry
186 It's You or No One
339 Teach Me Tonight

Tom Canning
62 Breakin' Away

Truman Capote
309 A Sleepin' Bee

Bill Carey
382 You've Changed

John Carisi
181 Israel

Hoagy Carmichael
133 Georgia on My Mind
159 I Get Along Without You Very Well (Except Sometimes)
177 In the Cool, Cool, Cool of the Evening
214 Lazy River
254 The Nearness of You
295 Riverboat Shuffle
328 Star Dust

Harry Carney
296 Rockin' in Rhythm

Lou Carter
100 Detour Ahead
166 I Told Ya I Love Ya Now Get Out

Ron Carter
56 Blues for D.P.
109 Eight
121 First Trip
208 Last Resort
218 Little Waltz
255 Nearly
347 The Third Plane

Leonello Casucci
191 Just a Gigolo

Dory Caymmi
213 Like a Lover (O Cantador)

Bill Champlin
182 Is It You?

Newell Chase
252 My Ideal

Billy Childs
117 The End of Innocence
125 Flanagan
188 Jazzmania

Kenny Clark
116 Epistrophy

Grant Clarke
236 Mandy Make Up Your Mind

Al Cohen
67 Can't Take You Nowhere

John Coltrane
22 After the Rain
26 Alabama
42 Bessie's Blues
43 Big Nick
52 Blue Train (Blue Trane)
80 Chasin' the Trane
85 Cousin Mary
88 Dahomey Dance
118 Equinox
130 Giant Steps
175 Impressions
231 Moment's Notice
253 Naima (Niema)

Leo Corday
47 Blue Flame

Chick Corea
32 Armando's Rhumba
37 Baja Bajo
94 Crystal Silence
123 500 Miles High
132 Friends
212 La Fiesta
303 Senor Mouse
371 Windows
374 You're Everything

Harold Cornelius
45 A Blossom Fell

Sam Coslow
81 Cocktails for Two
194 Just One More Chance
251 My Old Flame

Jimmie Cox
261 Nobody Knows You When You're Down and Out

Hoyt Curtin
123 (Meet) The Flintstones

Tadd Dameron
210 Lady Bird
311 So Easy

Hal David
26 Alfie
375 Wives and Lovers (Hey, Little Girl)

Mack David
98 Don't You Know I Care
 (Or Don't You Care to Know)
173 I'm Just a Lucky So and So

Charlie Davis
89 Copenhagen

Miles Davis
311 Sippin' at Bells

Sylvia Dee
327 Stardreams

Jack DeJohnette
218 Lydia
306 Silver Hollow

Vinicius de Moraes
22 Agua De Beber (Water to Drink)
264 O Morro Nao Tem Vez (Favela)
 (Somewhere in the Hills)
266 Once I Loved (Amor Em Paz)
 (Love in Peace)
326 Someone to Light Up My Life
 (Se Todos Fossem Iguais a Voce)

Aloysio de Oliveira
103 Dindi
170 If You Never Come to Me
 (Inutil paisagem)

Gene DePaul
339 Teach Me Tonight
380 You Don't Know What Love Is

Paul Desmond
55 Blues in Time
57 Bossa Antigua
114 El Prince
115 Eleven Four
208 Late Lament
298 Samba Cantina
340 Take Five
340 Take Ten
355 Two of a Mind
362 Wendy
372 Wintersong

B.G. DeSylva
171 I'll Build a Stairway to Paradise
174 I'm a Dreamer Aren't We All
318 Somebody Loves Me

Ray Dewey
29 And I Think About It All the Time

Al di Meola
170 If We Meet Again, Part One
192 July
283 Purple Orchids
293 Ritmo De La Noche
314 Smile from a Stranger

Alberto Dominguez
131 Frenesi
275 Perfidia

Walter Donaldson
203 Little White Lies
206 Love Me or Leave Me
220 Makin' Whoopee!
247 My Baby Just Cares for Me
377 You're Driving Me Crazy!
 (What Did I Do?)

Lew Douglas
284 Pretend

Ervin Drake
139 Good Morning Heartache

Vernon Duke
31 April in Paris
36 Autumn in New York
364 What Is There to Say

Eddie Durham
353 Topsy

Sherman Edwards
127 For Heaven's Sake

Edward Eliscu
372 Without a Song

Duke Ellington
47 Black and Tan Fantasy
73 Caravan
90 The Creole Love Call
98 Don't You Know I Care
 (Or Don't You Care to Know)
111 Drop Me Off in Harlem
110 East St. Louis Toodle-oo
154 I Ain't Got Nothin' but the Blues
158 I Didn't Know About You
157 I Got It Bad and That Ain't Good
160 I Let a Song Go out of My Heart
175 I'm Gonna Go Fishin'
173 I'm Just a Lucky So and So
176 In a Sentimental Mood
181 It Don't Mean a Thing
 (If It Ain't Got That Swing)
219 Love You Madly
240 The Mooch
225 Mood Indigo

282 Prelude to a Kiss
294 Ring Dem Bells
296 Rockin' in Rhythm
310 The Single Petal of a Rose
324 Sophisticated Lady

Mercer Ellington
343 Things Ain't What They Used to Be

Herb Ellis
100 Detour Ahead
166 I Told Ya I Love Ya Now Get Out

Michel Emer
169 If You Go

Peter Erskine
38 Bass Desires

Kevin Eubanks
23 Aftermath (Part II)
179 Inside
209 Livin'
334 Sun

Bill Evans
211 Laurie
276 Peri's Scope
287 Re: Person I Knew

Gil Evans
64 Buster's Last Stand
318 Solea

Ray Evans
210 Lonely Girl
222 Mona Lisa
237 Mr. Lucky
255 Never Let Me Go
352 To Each His Own

Donald Fagen
25 Aja

Sammy Fain
27 Alice in Wonderland
32 Are You Havin' Any Fun?
148 Here's to Your Illusions
319 Something I Dreamed Last Night
379 You Brought a New Kind of
 Love to Me

Art Farmer
55 Blueport

Leonard Feather
164 I Remember Bird

Victor Feldman
121 Falling in Love

Jose Feliciano
19 Affirmation

Dorothy Fields
28 Alone Too Long
289 Remind Me
378 You Couldn't Be Cuter

Carl Fischer
361 We'll Be Together Again
382 You've Changed

Dan Fisher
139 Good Morning Heartache

Marvin Fisher
162 I Keep Going Back to Joe's
365 When Sunny Gets Blue

Ralph Flanagan
150 Hot Toddy

Jimmy Forrest
259 Night Train

Frank Foster
64 Booze Brothers
73 Cecilia Is Love

David Foster
230 Mornin'

Ralph Freed
217 Love Lies
381 You Leave Me Breathless

Russ Freeman
98 Curves Ahead
167 I Watched Her Walk Away
224 Morocco
354 Tourist in Paradise

Russell Freeman
370 The Wind

John Frigo
100 Detour Ahead
166 I Told Ya I Love Ya Now Get Out

Dave Frishberg
67 Can't Take You Nowhere
214 Listen Here
227 My Attorney Bernie

Walter "Gil" Fuller
232 Mambo a La Savoy
221 Manteca
347 Things to Come

Kenny G
128 Forever in Love
138 Going Home
307 Silhouette
323 Songbird

Sammy Gallop
320 Somewhere Along the Way

Clarence Gaskill
155 I Can't Believe That You're in Love with Me

Lewis E. Gensler
203 Love Is Just Around the Corner

Don George
154 I Ain't Got Nothin' but the Blues

George Gershwin
171 I'll Build a Stairway to Paradise
318 Somebody Loves Me

Ira Gershwin
171 I'll Build a Stairway to Paradise

Andy Gibson
152 The Hucklebuck

Ray Gilbert
103 Dindi
120 The Face I Love
170 If You Never Come to Me (Inutil paisagem)
266 Once I Loved (Amor Em Paz) (Love in Peace)
120 The Face I Love

Dizzy Gillespie
30 Anthropology
46 Birk's Works
84 Con Alma
106 Down Under
221 Manteca
341 Tanga
347 Things to Come
376 Woodyn' You

Haven Gillespie
40 Beautiful Love

Norman Gimbel
22 Agua De Beber (Water to Drink)
335 Sway (Quien Sera)

Jerry Gladstone
370 The Wind

John L. Golden
282 Poor Butterfly

Benny Golson
56 Blues March
324 Stablemates

Luciano Pozo Gonzales
221 Manteca

Irving Gordon
282 Prelude to a Kiss
366 What Will I Tell My Heart

Berry Gordy
380 You've Made Me So Very Happy

Stuart Gorrell
133 Georgia on My Mind

Steve Graham
292 Rifftide

Jay Graydon
62 Breakin' Away
230 Mornin'

Benny Green
95 Cupcake
140 Greens
260 Nice Pants
276 Phoebe's Samba
277 The Place to Be
346 That's Right

Johnny Green
174 I'm Yours
271 Out of Nowhere
377 You're Mine You

Frank Grillo (Machito)
232 Mambo a La Savoy

Don Grolnick
270 Original Rays

Dave Grusin
302 Serengeti Walk (Slippin' in the Back Door)

Vince Guaraldi
76 Cast Your Fate to the Wind

Hal Hackady
134 Gettin' Over the Blues

James S. Hall
72 Careful
308 Simple Samba
360 Waltz New

Ord Hamilton
373 You're Blase

Oscar Hammerstein II
45 Bill
126 The Folks Who Live on the Hill
220 Make Believe
258 The Next Time It Happens
316 Softly as in a Morning Sunrise
368 Why Was I Born?

Herbie Hancock
69 Cantelope Island
77 Chameleon
106 Dolphin Dance
228 Maiden Voyage
266 One Finger Snap
342 Tell Me a Bedtime Story
359 Watermelon Man

W.C. Handy
35 Aunt Hagar's Blues
297 St. Louis Blues

William Hanna
123 (Meet) The Flintstones

E.Y. Harburg
31 April in Paris
108 Down with Love
148 Here's to Your Illusions
150 How Are Things in Glocca Morra
174 I'm Yours
199 Last Night When We Were Young
294 Right as the Rain
364 What Is There to Say

Bennie Harris
89 Crazyology

Eddie Harris
129 Freedom Jazz Dance

Lorenz Hart
54 The Blue Room
91 Dancing on the Ceiling
136 Glad to Be Unhappy
144 Happy Hunting Horn
168 I Wish I Were in Love Again
183 Isn't It Romantic?
185 It's Easy to Remember
206 Lover
249 Mountain Greenery
248 My Heart Stood Still
262 Nobody's Heart
306 A Ship Without a Sail
378 You Are Too Beautiful
382 You Took Advantage of Me
376 You're Nearer

Coleman Hawkins
163 I Mean You
292 Rifftide

Neal Hefti
136 Girl Talk
210 Lonely Girl

Ray Henderson
174 I'm a Dreamer Aren't We All

Herb Hendler
150 Hot Toddy

Joel Herron
171 I'm a Fool to Want You

Edward Heyman
52 Blame It on My Youth
53 Blue Star
204 Love Letters
252 My Silent Love
271 Out of Nowhere
377 You're Mine You

Irene Higginbotham
139 Good Morning Heartache

Bob Hilliard
27 Alice in Wonderland
178 In the Wee Small Hours of the Morning

Billie Holiday
197 Lady Sings the Blues

Frederick K. Hollander
381 You Leave Me Breathless

Patrice Holloway
380 You've Made Me So Very Happy

Brenda Holloway
380 You've Made Me So Very Happy

Larry Holofcener
239 Mr. Wonderful
353 Too Close for Comfort

Andre Hornez
78 C'est Si Bon (It's So Good)

Freddie Hubbard
66 Byrd Like
179 The Intrepid Fox
217 Little Sunflower
287 Red Clay

Raymond Hubbell
282 Poor Butterfly

Alberta Hunter
105 Down Hearted Blues

Paul Jackson
77 Chameleon

Al Jarreau
62 Breakin' Away
230 Mornin'

Will Jason
273 Penthouse Serenade

Gordon Jenkins
53 Blue Prelude
137 Good-Bye
285 P.S. I Love You
348 This Is All I Ask (Beautiful Girls Walk a Little Slower)

Antonio Carlos Jobim
22 Agua De Beber (Water to Drink)
20 Aguas De Marco (Waters of March)
30 Antigua
103 Dindi
170 If You Never Come to Me (Inutil paisagem)
207 Ligia
204 Look to the Sky
264 O Morro Nao Tem Vez (Favela) (Somewhere in the Hills)
266 Once I Loved (Amor Em Paz) (Love in Peace)
326 Someone to Light Up My Life (Se Todos Fossem Iguais a Voce)
356 Triste
360 Wave

Dominic John
45 A Blossom Fell

James P. Johnson
74 Carolina Shout

J.J. Johnson
211 Lament

Louie Johnson
302 Serengeti Walk (Slippin' in the Back Door)

Arthur Johnston
81 Cocktails for Two
194 Just One More Chance
236 Mandy Make Up Your Mind
251 My Old Flame

Thad Jones
63 Bluish Grey
81 A Child Is Born

Alan Rankin Jones
113 Easy Street

Isham Jones
269 The One I Love (Belongs to Somebody Else)

Irving Kahal
245 (There Ought to Be A) Moonlight Saving Time
379 You Brought a New Kind of Love to Me

Norman "Tiny" Kahn
67 Can't Take You Nowhere

Gus Kahn
99 Dream a Little Dream of Me
206 Love Me or Leave Me
220 Makin' Whoopee!
247 My Baby Just Cares for Me
269 The One I Love (Belongs to Somebody Else)

Bert Kalmar
349 Three Little Words

Bronislau Kaper
180 Invitation
268 On Green Dolphin Street

Buddy Kaye
172 I'll Close My Eyes

Nick Kenny
111 Drop Me Off in Harlem

Walter Kent
369 (There'll Be Bluebirds Over) The White Cliffs of Dover

Jerome Kern
45 Bill
126 The Folks Who Live on the Hill
176 In Love in Vain
220 Make Believe
289 Remind Me
351 Till the Clouds Roll By
368 Why Was I Born?
378 You Couldn't Be Cuter

Wayne King
40 Beautiful Love

Ted Koehler
33 As Long as I Live
44 Between the Devil and the Deep Blue Sea
97 Don't Worry 'Bout Me
161 I Gotta Right to Sing the Blues
190 I've Got the World on a String
367 When the Sun Comes Out

Eli Konikoff
130 Freetime

Manny Kurtz
176 In a Sentimental Mood

Frankie Laine
361 We'll Be Together Again

Burton Lane
83 Come Back to Me
150 How Are Things in Glocca Morra
158 I Hear Music
198 The Lady's in Love with You
358 Too Late Now

Jacques Larue
264 Nuages

Frank LaVere
284 Pretend

Jack Lawrence
366 What Will I Tell My Heart

Bob Leatherbarrow
195 Just the Way We Planned It

Peggy Lee
143 Happy with the Blues
175 I'm Gonna Go Fishin'

Gene Lees
326 Someone to Light Up My Life (Se Todos Fossem Iguais a Voce)

Jerry Leiber
265 On Broadway

John Lennon
262 Norwegian Wood (This Bird Has Flown)

Michael Leonard
172 I'm All Smiles

Alan Jay Lerner
83 Come Back to Me
358 Too Late Now

Edgar Leslie
244 Moon Over Miami

Oscar Levant
52 Blame It on My Youth

John Lewis
364 Two Degrees East, Three Degrees West

Abbey Lincoln
274 People in Me
331 Story of My Father
368 Wholey Earth
257 You Gotta Pay the Band

Jay Livingston
210 Lonely Girl
222 Mona Lisa
237 Mr. Lucky
255 Never Let Me Go
352 To Each His Own

John Jacob Loeb
302 Seems Like Old Times

Frank Loesser
158 I Hear Music
198 The Lady's in Love with You
199 Let's Get Lost
243 More I Cannot Wish You
198 The Lady's in Love with You

Carmen Lombardo
302 Seems Like Old Times

Joe Lovano
90 The Dawn of Time
154 Hypnosis
177 In the Land of Ephesus
190 Josie and Rosie
202 Lines and Spaces

Ballard MacDonald
318 Somebody Loves Me

Enric Madriguera
17 Adios

Herb Magidson
229 (I'm Afraid) The Masquerade Is Over
319 Something I Dreamed Last Night

Matt Malneck
325 Stairway to the Stars

Henry Mancini
226 Days of Wine and Roses
241 Moon River
237 Mr. Lucky

Johnny Mandel
305 The Shadow of Your Smile
322 Song from M*A*S*H (Suicide Is Painless)
359 Unless It's You

Chuck Mangione
124 Feels So Good

Barry Mann
265 On Broadway

David Mann
178 In the Wee Small Hours of the Morning

Bob Marley
200 Lively Up Yourself

Herbert Martin
172 I'm All Smiles

Bruno Martino
119 Estate

Harvey Mason
77 Chameleon
302 Serengeti Walk
       (Slippin' in the Back Door)

Bennie Maupin
77 Chameleon

Percy Mayfield
279 Please Send Me Someone to Love

Paul McCartney
262 Norwegian Wood
       (This Bird Has Flown)

Joe McCoy
369 Why Don't You Do Right
       (Get Me Some Money, Too!)

Loonis McGlohon
51 Blackberry Winter

Jimmy McHugh
155 I Can't Believe That You're in
       Love with Me
199 Let's Get Lost
205 A Lovely Way to Spend an Evening

Teddy McRae
58 Broadway

Walter Melrose
89 Copenhagen
94 Doctor Jazz

Nilo Mendez
141 Green Eyes (Aquellos Ojos Verdes)

Johnny Mercer
226 Days of Wine and Roses
146 Here's to My Lady
164 I Remember You
165 I Thought About You
177 In the Cool, Cool, Cool of the
       Evening
234 Laura
241 Moon River
267 One for My Baby
       (And One More for the Road)
285 P.S. I Love You
338 Tangerine
345 That Old Black Magic

Don Meyer
127 For Heaven's Sake

George Meyer
236 Mandy Make Up Your Mind

Joseph Meyer
217 Love Lies

Bub Miley
47 Black and Tan Fantasy
110 East St. Louis Toodle-oo

Marcus Miller
132 Full House
223 Maputo

Irving Mills
73 Caravan
160 I Let a Song Go out of My Heart
176 In a Sentimental Mood
181 It Don't Mean a Thing
       (If It Ain't Got That Swing)
240 The Mooch
225 Mood Indigo
282 Prelude to a Kiss
294 Ring Dem Bells
295 Riverboat Shuffle
296 Rockin' in Rhythm
324 Sophisticated Lady

Thelonious Monk
116 Epistrophy
163 I Mean You
178 In Walked Bud
265 Off Minor

John L. "Wes" Montgomery
124 Four on Six
363 West Coast Blues

Frank Morgan
58 Blues for Rosalinda
362 We Three Blues

Ferdinand "Jelly Roll" Morton
86 The Crave
238 Mr. Jelly-Lord
256 New Orleans Blues

Nelson Mota
213 Like a Lover (O Cantador)

Gerry Mulligan
36 Bark for Barksdale
298 Rocker (Rock Salt)
322 Song for Strayhorn

Oliver Nelson
116 Emancipation Blues
330 Stolen Moments

Portia Nelson
134 Gettin' Over the Blues
336 Sunday in New York

Henry Nemo
160 I Let a Song Go out of My Heart

Sammy Nestico
128 Freckle Face

Anthony Newley
281 Pure Imagination

Herbert Nichols
197 Lady Sings the Blues

James Noble
47 Blue Flame

Ray Noble
205 Love Is the Sweetest Thing
357 The Very Thought of You

Pierre Norman
379 You Brought a New Kind of Love
       to Me

Joseph "King" Oliver
104 Dippermouth Blues
94 Doctor Jazz

Sy Oliver
112 Easy Does It

Jack Palmer
187 I've Found a New Baby
       (I Found a New Baby)

Eddie Palmieri
290 Resemblance

Rique Pantoja
366 What Do You See

Mitchell Parish
295 Riverboat Shuffle
324 Sophisticated Lady
325 Stairway to the Stars
328 Star Dust

Charlie Parker
30 Anthropology
54 Blues for Alice
300 Segment
358 Visa

Dorothy Parker
168 I Wished on the Moon

Cliff Parman
284 Pretend

Geoffrey Parsons
169 If You Go

John Patitucci
37 Baja Bajo
80 Change of Season
142 Growing
300 Searching, Finding

Art Pepper
221 Make a List (Make a Wish)
226 Mr. Big Falls His J.G. Hand
332 Straight Life
336 Surf Ride

G. Pingarilno
120 The Face I Love

Cole Porter
34 At Long Last Love
109 Dream Dancing
118 Ev'rything I Love
156 I Am in Love
248 Most Gentlemen Don't Like Love
291 Ridin' High
313 So in Love

Neville Potter
123 500 Miles High
374 You're Everything

Miguel Prado
350 Time Was

Ralph Rainger
107 Easy Living
168 I Wished on the Moon
165 If I Should Lose You
195 June in January
278 Please
344 Thanks for the Memory

David Raksin
234 Laura

Milton Raskin
272 Passion Flower

Don Raye
380 You Don't Know What Love Is

Andy Razaf
46 (What Did I Do to Be So) Black and Blue
196 Keepin' out of Mischief Now

John Redmond
160 I Let a Song Go out of My Heart

Jimmy Reed
148 Honest I Do

Billy Reid
172 I'll Close My Eyes

Django Reinhardt
100 Dimunushing
234 Manoir De Mes Reves (Django's Castle)
264 Nuages
338 Swing 41
356 Ultrafox

Emelia Renaud
318 Somebody Loves Me

Harry Richman
245 (There Ought to Be A) Moonlight Savings Time

Lee Ritenour
65 Bullet Train
68 Captain Fingers
92 Cross My Heart
102 Dolphin Dreams
182 Is It You?

Leo Robin
107 Easy Living
165 If I Should Lose You
176 In Love in Vain
195 June in January
203 Love Is Just Around the Corner
252 My Ideal
278 Please
344 Thanks for the Memory

Williard Robinson
101 Don't Smoke in Bed

William "Smokey" Robinson
250 My Girl

Richard Rodgers
54 The Blue Room
91 Dancing on the Ceiling
136 Glad to Be Unhappy
144 Happy Hunting Horn
168 I Wish I Were in Love Again
183 Isn't It Romantic?
185 It's Easy to Remember
206 Lover
249 Mountain Greenery
248 My Heart Stood Still
258 The Next Time It Happens
262 Nobody's Heart
306 A Ship Without a Sail
312 Slaughter on Tenth Avenue
378 You Are Too Beautiful
382 You Took Advantage of Me
376 You're Nearer

Sigmund Romberg
316 Softly as in a Morning Sunrise

William Rose
372 Without a Song

Harry Ruby
349 Three Little Words

Pablo Beltran Ruiz
335 Sway (Quien Sera)

Bob Russell
158 I Didn't Know About You

Leon Russell
350 This Masquerade

S.K. Russell
61 Brazil
350 Time Was

Joe Sample
34 Ashes to Ashes
59 Born to Be Bad

David Sanborn
132 Full House
147 Hideaway
186 It's You

Arturo Sandoval
162 I Left This Space for You

Victor Schertzinger
164 I Remember You
338 Tangerine

Lalo Schifrin
219 Mission: Impossible Theme

Tom Schuman
130 Freetime

Wilbur Schwandt
99 Dream a Little Dream of Me

Arthur Schwartz
28 Alone Too Long

John Scofield
315 So You Say
330 Still Warm

Jerry Seelen
78 C'est Si Bon (It's So Good)

Jack Segal
162 I Keep Going Back to Joe's
365 When Sunny Gets Blue

Artie Shaw
311 So Easy

George Shearing
84 Conception
246 Lullaby of Birdland

Bruce Sievier
373 You're Blase

Carl Sigman
217 Love Lies

Frank Signorelli
325 Stairway to the Stars

Horace Silver
122 Filthy McNasty
222 Me and My Baby
272 Peace
333 Strollin'

Lewis C. Simpkins
259 Night Train

Frank Sinatra
171 I'm a Fool to Want You

Sunny Skylar
41 Besame Mucho (Kiss Me Much)

Chris Smith
71 Cake Walking Babies from Home

Johnny Smith
357 Walk Don't Run

Anna Sosenko
91 Darling, Je Vous Aime Beaucoup

Charles Spivak
327 Stardreams

Mike Stern
18 After All
40 Before You Go
82 Chromozone
216 Little Shoes
270 Original Rays

Mike Stoller
265 On Broadway

Billy Strayhorn
90 The Creole Love Call
272 Passion Flower

Jule Styne
142 Guess I'll Hang My Tears out to Dry
186 It's You or No One

Dana Suesse
252 My Silent Love

Steve Swallow
120 Falling Grace

Eric Tagg
92 Cross My Heart
182 Is It You?

Jean "Toots" Thielemans
55 Blues on Time

Claude Thornhill
64 Buster's Last Stand

Bobby Timmons
96 Dat Dere

Pete Tinturin
366 What Will I Tell My Heart

Juan Tizol
73 Caravan

Bobby Troup
136 Girl Talk

Henry Troy
71 Cake Walking Babies from Home

Roy Turk
236 Mandy Make Up Your Mind

Thomas Turrentine
194 June Bug

McCoy Tyner
24 Aisha
126 Fly with the Wind
270 Passion Dance
301 Senor Carlos

Adolfo Utrera
141 Green Eyes (Aquellos Ojos Verdes)

Marcos Valle
120 The Face I Love

Paulo Valle
120 The Face I Love

Egbert Van Alstyne
40 Beautiful Love

Jimmy Van Heusen
66 Call Me Irresponsible
165 I Thought About You
184 It Could Happen to You
244 Moonlight Becomes You
334 Suddenly It's Spring

Consuelo Velazquez
41 Besame Mucho (Kiss Me Much)

Dick Voynow
295 Riverboat Shuffle

Fats Waller
46 (What Did I Do to Be So) Black and Blue
191 Jitterbug Waltz
196 Keepin' out of Mischief Now

George Wallington
135 Godchild
215 Lemon Drop

Ned Washington
153 A Hundred Years from Today
254 The Nearness of You
268 On Green Dolphin Street
327 Stella by Starlight

Oscar Washington
259 Night Train

Ernie Watts
29 And I Think About It All the Time
65 Bullet Train
85 Continental Blues
195 Just the Way We Planned It
268 On the Border
366 What Do You See

Paul Francis Webster
48 Black Coffee
157 I Got It Bad and That Ain't Good
180 Invitation
305 The Shadow of Your Smile

Cynthia Weil
265 On Broadway

Kurt Weill
242 Mack the Knife

George David Weiss
246 Lullaby of Birdland
239 Mr. Wonderful
353 Too Close for Comfort

Carel Werver
76 Cast Your Fate to the Wind

Ronald White
250 My Girl

Richard A. Whiting
252 My Ideal

Alec Wilder
51 Blackberry Winter

Ernest B. Wilkins
331 Stereophonic

Buster Williams
24 Air Dancing
79 Christina
93 Deceptacon
352 Toku-Do

Clarence Williams
71 Cake Walking Babies from Home

Paul Williams
286 The Rainbow Connection

Spencer Williams
187 I've Found a New Baby
(I Found a New Baby)

Frank E. Wilson
380 You've Made Me So Very Happy

P.G. Wodehouse
45 Bill
351 Till the Clouds Roll By

Jack Wolf
171 I'm a Fool to Want You

Henri Woode
58 Broadway

Eddie Woods
17 Adios

Allie Wrubel
229 (I'm Afraid) The Masquerade Is Over

Jack Yellen
23 Ain't She Sweet
32 Are You Havin' Any Fun?
319 Something I Dreamed Last Night

Vincent Youmans
372 Without a Song

Jimmy Young
112 Easy Does It

Joe Young
153 A Hundred Years from Today

Victor Young
40 Beautiful Love
53 Blue Star
153 A Hundred Years from Today
204 Love Letters
327 Stella by Starlight

Josef Zawinul
50 Black Market
72 Cannonball
228 Mr. Gone
288 A Remark You Made

Anne Zindars
152 How My Heart Sings

Earl Zindars
152 How My Heart Sings

ADIOS

English Words by EDDIE WOODS
Spanish Translation and Music by ENRIC MADRIGUERA

AFTER ALL

By MIKE STERN

Copyright © 1988 Little Shoes Music (ASCAP)

AFFIRMATION

By JOSE FELICIANO

Copyright © 1975 J & H Publishing Company (ASCAP)
All Rights Administered by Stollman & Stollman o/b/o J & H Publishing Company

ÁGUAS DE MARÇO
(Waters of March)

Copyright © 1973 Antonio Carlos Jobim
Published by Corcovado Music Corp.

Words and Music by
ANTONIO CARLOS JOBIM

Moderately

A stick, a stone, it's the end of the road. It's the rest of a stump, it's a lit-tle a-lone.
It's a sli-ver of glass, it is life, it's the sun it is night, it is death,
it's a trap, it's a gun. The oak when it blooms, a fox in the brush, the knot in the wood,
the song of a thrush, the wood of the wind, a cliff, a fall, a scratch, a lump,
it is noth-ing at all. It's the wind blow-ing free, it's the end of the slope,
it's a beam, it's a void, it's a hunch, it's a hope, and the riv-er bank talks of the Wa-ters of March.
It's the end of the strain, it's the joy in your heart. The foot, the ground, the flesh and the bone,
the beat of the road, a sling-shot stone, a fish, a flash, a sil-ver-y glow.
a fight, a bet, the range of a bow, the bed of the well, the end of the line,
the dis-may in the face, it's a loss, it's a find. A spear, a spike, a point, a
nail, a drip, a drop, the end of the tale, a truck-load of bricks in the soft morn-ing light,
the shot of a gun in the dead of the night. A mile, a must, a thrust, a bump,

Am6 Fm6/A♭ C6add9/G Gm7 C9
it's a girl, it's a rhyme, it's a cold, it's the mumps. The plan of the house, the bod - y in bed,
D/C Fm/C C6/G Gm7/C C7
and the car that got stuck, it's the mud, it's the mud. A float, a drift, a flight, a wing,
D7/C Fm6add9/C CM7 C7/G
a hawk, a quail, the prom-ise of spring, and the riv - er-bank talks of the Wa-ters Of March.
Am6/F♯ Fm♯7 Fm6 C6 F♯/E E♭/D♭ C/B♭
It's the prom-ise of life, it's the joy in your heart.
Am6 Fm6/A♭ CM7/G G♭7♭5 FM7 Fm6 C6 C/B♭ Am6 Fm6/A♭
CM7/G C/B♭ Am6 Fm6/A♭
A snake, a stick, it is John, it is Joe, it's a thorn in your hand, and a cut on your toe.
C6add9/G C/B♭ Am6 Fm6/A♭ C6add9/G
A point, a grain, a bee, a bite, a blink, a buz-zard, a sud-den stroke of night. A pin, a
C/B♭ Am6 Fm6/A♭ CM7/G
nee - dle, a sting, a pain, a snail, a rid - dle, a wasp, a stain, a pass in the moun -
Cm7 D/C Fm6/C C
- tains, a horse and a mule, in the dis-tance the shelves rode three shad-ows of blue, and the riv - er-bank
Cm7 D/C D♭/C C/G C
talks of the Wa-ters Of March. It's the prom-ise of life, in your heart, in your heart. A stick, a
C/B♭ Am6 Fm6/A♭ C6add9/G
stone, the end of the load, the rest of a stump, a lone - some road, a sli - ver of glass,
Gm7 C7 D13/C Fm6 G♯dim/C CM7/G
a life, the sun, a night, a death, the end of the run, and the riv - er-bank
Gm7 C7 D13/C Fm6 C6add9
3 3
talks of the Wa - ters Of March. It's the end of all strain, it's the joy in your heart.

AFTER THE RAIN

By JOHN COLTRANE

Copyright © 1977 JOWCOL MUSIC

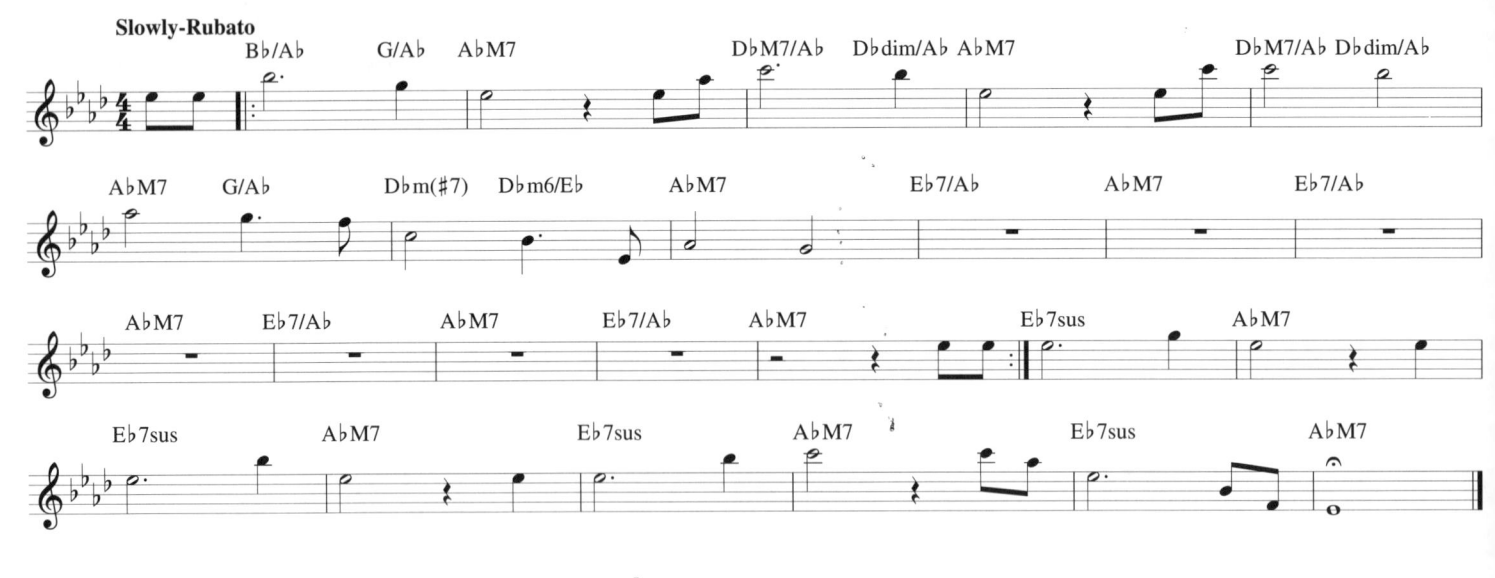

Slowly-Rubato

ÁGUA DE BEBER
(Water to Drink)

© Copyright 1965 by BUTTERFIELD MUSIC
Copyright Renewed
All Rights Controlled and Administered by MCA MUSIC PUBLISHING,
A Division of UNIVERSAL STUDIOS, INC.

Original Words by VINICIUS DE MORAES
English Words by NORMAN GIMBEL
Music by ANTONIO CARLOS JOBIM

Moderately

Your love is rain, my heart the flow - er.
 on dis - tant de - serts.

I need your love or I will die.
The rain can fall up - on the sea.

My ver - y life is in your pow - er.
The rain can fall up - on the flow - er.

Will I with - er and fade or bloom to the sky?
Since the rain has to fall let it fall on me.

Á - gua De Be - ber, give the flow - er wa - ter to drink.
Á - gua De Be - ber, Á - gua De Be - ber ca - ma - rá.

Á - gua De Be - ber, give the flow - er wa - ter to drink.
Á - gua De Be - ber, Á - gua De Be - ber

The rain can fall ca - ma - rá.

AFTERMATH (PART II)

Written by KEVIN EUBANKS

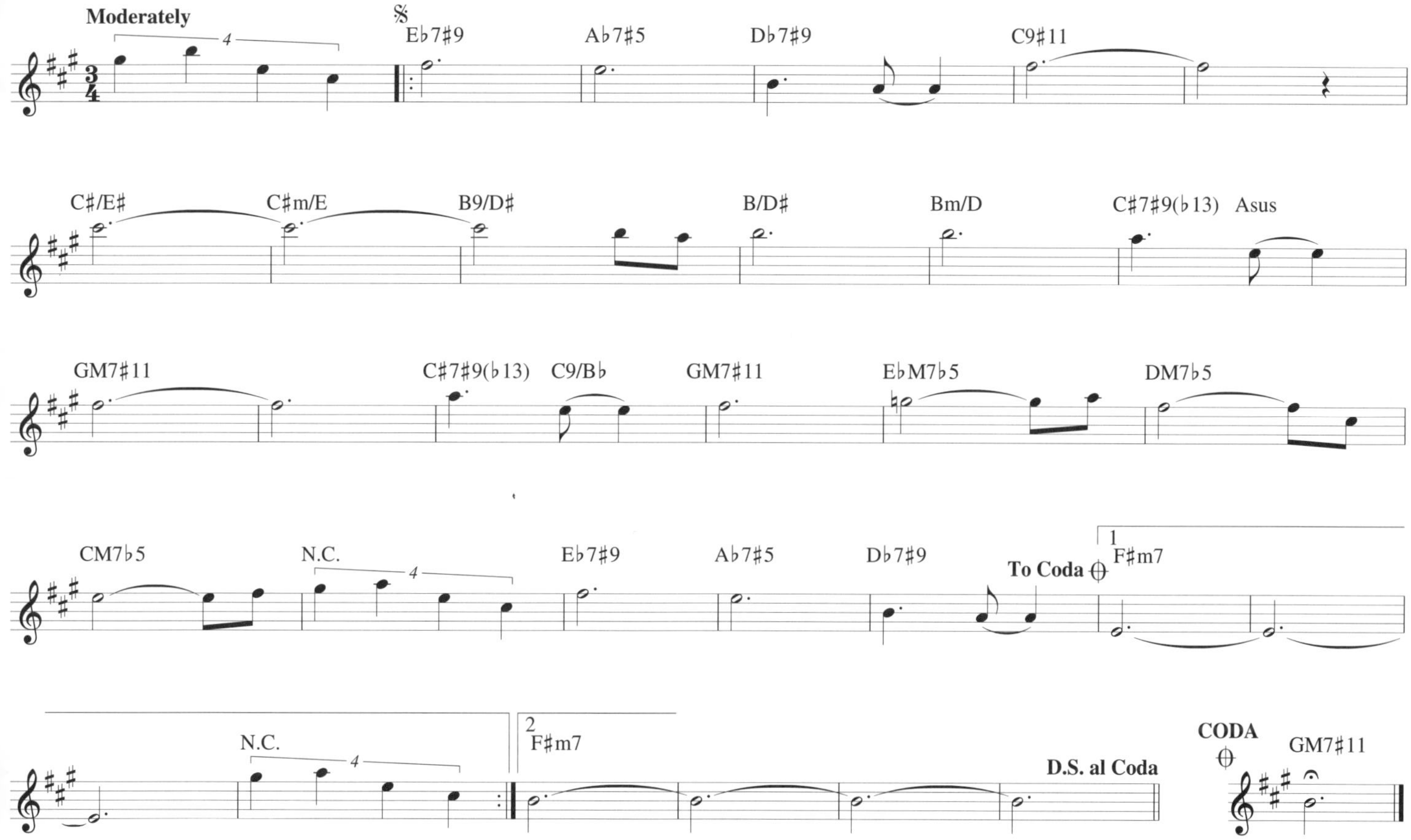

AIN'T SHE SWEET

Words by JACK YELLEN
Music by MILTON AGER

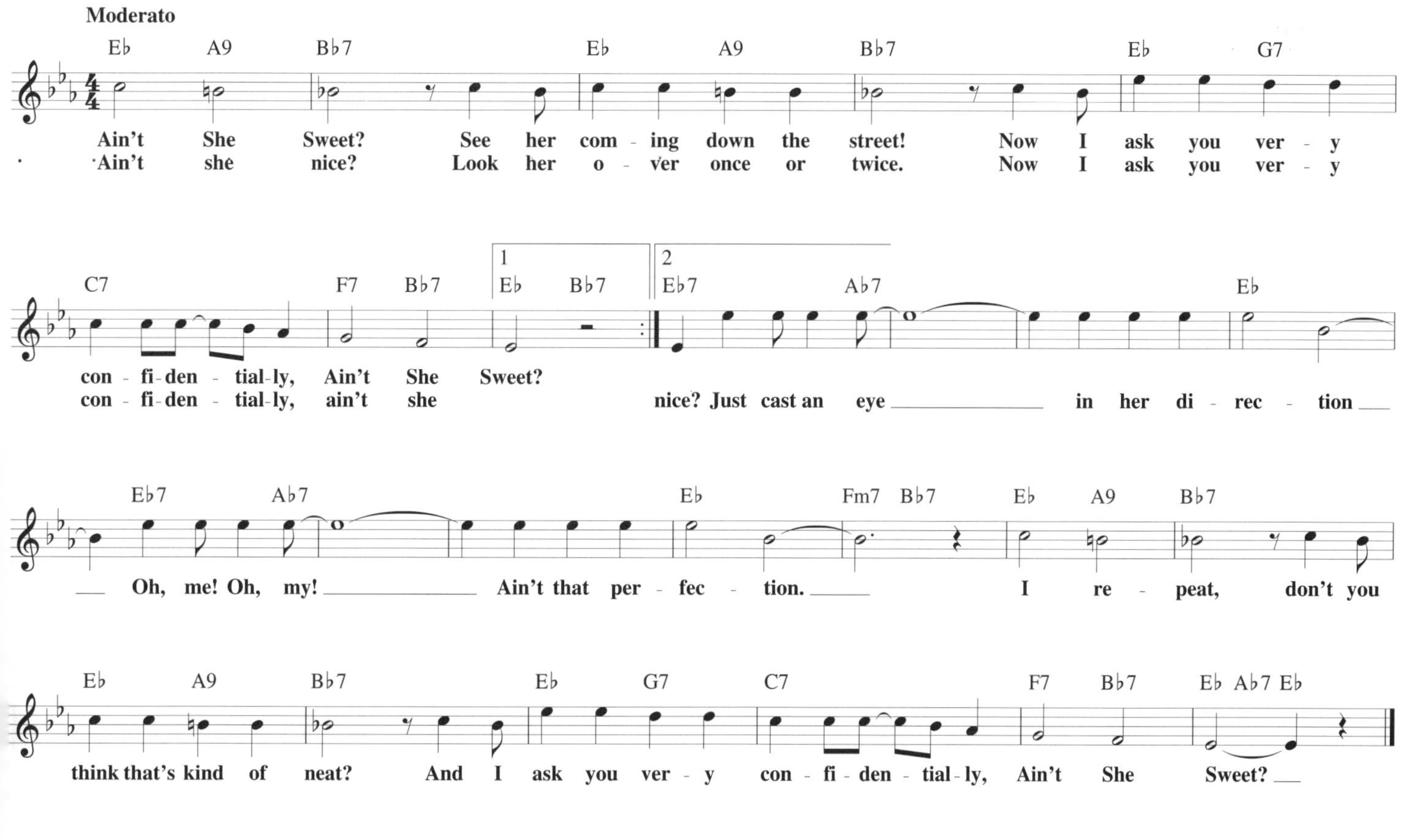

AIR DANCING

By BUSTER WILLIAMS

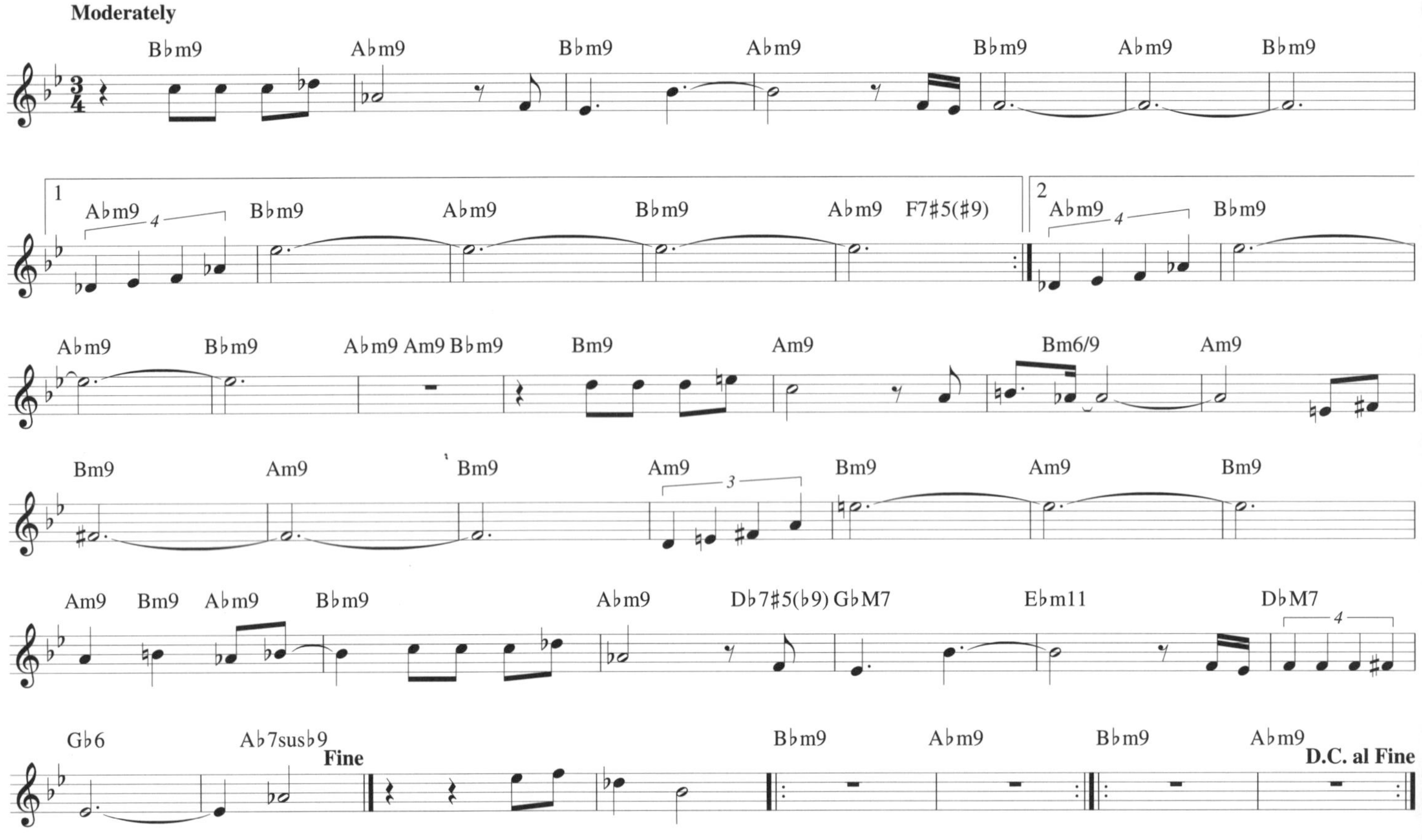

AISHA

By McCOY TYNER

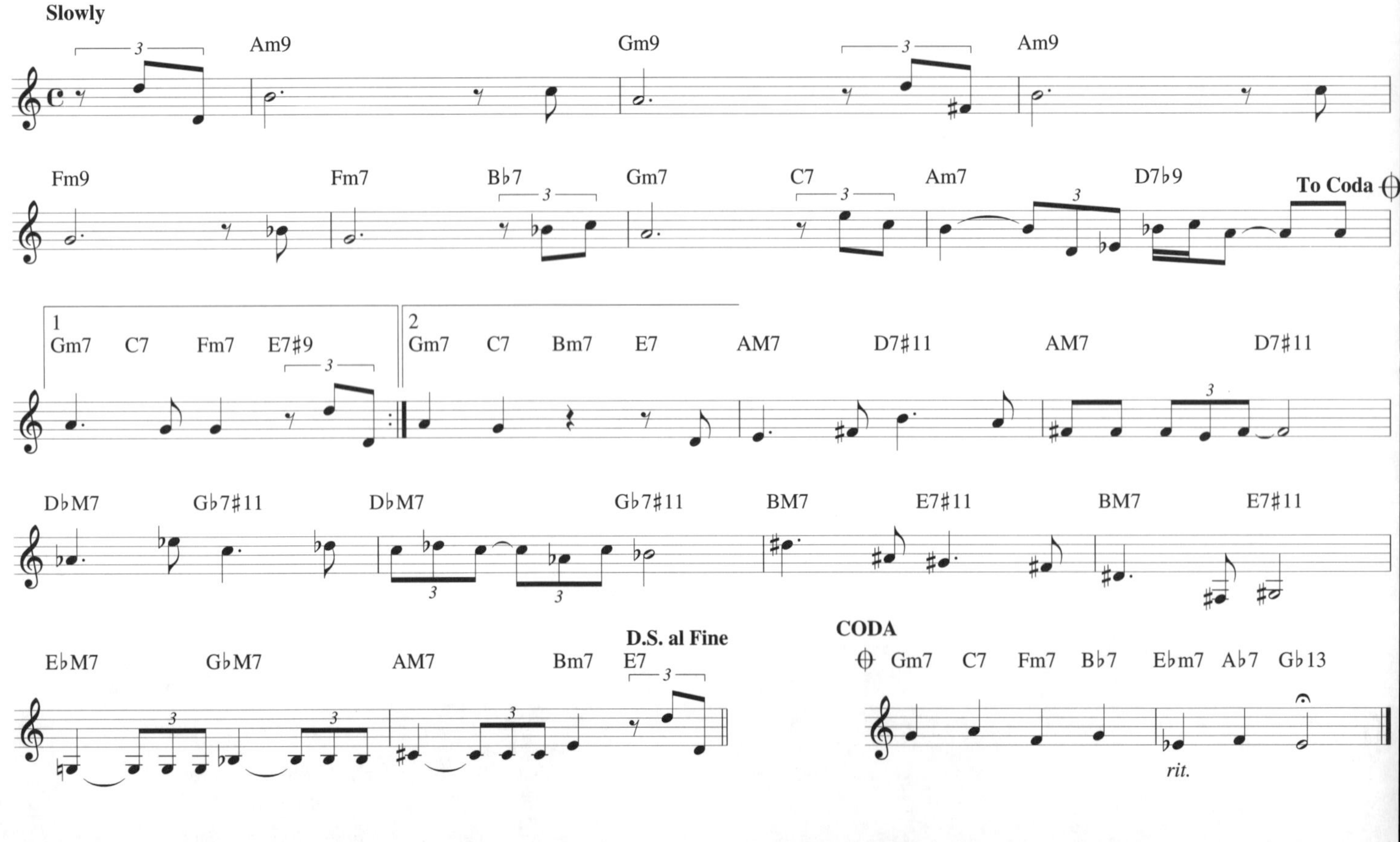

AJA

*© Copyright 1977, 1978 by MCA MUSIC PUBLISHING,
A Division of UNIVERSAL STUDIOS, INC.*

Words and Music by WALTER BECKER
and DONALD FAGEN

Moderately

1. Up-on the hill __ peo-ple nev-er stare, __ they just don't care.
2., 3. *(See additional lyrics)*

Chin-ese mu-sic un-der ban-yan __ trees __ here at the dude ranch a-bove the sea. A - ja, when all my dime danc-in' is through I run to you. __

Instrumental

Additional Lyrics

2. Upon the hill they've got time to burn.
   There's no return
   Double Helix in the sky tonight.
   Throw out the hardware
   Let's do it right.

3. Upon the hill they think I'm okay.
   Okay so they say.
   Chinese music always sets me free.
   Angular banjoes sound good to me.

ALABAMA

By JOHN COLTRANE

Copyright © 1977 JOWCOL MUSIC

Slowly, Pensively (Rubato)

ALFIE
Theme from the Paramount Picture ALFIE

Words by HAL DAVID
Music by BURT BACHARACH

Copyright © 1966 (Renewed 1994) by Famous Music Corporation

Very slowly, rubato

What's it all a-bout, Al - fie? Is it just for the mo-ment we live? What's it all a-bout when you sort it out, Al-fie? Are we meant to take more than we give, or are we meant to be kind? And if on-ly fools are kind, Al-fie, than I guess it is wise to be cruel. And if life be-longs on-ly to the strong, Al-fie, what will you lend on an old gold-en rule? As sure as I be-lieve there's a heav-en a-bove, Al-fie, I know there's some-thing much more, some-thing e-ven non - be-liev-ers

26

ALICE IN WONDERLAND
from Walt Disney's ALICE IN WONDERLAND

© 1951 Walt Disney Music Company
Copyright Renewed

Words by BOB HILLIARD
Music by SAMMY FAIN

Moderately

Al - ice In Won - der - land, how do you get to Won - der - land? O - ver the hill or un - der - land or just be - hind the tree. Where do stars go? Where is the cres - cent moon? They must be some - where in the sun - ny af - ter - noon. Al - ice In Won - der - land, where is the path to Won - der - land? O - ver the hill or here or there? I won - der where.

When clouds go roll - ing by, they roll a - way to and leave the sky. Where is the land be - yond the eye that peo - ple can - not see?

ALL ALONE

Words and Music by
IRVING BERLIN

© Copyright 1924 by Irving Berlin
Copyright Renewed

Moderately

All A - lone, I'm so All A - lone. There is no one else but you. All A - lone by the tel - e - phone wait - ing for a ring, a ting - a - ling. I'm All A - lone ev - 'ry eve - ning, All A - lone feel - ing blue, won - d'ring where you are, and how you are and if you are, All A - lone too. too.

ALONE TOO LONG
from BY THE BEAUTIFUL SEA

Words by DOROTHY FIELDS
Music by ARTHUR SCHWARTZ

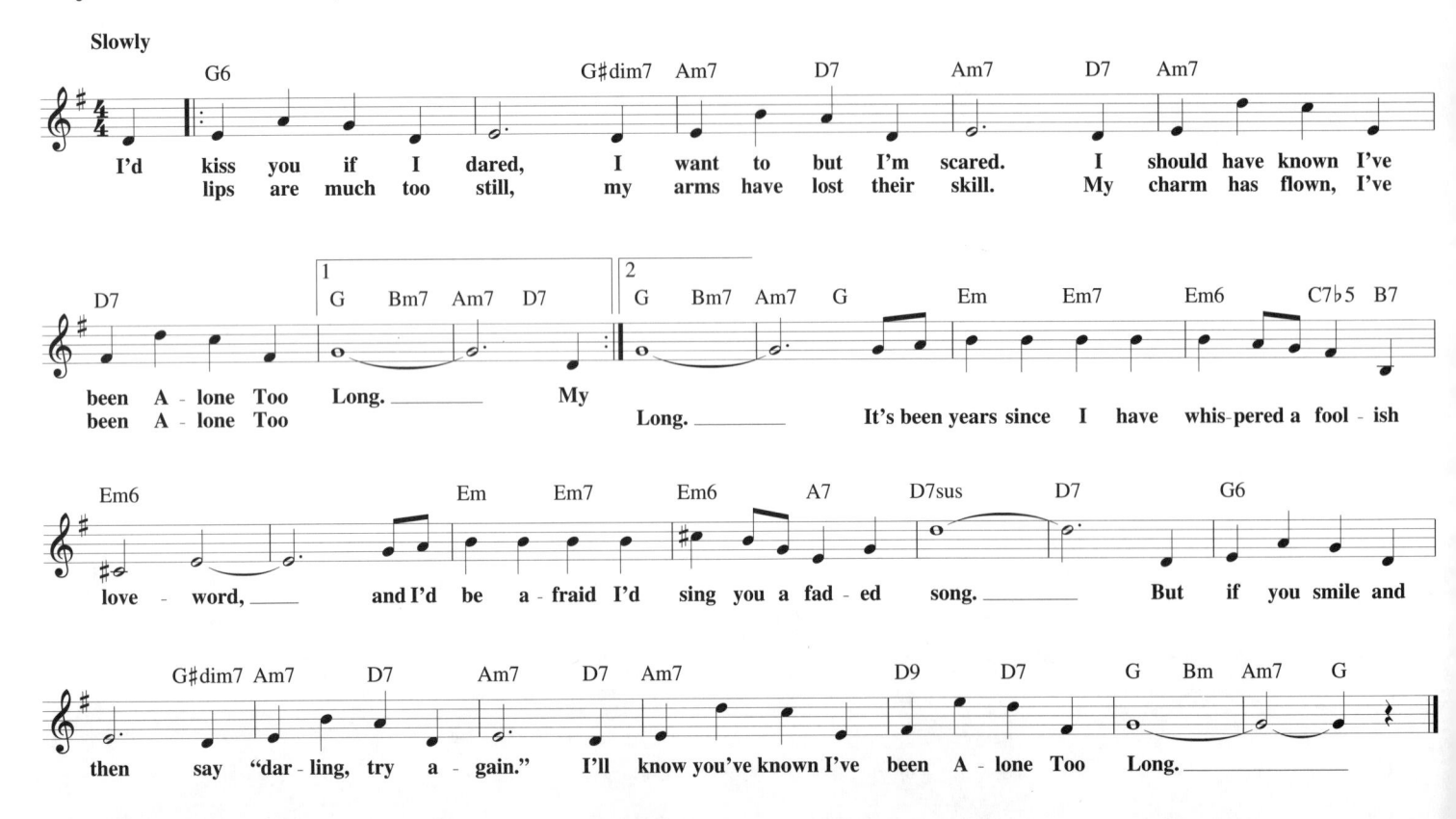

© 1954 (Renewed) ARTHUR SCHWARTZ and DOROTHY FIELDS
All Rights Controlled by EDWIN H. MORRIS & COMPANY, A Division of
MPL Communications, Inc. and ALDI MUSIC
All Rights for ALDI MUSIC Administered by THE SONGWRITERS GUILD OF AMERICA

Slowly

I'd kiss you if I dared, I want to but I'm scared. I should have known I've been A - lone Too Long. My
lips are much too still, my arms have lost their skill. My charm has flown, I've been A - lone Too Long. It's been years since I have whis - pered a fool - ish love - word, and I'd be a - fraid I'd sing you a fad - ed song. But if you smile and then say "dar - ling, try a - gain." I'll know you've known I've been A - lone Too Long.

AND I THINK ABOUT IT ALL THE TIME

By ERNIE WATTS
and RAY DEWEY

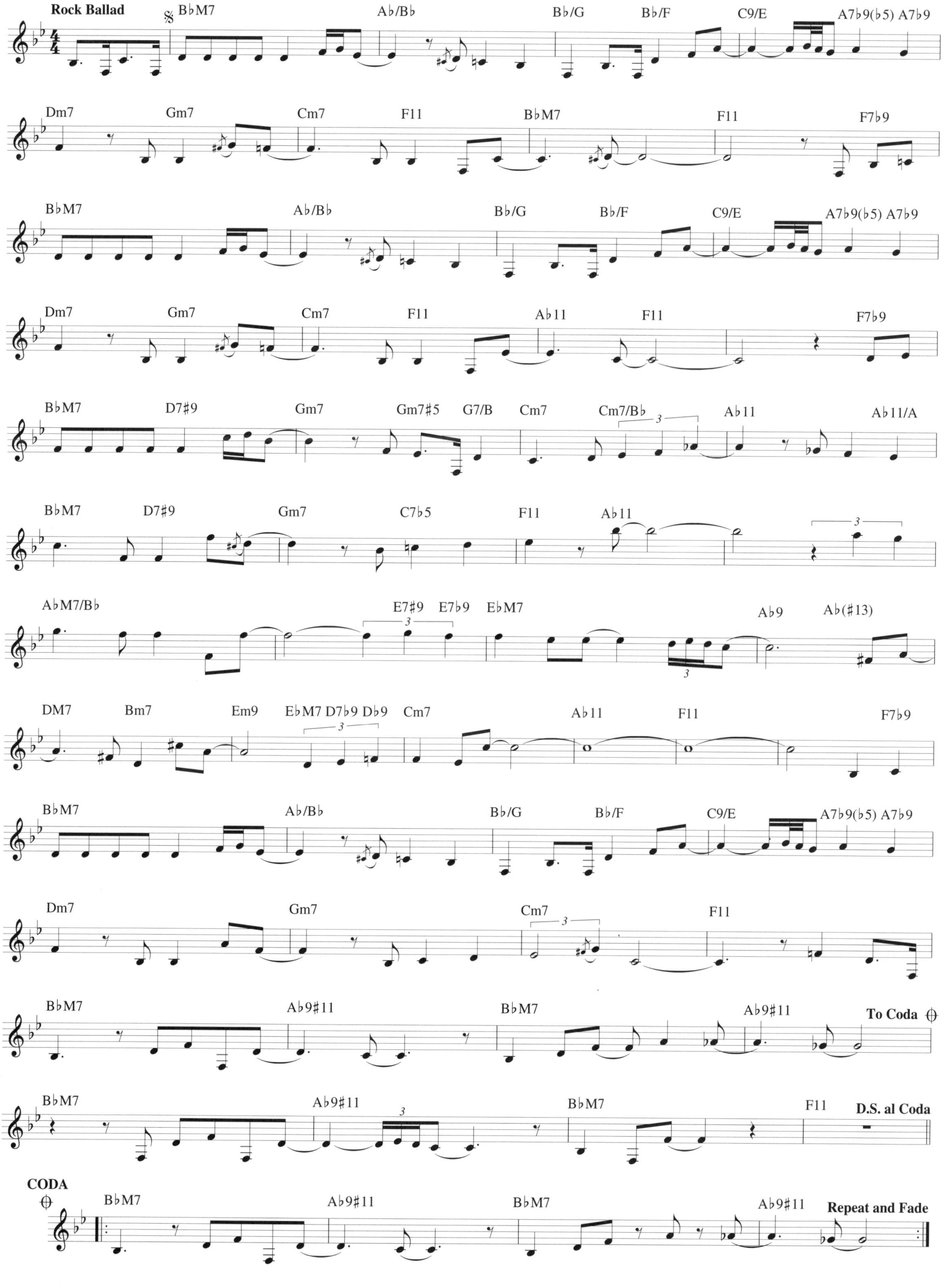

ANTHROPOLOGY

By CHARLIE PARKER and DIZZY GILLESPIE

Copyright © 1946, Renewed and Assigned to Atlantic Music Corp. and Music Sales Corporation

ANTIGUA

By ANTONIO CARLOS JOBIM

Copyright © 1967, 1968 Antonio Carlos Jobim
Copyright Renewed
Corcovado Music Corp., Publisher

APRIL IN PARIS

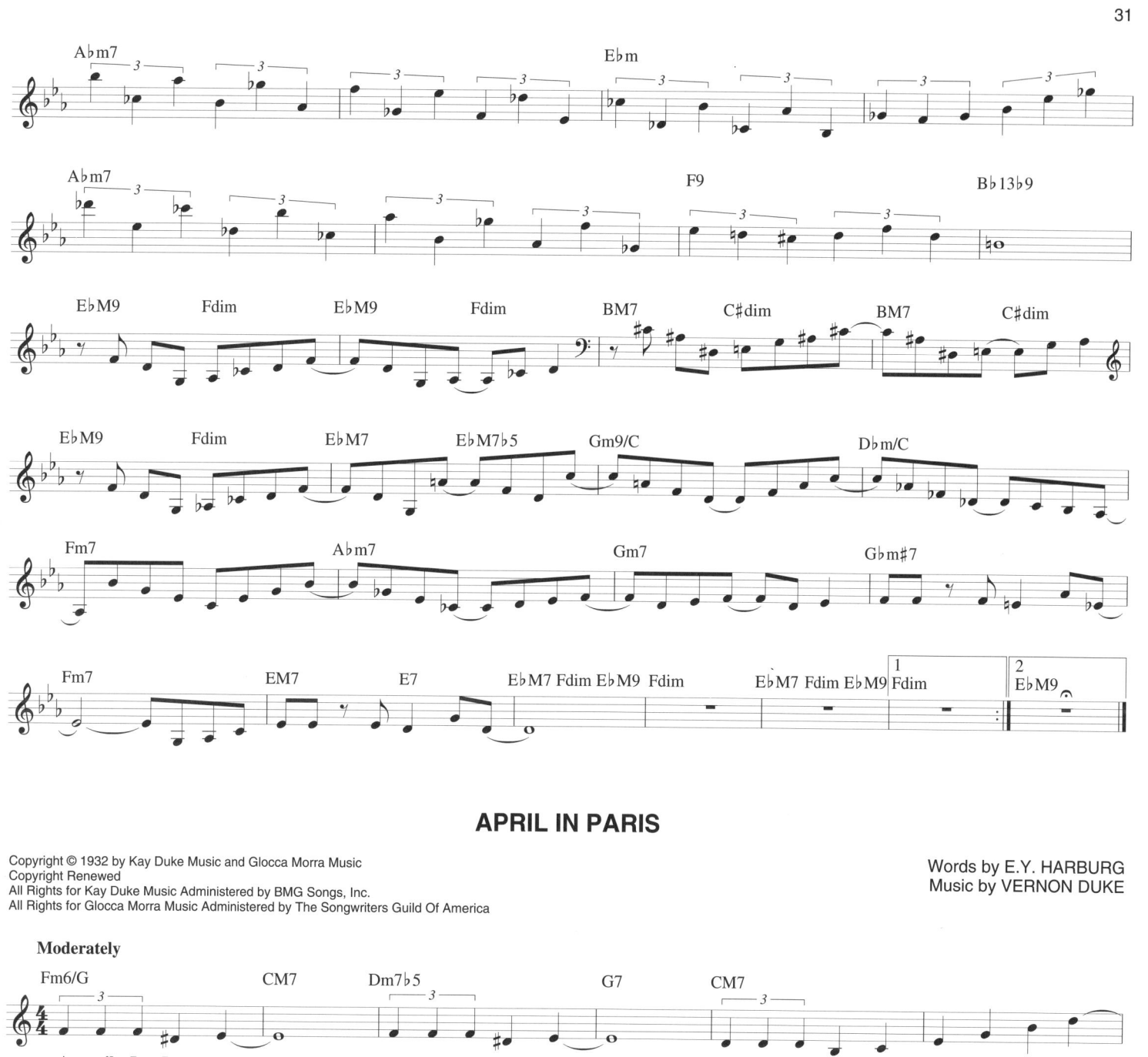

Words by E.Y. Harburg
Music by VERNON DUKE

Copyright © 1932 by Kay Duke Music and Glocca Morra Music
Copyright Renewed
All Rights for Kay Duke Music Administered by BMG Songs, Inc.
All Rights for Glocca Morra Music Administered by The Songwriters Guild Of America

Moderately

April In Paris, chestnuts in blossom, holiday tables under the trees. April In Paris, this is a feeling no one can ever reprise. I never knew the charm of spring, never met it face to face. I never knew my heart could sing, never missed a warm embrace, till April In Paris, whom can I run to, what have you done to my heart?

ARE YOU HAVIN' ANY FUN?
from GEORGE WHITE'S SCANDALS (1939 Edition)

Words by JACK YELLEN
Music by SAMMY FAIN

Copyright © 1939 by Chappell & Co. and Fain Music Co.
Copyright Renewed

Moderately bright

Are You Hav-in' An-y Fun? What y' get-tin' out o' liv-in? What good is what you've got if you're not hav-in' an-y fun? Are you hav-in' an-y laughs? Are you get-tin' an-y lov-in'? If oth-er peo-ple do so can you; Have a lit-tle fun.

{ Af-ter the hon-ey's in the comb lit-tle bees go out and play; E-ven the old grey mare down home has got to have hay. Hey!
  Why do you work and slave and save? Life is full of ifs and buts; You know the squir-rels save and save, and what have they got? Nuts! }

Bet-ter have a lit-tle fun. you ain't gon-na live for-ev-er; Be-fore you're old and gray still o-kay. Have your lit-tle fun, son! Have your lit-tle fun! Are You Hav-in' An-y fun!

ARMANDO'S RHUMBA

© Copyright 1976 by MCA MUSIC PUBLISHING,
A Division of UNIVERSAL STUDIOS, INC.

By CHICK COREA

Moderately

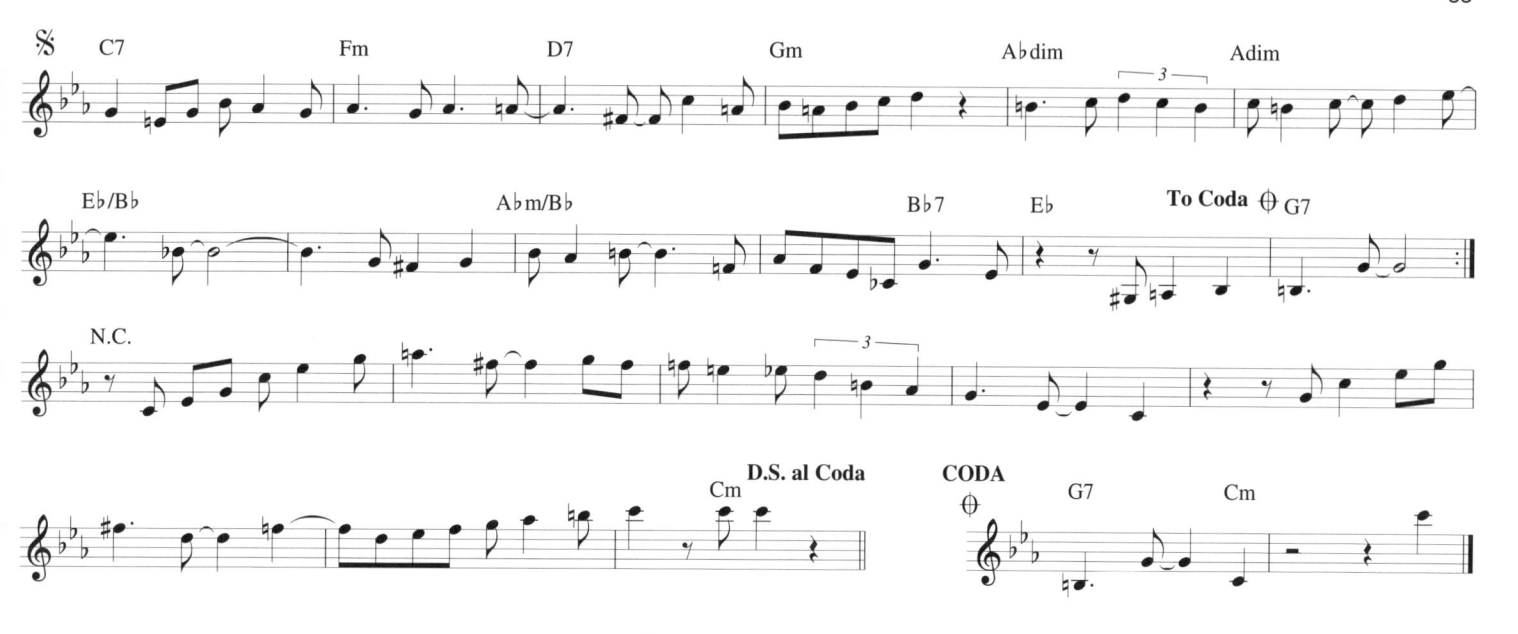

AS LONG AS I LIVE

© 1934 (Renewed 1962) TED KOEHLER MUSIC and S.A. MUSIC CO.
All Rights for TED KOEHLER MUSIC Administered by FRED AHLERT MUSIC CORPORATION

Lyric by TED KOEHLER
Music by HAROLD ARLEN

Moderately

May-be I can't live to love you as long as I want to, life is-n't long e-nough, ba-by, but I can love you As Long As I Live.

May-be I can't give you dia-monds and things like I want to, but I can prom-ise you, ba-by, I'm gon-na want to As Long As I Live. I

nev-er cared, but now I'm scared I won't live long enough, that's why I wear my rub-bers when it rains and eat an ap-ple ev-'ry day, then see a doc-tor an-y-way.

What if I can't live to love you as long as I want to, 'long as I prom-ise you, ba-by, I'm gon-na love you As Long As I Live.

AT LONG LAST LOVE
from YOU NEVER KNOW

Words and Music by
COLE PORTER

ASHES TO ASHES

Music by JOE SAMPLE

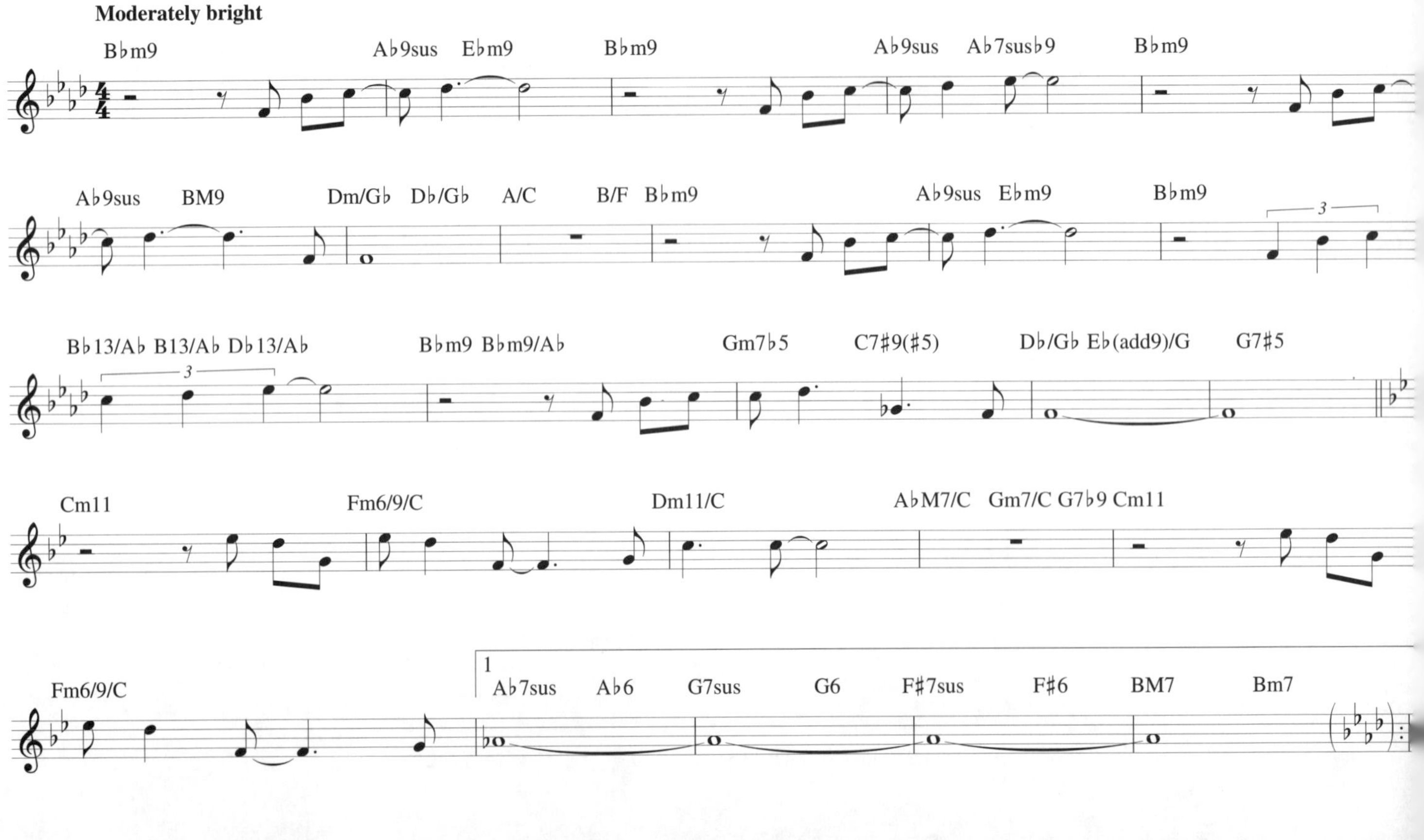

AUNT HAGAR'S BLUES

Words by J. TIM BRYMN
Music by W.C. HANDY

Copyright © 1998 by HAL LEONARD CORPORATION

Moderately

Old Deacon Splivin', his flock was givin' the way of livin' right, said he "No wing-in', no rag-time singin' to-night." Up jumped Aunt Ha-gar, and shout-ed out with all her might: Oh, 'taint no use o' preach-in', oh, 'taint no use o' teach-in', each mod-u-la-tion of syn-co-pa-tion just tells my feet to dance and I can't re-fuse when I hear the mel-o-dy they call the blues; those ev-er lov-in' blues. Just hear Aunt Ha-gar's chil-dren har-mon-iz-in' to that old mourn-ful tune, it's like a choir from on high broke loose. If the deb-bil brought it the good Lawd sent it right down to me, let the con-gre-ga-tion join while I sing those lov-in' Aunt Ha-gar's Blues.

AUTUMN IN NEW YORK

Words and Music by
VERNON DUKE

Copyright © 1934 by Kay Duke Music
Copyright Renewed
All Rights Administered by BMG Songs, Inc.

Au-tumn In New York, why does it seem so in-vit-ing? Au-tumn In New York,
Au-tumn In New York, the gleam-ing roof-tops at sun-down.

it spells the thrill of first night-ing. Glit-ter-ing crowds and shim-mer-ing clouds in
it lifts you up when you're run-down. Jad-ed rou-és and gay di-vor-cees who

can-yons of steel, they're mak-ing me feel I'm home. It's Au-tumn In New York,
lunch at the Ritz will tell you that "it's di-vine!" This Au-tumn In New York,

that brings the pro-mise of new love; Au-tumn In New York is of-ten min-gled with
trans-forms the slums in-to May-fair; Au-tumn In New York, you'll need no cas-tles in

pain. Dream-ers with emp-ty hands may sigh for ex-ot-ic lands; It's
Spain. Lov-ers that bless the dark on bench-es in Cen-tral Park greet

Au-tumn In New York, it's good to live it a-gain. gain.

BARK FOR BARKSDALE

By GERRY MULLIGAN

Copyright © 1954 (Renewed) Criterion Music Corp.

D.C. al Coda CODA

BAJA BAJO

By JOHN PATITUCCI and CHICK COREA

© Copyright 1988 by MCA MUSIC PUBLISHING, A Division of UNIVERSAL STUDIOS, INC.

BASS DESIRES

By PETER ERSKINE

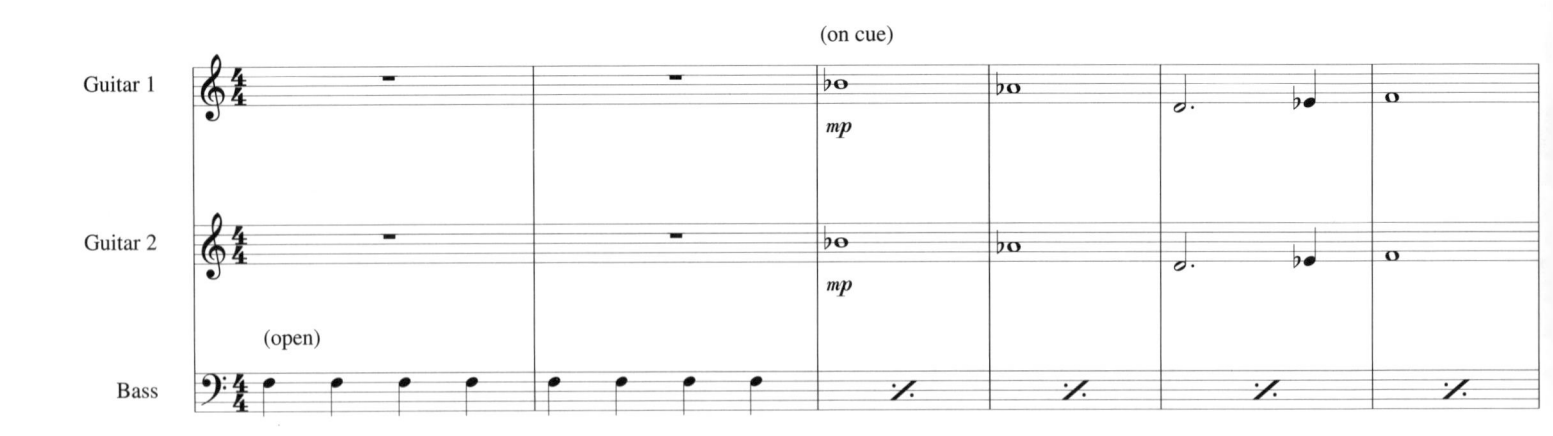

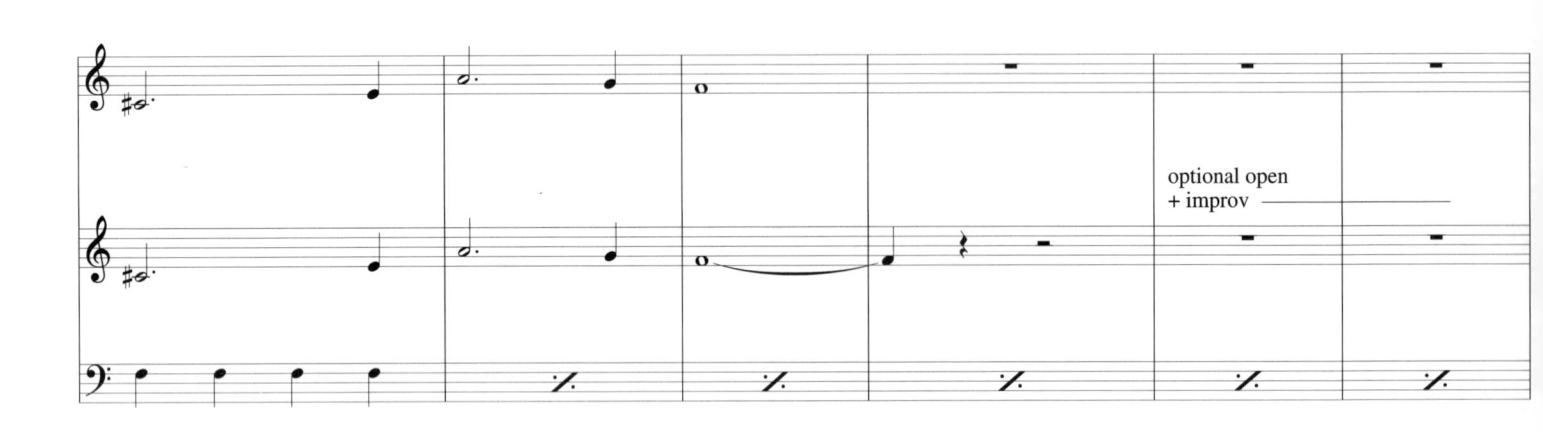

Copyright © 1985 Ersko Music

to improvisation
"time, no changes"...

BEAUTIFUL LOVE

Words by HAVEN GILLESPIE
Music by VICTOR YOUNG, WAYNE KING
and EGBERT VAN ALSTYNE

BEFORE YOU GO

By MIKE STERN

BÉSAME MUCHO
(Kiss Me Much)

Original Words and Music by CONSUELO VELAZQUEZ
English Words by SUNNY SKYLAR

BESSIE'S BLUES

By JOHN COLTRANE

THE BEST THING FOR YOU

from the Stage Production CALL ME MADAM

Words and Music by
IRVING BERLIN

BETTER LUCK NEXT TIME

from the Motion Picture Irving Berlin's EASTER PARADE

Words and Music by
IRVING BERLIN

BIG NICK

By JOHN COLTRANE

BETWEEN THE DEVIL AND THE DEEP BLUE SEA

from RHYTHMANIA

Lyric by TED KOEHLER
Music by HAROLD ARLEN

BIJOU

Music by RALPH BURNS

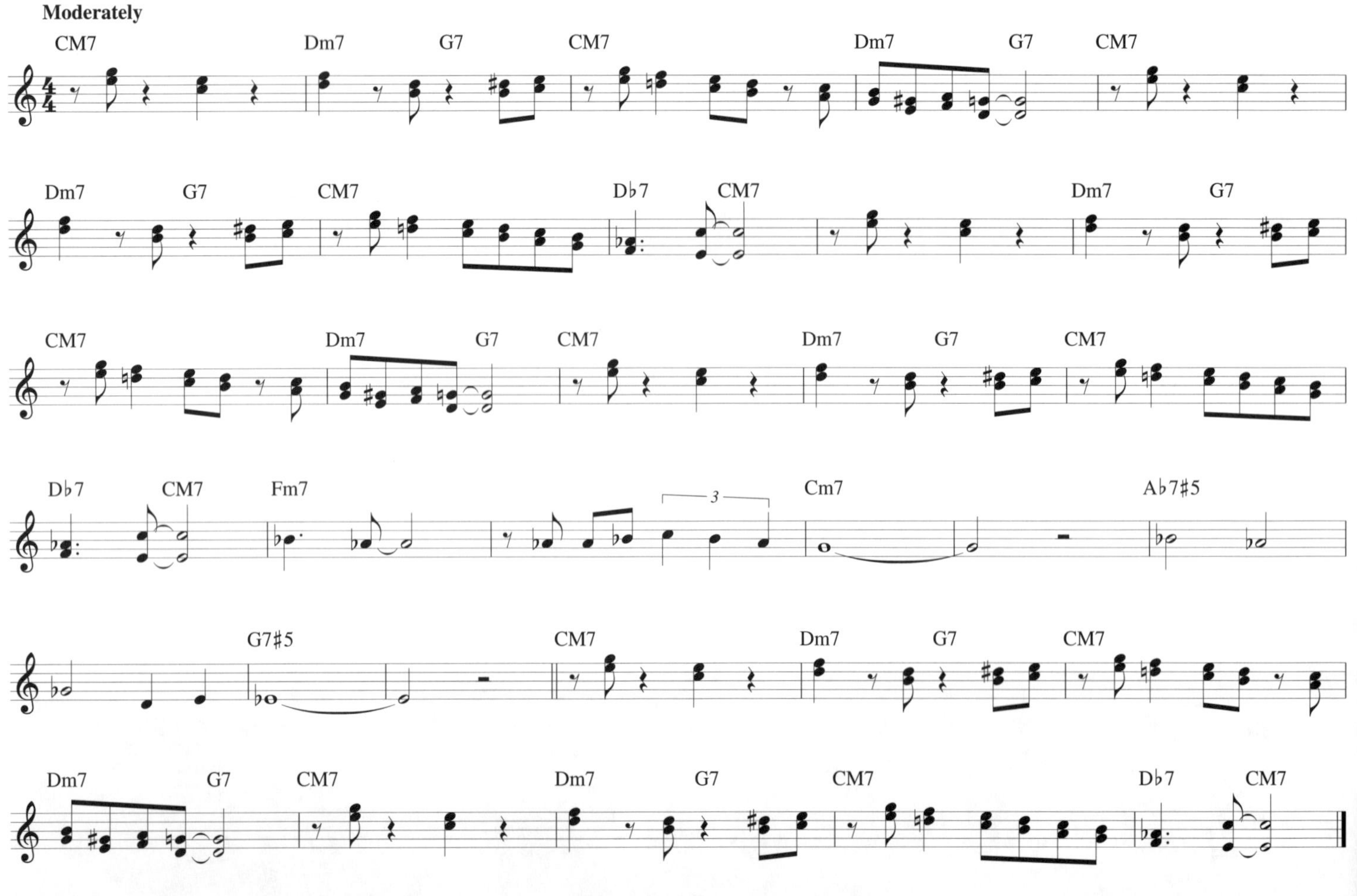

BILL
from SHOW BOAT

Lyrics by P.G. WODEHOUSE and OSCAR HAMMERSTEIN II
Music by JEROME KERN

A BLOSSOM FELL

Words and Music by HOWARD BARNES,
HAROLD CORNELIUS and DOMINIC JOHN

BIRK'S WORKS

Music by JOHN "DIZZY" GILLESPIE

(What Did I Do to Be So)
BLACK AND BLUE
from AIN'T MISBEHAVIN'

Words by ANDY RAZAF
Music by HARRY BROOKS and FATS WALLER

BLACK AND TAN FANTASY

By DUKE ELLINGTON
and BUB MILEY

BLUE FLAME

Lyric by LEO CORDAY
Music by JAMES NOBLE and JOE BISHOP

BLACK COFFEE

Words and Music by PAUL FRANCIS WEBSTER
and SONNY BURKE

Copyright © 1948 (Renewed) Webster Music Co. and Sondot Music Corporation

Slow Blues

I'm feel-in' might-y lone-some, have-n't slept a wink, I walk the floor and watch the door and
feel-in' might-y lone-some, have-n't slept a wink, I walk the floor and watch the door and

in be-tween I drink Black Cof-fee. Love's a hand-me-down broom. I'll
in be-tween I drink Black Cof-fee. Since my gal went a-way. My

nev-er know a Sun-day, in this week-day room. I'm
nerves have gone to piec-es and my hair's turn-in' gray. I'm

talk-in' to the shad-ows, one o'-clock to four. And Lord, how slow the mo-ments go when
talk-in' to the shad-ows, one o'-clock to four. And Lord, how slow the mo-ments go when

all I do is pour Black Cof-fee. Since the blues caught my eye. I'm
all I do is pour Black Cof-fee. Love's a sor-ry af-fair. I

hang-in' out on Mon-day my Sun-day dreams to dry. Now a
know where all the blues are, 'cause, ba-by, I've been there. Now a

man is born to go a-lov-in', a wom-an's born to weep and
man is born to love a wom-an, to work and slave to pay her

fret, to stay at home and tend her ov-en, and drown her past re-grets in
debts. And just be-cause he's on-ly hu-man, to drown his past re-grets in

cof-fee and cig-a-rettes! I'm moon-in' all the morn-in', and mourn-in' all the night, and
cof-fee and cig-a-rettes! I'm moon-in' all the morn-in', and mourn-in' all the night, and

in be-tween it's nic-o-tine and not much heart to fight Black Cof-fee.
in be-tween it's nic-o-tine and not much heart to fight Black Cof-fee.

BLACK ORPHEUS

Words and Music by LUIZ BONFA

Copyright © 1968 by Chappell & Co.
Copyright Renewed

BLACK MARKET

Music by JOSEF ZAWINUL

© 1976 MULATTO MUSIC

BLACKBERRY WINTER

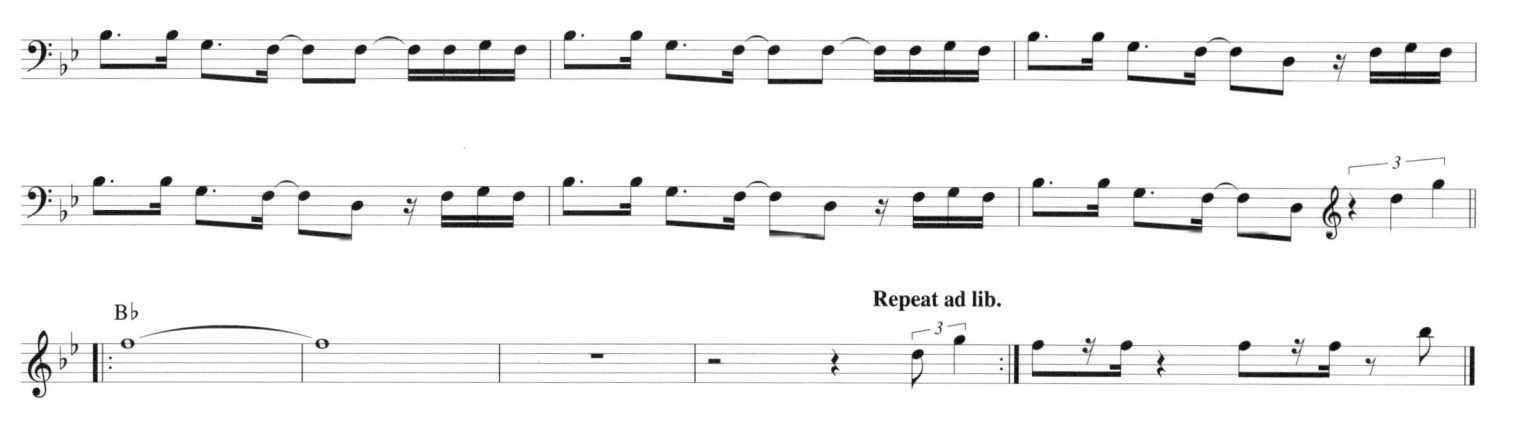

TRO - © Copyright 1976 Ludlow Music, Inc., New York, NY

Words and Music by ALEC WILDER
and LOONIS McGLOHON

Expressively

Black - ber - ry Win - ter comes with-out a warn - ing just when you think that spring's a - round to
Black - ber - ry Win - ter on - ly lasts a few days, just long e - nough to get you feel - ing

stay, so you wake up on a cold rain - y morn - ing and won - der what on earth be - came of
sad when you think of all the love that you wast - ed on some - one whom you nev - er real - ly

May. had. I'll nev - er get o - ver los - ing you, but I've had to

learn that life goes on. And the mem - o - ries grow dim like a half - for - got - ten song, 'til a

Black - ber - ry Win - ter re - minds me you are gone. And I get so lone - ly

most of all in spring - time. I wish I could en - joy the first of May, but I know it means that

Black - ber - ry Win - ter is not too far a - way.

BLAME IT ON MY YOUTH

Words by EDWARD HEYMAN
Music by OSCAR LEVANT

Copyright © 1934 PolyGram International Publishing, Inc. and Oscar Levant Music
Copyright Renewed
All Rights on behalf of Oscar Levant Music Administered by The Songwriters Guild of America

If I expected love when first we kissed, Blame It On My Youth;
If only just for you I did exist, Blame It On My Youth.
I believed in ev'rything like a child of three. You meant more than anything, all the world to me! If you were on my mind all night and day, Blame It On My Youth; If I forgot to eat and sleep and pray, Blame It On My Youth. If I cried a little bit when first I learned the truth, don't blame it on my heart, Blame It On My Youth.

BLUE TRAIN
(Blue Trane)

By JOHN COLTRANE

Copyright © 1957 (Renewed 1985) JOWCOL MUSIC

Medium Blues

BLUE PRELUDE

Copyright © 1933 (Renewed) by Music Sales Corporation (ASCAP)

Words by GORDON JENKINS
Music by JOE BISHOP

Slow Blues

Let me sigh, let me cry when I'm blue. Let me go 'way from this lone-ly town. Won't be long till my song will be thru', 'cause I know I'm on my last go round. All the love I could steal, beg or bor-row would-n't heal all this pain in my soul. What is love, but a pre-lude to sor-row with a heart-break a-head for your goal. Here I go, now you know why I'm leav-ing; Got the blues, what can I lose, good-bye.

BLUE STAR

Copyright © 1955 by Chappell & Co.
Copyright Renewed

Words by EDWARD HEYMAN
Music by VICTOR YOUNG

Slowly

Blue Star when I am blue, all I do is look at you. For I seem to find peace of mind, and I nev-er get lone-ly when you shine from a-far. With you a-way up there, I don't dare to have a care. For I want to show that your glow let's me know that you know that I'm not blue. Blue Star. Blue Star.

THE BLUE ROOM
from THE GIRL FRIEND

Words by LORENZ HART
Music by RICHARD RODGERS

Slowly, with expression

We'll have a blue room, a new room, for two room, where ev-'ry day's a hol-i-day be-cause you're mar-ried to me. Not like a ball-room a small room, a hall room, where {I/you} can smoke {my/your} pipe a-way, with {your/my} wee head up-on {my/your} knee. We will thrive on, keep a-live on just noth-ing but kiss-es, with Mis-ter and Mis-sus on lit-tle blue chairs. {You sew your/I'll wear my} trous-seau, and Rob-in-son Cru-soe is not so far from world-ly cares as our blue room far a-way up-stairs! stairs!

BLUES FOR ALICE

By CHARLIE PARKER

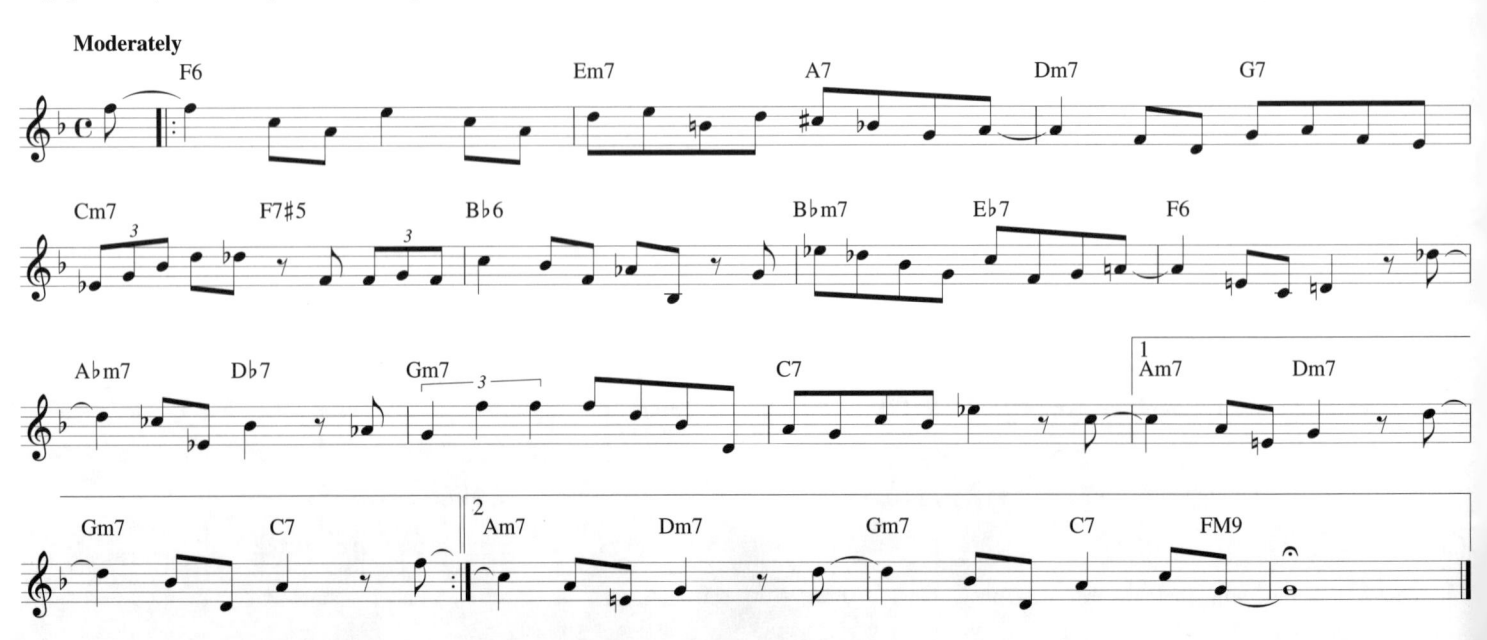

Moderately

BLUEPORT

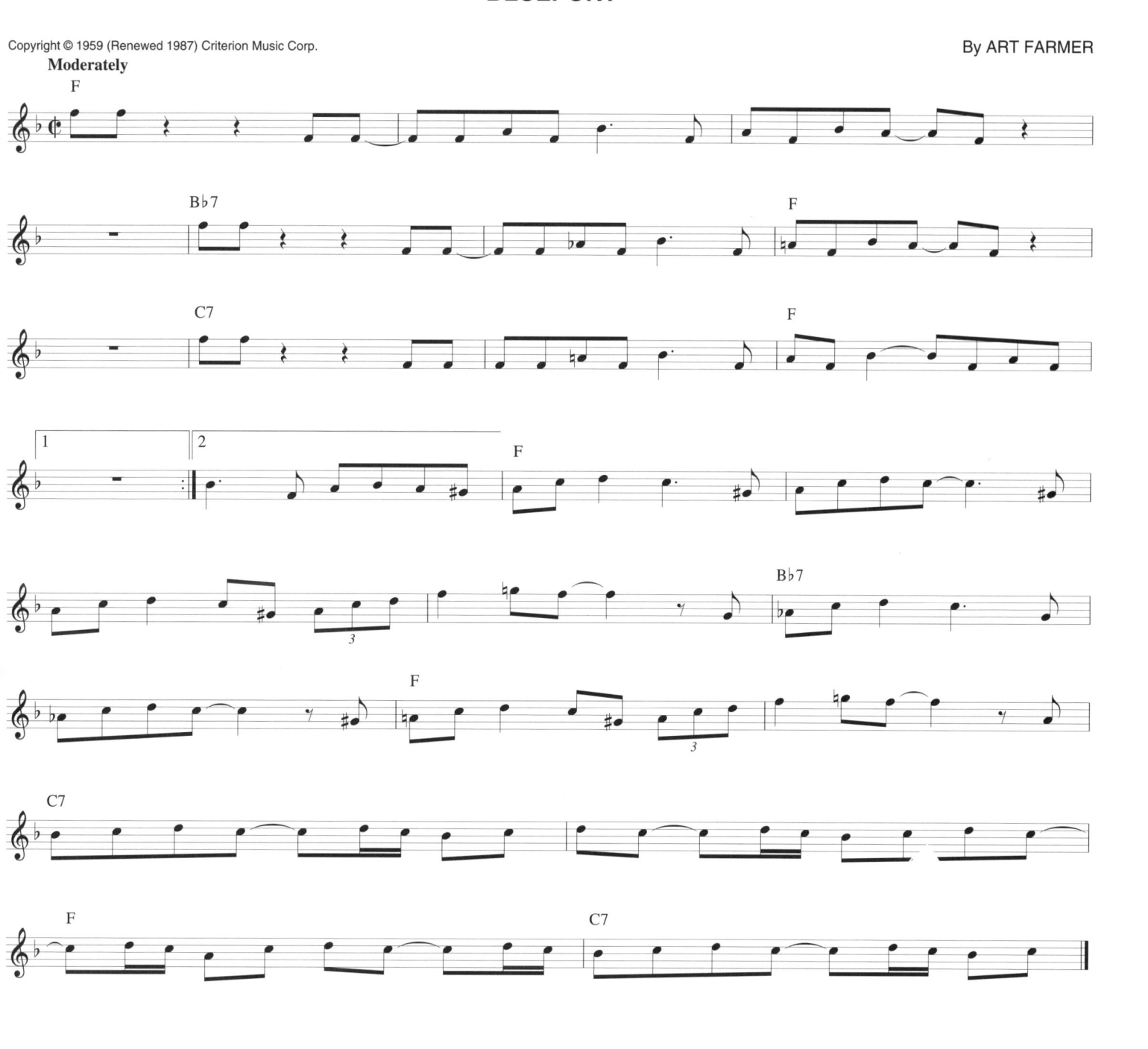

By ART FARMER

Copyright © 1959 (Renewed 1987) Criterion Music Corp.

BLUES IN TIME

By PAUL DESMOND

© 1957 (Renewed) Desmond Music Company

BLUES FOR D.P.

Written by RON CARTER

Copyright © 1981 RETRAC PRODUCTIONS, INC.

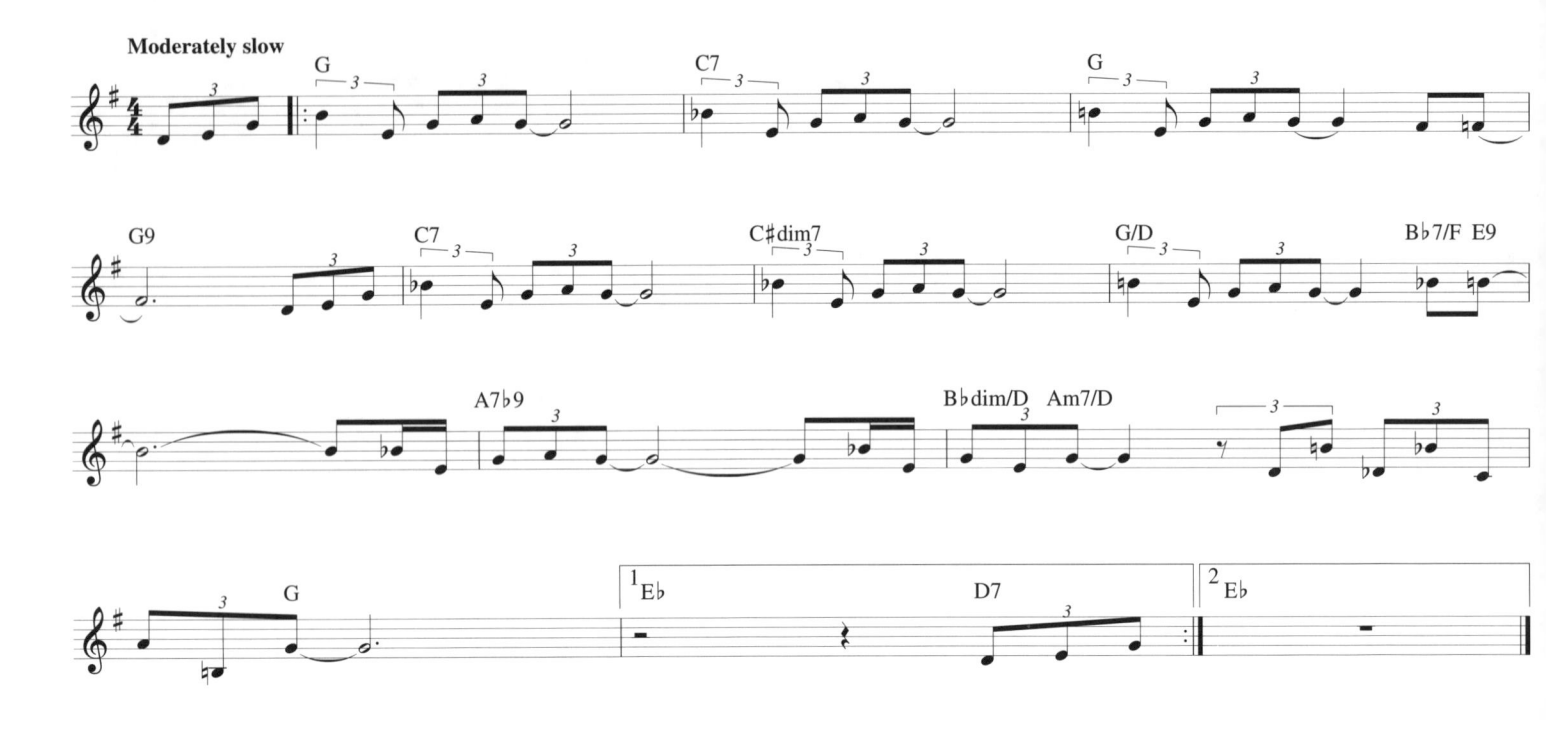

BLUES MARCH

By BENNY GOLSON

Copyright © 1958 (Renewed 1986) TIME STEP MUSIC (ASCAP)
All Rights Administered by MAYFLOWER MUSIC CORPORATION (ASCAP)

BLUES FOR JUNIOR
(Pyramid)

By RAY BROWN

BOSSA ANTIGUA

By PAUL DESMOND

BLUES FOR ROSALINDA

By FRANK MORGAN

Copyright © 1985 Sabirah Music (BMI)

BROADWAY

Words and Music by BILL BYRD, TEDDY McRAE and HENRI WOODE

Copyright © 1940 by Intersong U.S.A., Inc.
Copyright Renewed

Broad-way, Broad-way, ev-'ry-bod-y's hap-py and gay where the night is bright-er than day, all a-long Broad-way. Sweet-hearts and beaus on their way to mo-vies and shows dressed up in their Sun-day best clothes up and down Broad-way. Out of town, I'm low down when I walk a-long the main street. An-y-where, I don't care, but I al-ways find a main street just an-oth-er plain street. Broad-way, Broad-way, take a lit-tle time out for play where the joy of liv-ing holds sway all a-long Broad-way.

BORN TO BE BAD

Music by JOE SAMPLE

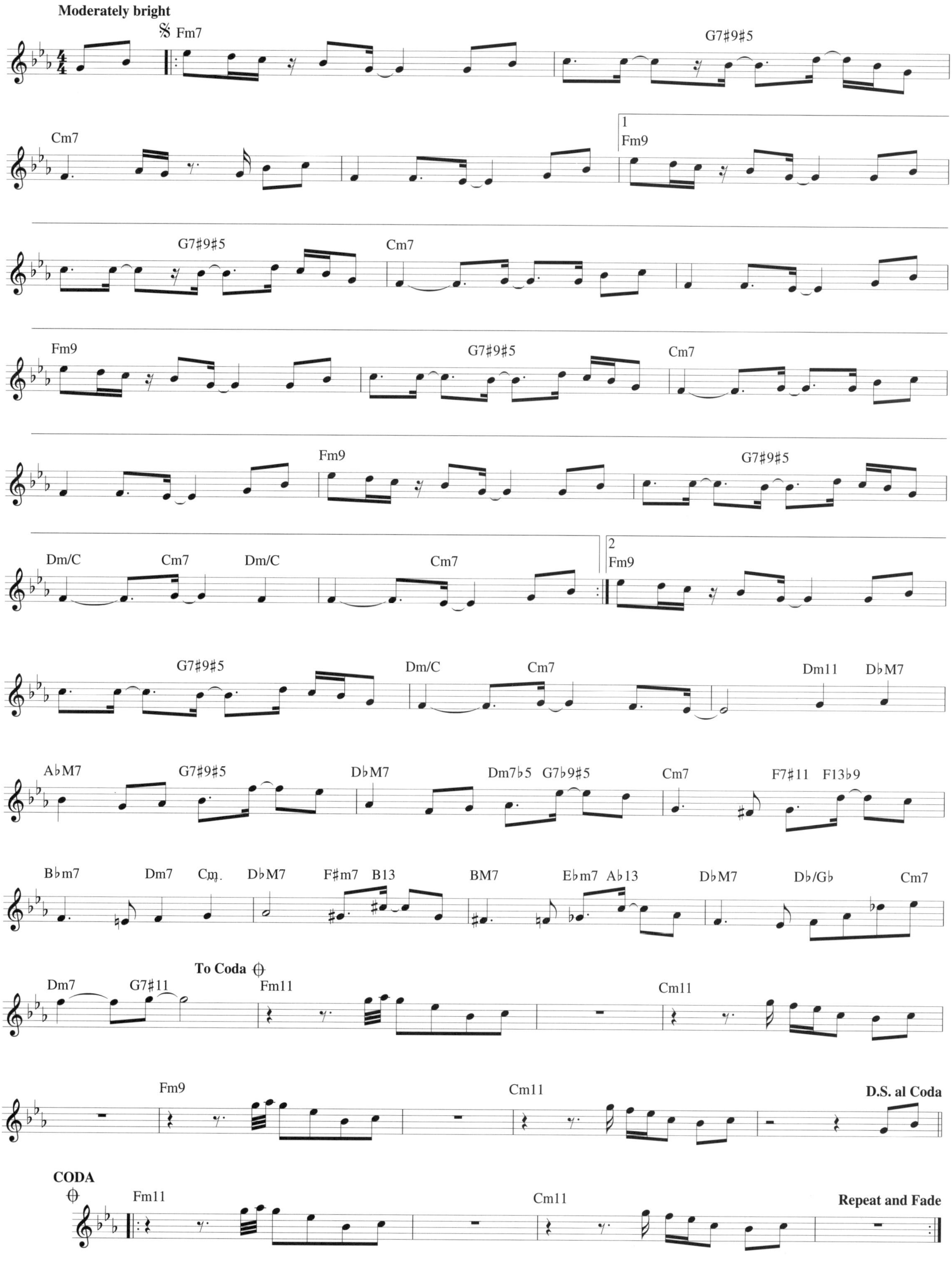

BOTH SIDES OF THE COIN

By MICHAEL BRECKER

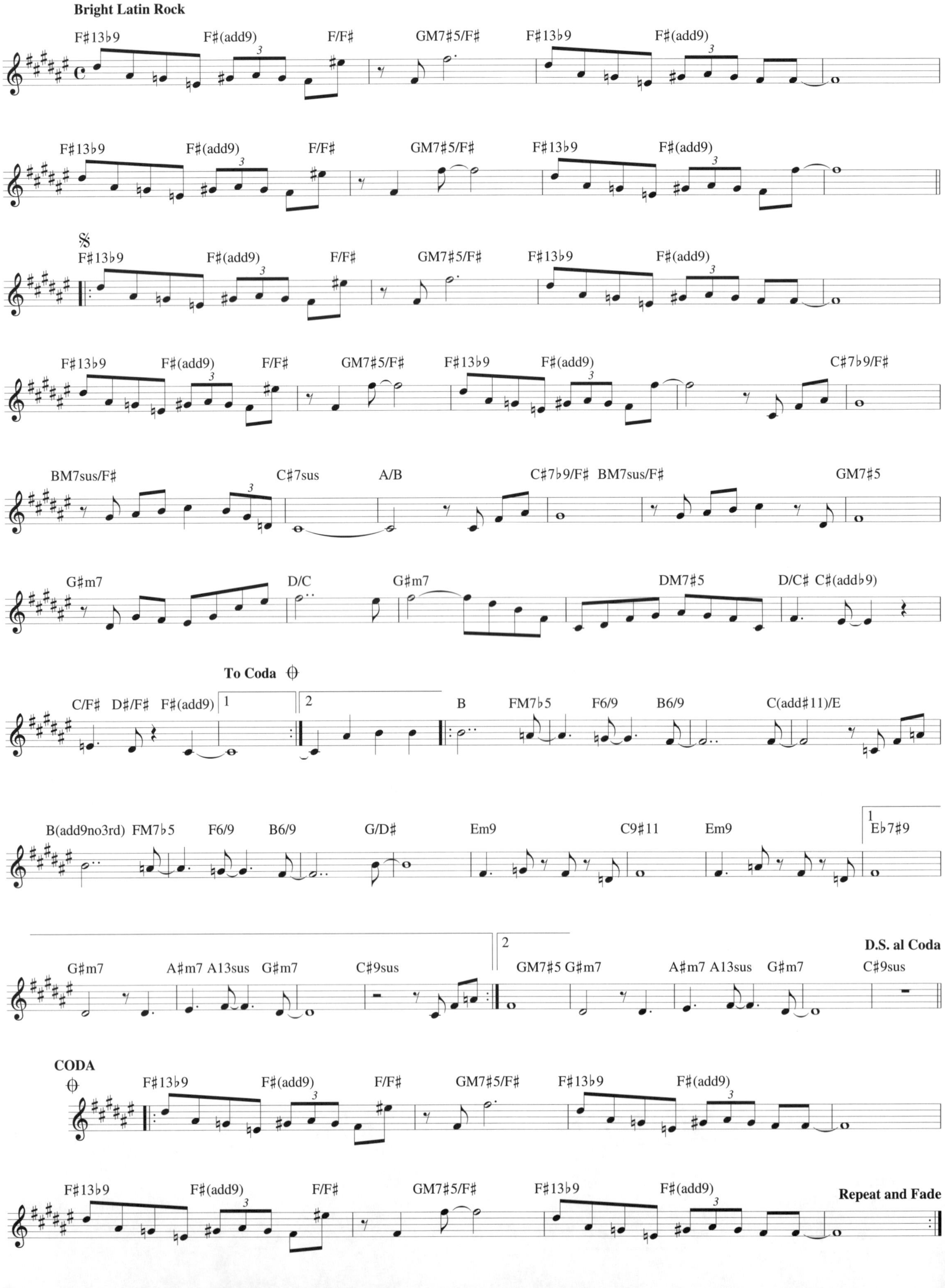

BRAZIL

Words and Music by S.K. RUSSELL
and ARY BARROSO

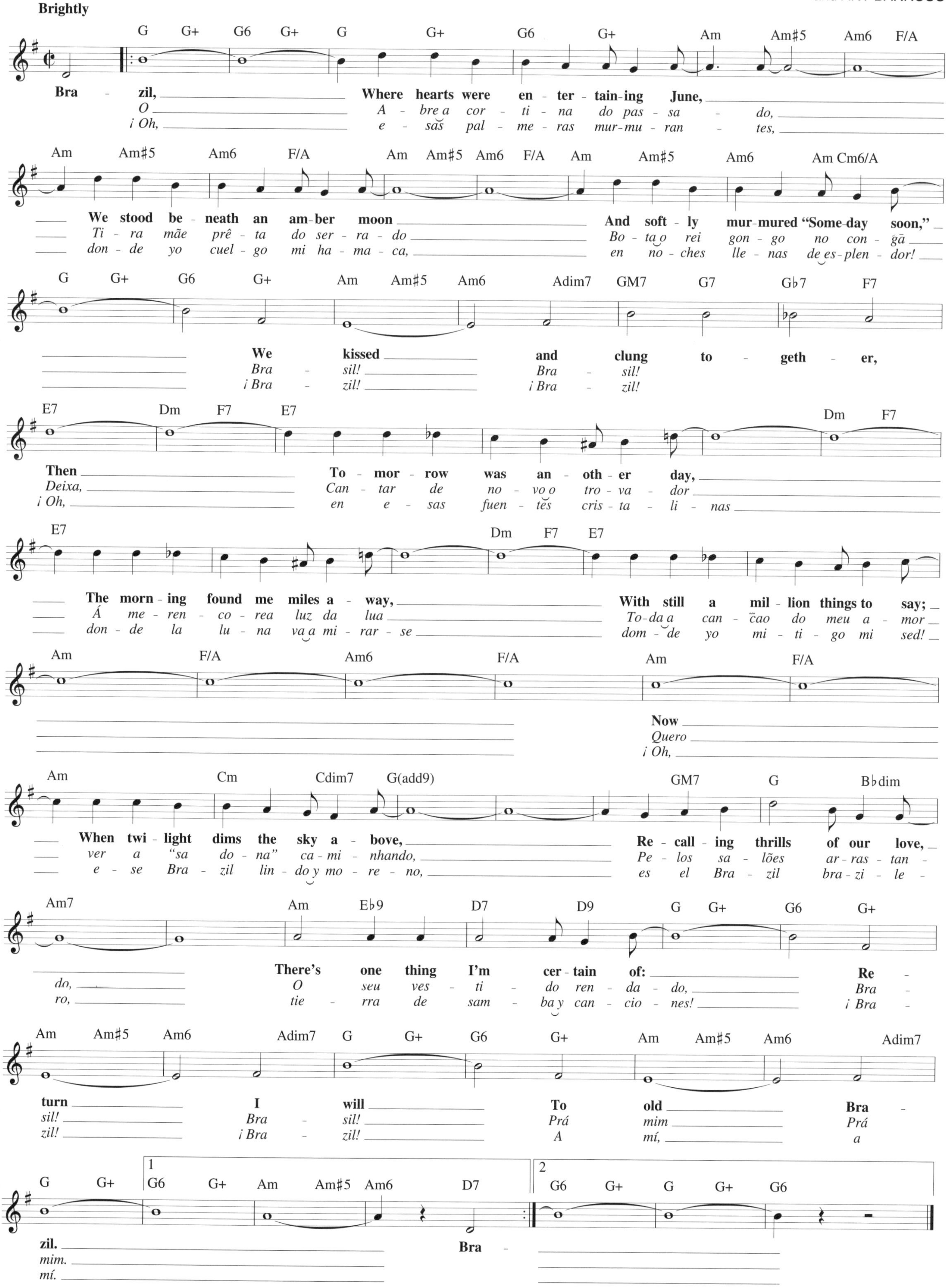

BREAKIN' AWAY

Words and Music by AL JARREAU,
JAY GRAYDON and TOM CANNING

63

Just Break-in' A - way, ___ your love ___ has o - pened eyes ___ that could - n't see.

Break - in' A - way, ___ your bea - con in ___ the night ___

___ dis - cov - ered me

Repeat and Fade

Break - in' A - way, ___

BLUES ON TIME

Copyright © by Toots Music

By JEAN "TOOTS" THIELEMANS

Slow Blues

BLUISH GREY

Copyright © 1987 Jazz Editions

Composed by THAD JONES

Moderately slow

BOOZE BROTHERS

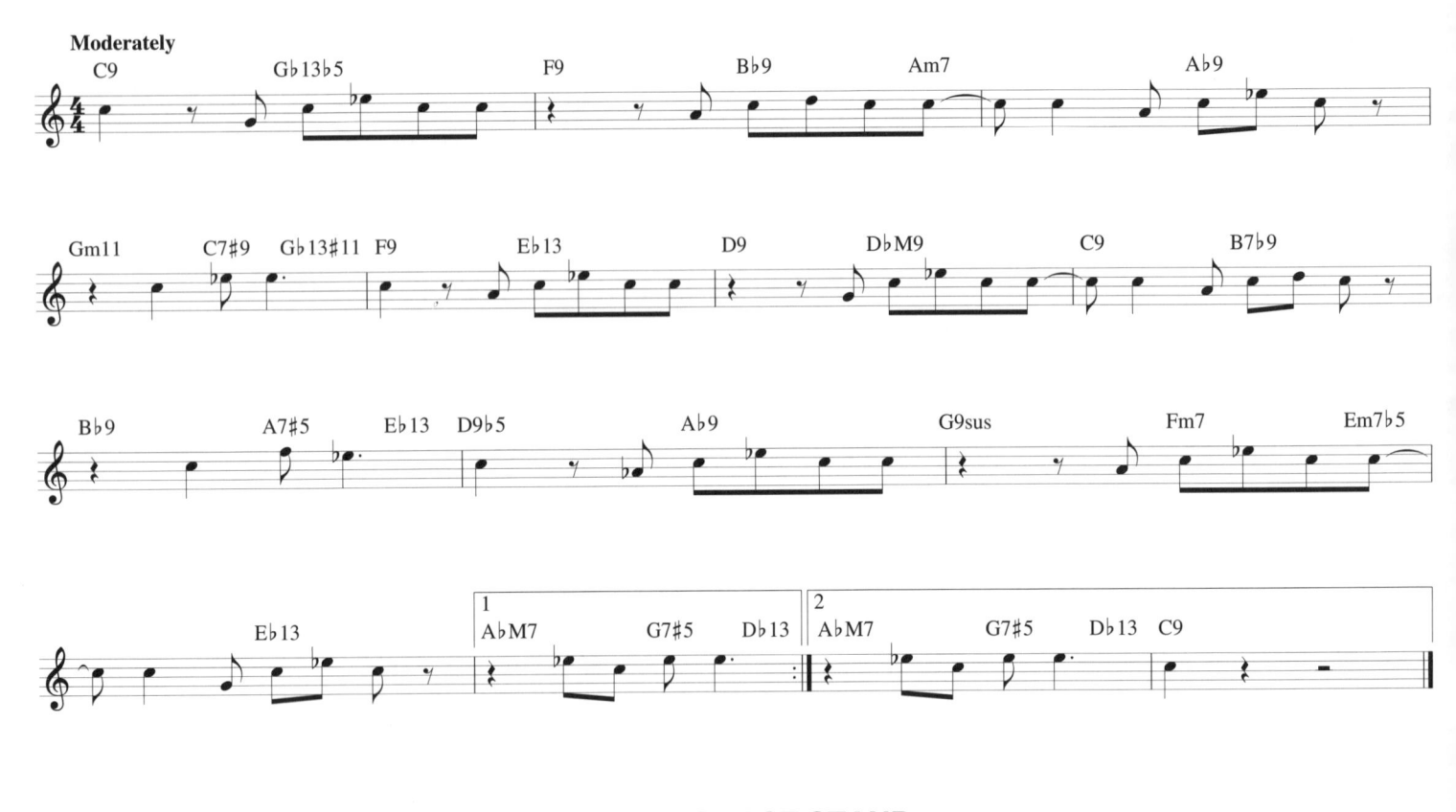

Composed by FRANK FOSTER

Copyright © 1989 by Swing That Music, Inc., Scarsdale, NY 10583

BUSTER'S LAST STAND

Written by GIL EVANS and CLAUDE THORNHILL

Copyright © 1942 (Renewed 1970) BOPPER SPOCK SUNS MUSIC and CHAPPELL & CO.

BULLET TRAIN

By LEE RITENOUR
and ERNIE WATTS

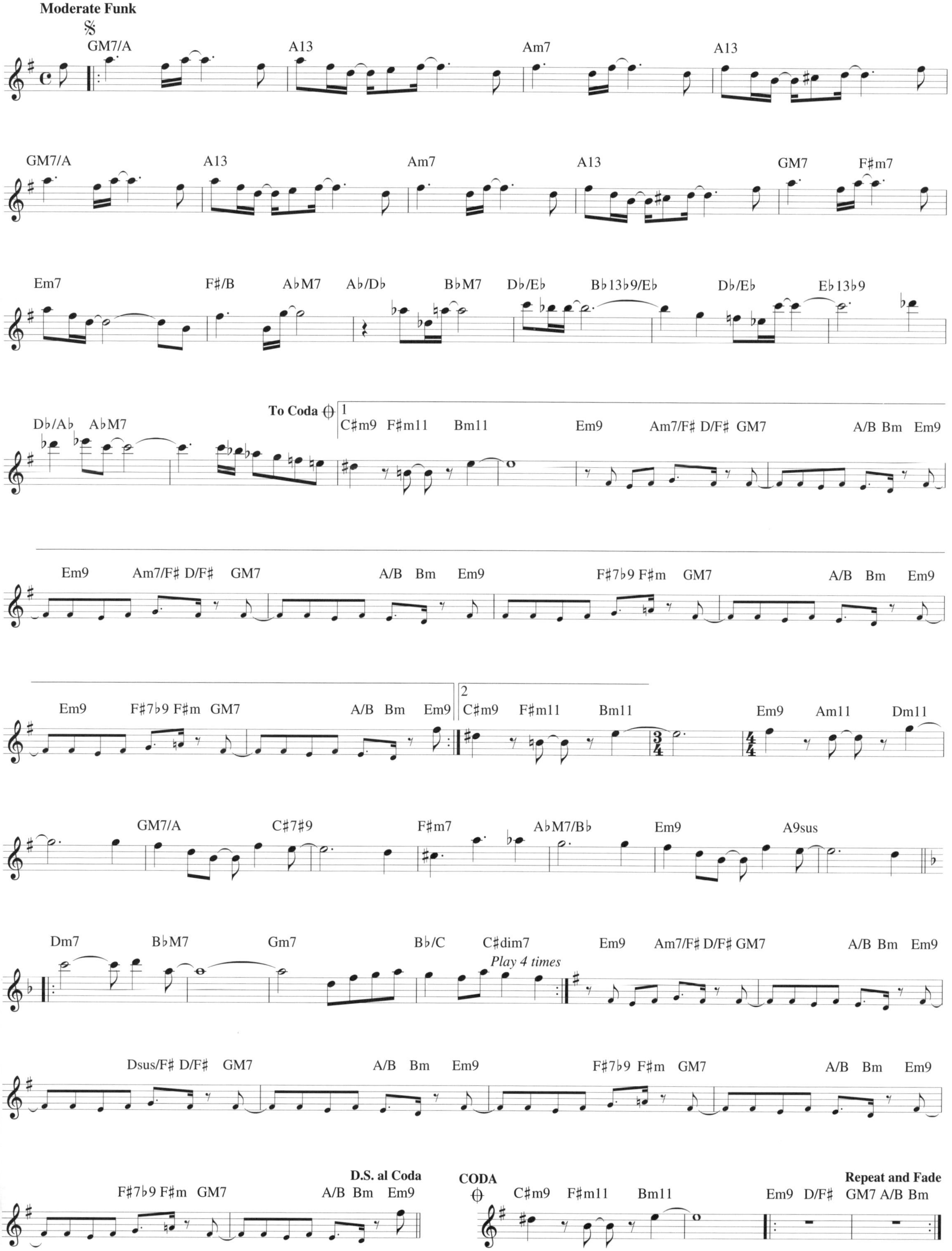

BYRD LIKE

By FREDDIE HUBBARD

CALL ME IRRESPONSIBLE

from the Paramount Picture PAPA'S DELICATE CONDITION

Words by SAMMY CAHN
Music by JAMES VAN HEUSEN

Can't Take You Nowhere

© 1987 Swiftwater Music

Music by TINY KAHN and AL COHEN
Words by DAVE FRISHBERG

Loose Swing

You knock back the schnapps, you talk back to cops, you walk in the room, and con-ver-sa-tion stops. I Can't Take You No-where. No, I Can't Take You No-where.

loud and you're lewd, you tend toward the crude, my friends are dis-gust-ed with your at-ti-tude.

You {stag-ger, you sag, you're half in the bag, one glass of beer and you're a to-tal drag. I Can't Take You No-where. No, I Can't Take You No-where.
     {mum-ble, you moan, you grum-ble, you groan, you called Hon-o-lu-lu on my tel-e-phone.

{I buy three or four, you mooch plen-ty more. The check comes a-round and you are out the door. I Can't Take You No-where. No, I Can't Take You No-where. I don't
{I hear peo-ple say you won't go a-way. You drop by for break-fast and you stay all day.

wan-na watch you fall on your face. You're Take You No-where.

That's right! Try not to get up tight.
way. So have a real nice day."

But I Can't Take You No-where, 'cause I don't know a place where you can show your face, and an-y-way, I'd just like to say, "So sad to see you must be on your way." must be on your way." What a pit-y to say, "So long!"

CAPTAIN FINGERS

By LEE RITENOUR

Copyright © 1977 RIT OF HABEAS MUSIC

CANTELOPE ISLAND

Copyright © 1964 (Renewed) by Hancock Music Co.

By HERBIE HANCOCK

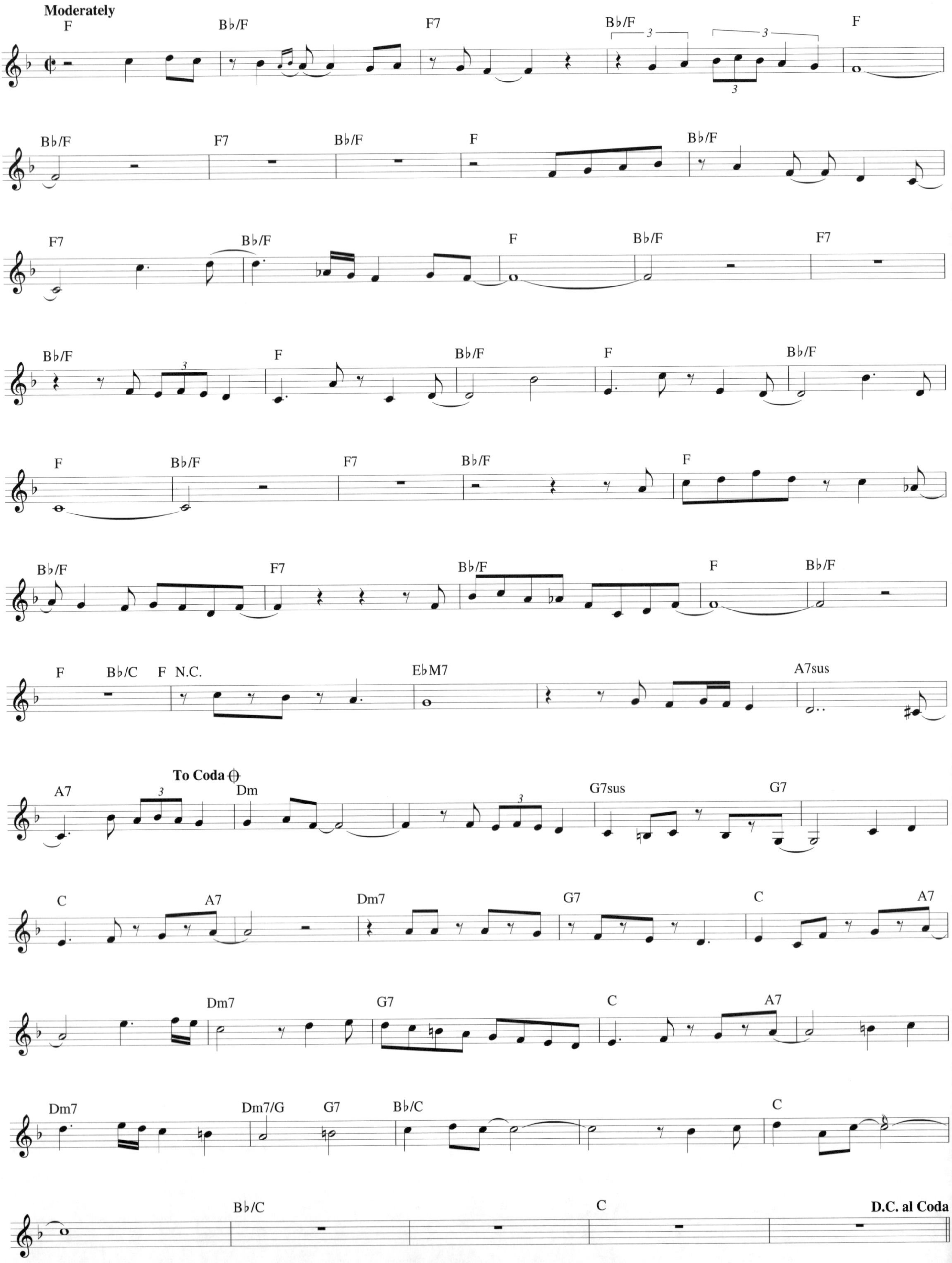

CAKE WALKING BABIES FROM HOME

Words and Music by HENRY TROY, CHRIS SMITH and CLARENCE WILLIAMS

Here they come, look at 'em {demonstratin'. / syncopatin'.} Goin' some, ain't they {syncopatin'? / demonstratin'?} Talk of the town, easin' 'round, pickin' 'em up and layin' 'em down. Dancin' fools, ain't they {demonstratin'? / syncopatin'?} They're in a class of their own. Now the only way to win is to cheat 'em, you may tie 'em but you'll never beat 'em. Strut your stuff, they're the Cake Walkin' Babies From Home. Strut your stuff, strut your stuff, Cake Walkin' Babies From Home.

CAREFUL

By JAMES S. HALL

Copyright © 1960 (Renewed 1988) by MJQ Music, Inc.

CANNONBALL

Music by JOSEF ZAWINUL

© 1976 MULATTO MUSIC

CARAVAN
from SOPHISTICATED LADIES

Words and Music by DUKE ELLINGTON,
IRVING MILLS and JUAN TIZOL

Copyright © 1937 (Renewed 1965) and Assigned to Famous Music Corporation and EMI Mills Music Inc. in the U.S.A.
Rights for the world outside the U.S.A. Controlled by EMI Mills Music Inc. and Warner Bros. Publications Inc.

Moderately

Night _____ and stars a - bove that shine so bright _____ the mys - t'ry
Sleep _____ up - on my shoul - der as we creep _____ a - cross the
you, _____ be - side me here be - neath the blue _____ my dream of

of their fad - ing light _____ that shines up - on our Car - a -
sands so I may keep _____ this mem - 'ry of our Car - a -
love is com - ing true _____ with - in our de - sert Car - a -

van.
van.
van.

This _____ is so ex - cit - ing, you _____ are so in -

D.C. al Fine

vit - ing rest - ing in my arms as I thrill to _____ the mag - ic charms _____ of

CECILIA IS LOVE

Copyright © 1971 by Swing That Music, Inc., Scarsdale, NY 10583

Composed by FRANK FOSTER

Moderately fast Bossa Nova

CAROLINA SHOUT

By JAMES P. JOHNSON

© Copyright 1925 by MCA MUSIC PUBLISHING, A Division of UNIVERSAL STUDIOS, INC.
Copyright Renewed

1 G F♯7 Bm F♯7 Bm Am D7
2 G G7/F
C/E Cm/E♭ G/D D7 G/B C♯dim G7
C C♯dim G7
1 C C♯dim G7 C C♯dim7
G/D D7 G/B C♯dim
2 C B B♭ A A7/C♯ Dm
C/G D7/A G7/B C7 F6 F♯dim C7 F6 F♯dim
3
1 C7 F6 F♯dim C B7 Em C7
2 C7 Gm/B♭ A7 Dm C/G D7/A G7/B C C♯dim
G7 C C♯dim G7/D G7 C C♯dim G7/D G7 C C♯dim
D7 G C♯dim G7/D G7 C C♯dim G7/D G7 C Gm/B♭
A7 Dm/F Fm/A♭ C/G D7/A G7/B C C♯dim G7/D G7 C C♯dim
G7/D G7
1 C C♯dim G7/D G7 C G/D D7 G/B C♯dim
2 C7/B♭ Gm/B♭ A7 Dm Fm C/G D7/A G/B C G7 C N.C.
E♭7 A♭7 G7 C N.C. G7♯5 C6
(8va)

CAST YOUR FATE TO THE WIND

Words and Music by VINCE GUARALDI and CAREL WERVER

A month of nights, a year of days, Octobers drifting into Mays. You set your sail when the tide comes in and you just Cast Your Fate To The Wind. You shift your course along the breeze, won't sail up-wind on memories. The empty sky is your best friend and you just Cast Your Fate To The Wind. That time has such a way of changing a man throughout the years. And now you're re-arranging your life thru all your tears alone, alone. There never was, there couldn't be a place in time for men to be, who'd drink the dark and laugh at day and let their wildest dreams blow away.

now you're old, you're wise you're smart, you're just a man with half a heart. You wonder how it might have been had you not Cast Your Fate To The Wind.

So Cast Your Fate To The Wind.

CHAMELEON

By HERBIE HANCOCK, PAUL JACKSON,
HARVEY MASON and BENNIE MAUPIN

CHANGE PARTNERS
from the RKO Radio Motion Picture CAREFREE

Words and Music by
IRVING BERLIN

C'EST SI BON
(It's So Good)

English Words by JERRY SEELEN
French Words by ANDRE HORNEZ
Music by HENRI BETTI

© Copyright 1947 by ARPEGE EDITIONS
Copyright Renewed
All Rights for the USA and Canada Controlled and Administered by
MCA MUSIC PUBLISHING, A Division of UNIVERSAL STUDIOS, INC.

Moderately

"C'est Si Bon," lov-ers say that in France, when they thrill to ro-mance, it means that it's so good. C'est Si Bon, so I say it to you, like the French peo-ple do, Be-cause it's oh, so good. Ev-'ry word, ev-'ry sigh, ev-'ry kiss, dear, leads to on-ly one thought and it's this, dear. It's so good, noth-ing else can re-place, just your slight-est em-brace. And if you on-ly would, be my

"C'est Si Bon," De par-tir n'im-porte où, Bras des-sus bras des-sous En chan-tant des chan-sons. C'est Si Bon, De se dir' 'des mots doux. Des pe-tits riens du tout Mais qui en di-sent long. En voy-ant no-tre mine a-mi ne ra-vi e, Les pas-sant dans la rue, nous en vient. dear. C'est Si Bon, De guet-ter dans ses yeux Un es-poir mer-veil-leux. And if you on-ly would, Qui don-ne le fris-son. C'est Si

"C'est Si Bon," De pou-voir l'em-bras-ser Et puis de r'com-men-cer A la moindre oc-ca-sion. C'est Si Bon, De jou-er du pla-no. Tout le long de son dow C'est i-tan-dis que nous dan-sons. Sans par-ler de c'que je n'peux pas dire. C'est Si Bon, Quand j'la tiens dans mes bras, De me dir' que tout ca C'est á moi pour de bon. C'est Si

CHRISTINA

© 1983 Buster Williams Productions, Inc. (SESAC)
All Rights Administered by Soroka Music Ltd.

By BUSTER WILLIAMS

CHANGE OF SEASON

CHASIN' THE TRANE

A CHILD IS BORN

By THAD JONES

COCKTAILS FOR TWO

from the Paramount Picture MURDER AT THE VANITIES

Words and Music by ARTHUR JOHNSTON
and SAM COSLOW

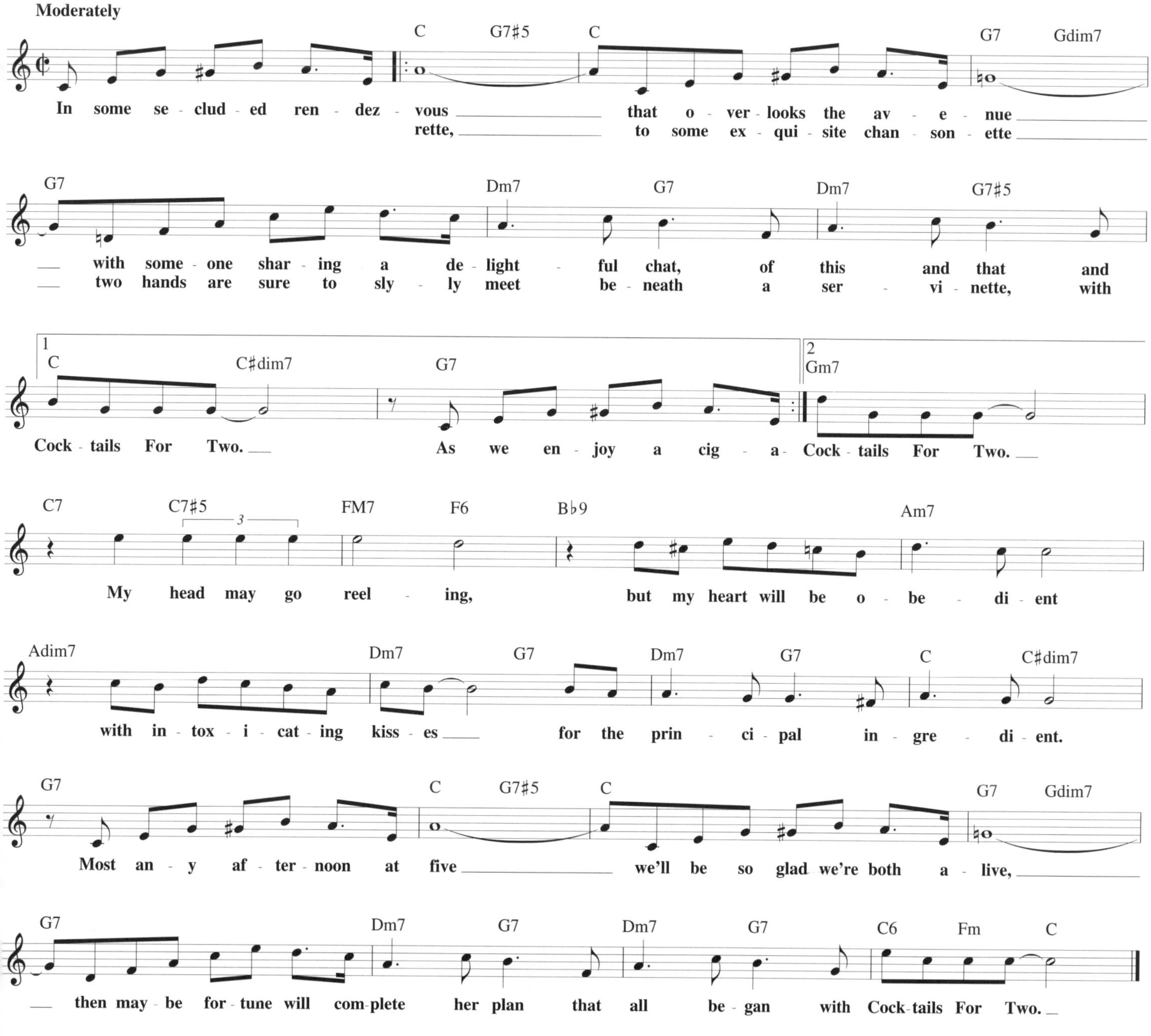

CHROMOZONE

By MIKE STERN

Copyright © 1988 Little Shoes Music (ASCAP)

COME BACK TO ME
from ON A CLEAR DAY YOU CAN SEE FOREVER

Lyrics by ALAN JAY LERNER
Music by BURTON LANE

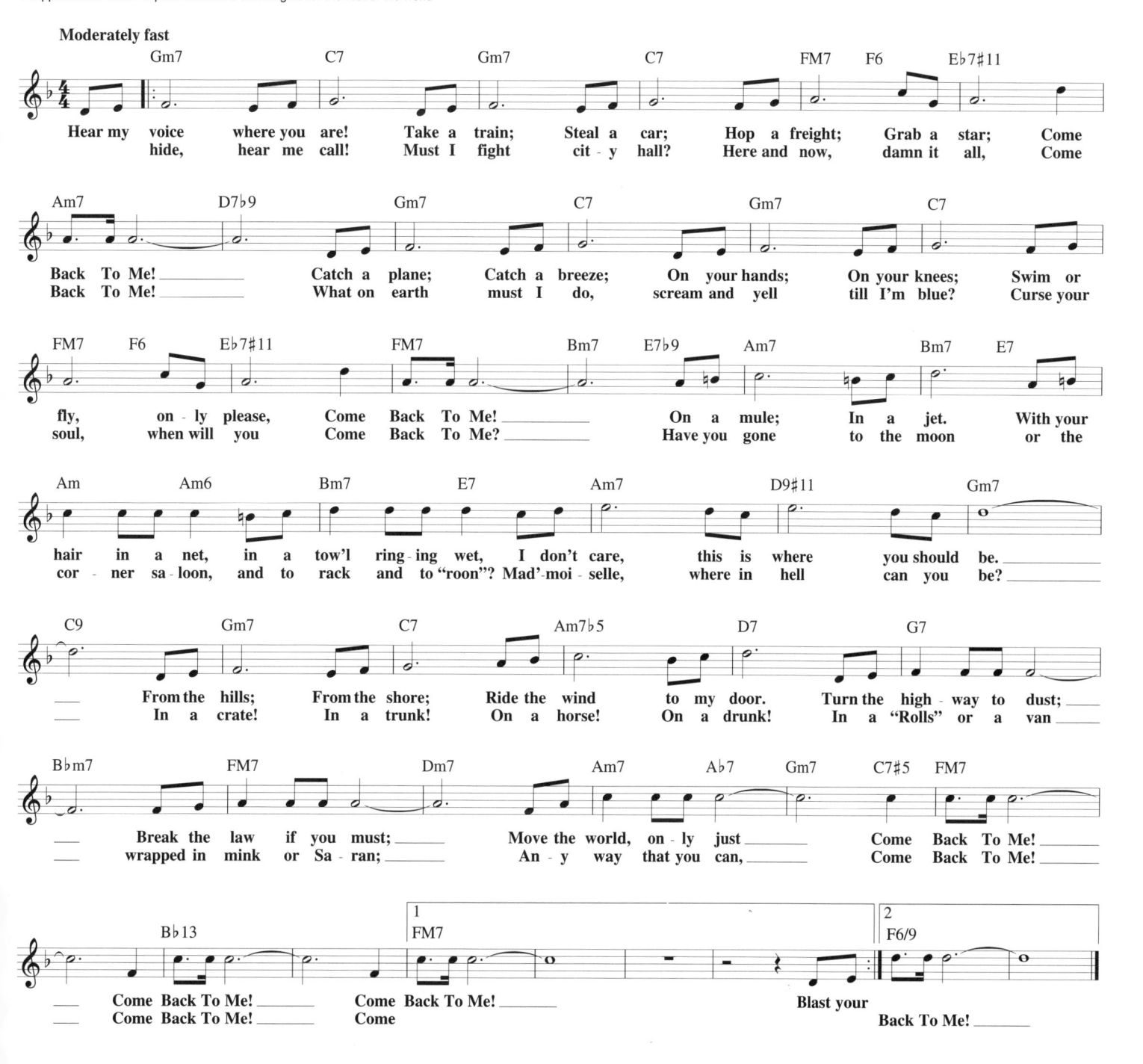

Moderately fast

Hear my voice where you are! Take a train; Steal a car; Hop a freight; Grab a star; Come
hide, hear me call! Must I fight cit-y hall? Here and now, damn it all, Come

Back To Me! Catch a plane; Catch a breeze; On your hands; On your knees; Swim or
Back To Me! What on earth must I do, scream and yell till I'm blue? Curse your

fly, on-ly please, Come Back To Me! On a mule; In a jet. With your
soul, when will you Come Back To Me? Have you gone to the moon or the

hair in a net, in a tow'l ring-ing wet, I don't care, this is where you should be.
cor-ner sa-loon, and to rack and to "roon"? Mad'-moi-selle, where in hell can you be?

From the hills; From the shore; Ride the wind to my door. Turn the high-way to dust;
In a crate! In a trunk! On a horse! On a drunk! In a "Rolls" or a van

Break the law if you must; Move the world, on-ly just Come Back To Me!
wrapped in mink or Sa-ran; An-y way that you can, Come Back To Me!

Come Back To Me! Come Back To Me! Blast your
Come Back To Me! Come Back To Me! Come Back To Me!

CON ALMA

Music by JOHN "DIZZY" GILLESPIE

Copyright © 1956 by Jatap Publishing Co., Inc.
Copyright Renewed 1984 by John Dizzy Gillespie

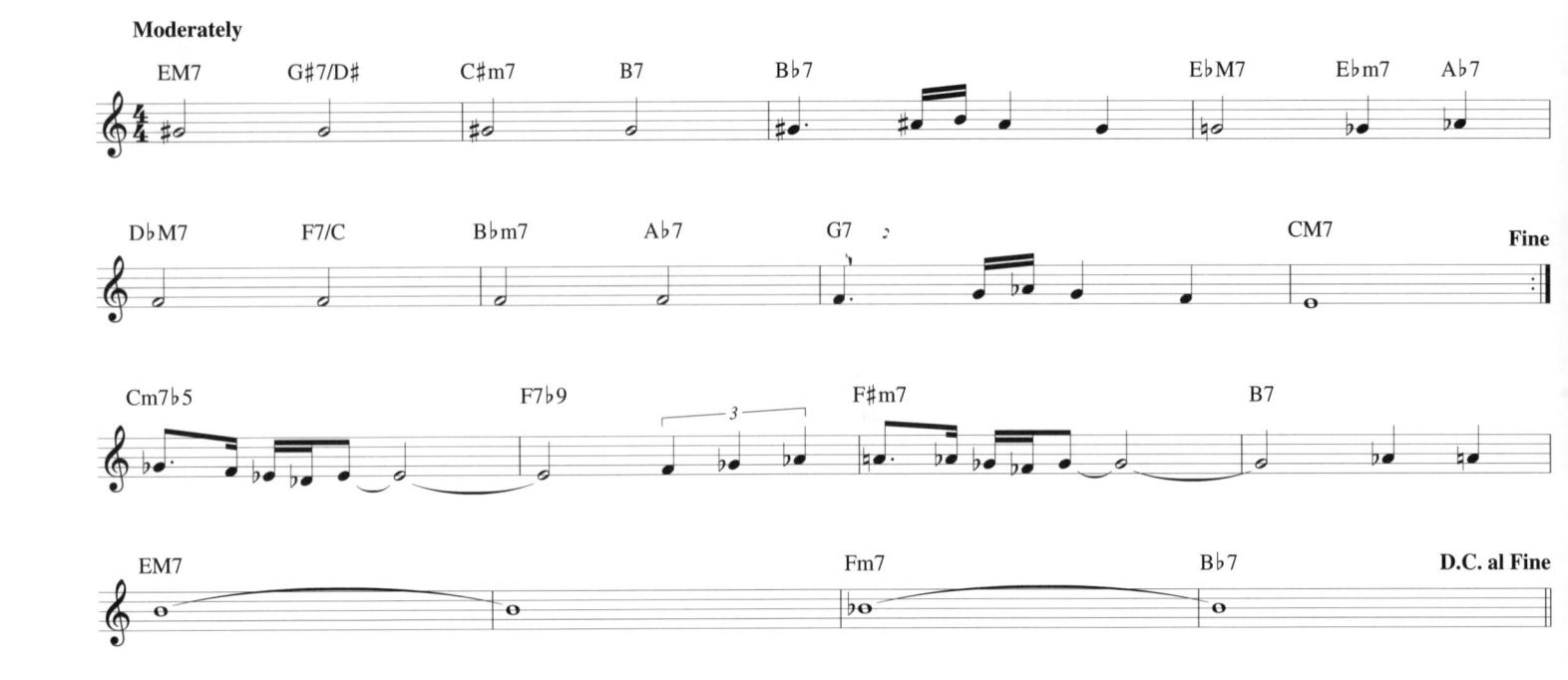

CONCEPTION

By GEORGE SHEARING

© 1950 (Renewed 1978) SCREEN GEMS-EMI MUSIC INC.

CONTINENTAL BLUES

By ERNIE WATTS

COUSIN MARY

By JOHN COLTRANE

THE CRAVE

© 1939 TEMPO MUSIC PUBLISHING CO.
© Renewed 1967 EDWIN H. MORRIS & COMPANY, A Division of MPL Communications, Inc.

By FERDINAND "JELLY ROLL" MORTON

F Abdim C7 C7#5
F N.C. F
Cm F7 Bb Bdim F C7
F N.C. Bb N.C. Bb
Edim Cm F7
Bb Edim F7 N.C. Bb N.C.
Bb A Dm
A7 Dm N.C. F7
Bb
F7 3 3 Bb
Bb7 Eb
Edim 8va Bb Edim F7
Bb Gdim F7 Bb N.C. Bb N.C.

DAHOMEY DANCE

By JOHN COLTRANE

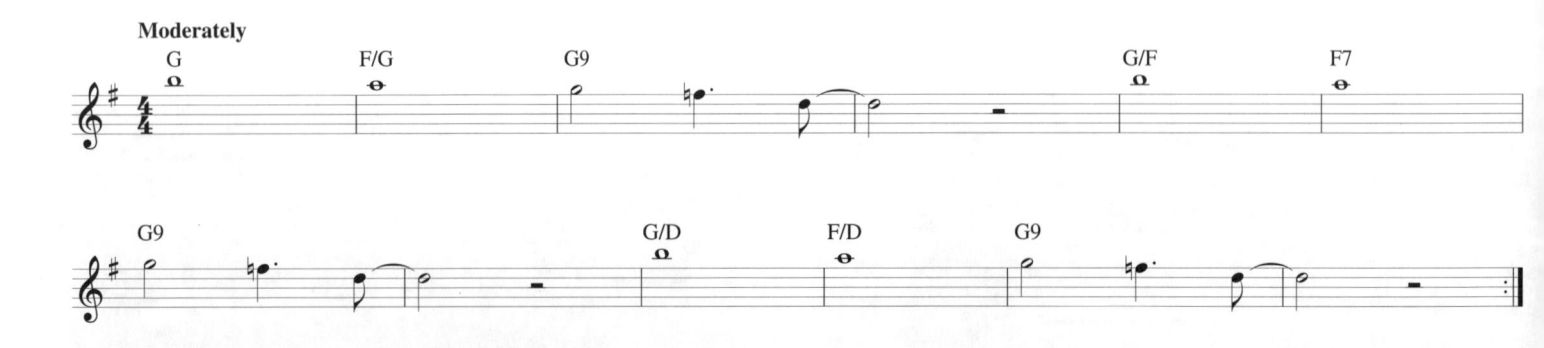

Copyright © 1977 JOWCOL MUSIC

COPENHAGEN

Lyric by WALTER MELROSE
Music by CHARLIE DAVIS

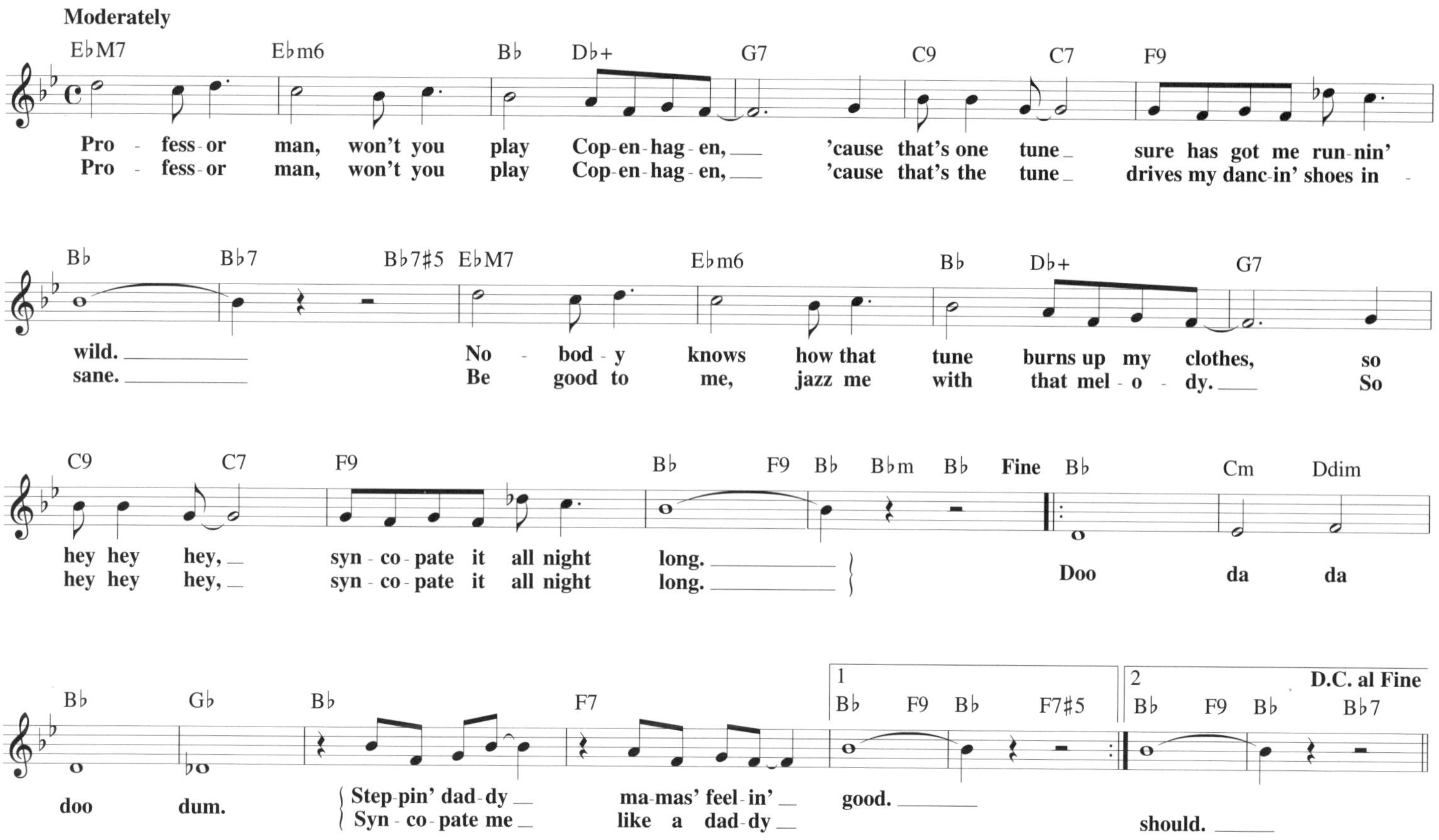

CRAZYOLOGY

By BENNIE HARRIS

THE CREOLE LOVE CALL

By DUKE ELLINGTON

THE DAWN OF TIME

Written by JOE LOVANO

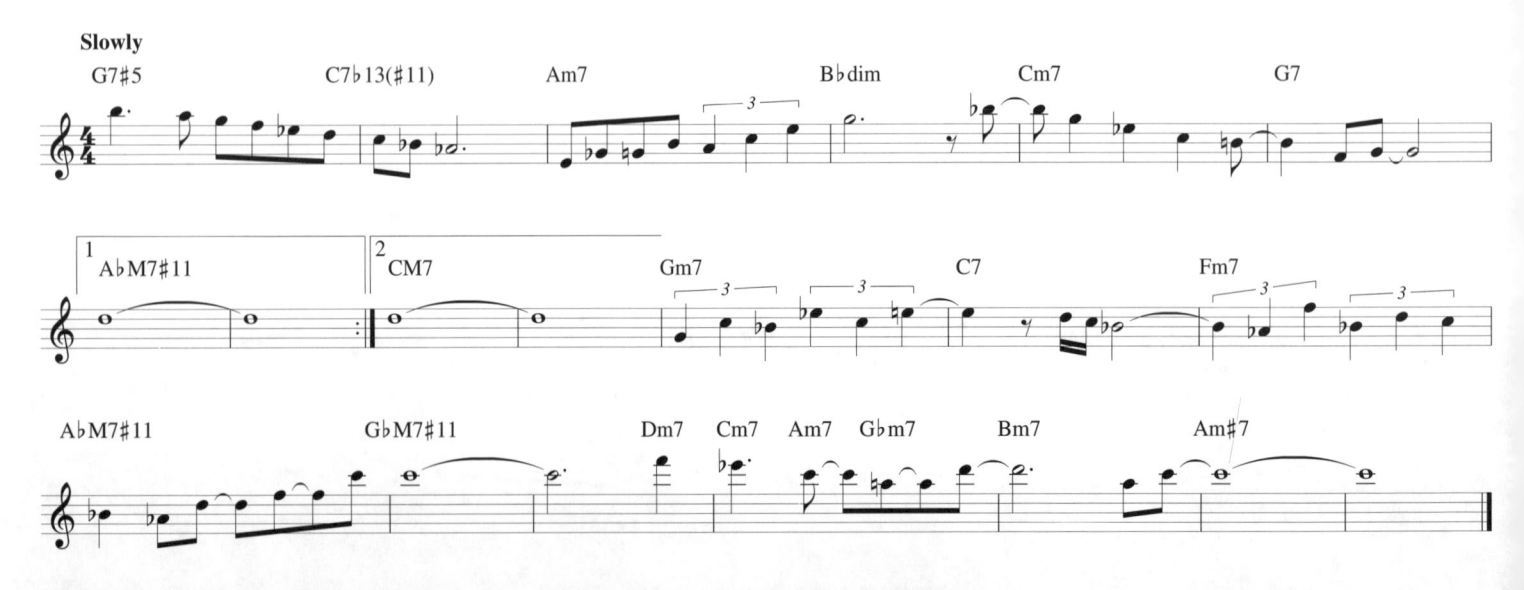

DANCING ON THE CEILING
from SIMPLE SIMON

Copyright © 1931 by Williamson Music and The Estate Of Lorenz Hart in the United States
Copyright Renewed
All Rights on behalf of The Estate Of Lorenz Hart Administered by WB Music Corp.

Words by LORENZ HART
Music by RICHARD RODGERS

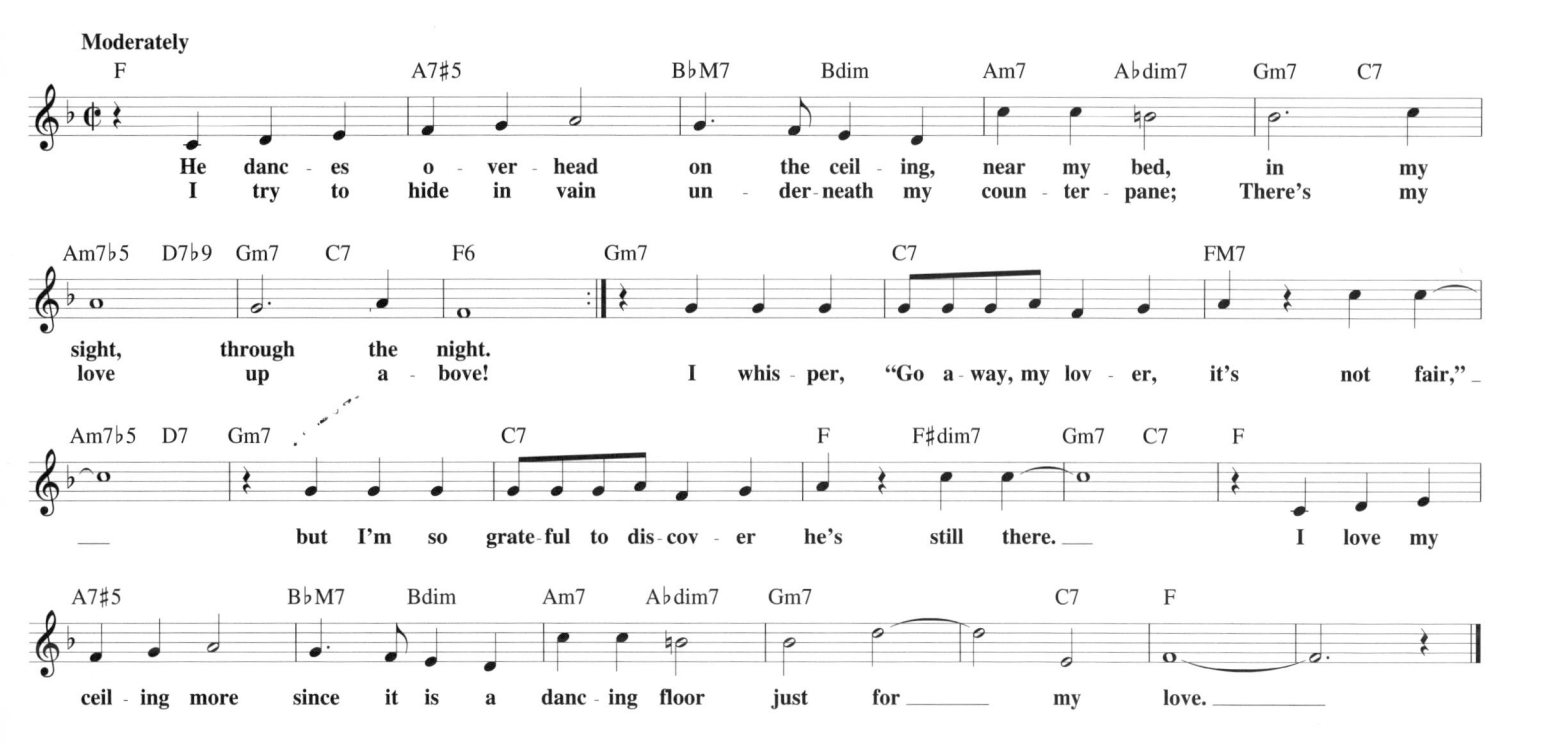

He danc-es o-ver-head on the ceil-ing, near my bed, in my sight, through the night.
I try to hide in vain un-der-neath my coun-ter-pane; There's my love up a-bove!

I whis-per, "Go a-way, my lov-er, it's not fair," but I'm so grate-ful to dis-cov-er he's still there. I love my ceil-ing more since it is a danc-ing floor just for my love.

DARLING, JE VOUS AIME BEAUCOUP
from LOVE AND HISSES

Copyright © 1935 by Francis Day S.A.
Copyright Renewed
All Rights for the U.S.A. Controlled by Chappell & Co.

Words and Music by ANNA SOSENKO

Dar-ling, Je Vous Aime Beau-coup, Je ne sais pas. What to do, you know you've com-plete-ly sto-len my heart. Morn-ing, noon and night-time too, Tou-jours won-d'ring what you do. That's the way I've felt right from the start. Ah, Cher-ie! my love for you is trés, trés, fort; Wish my French were good e-nough, I'd tell you so much more. But I hope that you com-pree all the things you mean to me.

1. Dar-ling, Je Vous Aime Beau-coup, I love you!
2. Aime Beau-coup, I love you, yes, I do.

CROSS MY HEART

Copyright © 1982 RIT OF HABEAS MUSIC and CAPTAIN FINGERS PRODUCTIONS

By LEE RITENOUR and ERIC TAGG

With a beat

You asked me all about my past, my oth-er love af-fair. 'Cause you're not sure, though this love will last, 'bout if I'd ev-er leave you.

You saw me with an-oth-er girl, you think that I'm un-true. For all the gold that was in the world, I would nev-er trade your love.

Can't you see, you're the on-ly one. Why won't you be-lieve in me? But I don't know what you think I've done, can't look you in the eyes.

Cross My Heart, I'd nev-er de-ceive you. So Cross My Heart, I would

1. nev-er tell you lies.
2. nev-er leave your love.

Cross My Heart, I'd nev-er de-ceive you. So Cross My Heart, I would nev-er tell you lies. You don't have to wor-ry 'bout me,

DECEPTACON

© 1986 Buster Williams Productions, Inc. (SESAC)
All Rights Administered by Soroka Music Ltd.

By BUSTER WILLIAMS

DOCTOR JAZZ
from JELLY'S LAST JAM

Lyric by WALTER MELROSE
Music by JOSEPH "KING" OLIVER

CRYSTAL SILENCE

Music by CHICK COREA

CUPCAKE

Copyright © 1993 Benny Green Music (BMI)

By BENNY GREEN

Moderately slow

DAT DERE

Music by BOBBY TIMMONS
Lyrics by OSCAR BROWN, JR.

Copyright © 1960 (Renewed 1988) by UPAM MUSIC CO., a division of Gopam Enterprises, Inc.

Moderately

Hey, dad-dy, what Dat Dere? 'N' why dat un-der dere? 'N' oh, dad-dy, oh,
who dat in my chair? 'N' what she do-in' dere? 'N' oh, dad-dy, oh,

hey, dad-dy hey look it ob-er dere. Hey, where dey go-in' dere? 'N'
hey, dad-dy can I go ob-er dere? Hey, dad-dy what's a square? 'N'

what dey do in dere? 'N' dad-dy, can I ha' dat big el-e-phant ob-er dere?
where do we get air? 'N' dad-dy, can I ha' dat big el-e-phant ob-er dere?

Hey My quiz-za-cal kid, man he does-n't want

an-y thing hid, he's for-ev-er de-mand-ing to know who, 'n' what 'n' why 'n' where.

In qui-sa-tive child and some-times the ques-tions are wild, like dad-dy can

I ha' dat big ele-punt ob-er dere? Don' wan-na comb my hair 'n'

where my ted-dy bear? 'N' oh, dad-dy, oh, hey look a dat cow-boy com-in' dere!

To Coda

Hey, can I hab a pair o' boots like dat to wear? 'N' dad-dy, can

I ha' dat big el-e-punt ob-er dere? The time will march, the
life's par-ade goes

years will go, the lit-tle fel-la's gon-na grow. I got-ta tell him what he
trudg-in' by, he'll need to know some rea-sons why. I don't have all the an-swers

DON'T WORRY 'BOUT ME
from COTTON CLUB PARADE

Copyright © 1939 (Renewed) Ted Koehler Music and EMI Mills Music Inc.
All rights for the extended term administered by Fred Ahlert Music Corporation
on behalf of Ted Koehler Music

Lyric by TED KOEHLER
Music by RUBE BLOOM

Moderately

Don't Wor-ry 'Bout Me, I'll get a-long; For-get a-bout me, be hap-py, my love. Let's say that our lit-tle show is o-ver and so, the sto-ry ends; Why not call it a day the sen-si-ble way, and still be friends. "Look out for your-self" should be the rule; Give your heart and your love to whom-ev-er you love, don't be a fool. Dar-ling, why should you cling to some fad-ing thing that used to be? If you can for-get, Don't Wor-ry 'Bout Me.

DON'T YOU KNOW I CARE
(Or Don't You Care to Know)

Words by MACK DAVID
Music by DUKE ELLINGTON

Slowly

Don't You Know I Care or don't you care to know?_ If you know I care how can you hurt me so?_ Dar-ling, you are part of ev-'ry breath I take,_ will you break my heart or give my heart a break?_ I can't fig-ure out_ what love's all a-bout_ and where I fit in-to your scheme._ Am I wast-ing time,_ please tell me 'cause I'm down to my last dream? Won't you please be fair, love me or let me go._ Don't You Know I Care or don't you care to know?_

CURVES AHEAD

By RUSS FREEMAN

Moderate Latin Rock

DREAM A LITTLE DREAM OF ME

TRO - © Copyright 1930 (Renewed) and 1931 (Renewed) Essex Music, Inc., Words and Music, Inc., New York, NY,
Don Swan Publications, Miami, FL and Gilbert Keyes Music, Hollywood, CA

Words by GUS KAHN
Music by WILBUR SCHWANDT
and FABIAN ANDREE

Moderately

Stars shining bright above you, night breezes seem to whisper, "I love you," birds singing in the sycamore tree, "Dream A Little Dream Of Me." Say "Nightie-night" and kiss me, just hold me tight and tell me you'll miss me; While I'm alone and blue as can be, Dream A Little Dream Of Me. Stars fading, but I linger on, dear, still craving your kiss; I'm longing to linger till dawn, dear, just saying this: Sweet dreams till sunbeams find you, sweet dreams that leave all worries behind you, but in your dreams whatever they be, Dream A Little Dream Of Me. Me.

DETOUR AHEAD

By HERB ELLIS, JOHN FRIGO and LOU CARTER

Copyright © 1948 (Renewed 1976) by Woodrow Music Inc.

Slowly

Smooth road, clear day, but why am I the only one trav-'lin' this
Wake up, slow down be-fore you crash and break your heart, gull-i-ble
way? How strange the road to love should be so eas-y,
clown. You fool, you're head-ed in the wrong di-rec-tion,

1. can there be a De-tour A-head?
2. can't you see the De-tour A-head? The far-ther you trav-el, the hard-er to un-rav-el the web he spins a-round you. Turn back while there's time, can't you see the dan-ger sign; soft shoul-ders sur-round you. Smooth road, clear night; oh, luck-y me, that sud-den-ly I saw the light. I'm turn-ing back a-way from all this trou-ble. Smooth road, smooth road, no De-tour A-head.

DIMINUSHING

Copyright © 1958 (Renewed) by Publications Francis Day S.A.
All Rights in the U.S.A. and Canada Controlled by Jewel Music Publishing Co., Inc.

By DJANGO REINHARDT

Moderately slow

DON'T SMOKE IN BED

© Copyright 1948 by MCA MUSIC PUBLISHING, A Division of UNIVERSAL STUDIOS, INC.
Copyright Renewed

By WILLIARD ROBINSON

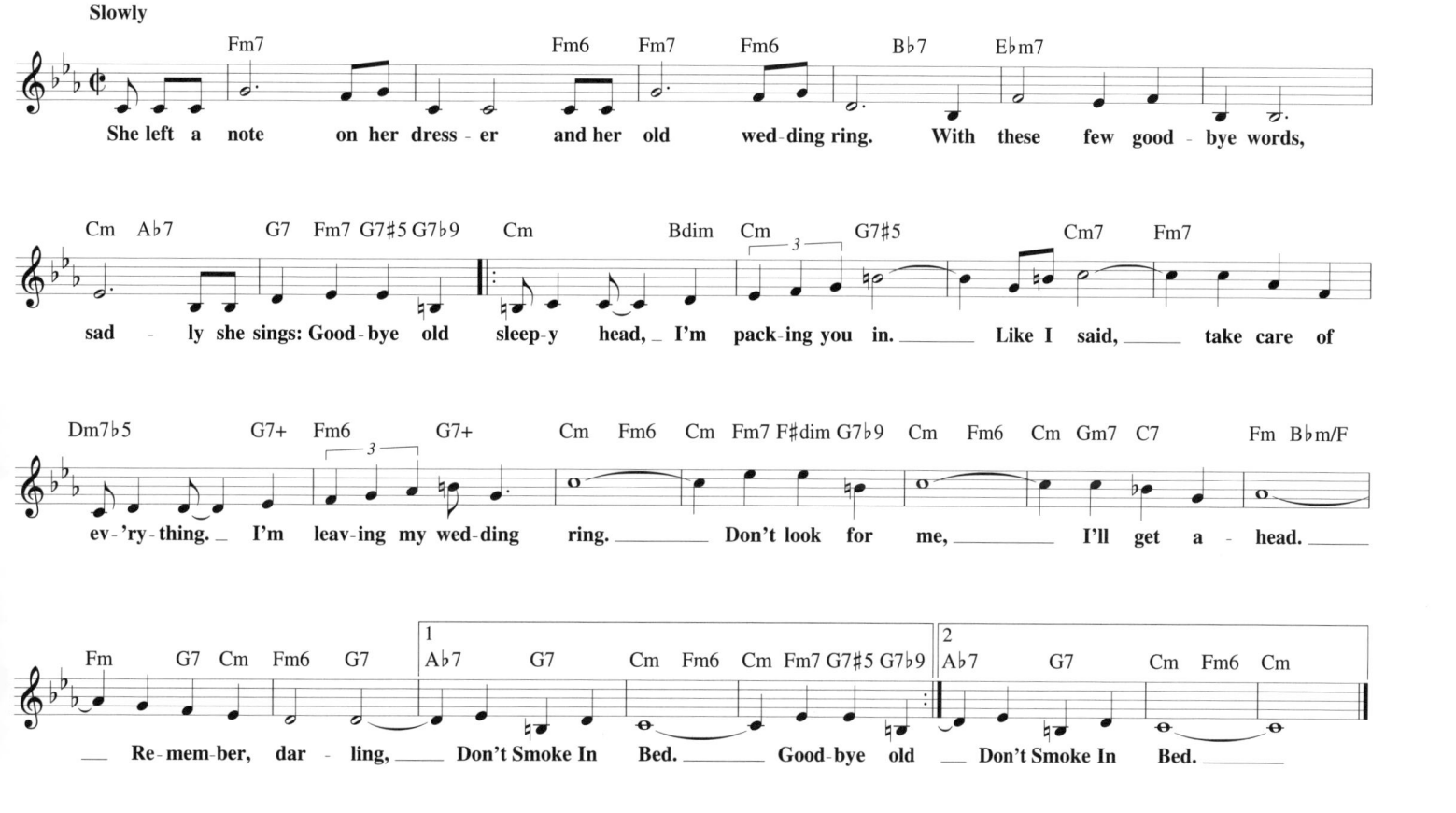

Slowly

She left a note on her dress-er and her old wed-ding ring. With these few good-bye words, sad-ly she sings: Good-bye old sleep-y head, I'm pack-ing you in. Like I said, take care of ev-'ry-thing. I'm leav-ing my wed-ding ring. Don't look for me, I'll get a-head. Re-mem-ber, dar-ling, Don't Smoke In Bed. Good-bye old Don't Smoke In Bed.

DOLPHIN DREAMS

By LEE RITENOUR

Copyright © 1977, 1984 RIT OF HABEAS MUSIC

DINDI

Music by ANTONIO CARLOS JOBIM
Portuguese Lyrics by ALOYSIO DE OLIVEIRA
English Lyrics by RAY GILBERT

Copyright © 1965 Ipanema Music Corp.
Copyright Renewed, Assigned to Corcovado Music Corp., Ipanema Music Corp. and Luiz Oliveira

Sky, so vast is the sky, with far-a-way clouds just wan-der-ing by. Where do they go? Oh, I don't know, don't know; Wind that speaks to the leaves, tell-ing stor-ies that no one be-lieves. Stor-ies of love be-long to you and me. Oh, Din-di, if I on-ly had words I would say all the beau-ti-ful things that I see when you're with me, oh, my Din-di. Oh, Din-di, like the song of the wind in the trees, that's how my heart is sing-ing Din-di, hap-py Din-di, when you're with me. I love you more each day, yes, I do, yes, I do; I'd let you go a-way if you take me with you. Don't you know, Din-di, I'd be run-ning and search-ing for you like a riv-er that can't find the sea, that would be me with-out you, my Din-di.

DIPPERMOUTH BLUES

Music by JOSEPH OLIVER

© Copyright 1926 by MCA MUSIC PUBLISHING, A Division of UNIVERSAL STUDIOS, INC.
Copyright Renewed

DOWN HEARTED BLUES

Words by ALBERTA HUNTER
Music by LOVIE AUSTIN

Moderately

Gee, but it's hard to love some-one when that some-one don't love you. I'm so dis-gust-ed, heart-bro-ken, too. I've got those Down Heart-ed Blues. Once I was cra-zy 'bout a {man/gal}. {He/She} mis-treat-ed me all the time. The next {man/gal} I get {he's/she's} got to prom-ise me to be mine, all mine.

1. Trou-ble, trou-ble, I've had it all my days.
2. world in a jug, the stop-per's in my hand.
3.-6. See additional lyrics

If I could on-ly find the {man/gal} oh how hap-py I would be. To the Good Lord ev-'ry night I pray. Please send my {man/gal} back to me. I've al-most wor-ried my-self to death won-d'ring why {he/she} went a-way. But just wait and see {he's/she's} gon-na want me back some sweet day.

Trou-ble, trou-ble, I've had it all my days. It seems that trou-ble's going to fol-low me to my grave.
Got the world in a jug. The stop-per's in my hand. Going to hold it ba-by, till you come un-der my com-mand.

Got the _____ Say I

Additional Choruses (Ad lib.)

Chorus 3: Say, I ain't never loved but three {men/women} in my life.
No, I ain't never loved but three {men/women} in my life,
'Twas my {father, brother / mother, sister} and the {man/woman} who wrecked my life.

Chorus 4: 'Cause {he/she} mistreated me and {he/she} drove me from {his/her} door,
Yes, {he/she} mistreated me and {he/she} drove me from {his/her} door,
But the Good Book says you'll reap just what you sow.

Chorus 5: Oh, it may be a week and it may be a month or two,
Yes, it may be a week and it may be a month or two,
But the day you quit me honey, it's coming home to you.

Chorus 6: Oh, I walked the floor and I wrung my hands and cried,
Yes, I walked the floor and I wrung my hands and cried,
Had the Down Hearted Blues and couldn't be satisfied.

DOWN UNDER

By DIZZY GILLESPIE

© 1943 (Renewed) EDWIN H. MORRIS & COMPANY, A Division of MPL Communications, Inc.

DOLPHIN DANCE

By HERBIE HANCOCK

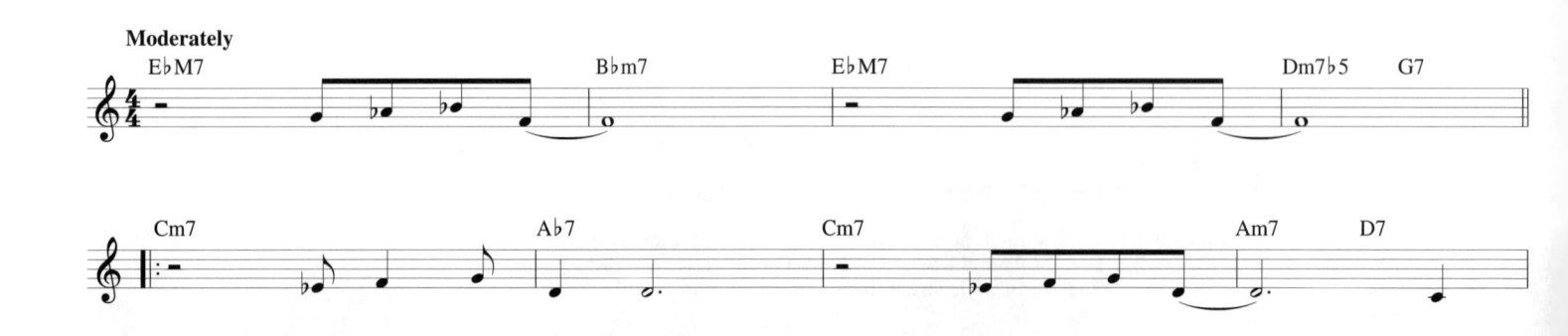

Copyright © 1966 (Renewed) by Hancock Music Co.

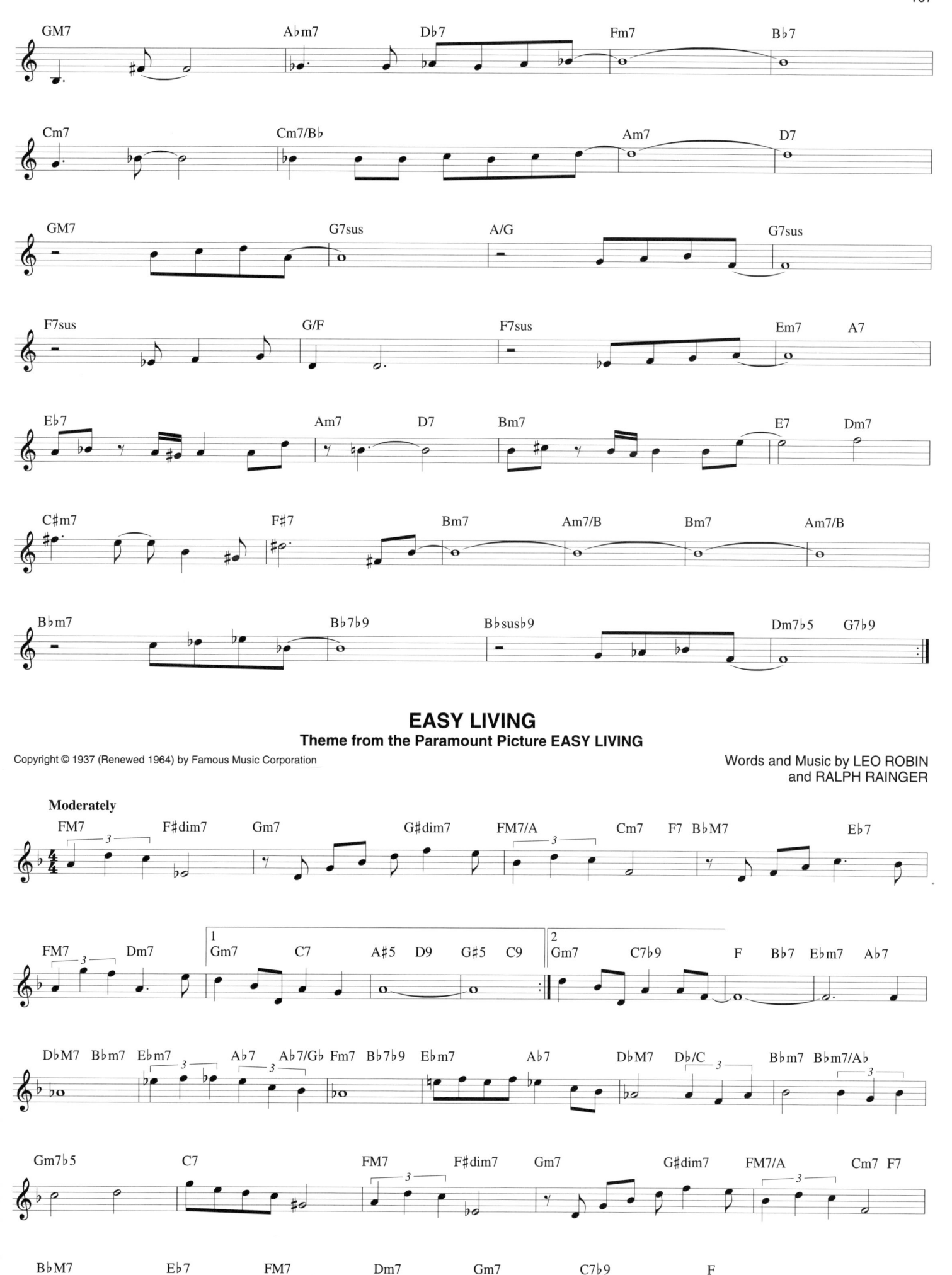

EASY LIVING
Theme from the Paramount Picture EASY LIVING

Copyright © 1937 (Renewed 1964) by Famous Music Corporation

Words and Music by LEO ROBIN
and RALPH RAINGER

DOWN WITH LOVE

from the Musical Production HOORAY FOR WHAT!

Lyric by E.Y. HARBURG
Music by HAROLD ARLEN

DREAM DANCING

Words and Music by
COLE PORTER

Copyright © 1941 by Chappell & Co.
Copyright Renewed, Assigned to John F. Wharton, Trustee of the Cole Porter Musical and Literary Property Trusts
Chappell & Co. owner of publication and allied rights throughout the world

Moderately

When day is gone and night comes on, un-til the dawn what do I do? ___ I clasp your hand and wan-der through slumb-er-land, ___ Dream Danc-ing ___ with you. ___ We dance be-tween a sky se-rene and fields of green, spark-ling with dew. ___ It's joy sub-lime, when-ev-er I spend my time ___ Dream Danc-ing ___ with you. ___ Dream Danc-ing, ___ oh, what a luck-y wind-fall! Touch-ing you, clutch-ing you all ___ the night through. ___ So say you love me dear, and let me make my ca-reer ___ Dream Danc-ing, ___ to par-a-dise pranc-ing, ___ Dream Danc-ing ___ with you. ___ When you. ___

EIGHT

Written by RON CARTER

Copyright © 1978 RETRAC PRODUCTIONS, INC.

Moderately fast

EAST ST. LOUIS TOODLE-OO

By DUKE ELLINGTON
and BUB MILEY

DROP ME OFF IN HARLEM

Words by NICK KENNY
Music by DUKE ELLINGTON

Copyright © 1933 (Renewed 1960) and Assigned to Famous Music Corporation and EMI Mills Music Inc. in the U.S.A.
Rights for the world outside the U.S.A. Controlled by EMI Mills Music Inc. and Warner Bros. Publications Inc.

Moderately

Drop Me Off__ In Har - lem,_____ an - y place__ in Har - lem._____ There's some - one wait - ing there who makes it seem like Heav - en up in Har - lem._____ I don't want__ your Dix - ie,_____ you can keep__ your Dix - ie._____ There's no one down in Dix - ie who can take me 'way from my own Har - lem._____ Har - lem has__ those south - ern skies, they're in my ba - by's smile.__ I i - dol - ize__ my ba - by's eyes__ and class - y up - town style. If Har - lem moved__ to Chi - na,_____ I know of noth - ing fin - er_____ than to stow a - way__ on a 'plane some day and have them Drop Me Off In Har - lem._____

EASY DOES IT

Words by SY OLIVER
Music by SY OLIVER and JIMMY YOUNG

© Copyright 1940 by MCA MUSIC PUBLISHING, A Division of UNIVERSAL STUDIOS, INC.
Copyright Renewed

Moderately

Eas-y on the beat, you take it eas-y, nev-er turn-in' on the heat, and keep it eas-y, just a stead-y e-ven beat. Eas-y Does It ev-'ry time. You'll hear the danc-ers feet, an eas-y shuf-fle. Boy, it real-ly is a treat. No nois-y scuf-fle sor-ta rid-in' with the beat Eas-y Does It. Watch 'em fall in line. Rhy-thm's for the feet, and when it's eas-y you can nev-er miss the beat, and it-'ll send you 'cause it's sol-id-ly a treat. Eas-y Does It all the time.

EASY RIDER
(I Wonder Where My Easy Rider's Gone)

By SHELTON BROOKS

Copyright © 1998 by HAL LEONARD CORPORATION

Moderately

I won-der where my Eas-y Rid-er's Gone to-day, he nev-er told me he was goin' a-way; If he was here, he'd win the race. If not first, he'd get a "place." Cash

won-der where my Eas-y Rid-er's Gone, dog-gone! *(Maybe Kansas City where the girls are pretty)* He went and put my brand new watch in pawn; *(Had an Elgin movement with all the late improvements.)* He had those fas-ci-nat-in' eyes, that just seem to hip-no-tize. I'm

EASY STREET

© 1941 (Renewed 1969) BEECHWOOD MUSIC CORP.

By ALAN RANKIN JONES

EL PRINCE

By PAUL DESMOND

© 1963 (Renewed) Desmond Music Company

ELEVEN FOUR

By PAUL DESMOND

© 1961 (Renewed) Desmond Music Company

EMANCIPATION BLUES

By OLIVER NELSON

Copyright © 1963, 1964 by Oliver E. Nelson
Copyright Renewed
Sole Licensing and Selling Agent: Alameda Music Co.

EPISTROPHY

By THELONIOUS MONK and KENNY CLARK

Copyright © 1947 (Renewed 1975) by Embassy Music Corporation and Music Sales Corporation

THE END OF INNOCENCE

Copyright © 1992 Lunacy Music (BMI)

By BILLY CHILDS

Moderately slow

EQUINOX

By JOHN COLTRANE

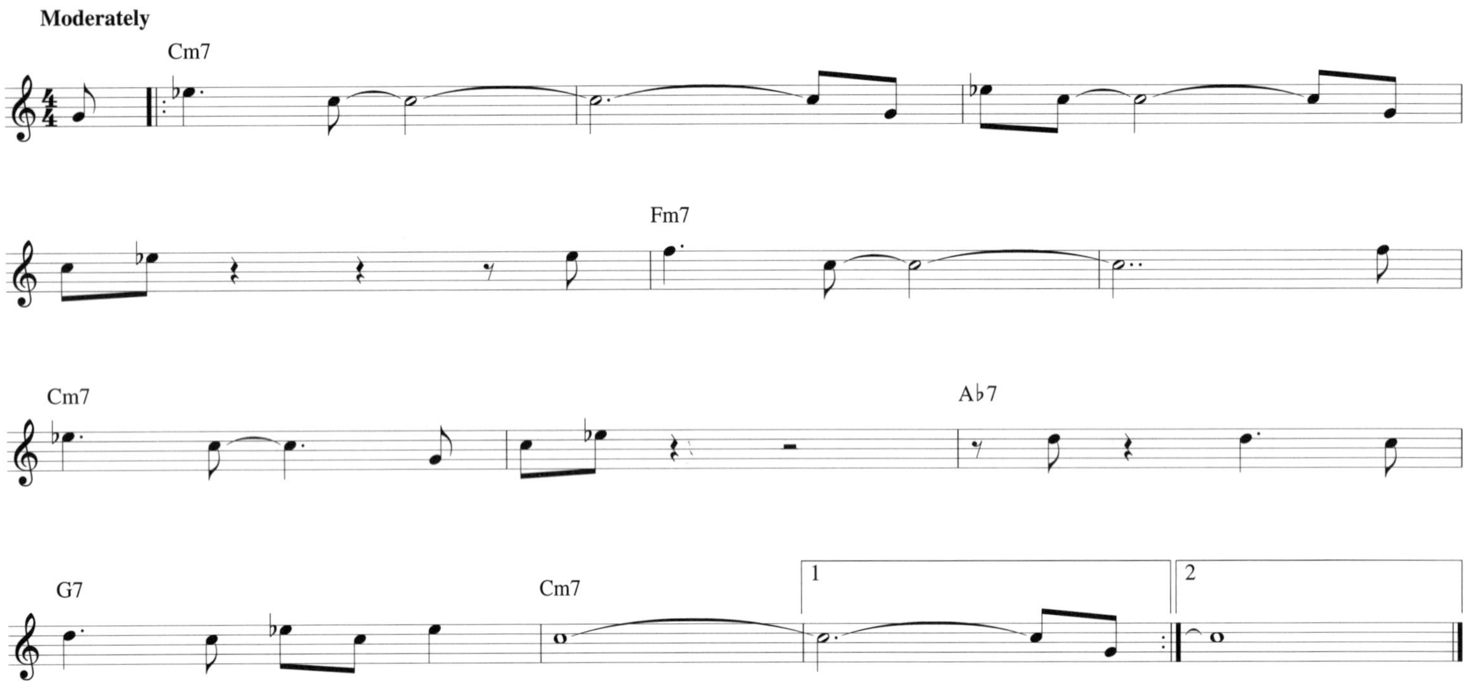

EV'RYTHING I LOVE

Words and Music by
COLE PORTER

ESTATE

© Copyright 1960 by SANTA CECILIA CASA MUSICALE
Copyright Renewed
All Rights for United States and Canada Controlled and Administered by MCA MUSIC PUBLISHING,
A Division of UNIVERSAL STUDIOS, INC.

Music by BRUNO MARTINO
Lyrics by BRUNO BRIGHETTI

Slowly

E - sta - te ___ sei cal - da co - me i ba - ci che ho per - du - to ___ sei pic - na di un a - mo - re che è pas - sa - to ___ che il cuo - re mio vorrabbe ___ cancel - lar. ___ O - dio l'e - sta - te! Il so - le che o - gni giorno ci scal - da - va, ___ che splendi - di tramon - ti di - pin - ge - va ___ a - des - so bru - nia so - lo con fu - ror... ___ Tor - ne - rà un al - tro in - ver - no, ca - dranno mil - le pe - ta - li di ro - se ___ la ne - ve co - pri - rà tut - te le co - se ___ e forse un po' di pa - ce tor - ne - rà! ___ O - dio l'e - sta - te! ___ che ha dato il suo profumo ad o - gni fio - re, ___ l'e - state ___ che ha creato il nostro ___ a - mo - re ___ per far - mi poi mor - ri - ro di do - lor! O - dio l'e - sta - te! ___

1. O - dio l'a - sta - te! ___
2. E - O - dio l'e - sta - te! ___

THE FACE I LOVE

Lyric by RAY GILBERT
Music by MARCOS VALLE
Portuguese Lyric by PAULO VALLE and G. PINGARILNO

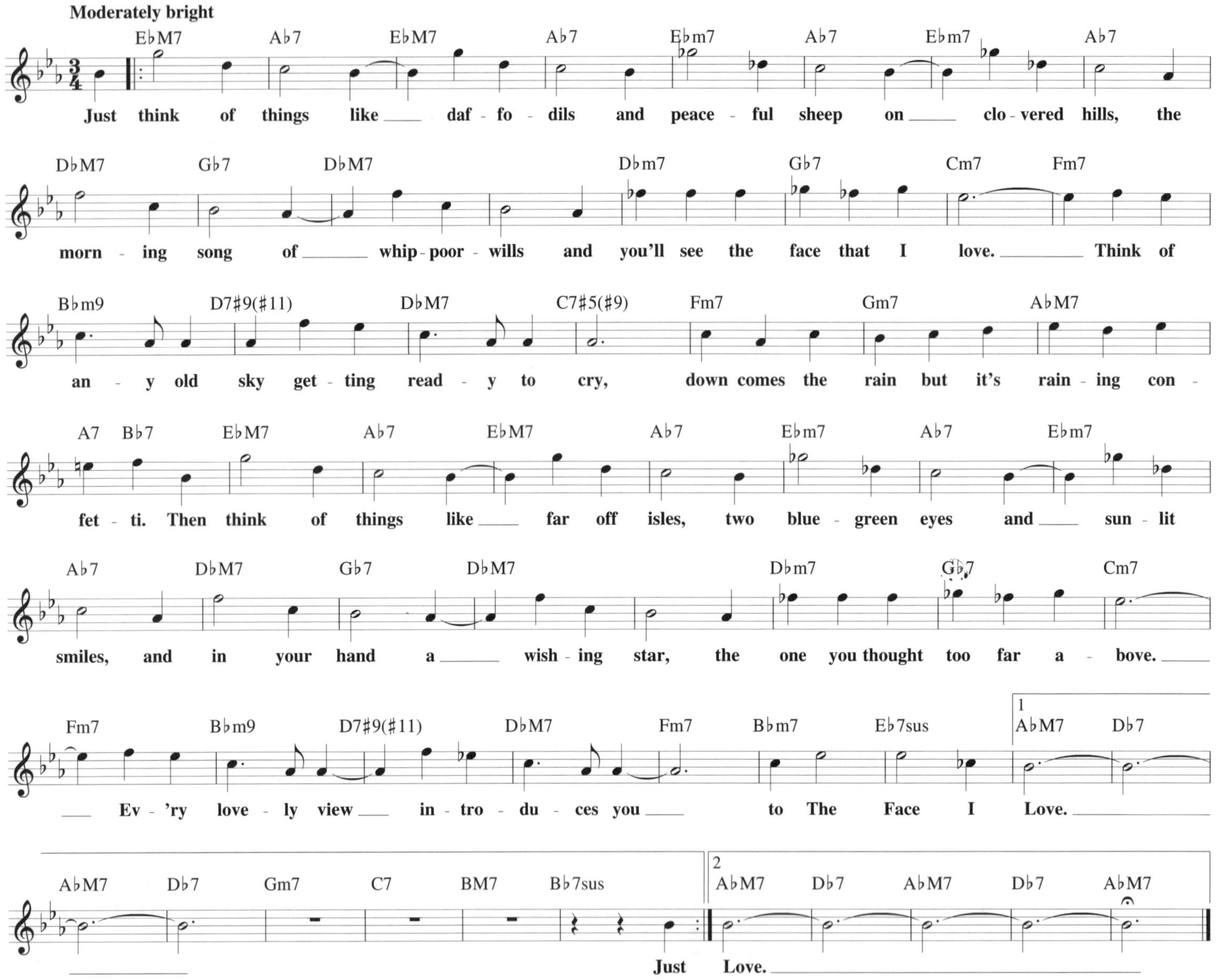

FALLING GRACE

By STEVE SWALLOW

FALLING IN LOVE

Music by VICTOR FELDMAN

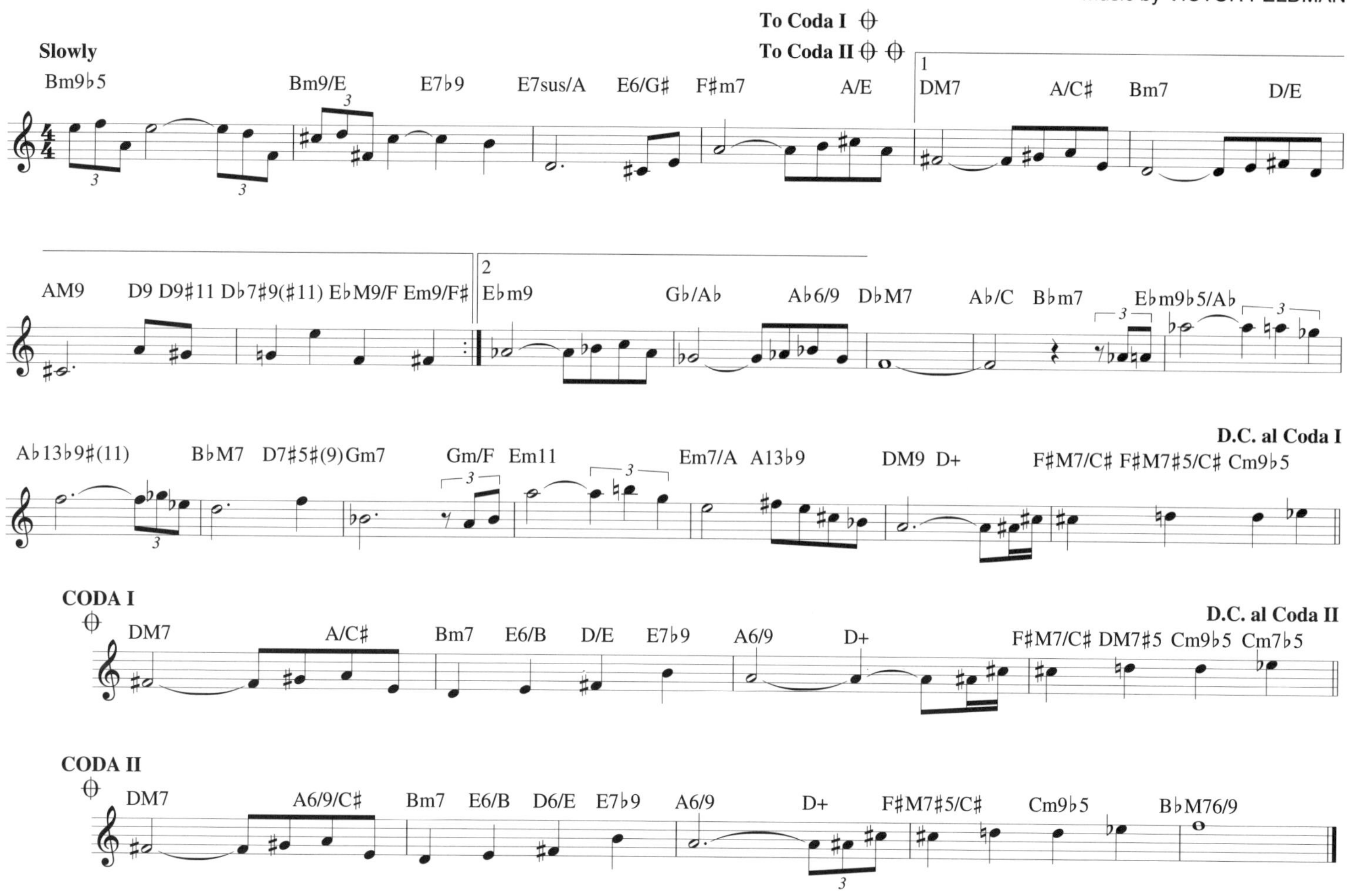

FIRST TRIP

Written by RON CARTER

FILTHY McNASTY

Words and Music by
HORACE SILVER

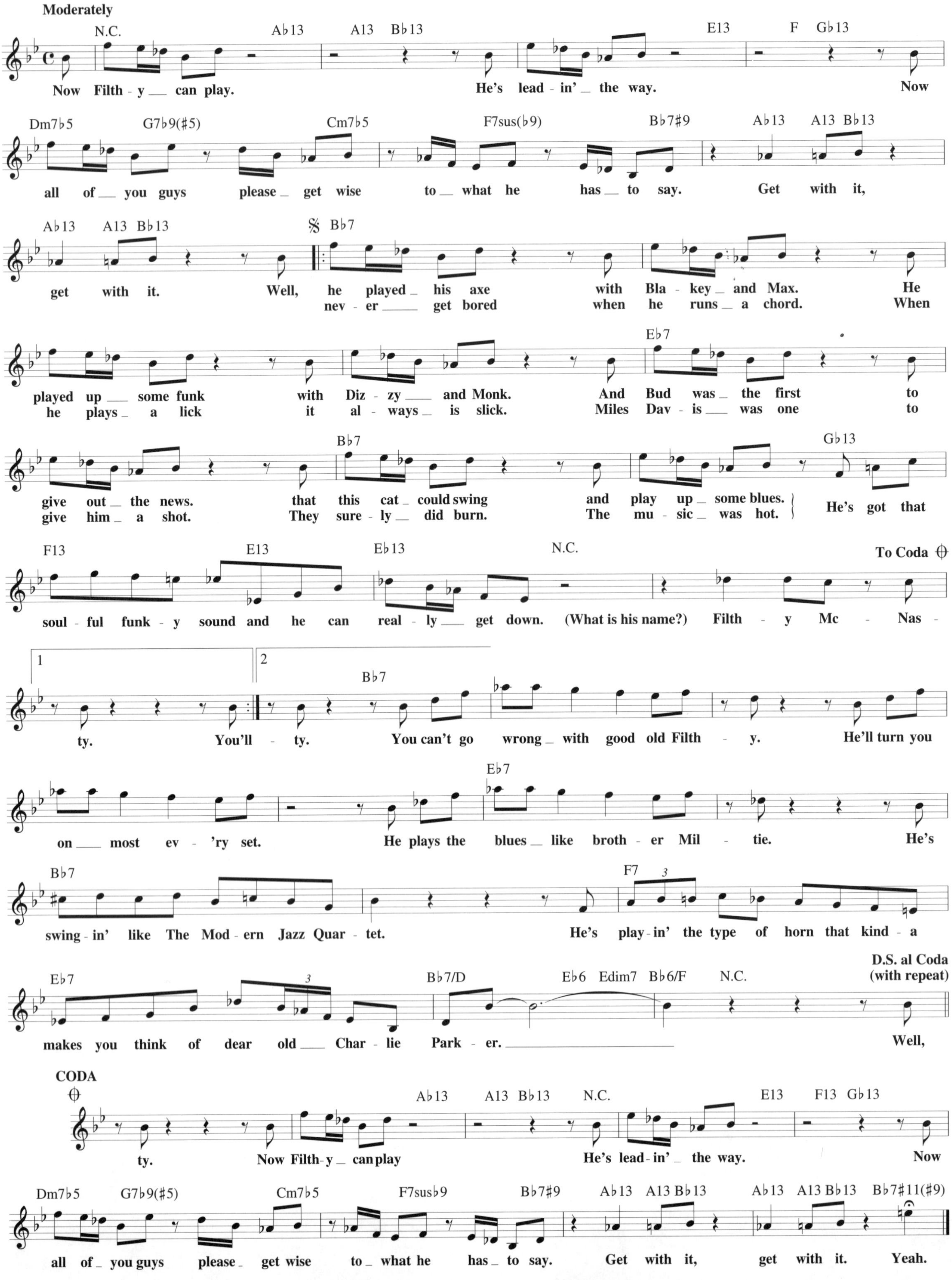

500 MILES HIGH

Lyric by NEVILLE POTTER
Music by CHICK COREA

Medium Latin

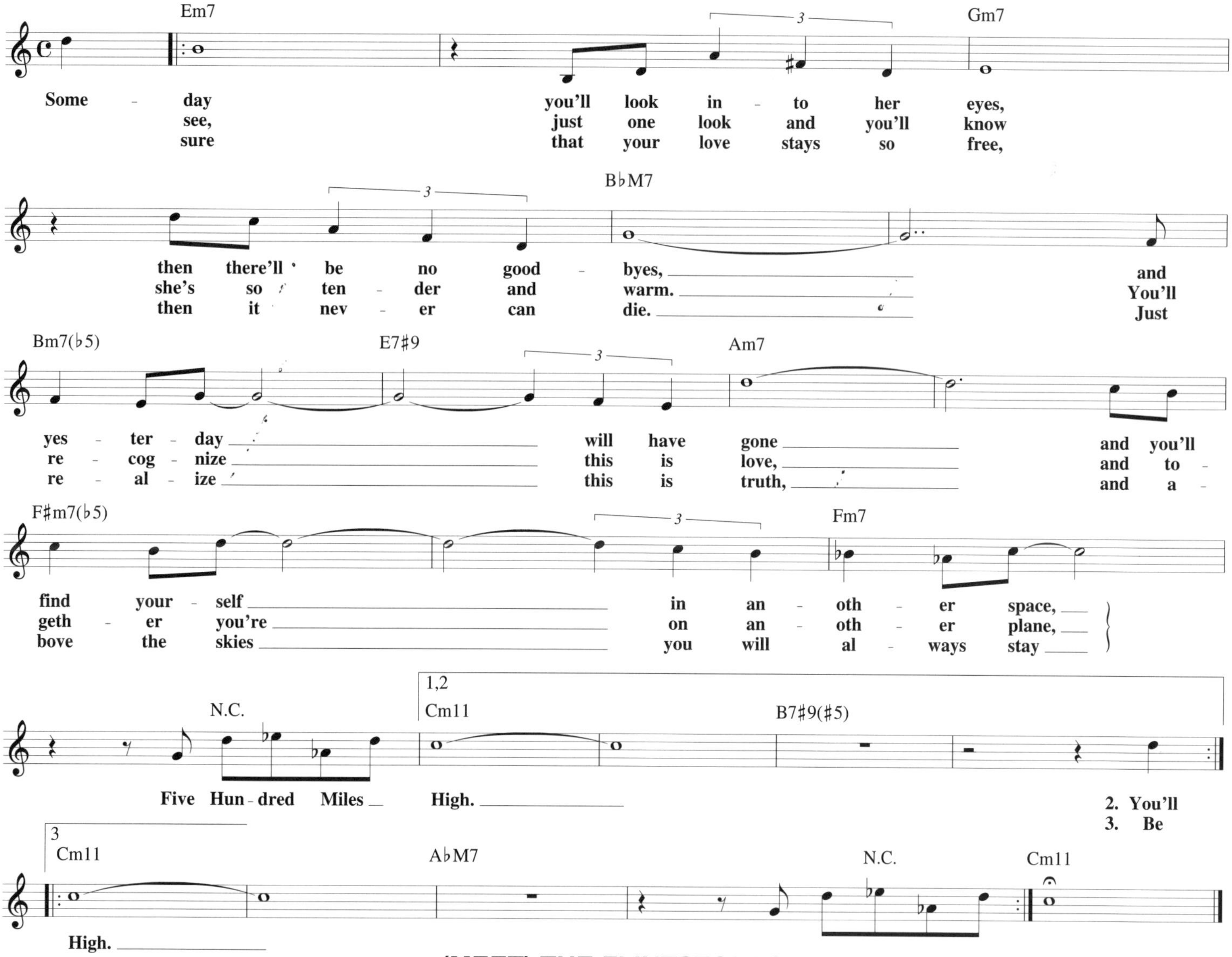

(MEET) THE FLINTSTONES
from THE FLINTSTONES

Words and Music by WILLIAM HANNA, JOSEPH BARBERA and HOYT CURTIN

Quickly

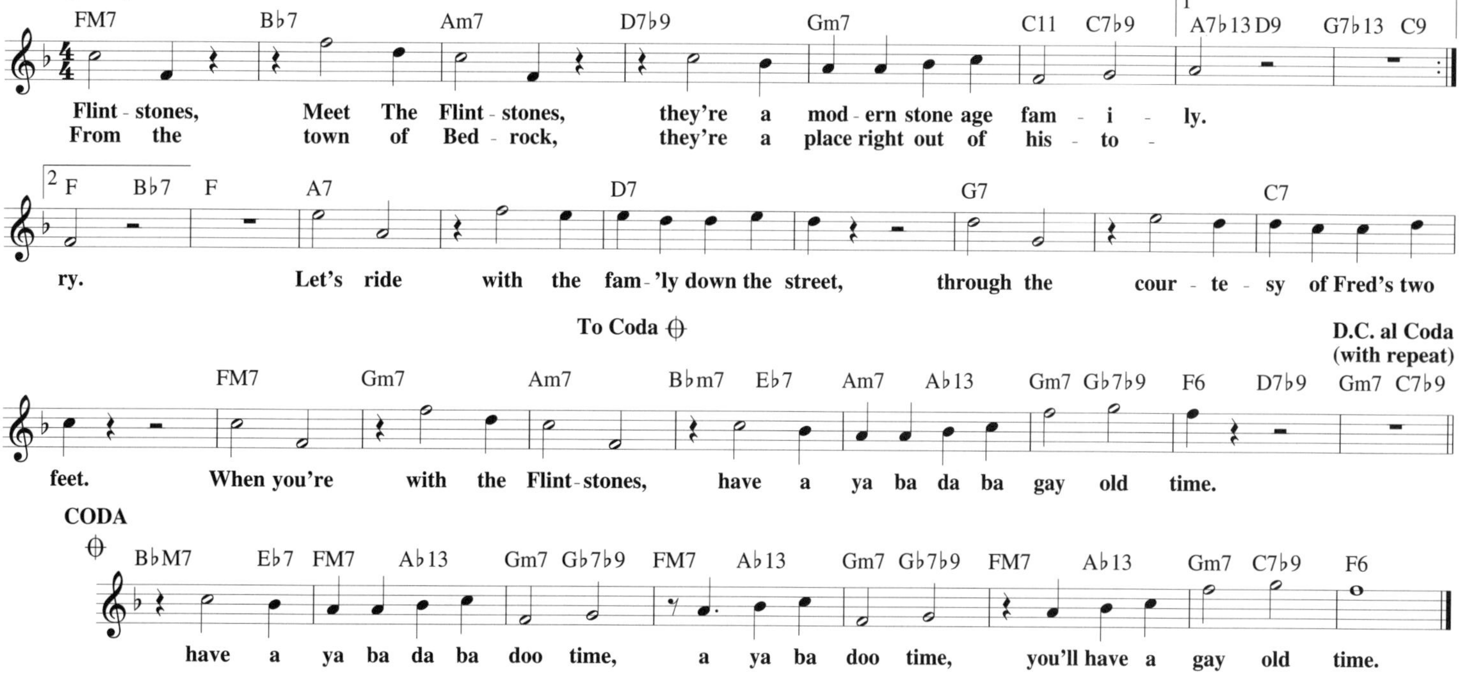

124

FOUR ON SIX

Copyright © 1960 (Renewed) by TAGGIE MUSIC CO., a division of Gopam Enterprises, Inc.

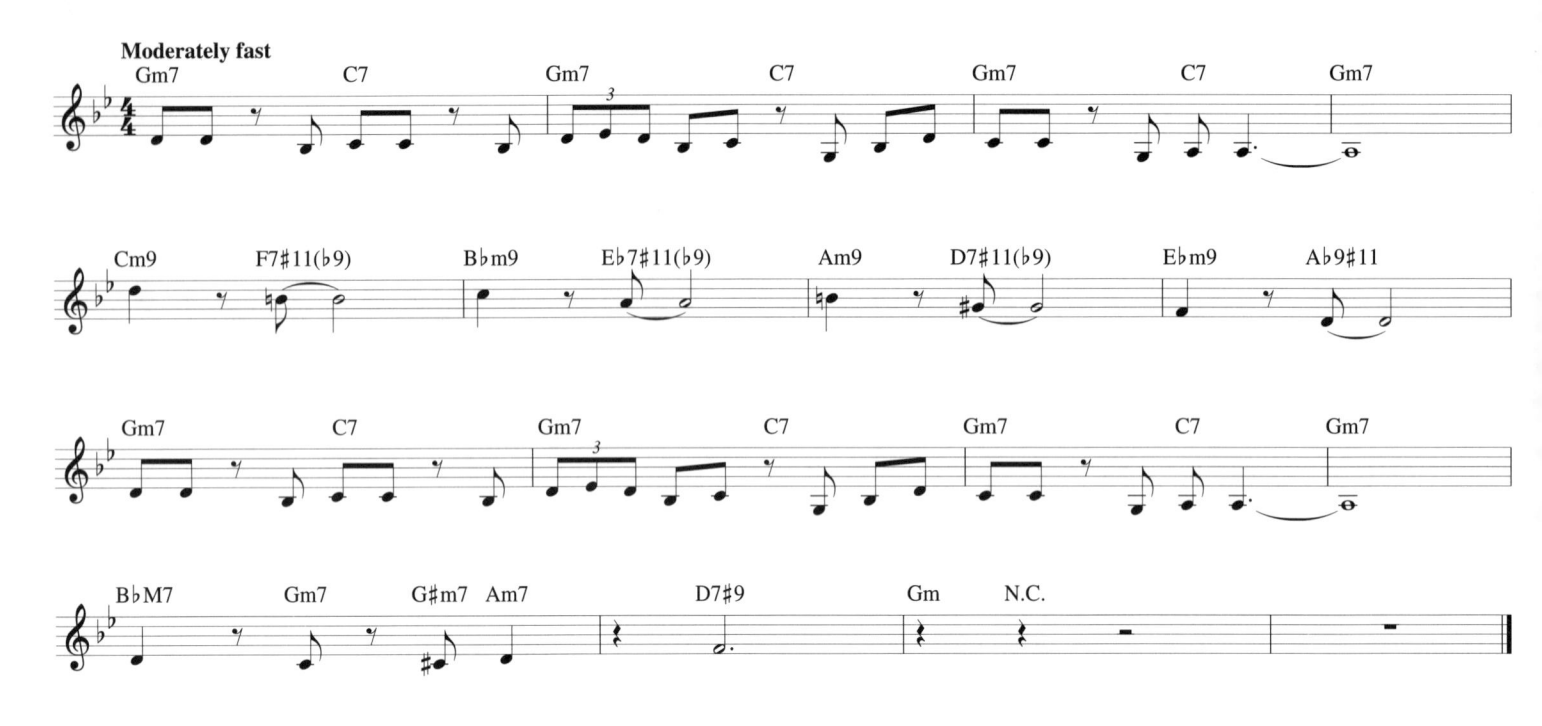

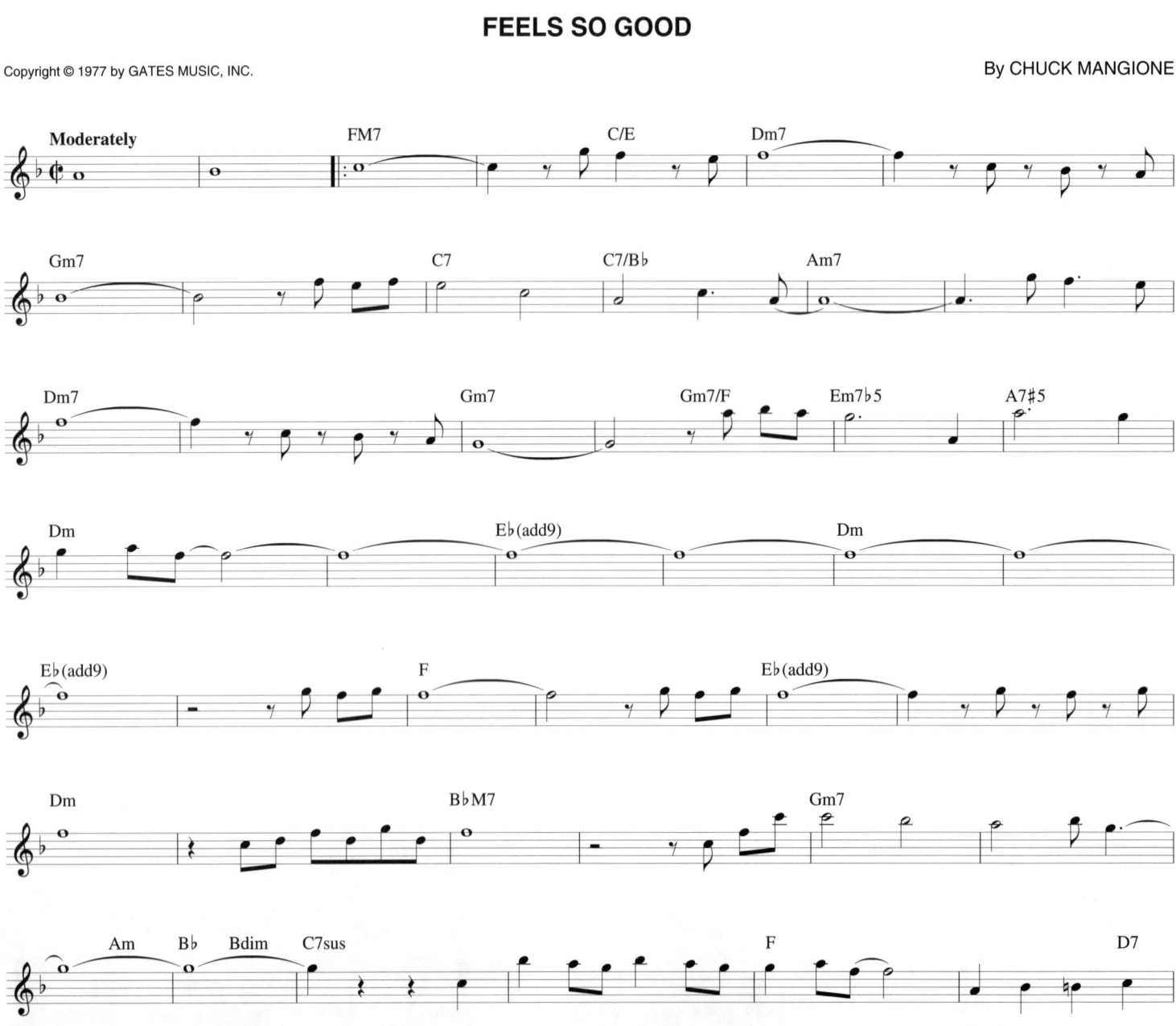

By JOHN L. "WES" MONTGOMERY

FEELS SO GOOD

Copyright © 1977 by GATES MUSIC, INC.

By CHUCK MANGIONE

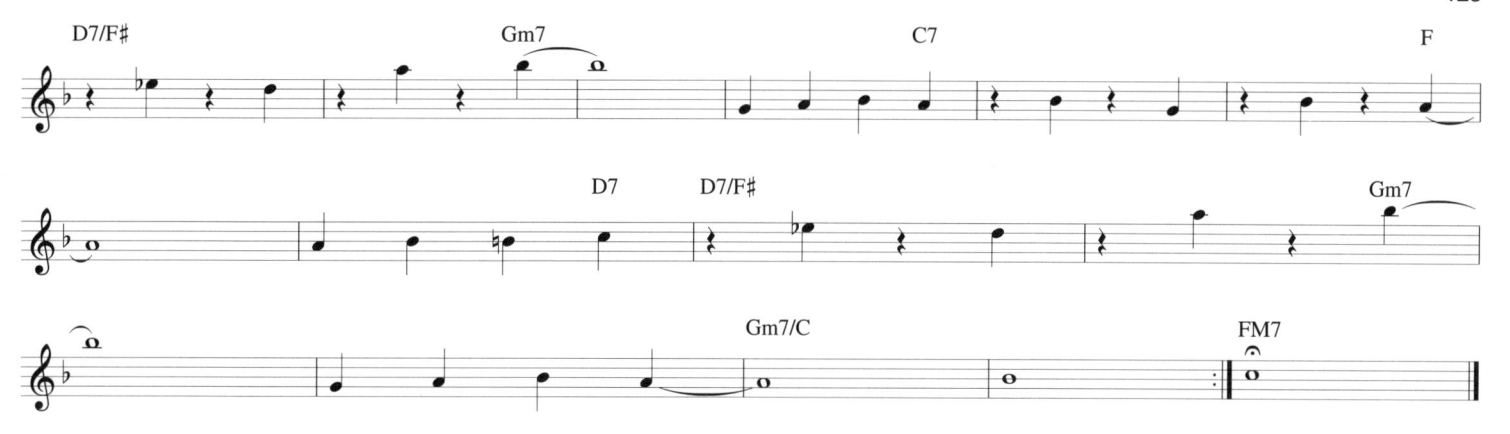

FLANAGAN

By BILLY CHILDS

Copyright © 1992 Lunacy Music (BMI)

FLY WITH THE WIND

By McCOY TYNER

THE FOLKS WHO LIVE ON THE HILL

from HIGH, WIDE AND HANDSOME

Lyrics by OSCAR HAMMERSTEIN II
Music by JEROME KERN

will com-mand a view of mead-ows green, the sort of view that seems to want to be seen. And when the kids grow up and leave us, we'll sit and look at that same old view, just we two. Dar-by and Joan, who used to be Jack and Jill, the folks who like to be called what they have al-ways been called, "The Folks Who Live On The Hill."

FOR HEAVEN'S SAKE

© Copyright 1948 by MCA-DUCHESS MUSIC CORPORATION
Copyright Renewed

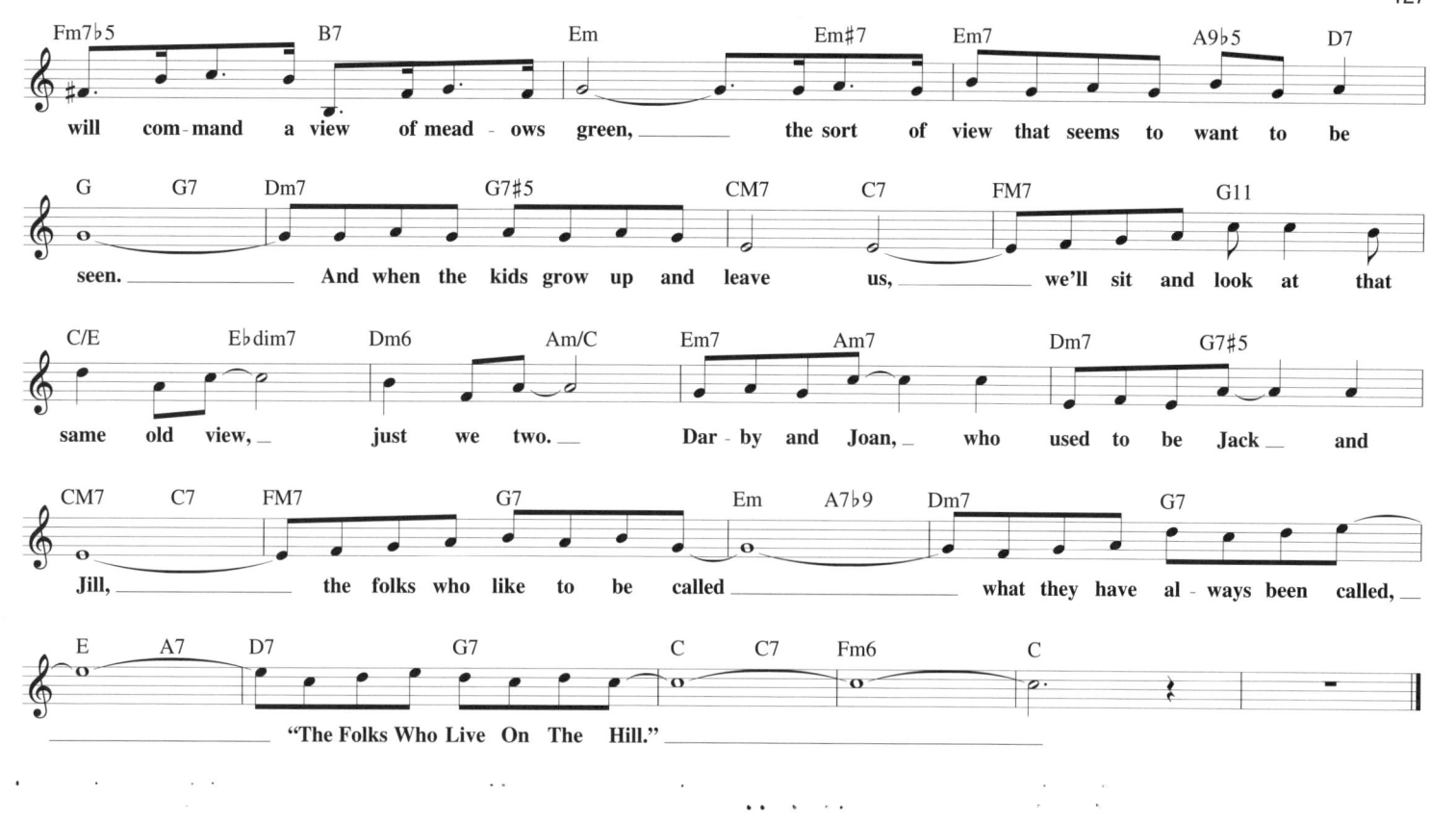

Words and Music by DON MEYER,
ELISE BRETTON and SHERMAN EDWARDS

Moderately

For Heav-en's Sake let's fall in love; It's no mis-take to call it love. An an-gel's hold-ing hands with me, how heav-en-ly Heav-en can be. Here is ro-mance for us to try, Here is the chance we can't de-ny; While Heav-en's giv-ing us the break, let's fall in love, for Heav-en's Sake. {Don't say a word, my dar-ling. Don't break a spell like this; Oh, what a love-ly mo-ment. Oh, what a night is this; {Just hold me tight, we're a-lone in the night, And Heav-en is here in a {Moon all a-glow, seems to want us to know, That Heav-en is here in a kiss.} This pair of eyes can see a star; So Par-a-dise can't be so far, since Heav-en's kiss.} what we're dream-ing of, For Heav-en's Sake let's fall in love. For Heav-en's love.

FRECKLE FACE

By SAMMY NESTICO

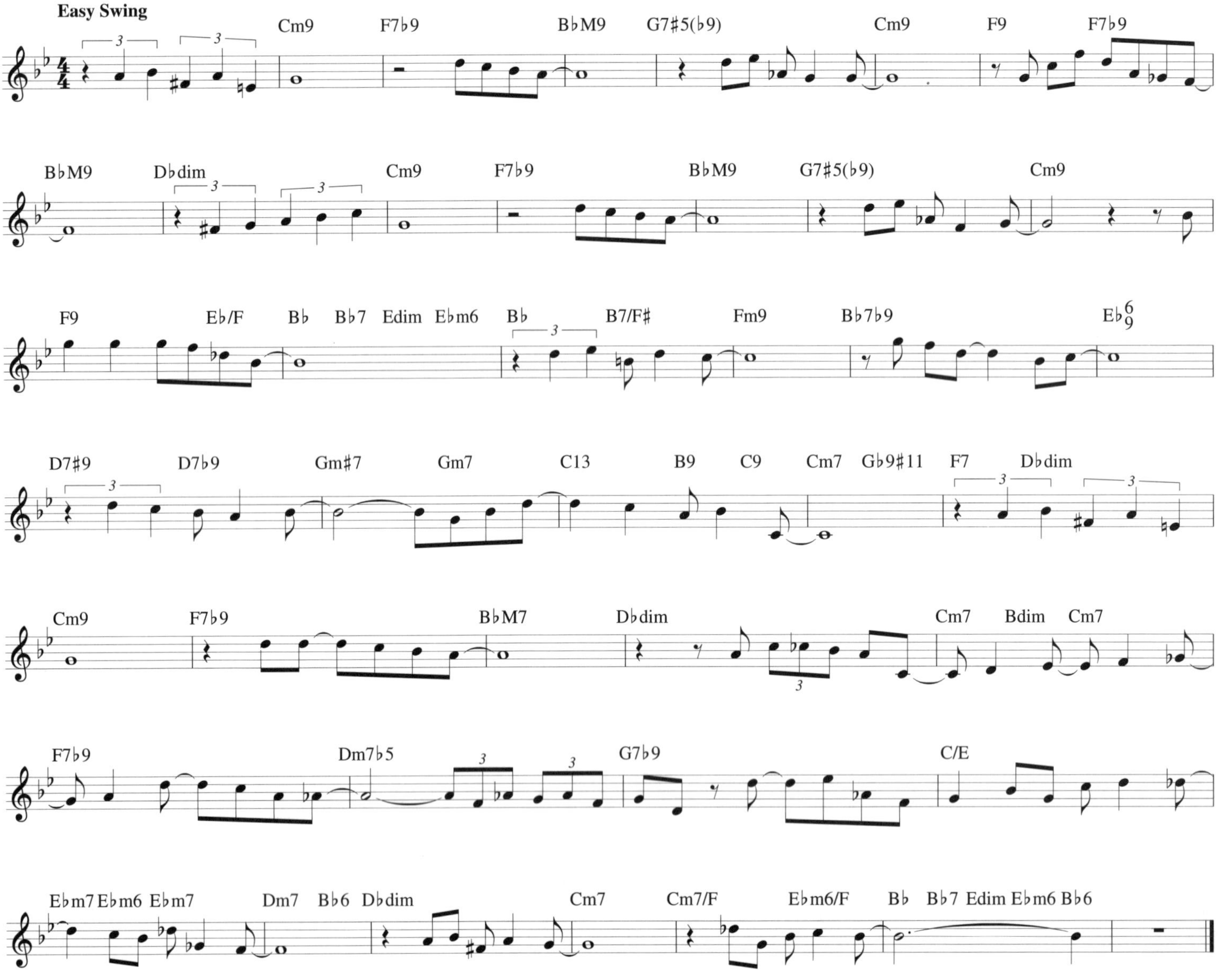

FOREVER IN LOVE

By KENNY G

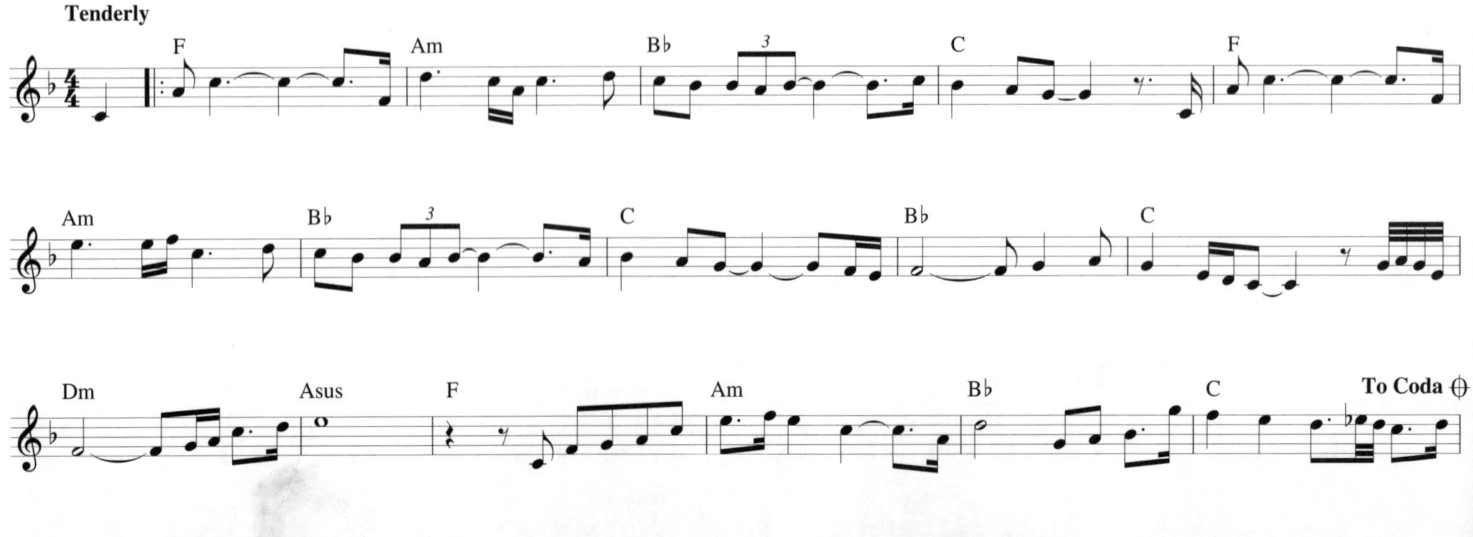

FREEDOM JAZZ DANCE

By EDDIE HARRIS

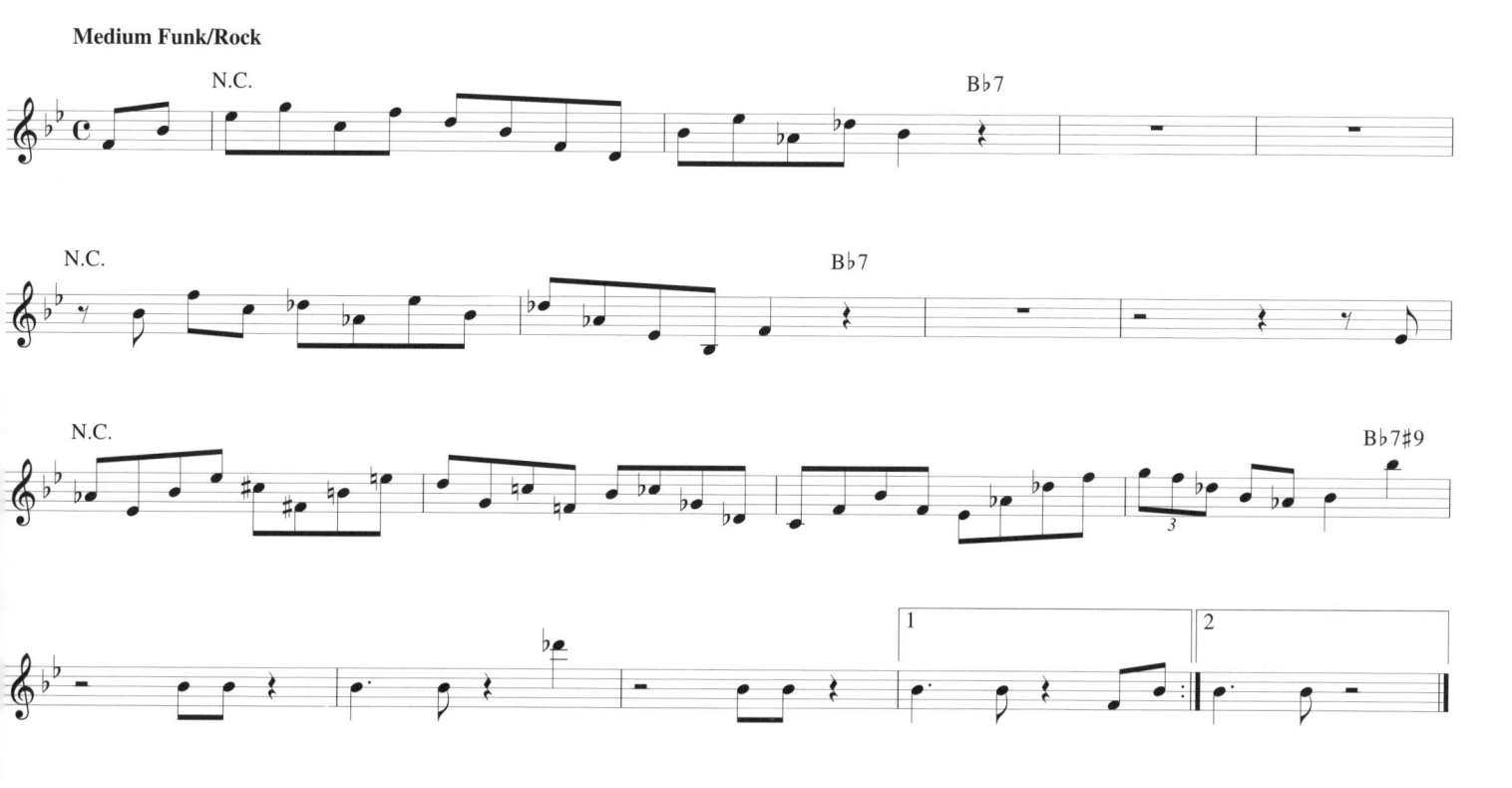

Copyright © 1965 by SEVENTH HOUSE MUSIC
Copyright Renewed
All Rights Administered by THE SONGWRITERS GUILD OF AMERICA

FREETIME

By TOM SCHUMAN
and ELI KONIKOFF

GIANT STEPS

By JOHN COLTRANE

FRENESI

131

Copyright © 1939 by Peer International Corporation
Copyright Renewed

Words and Music by
ALBERTO DOMINGUEZ

Moderate Latin

It was Fi-es-ta down in Mex-i-co, And so I stopped a-while to
Quie-ro que vi-vas só-lo pa-ra mí y que tú va-yas por don-

see the show, I knew that Fre-ne-si meant "please love me"
de yo voy, pa-ra que mi al-ma sea no-más de ti,

And I could say Fre-ne-si. A love-ly se-ño-ri-ta
bé-sa-me con fre-ne-sí. Da-me la luz que tie-ne

caught my eye, I stood en-chant-ed as she wan-der'd by,
tu mi-rar y la an-sie-dad que en-tre tus la-bios vi,

And nev-er know-ing that it came from me I gent-ly sighed Fre-ne-si.
e-sa lo-cu-ra de vi-vir y a-mar, que es más que a-mor, fre-ne-sí.

She stopped and raised her eyes to mine, Her lips just plead-ed to be
Hay en el be-so que te dí, al-ma, pie-dad, co-ra-

kissed, Her eyes were soft as can-dle-shine, So how was I to re-
zón; di-me que sa-bes tu sen-tir, lo mis-mo que sien-to

sist? And now with-out a heart to call my own, A great-er hap-pi-ness I've
yo. Quie-ro que vi-vas só-lo pa-ra mí y que tú va-yas por don-

nev-er known Be-cause her kiss-es are for me a-lone,
de yo voy, pa-ra que mi al-ma sea no-más de tí,

1.
Who would-n't say Fre-ne-si. It was Fi-es-ta down in
bé-sa-me con fre-ne-sí. Quie-ro que vi-vas só-lo

2.
si. who would-n't say Fre-ne-si!
sí, bé-sa-me con fre-ne-sí.

FRIENDS

By CHICK COREA

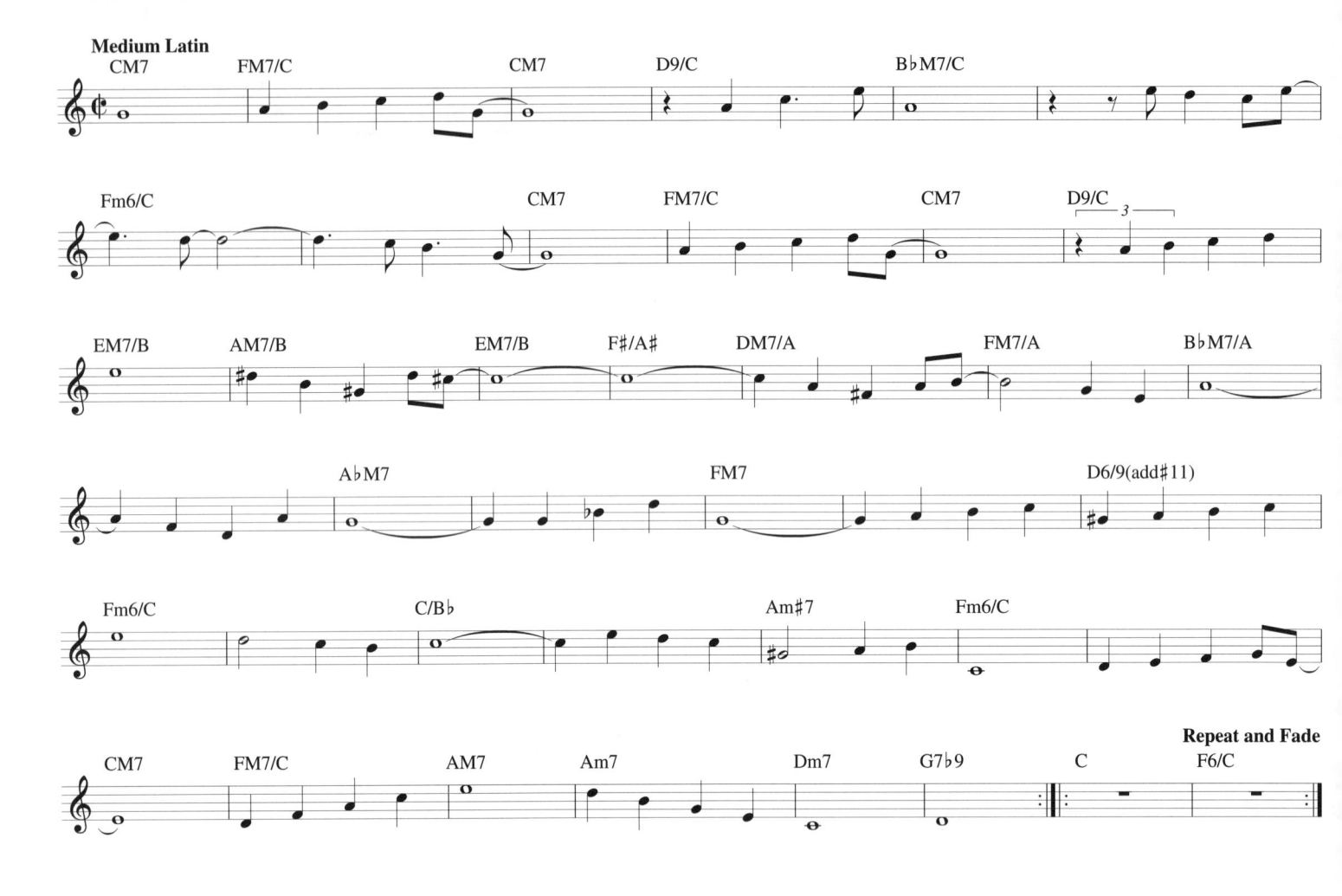

GEORGIA ON MY MIND

Words by STUART GORRELL
Music by HOAGY CARMICHAEL

Copyright © 1930 by Peermusic Ltd.
Copyright Renewed

GETTIN' OVER THE BLUES

Words and Music by PORTIA NELSON
and HAL HACKADY

Copyright © 1963 (Renewed 1991) Atlantic Music Corp.

Moderately slow

There's a song I don't sing an-y-more, there's a
note that I no long-er read, there's a
cock-tail I won't drink a-lone. There's a smile and a face that I
pho-to I've turned to the wall. There's a mil-lion and one fool-ish
try to e-rase, and a num-ber I try not to phone. Go-in' my
things that I've done, but they don't seem to help me at all. I'm what you'd
own } Get-tin' O-ver The Blues. There's a
call

Blues. I keep liv-ing it o-ver and
o-ver a-gain, ev-'ry look, ev-'ry sigh, ev-'ry kiss. But the
more I re-mem-ber, the deep-er the pain. How could some-thing so won-der-ful
end like this? There are friends I don't see an-y-more, (Boy) there are
(Girl) (There's a
cuff links I no long-er wear. There's a lit-tle ca-fe I go
flow-er)
out of my way to a-void on the chance she'll be there. But what-
ev-er I do, it's in-creas-ing-ly true that a torch is a one way af-

GODCHILD

Composed by GEORGE WALLINGTON

Copyright © 1950 (Renewed 1987) Jazz Editions

GIRL TALK
from the Paramount Picture HARLOW

Words by BOBBY TROUP
Music by NEAL HEFTI

Copyright © 1965 (Renewed 1993) by Famous Music Corporation

Slowly and Bluesy

They / We like to chat a-bout the dress-es {they / we} will wear to-night, {they / we} chew the fat a-bout {their / our} tress-es and the neigh-bor's fight. In-con-se-quen-tial things that men don't real-ly care to know be-come es-sen-tial things that wom-en find so "ap-pro-po." But that's a dame, {they're / we're} all the same; it's just a game. {They / We} call it Girl Talk, Girl Talk. {They / We} all me-ow a-bout the ups and downs of all {their / our} friends the "who," the "how," the "why," {they / we} dish the dirt, it nev-er ends. The weak-er sex, the speak-er sex {we / you} mor-tal males be-hold, but tho' we joke we would-n't trade you for a ton of gold. So ba-by stay and gab a-way, but hear me say that af-ter / It's all been planned, so take my hand, please un-der-stand the sweet-est Girl Talk, talk to me. / Girl Talk, talks of you.

GLAD TO BE UNHAPPY
from ON YOUR TOES

Words by LORENZ HART
Music by RICHARD RODGERS

Copyright © 1936 by Williamson Music and The Estate Of Lorenz Hart in the United States
Copyright Renewed
All Rights on behalf of The Estate Of Lorenz Hart Administered by WB Music Corp.

Reflectively

Fools rush in, so here I am ver-y Glad To Be Un-hap-py; I can't win, but here I am, more than Glad To Be Un-hap-py. Un-re-quit-ed love's a

137

bore, and I've got it pretty bad. But for some-one you a-dore,

it's a plea-sure to be sad. Like a stray-ing ba-by lamb, with no mam-my and no

pap-py, I'm so un-hap-py, but oh, so glad!

GOOD-BYE

© Copyright 1935 by MCA MUSIC PUBLISHING, A Division of UNIVERSAL STUDIOS, INC.
Copyright Renewed

Words and Music by
GORDON JENKINS

I'll nev-er for-get you, I'll nev-er for-get you. I'll

nev-er for-get how we prom-ised one day, to love one an-oth-er for-

ev-er that way. We said we'd nev-er say, Good-bye.

But that was long a-go, now you've for-got-ten, I know.

No use to won-der why, let's say fare-well with a sigh; Let love

die. But we'll go on liv-ing our own way of liv-ing, so

you take the high road and I'll take the low. It's time that we part-ed, it's

much bet-ter so. But kiss me as you go, Good-bye.

GOING HOME

By KENNY G and WALTER AFANASIEFF

GOOD MORNING HEARTACHE

Words and Music by DAN FISHER,
IRENE HIGGINBOTHAM and ERVIN DRAKE

Copyright © 1945 Sony/ATV Tunes LLC and Lindabet Music
Copyright Renewed
All Rights on behalf of Sony/ATV Tunes LLC Administered by Sony/ATV Music Publishing,
8 Music Square West, Nashville, TN 37203

Good Morn-ing Heart-ache, you old gloom-y sight. Good Morn-ing Heart-ache, tho't we said good-bye last night.
I tossed and turned un-til it seemed you had gone, but here you are with the dawn.
Wish I'd for-get you but you're here to stay. It seems I met you when my love went a-way.
Now ev-'ry day I start by say-ing to you, Good Morn-ing Heart-ache, what's new?
Stop haunt-ing me now. Can't shake you no - how. Just leave me a - lone. I've
got those Mon - day blues straight thru Sun - day blues. Good Morn-ing Heart-ache, here we go a-gain.
Good Morn-ing Heart-ache, you're the one who knew me when. Might as well get used to you hang-in' a-round.
Good Morn-ing Heart-ache sit down! down!

GRAVY WALTZ

Lyrics by STEVE ALLEN
Music by RAY BROWN

© 1962, 1963 (Renewed 1990, 1991) SCREEN GEMS-EMI MUSIC INC.

Moderately

Miss Mi-ran-da's / Pret-ty ma-ma's } in the kit-chen this glor-i-ous day, Smell the gra-vy sim-mer-in' near-ly half a mile a-way. La-dy Morn-in' Glo-ry, I say good morn-in' to you, Chir-py lit-tle chick-a-dee told me that my ba-by was true. { Miss Mi-ran-da / Well, she real-ly } ran to get her fry-in' pan when she saw me com-in'. Gon-na get a taste be-fore it goes to waste, this hon-ey-bee's hum-min'. Mis-ter Weep-in' Wil-low, I'm thru with all of my faults, 'cause { Mir-an-da's / my ba-by's } rea-dy to do the ev-er new Gra-vy Waltz.

GREENS

By BENNY GREEN

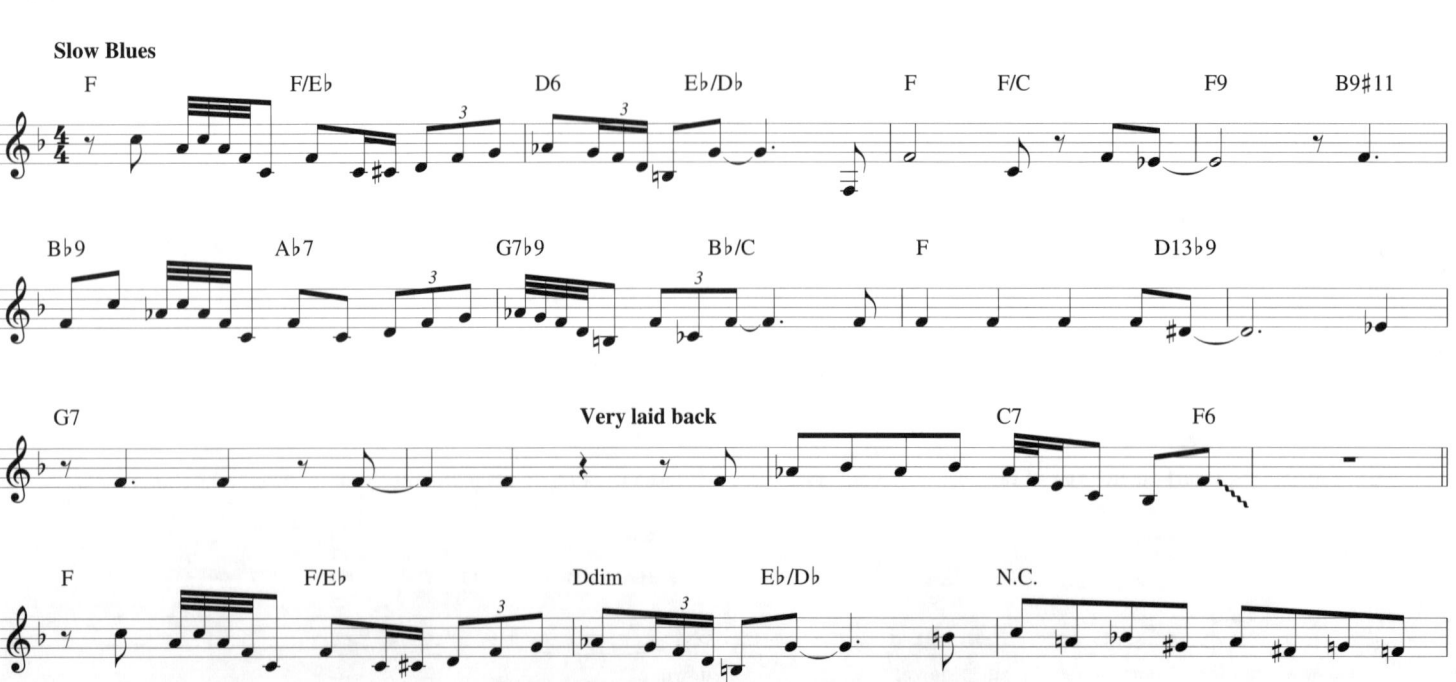

Copyright © 1991 Benny Green Music (BMI)

Slow Blues

Very laid back

GREEN EYES
(Aquellos Ojos Verdes)

Copyright © 1929 by Peer International Corporation
Copyright Renewed

Words and Music by ADOLFO UTRERA
and NILO MENDEZ

Moderately

Your Green Eyes with their soft lights, ___ Your eyes that promise sweet nights ___
A- que- llos o- jos ver- des de mi- ra- da se- re- na

Bring to my soul a long- ing ___ a thirst for love di- vine.
De- ja- ron en mi al- ma eter- na sed de a- mar

In dreams I seem to hold you ___ To find you and en- fold you ___
An- he- los de ca- ri- cias de be- sos y ter- nu- ras

Our lips meet, and our hearts too, ___ with a thrill so sub- lime.
de to- das las dul- zu- ras que sa- bi- an brin- dar

Those cool and lim- pid Green Eyes ___ A pool where- in my love lies ___
A- que- llos o- jos ver- des se- re- nos co- mo un la- go

so deep, that in my search- ing ___ For hap- pi- ness, I fear ___
en cu- yas quie- tas a- guas un di- a me mi- ré

That they will ev- er haunt me ___ All through my life they'll taunt me ___
No sa- ben las tris- te- zas que en mi al- ma han de- ja- do

But will they ev- er want me ___ Green Eyes make my dreams come
A- que- llos o- jos ver- des que yo nun- ca be- sa-

1. true. **2.** true.
ré. ré.

Your Green Eyes with their
A- que- llos o- jos

GUESS I'LL HANG MY TEARS OUT TO DRY
from GLAD TO SEE YOU

Words by SAMMY CAHN
Music by JULE STYNE

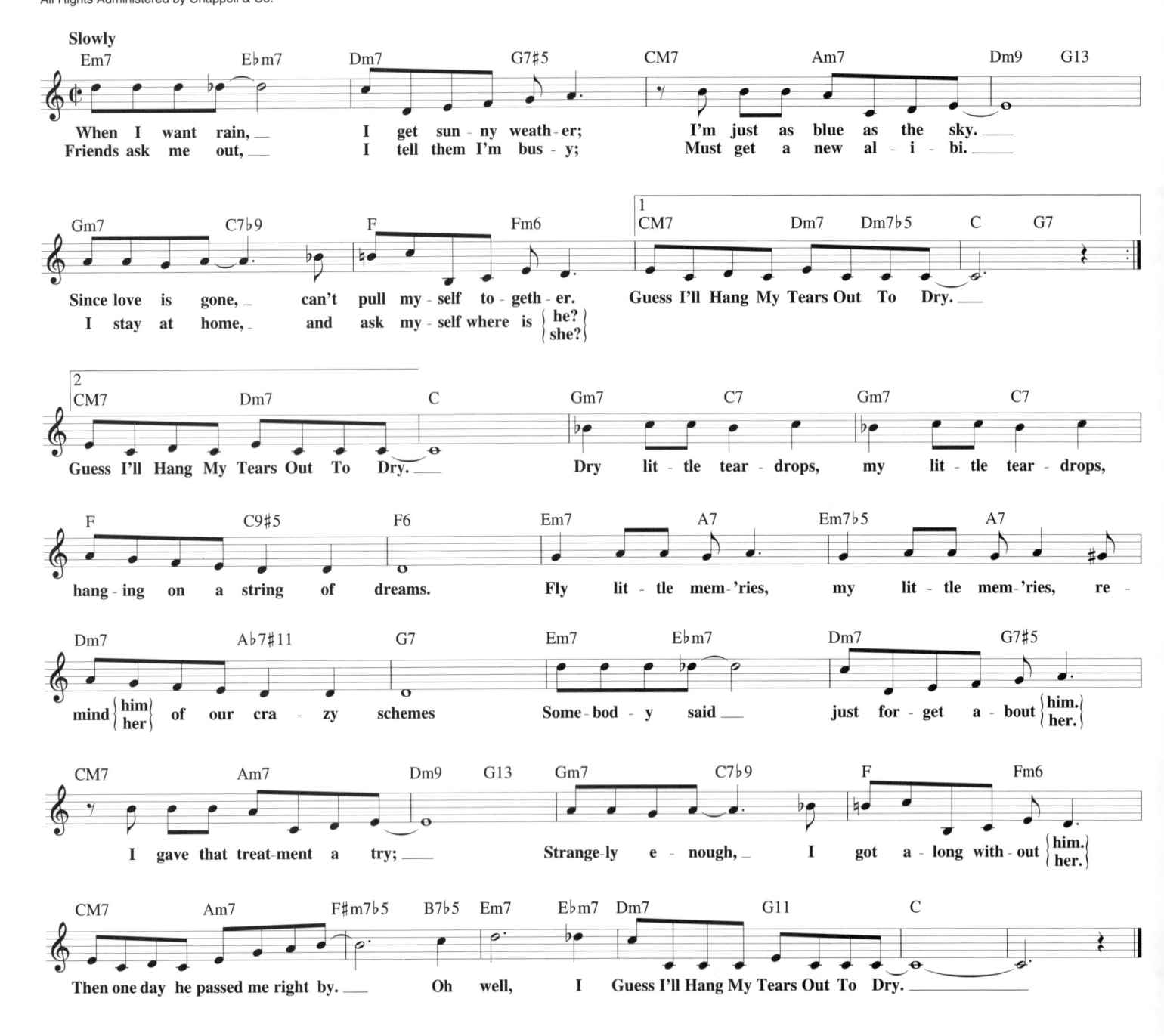

Copyright © 1944 by Chappell & Co. and Producers Music Publishing Co., Inc.
Copyright Renewed
All Rights Administered by Chappell & Co.

When I want rain, I get sunny weather; I'm just as blue as the sky.
Friends ask me out, I tell them I'm busy; Must get a new alibi.
Since love is gone, can't pull myself together.
I stay at home, and ask myself where is {he?/she?}
Guess I'll Hang My Tears Out To Dry.

Guess I'll Hang My Tears Out To Dry. Dry little teardrops, my little teardrops, hanging on a string of dreams. Fly little mem'ries, my little mem'ries, remind {him/her} of our crazy schemes. Somebody said just forget about {him./her.} I gave that treatment a try; Strangely enough, I got along without {him./her.} Then one day he passed me right by. Oh well, I Guess I'll Hang My Tears Out To Dry.

GROWING

By JOHN PATITUCCI

Copyright © 1988 Iccutitap Music

HAPPY WITH THE BLUES

Lyric by PEGGY LEE
Music by HAROLD ARLEN

© 1961, 1962 (Renewed) HARWIN MUSIC CO.

THE HAWK TALKS

By LOUIS BELLSON

Copyright © 1951, 1954 (Renewed) by Tempo Music, Inc. and Music Sales Corporation (ASCAP)
All Rights Administered by Music Sales Corporation

HAPPY HUNTING HORN
from PAL JOEY

Words by LORENZ HART
Music by RICHARD RODGERS

Copyright © 1951, 1952 by Chappell & Co.
Copyright Renewed

Brightly

Sound the hap-py hunt-ing horn, there's new game_ on the trail now._ We're hunt-ing for quail now,_ hap-py lit-tle hunt-ing horn. Play the horn but don't play corn, the mu-sic_ must be nice now._ We're hunt-ing for mice now_ hap-py lit-tle hunt-ing horn.

HELEN'S SONG

By GEORGE CABLES

© 1985 WEEAMARA MUSIC

HEEBIE JEEBIES

By BOYD ATKINS

HERE'S TO MY LADY

Lyric by JOHNNY MERCER
Music by RUBE BLOOM

Hideaway

By DAVID SANBORN

148

HERE'S TO YOUR ILLUSIONS

Copyright © 1951 by Chappell & Co.
Copyright Renewed

Words and Music by SAMMY FAIN
and E.Y. HARBURG

Slowly

Here's to all your dreams, Here's To Your Il - lu - sions.
May they al - ways lead you in - to my arms. Here's to all your hopes and those sweet con - fu - sions that charm you in - to see - ing my charms. Here's to that trick of ro - mance that be - guiles with a smile or a glance. As long as you're in this trance, I stand a chance with you. So here's to "love is blind," Here's To Your Il - lu - sions. Stay en - chant - ed, please, put my heart at ease for all the years to come.

HONEST I DO

Copyright © 1957 (Renewed) by Conrad Music, a division of Arc Music Corp.

By JIMMY REED
and EWART G. ABNER, JR.

Slowly

Don't you know that I love you Hon - est I Do. I nev - er placed no one a - bove you. Please tell me you love me,

HOW ABOUT ME?

HOT TODDY

Words and Music by HERB HENDLER
and RALPH FLANAGAN

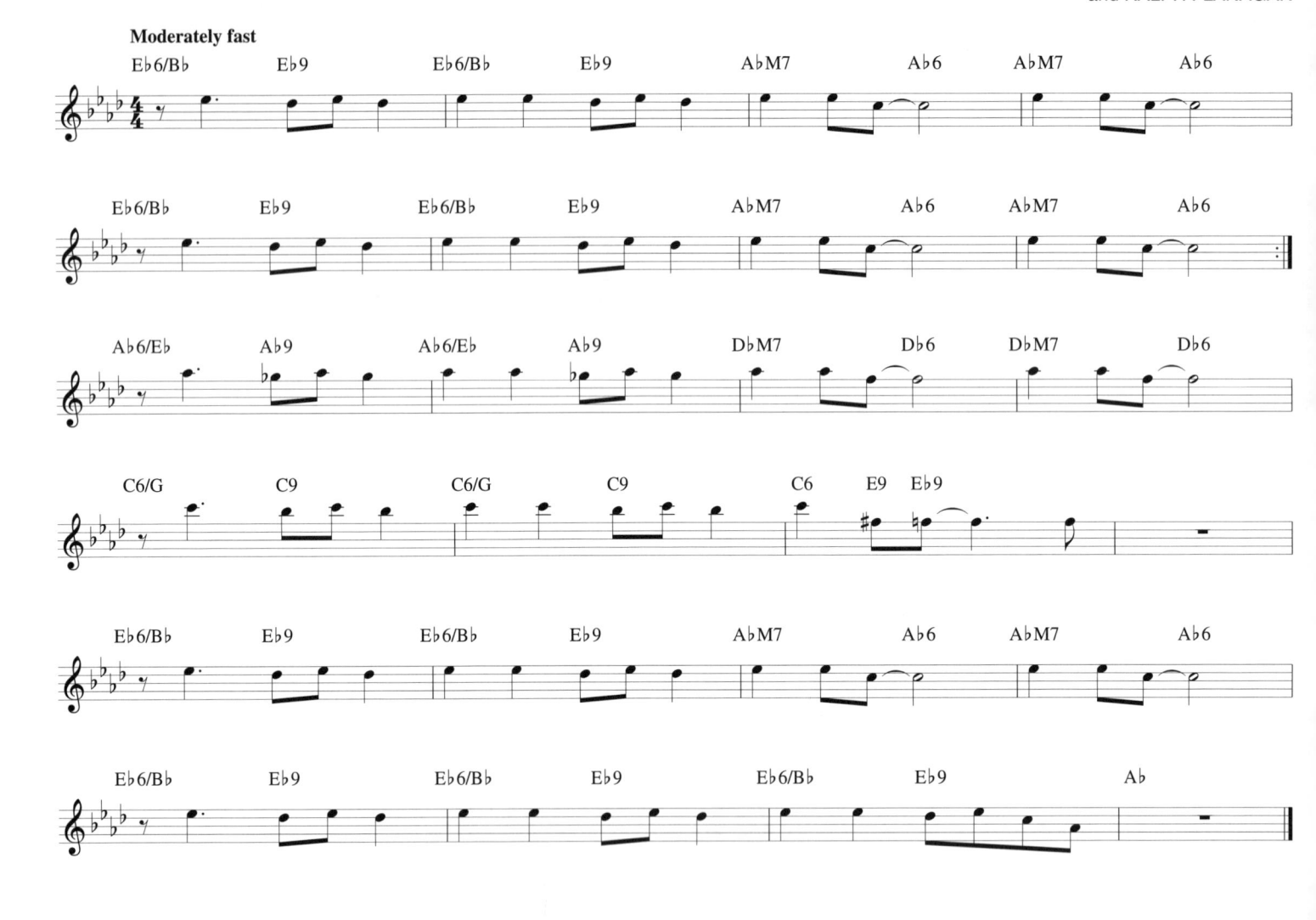

Copyright © 1953 (Renewed 1981) Valley Entertainment Enterprises, Inc.

HOW ARE THINGS IN GLOCCA MORRA
from FINIAN'S RAINBOW

Words by E.Y. HARBURG
Music by BURTON LANE

Copyright © 1946 by Chappell & Co.
Copyright Renewed

How Are Things In Glocca Morra? Is that little brook still leaping there? Does it still run down to Donny Cove, through Killybegs, Kilkerry and Kildare? How Are Things In Glocca Morra? Is that willow tree still weeping there? Does that laddie with the twinklin' eye come whistlin' by and does he walk away, sad and

(continued from previous page)

Gm7 ... **C7** ... **FM7**
dream-y there, not to see me there? _____ So I

B♭M7 ... **C7** ... **FM7** ... **Gm7** ... **C7** ... **FM7**
ask each weep-in' wil-low and each brook a-long the way, and each

B♭M7 ... **C7** ... **Em7♭5** **A7** **Am7** **D7**
lad that comes a whist-lin' Too-ra-lay, _____ How Are

Gm7 ... **C7** ... **FM7**
Things In Gloc-ca Mor-ra this fine day? _____

HOW DEEP IS THE OCEAN
(How High Is the Sky)

© Copyright 1932 by Irving Berlin
Copyright Renewed

Words and Music by
IRVING BERLIN

Slowly

Cm7 ... **Dm7♭5** **G7** **Cm7** ... **Am7♭5** **D7**
How much do I love you? I'll tell you no lie.

Gm7 ... **Am7** **D7** **Gm7** ... **C7** **Fm7** **B♭7**
How Deep Is The O-cean, how high is the sky?

E♭M7 ... **B♭m7** **E♭7** **A♭7**
How man-y times a day _____ do I think of you? _____

Cm7♭5 ... **F7** ... **B♭7** ... **Dm7♭5** **G7**
How man-y ros-es are sprink-led with dew? _____

Cm7 ... **Dm7♭5** **G7** **Cm7** ... **Am7♭5** **D7**
How far would I trav-el to be where you are?

Gm7 ... **Am7** **D7** **Gm7** ... **C7** **Fm7** **B♭7**
How far is the jour-ney from here to a star?

E♭M7 ... **Gm7♭5** **C7** **Fm7** ... **A♭m7** **D♭7**
And if I ev-er lost you, how much would I cry?

E♭M7 ... **F7** ... **Fm7** **B♭7** **E♭M7**
How Deep Is The O-cean, how high is the sky?

HOW MY HEART SINGS

Lyrics by ANNE ZINDARS
Music by EARL ZINDARS

Copyright Renewed 1991 Zindars Publishing Co.

Moderately

How My Heart Sings, when you hold me and you
laugh - ing, it's like danc - ing, and it's like

tell me that this is our love to be. The
fly - ing high - er than the love clouds can go. You

songs that soar thru me com - pel me so com - plete - ly,

I must sur - ren - der to you and set free all the

joys that make my heart take wing,

all the love that makes my heart sing! It's like

CODA

do all this to me and much more than you know,

that's How My Heart Sings.

THE HUCKLEBUCK

Lyrics by ROY ALFRED
Music by ANDY GIBSON

Copyright © 1948, 1949 by Bienstock Publishing Company, Jerry Leiber Music, Mike Stoller Music and Seven Eight Nine Music Assoc.
Copyright Renewed

Slow Blues

Here's a dance you should know when

the lights are down low, grab your ba - by

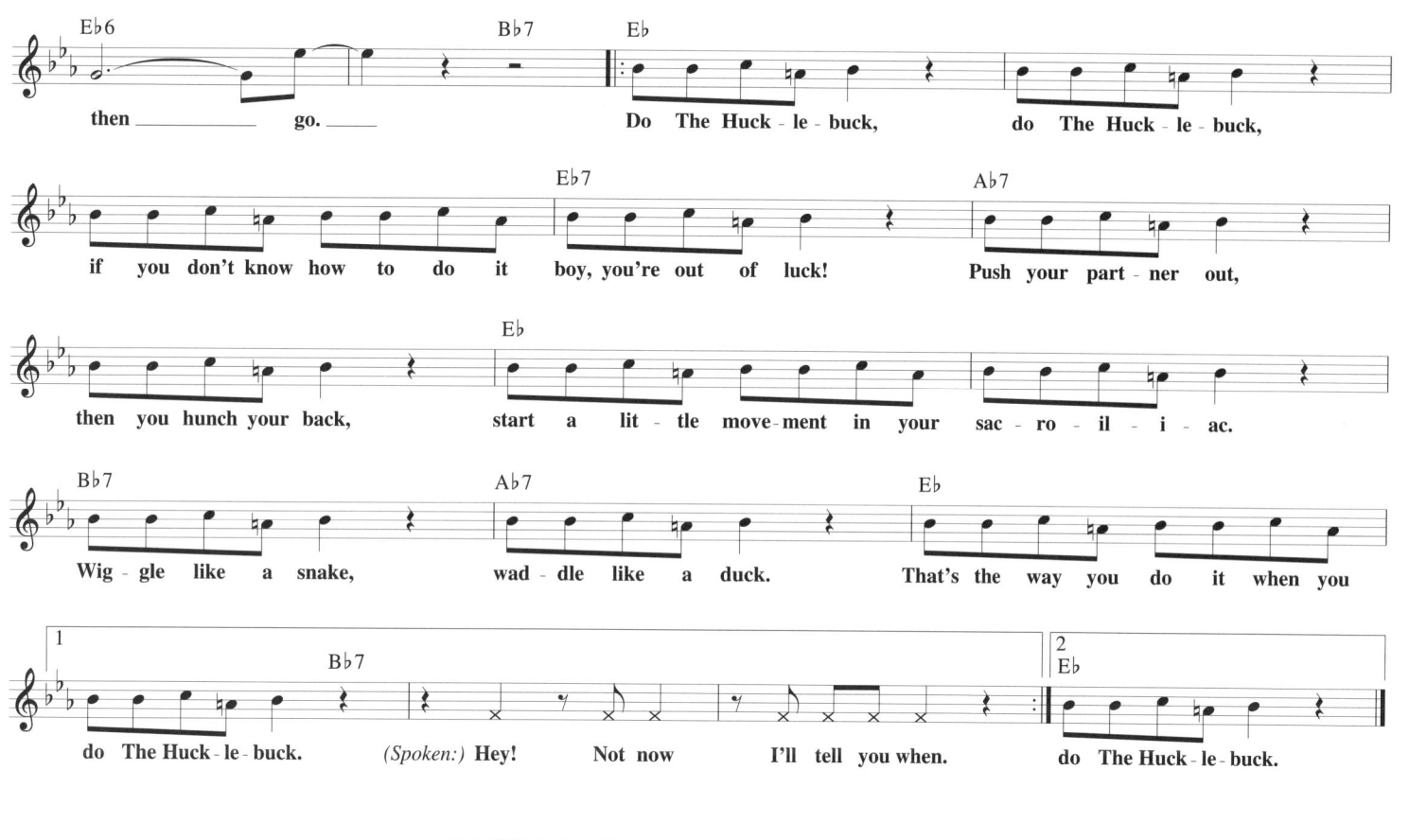

A HUNDRED YEARS FROM TODAY
from LEW LESLIE'S BLACKBIRDS OF 1934

© 1933 ROBBINS MUSIC CORPORATION
© Renewed 1961 WAROCK CORP. and EMI ROBBINS MUSIC CORPORATION

Lyric by JOE YOUNG and NED WASHINGTON
Music by VICTOR YOUNG

HYPNOSIS

Written by JOE LOVANO

Copyright © 1992 LOVO MUSIC (BMI)

I AIN'T GOT NOTHIN' BUT THE BLUES

Words by DON GEORGE
Music by DUKE ELLINGTON

Copyright © 1944 (Renewed 1971) and Assigned to Famous Music Corporation, Tempo Music, Inc.
c/o Music Sales Corporation and Ricki Music Co. in the U.S.A.
Rights for the world outside the U.S.A. Controlled by Ricki Music Co.

Slow Blues

Ain't got the change of a nick-el, ain't got no bounce in my shoes, ain't got no fan-cy to tick-le, I Ain't Got Noth-in' But The Blues.

Ain't got no cof-fee that's perk-in', ain't got no win-nings to lose, ain't got a dream that is work-in', I Ain't Got Noth-in' But The Blues.

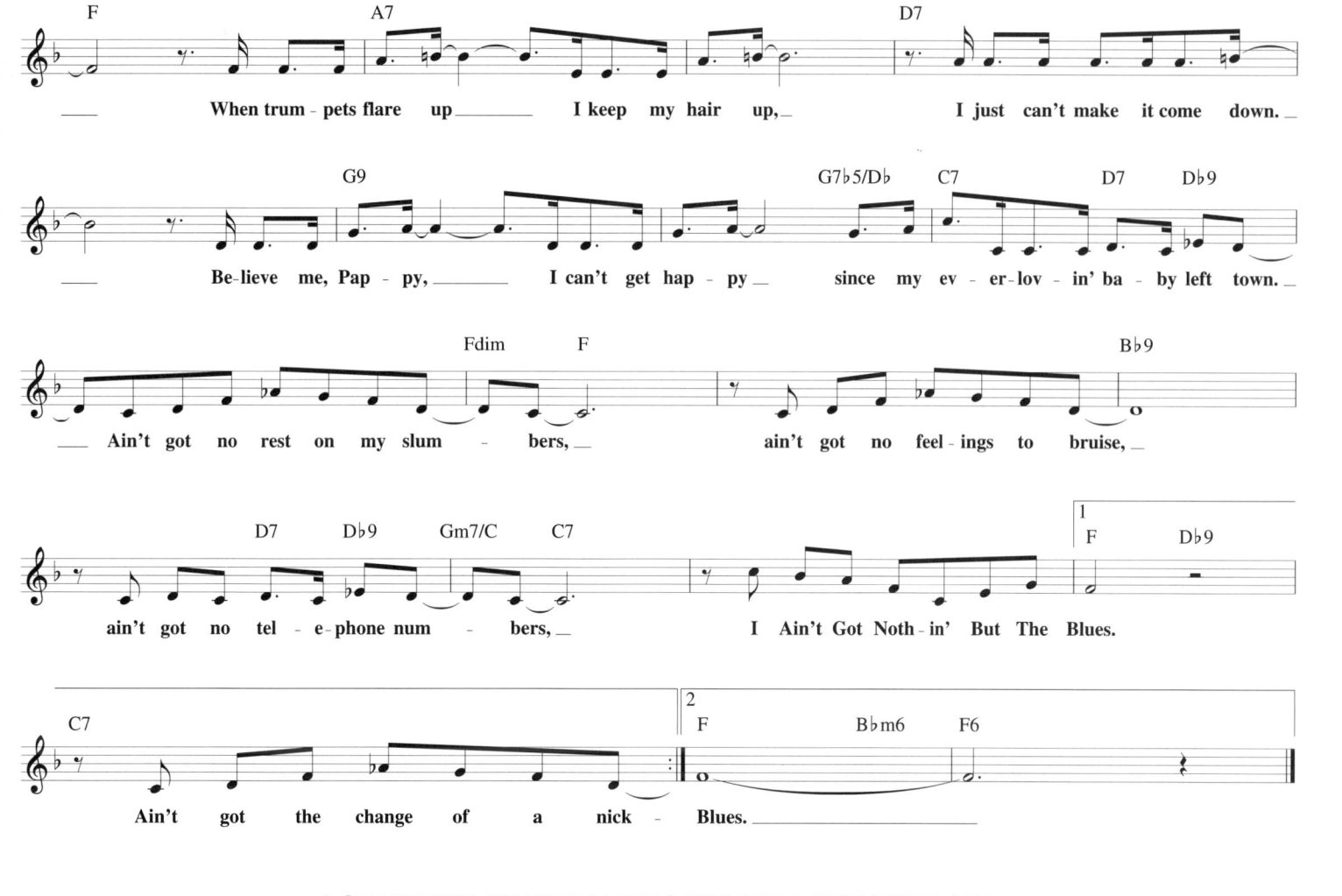

When trum-pets flare up, I keep my hair up, I just can't make it come down. Be-lieve me, Pap-py, I can't get hap-py since my ev-er-lov-in' ba-by left town. Ain't got no rest on my slum-bers, ain't got no feel-ings to bruise, ain't got no tel-e-phone num-bers, I Ain't Got Noth-in' But The Blues. Ain't got the change of a nick - Blues.

I CAN'T BELIEVE THAT YOU'RE IN LOVE WITH ME

Copyright © 1926 by Mills Music, Inc.
Copyright Renewed, Assigned to Ireneadele Publishing Company and EMI Mills Music Inc. for the United States
All Rights for Ireneadele Publishing Company Administered by The Songwriters Guild Of America

Words and Music by JIMMY McHUGH
and CLARENCE GASKILL

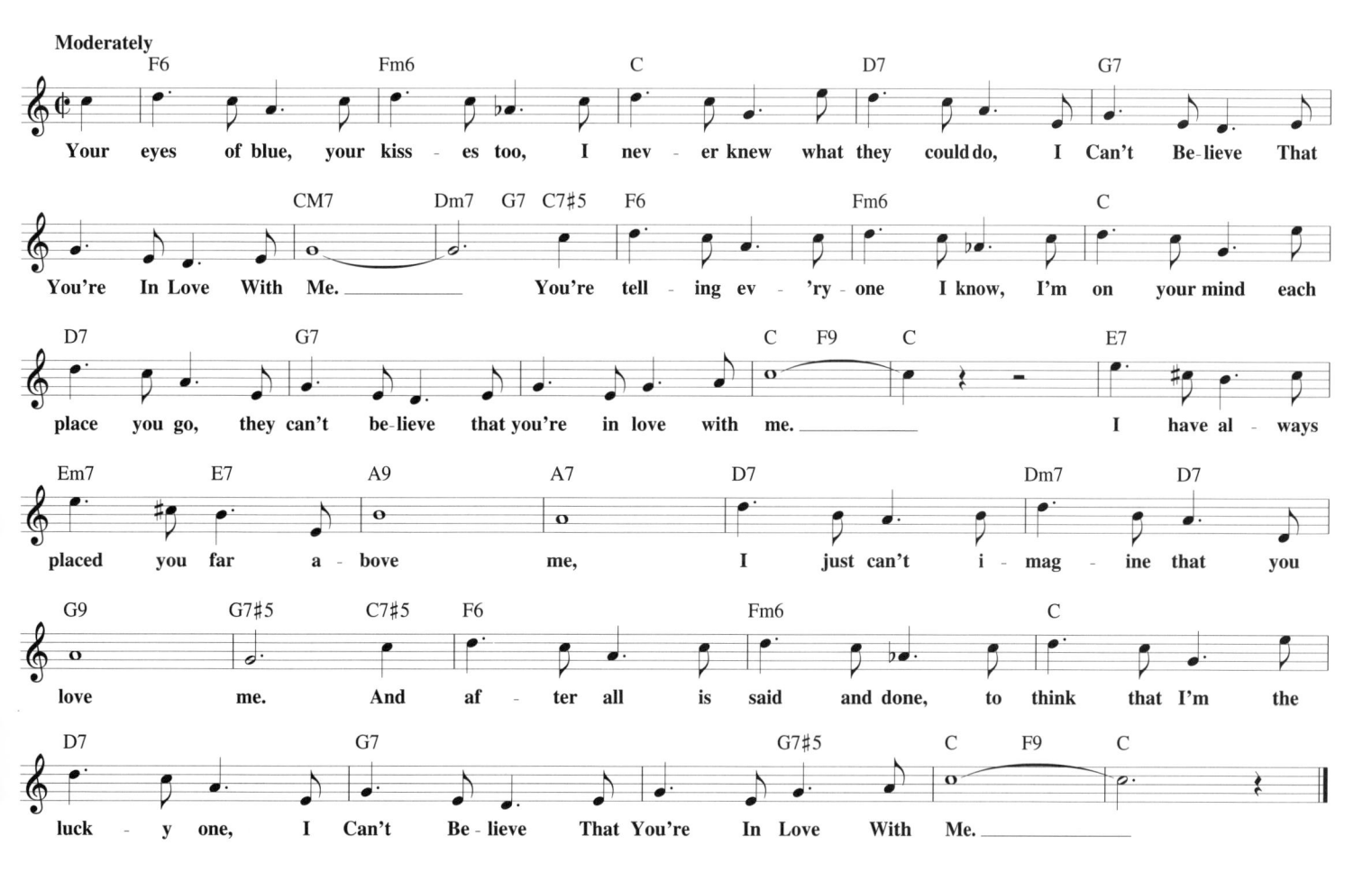

Moderately

Your eyes of blue, your kiss-es too, I nev-er knew what they could do, I Can't Be-lieve That You're In Love With Me. You're tell-ing ev-'ry-one I know, I'm on your mind each place you go, they can't be-lieve that you're in love with me. I have al-ways placed you far a-bove me, I just can't i-mag-ine that you love me. And af-ter all is said and done, to think that I'm the luck-y one, I Can't Be-lieve That You're In Love With Me.

I AM IN LOVE
from CAN-CAN

Words and Music by
COLE PORTER

Copyright © 1953 by Cole Porter
Copyright Renewed, Assigned to Robert H. Montgomery, Trustee of the
Cole Porter Musical and Literary Property Trusts
Chappell & Co. owner of publication and allied rights throughout the world

Moderately

I am de-ject-ed, I am de-pressed, yet res-ur-rect-ed and sail-ing the crest. Why this e-la-tion mixed with de-fla-tion? What ex-pla-na-tion? I ___ Am In Love! Such con-flict-ing ques-tions ride a-round ___ in my brain. Should I or-der cy-a-nide or or-der cham-pagne? Oh, what is this sud-den jolt? ___ I feel like a fright-ened colt ___ just hit by a thun-der-bolt; ___ I ___ Am In Love! I knew the odds were a-gainst me be-fore, I had no flare for flam-ing de-sire. But since the gods gave me you to a-dore, I may lose, but I re-fuse to fight the fire! So, come and en-light-en my days and nev-er de-part. You on-ly can bright-en the blaze that burns in my heart, for I am wild-ly in love with you and so in need of ___ a stam-pede of ___ love! I am de-pede of ___ love! ___

I GOT IT BAD AND THAT AIN'T GOOD

Words by PAUL FRANCIS WEBSTER
Music by DUKE ELLINGTON

I HEAR MUSIC
from the Paramount Picture DANCING ON A DIME

Copyright © 1940 (Renewed 1967) by Famous Music Corporation

Words by FRANK LOESSER
Music by BURTON LANE

I Hear Music, might-y fine mu-sic, the mur-mur of a morn-ing breeze up there, the rat-tle of the milk-man on the stair.
Sure that's mu-sic, might-y fine mu-sic, the sing-ing of a spar-row in the sky, the perk-ing of the cof-fee right near-by. There's my fa-v'rite mel-o-dy, You, my an-gel, phon-ing me.

I Hear Mu-sic, might-y fine mu-sic, and an-y-time I think my world is wrong, I get me out of bed and sing this song. song.

I DIDN'T KNOW ABOUT YOU

Copyright © 1944 Robbins Music Corp.
Copyright Renewed 1972 Harrison Music Corp. and EMI Robbins Catalog Inc.

Words by BOB RUSSELL
Music by DUKE ELLINGTON

I ran a-round with my own lit-tle crowd, the u-su-al laughs, not of-ten but loud. And in the world that I knew, I Did-n't Know A-bout You. Chas-ing af-ter the ring on the mer-ry-go-round, just tak-ing my fun where it could be found, and yet what else could I do? I Did-n't Know A-bout You. Dar-ling, now I know I

had the lone-li-est yes-ter-day, ev'-ry-day. In your arms I
know for once in my life I'm liv-ing. Had a good time ev'-ry
time I went out, ro-mance was a thing I kid-ded a-bout. How could I
know a-bout love? I Did-n't Know A-bout You.

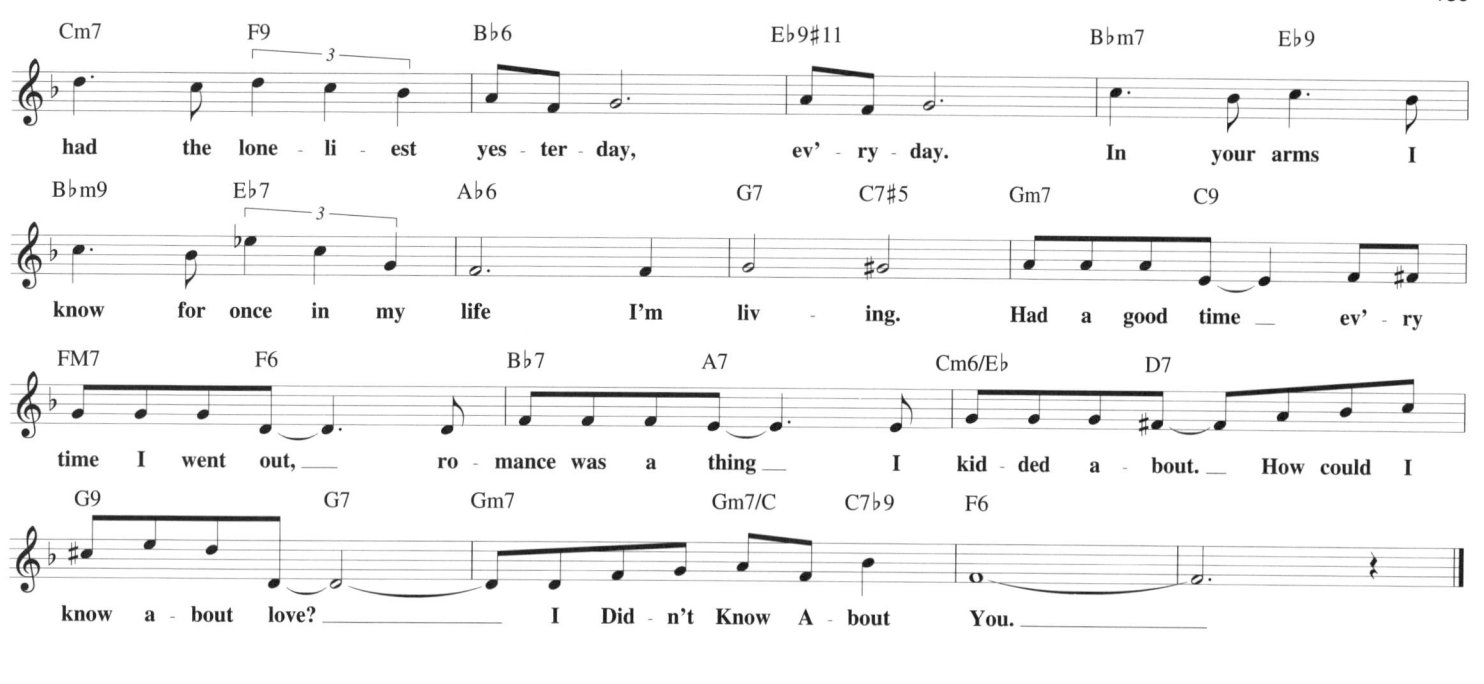

I GET ALONG WITHOUT YOU VERY WELL
(Except Sometimes)

Copyright © 1938, 1939 Hoagy Publishing Company
Copyrights Renewed 1965, 1966

Words and Music by HOAGY CARMICHAEL
Inspired by a poem written by J.B. THOMPSON

Slowly with expression

I Get A-long With-out You Ver-y Well, of course I do, ex-cept when
I Get A-long With-out You Ver-y Well, of course I do, ex-cept per-

soft rains fall and drip from leaves. Then I re-call the thrill of be-ing
haps in spring. But I should nev-er think of spring, for that would sure-ly

To Coda ⊕

shel-tered in your arms, of course I do, but I Get A-long With-
break my heart in

out You Ver-y Well, I've for-got-ten you, just like I should, of course I have,

ex-cept to hear your name or some-one's laugh that is the same, but I've for-got-ten

you just like I should. What a guy! What a fool am I

to think my break-ing heart could kid the moon; What's in store? Should I

D.C. al Coda **CODA** ⊕

'phone once more? No it's best that I stick to my tune. two.

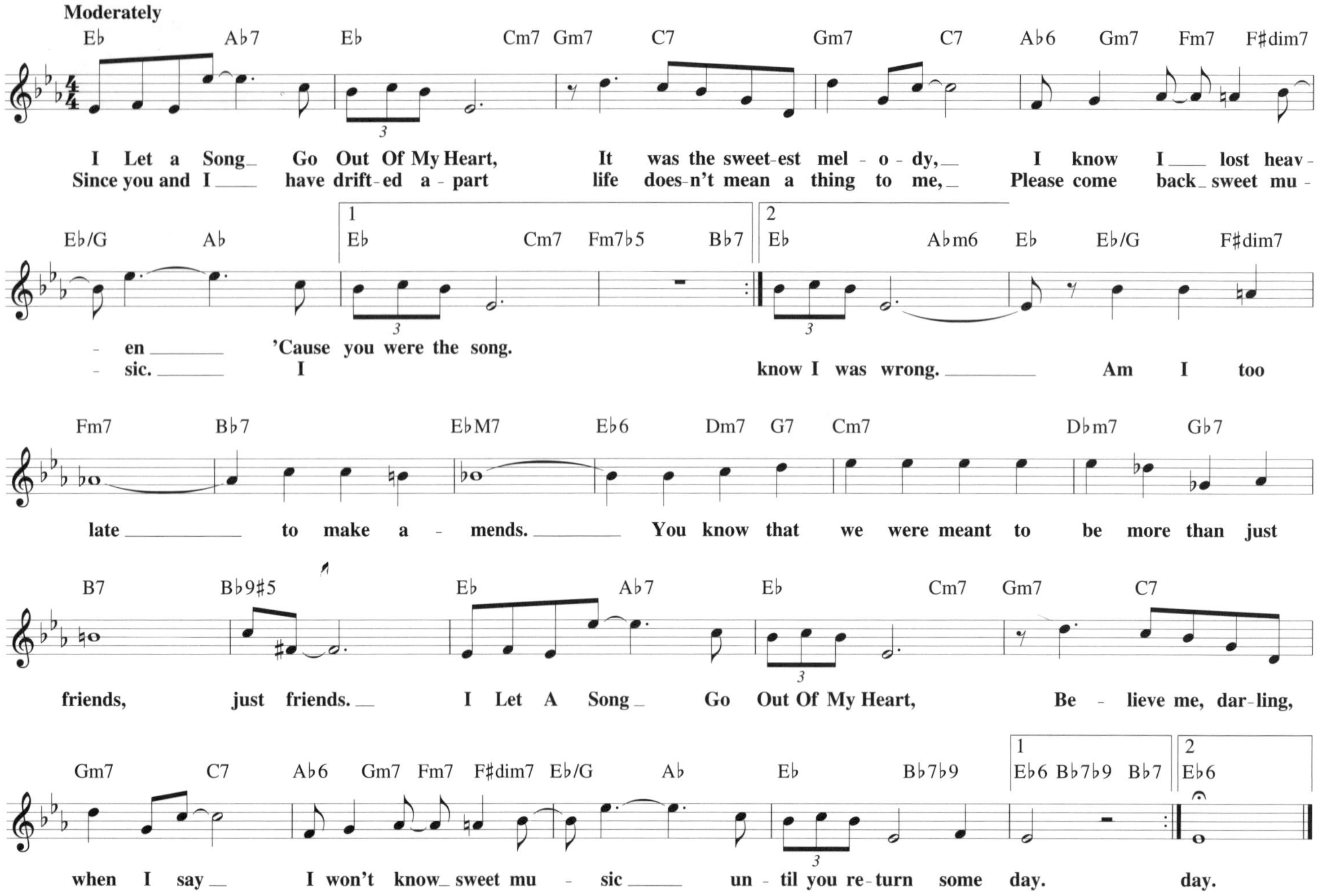

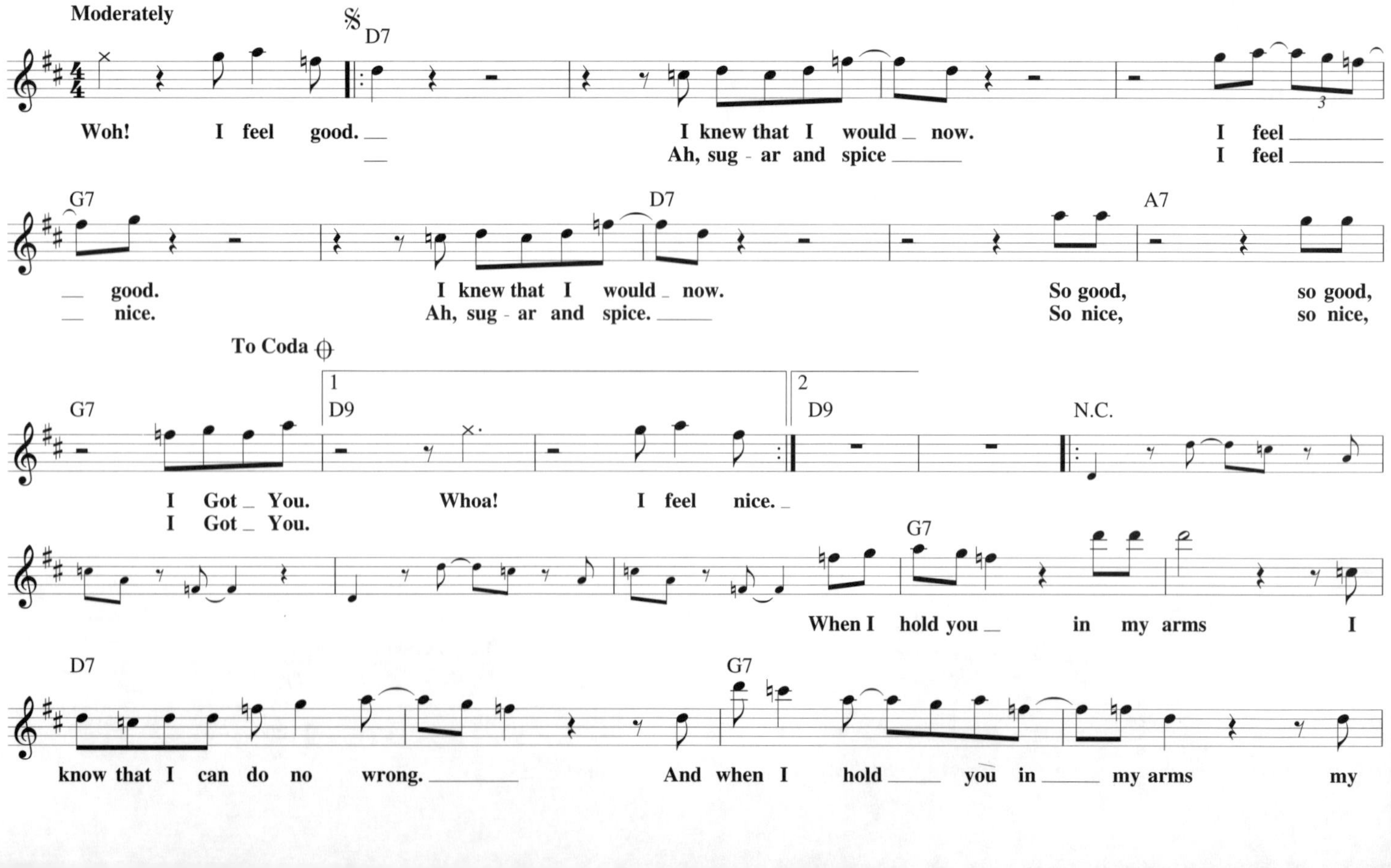

I GOTTA RIGHT TO SING THE BLUES

Words by TED KOEHLER
Music by HAROLD ARLEN

© 1932 (Renewed) WARNER BROS. INC. and S.A. MUSIC CO.

I KEEP GOING BACK TO JOE'S

Words and Music by MARVIN FISHER
and JACK SEGAL

I LEFT THIS SPACE FOR YOU

Written by ARTURO SANDOVAL

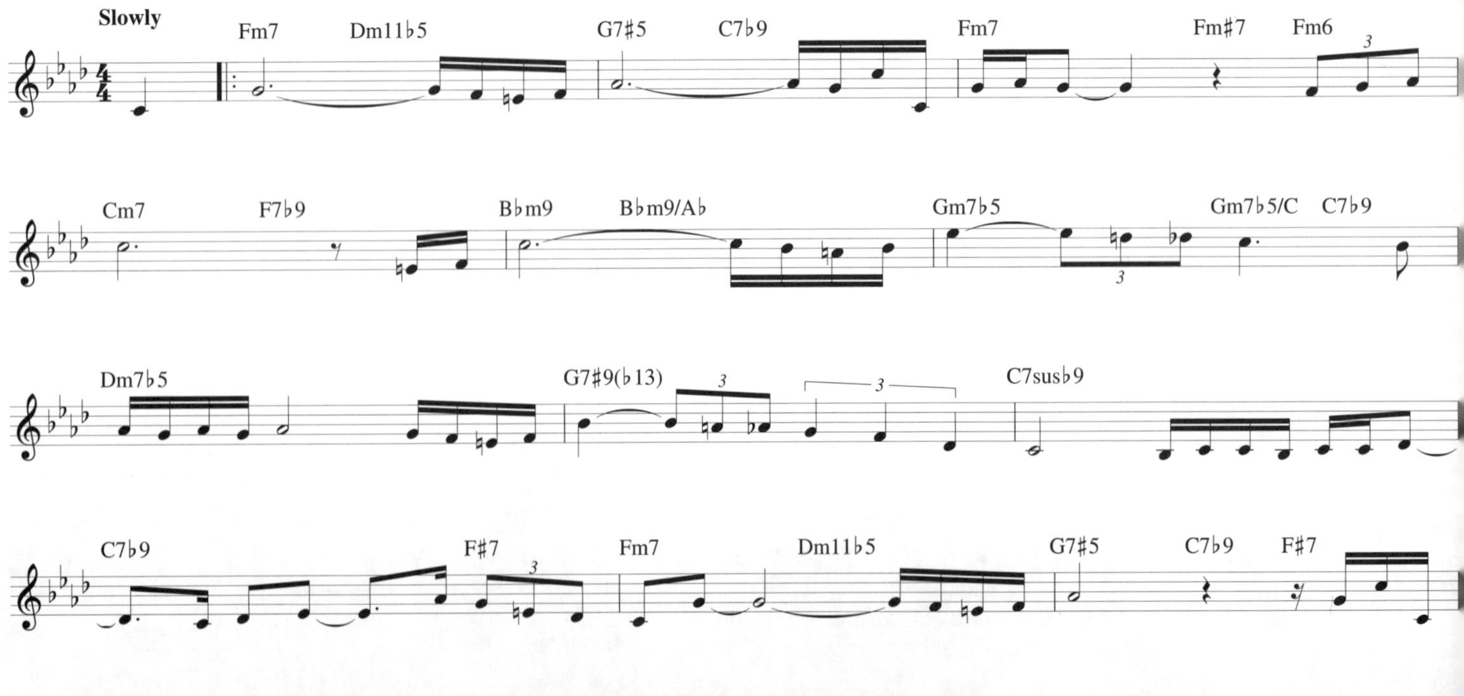

I MEAN YOU

By THELONIOUS MONK
and COLEMAN HAWKINS

I REMEMBER BIRD

By LEONARD FEATHER

Copyright © 1967 (Renewed) Model Music Co.

Moderately slow

He brought a new sound, and cov-ered new ground, but then he soon found good for-tune nev-er seems to bless the pi-o-neer. The things he taught us, the joy he brought us, this mood has caught us un-til there's Bird to-day in ev-'ry note we hear. We can't for-get him be-cause his soul's with us, we all re-mem-ber Bird through the years. In far off plac-es, you'll hear Bird's trac-es. De-spite new fac-es, the things he gave we had to save un-til to-day. The leg-end's grow-ing, no way of know-ing, how much is ow-ing. We owe him dues for ev-'ry blues we try to play. He'll live for-ev-er, that's why we're we're still hear-ing the Bird, be-cause he's with us to-day.

I REMEMBER YOU

from the Paramount Picture THE FLEET'S IN

Copyright © 1942 (Renewed 1969) by Paramount Music Corporation

Words by JOHNNY MERCER
Music by VICTOR SCHERTZINGER

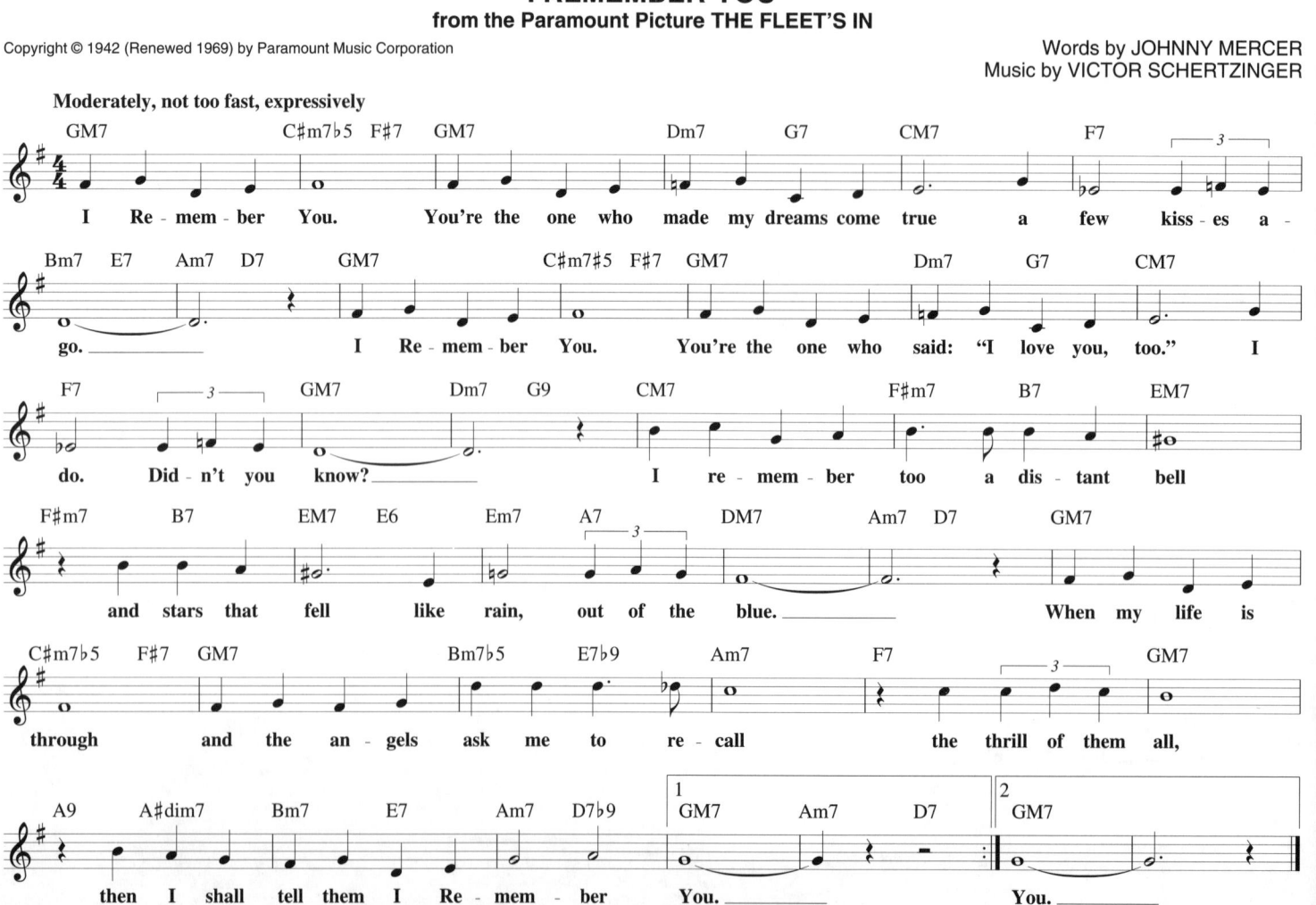

Moderately, not too fast, expressively

I Re-mem-ber You. You're the one who made my dreams come true a few kiss-es a-go. I Re-mem-ber You. You're the one who said: "I love you, too." I do. Did-n't you know? I re-mem-ber too a dis-tant bell and stars that fell like rain, out of the blue. When my life is through and the an-gels ask me to re-call the thrill of them all, then I shall tell them I Re-mem-ber You. You.

I THOUGHT ABOUT YOU

Copyright © 1939 (Renewed) by Music Sales Corporation (ASCAP) and Commander Music

Words by JOHNNY MERCER
Music by JIMMY VAN HEUSEN

Moderately slow

I took a trip on the train and I Thought A-bout You, I passed a shad-ow-y lane and I Thought A-bout You. Two or three cars parked un-der the stars, a wind-ing stream. Moon shin-ing down on some lit-tle town and with each beam, same old dream. At ev-'ry stop that we made, oh, I Thought A-bout You, but when I pulled down the shade, then I real-ly felt blue. I peeked through the crack and looked at the track, the one go-ing back to you, and what did I do? I Thought A-bout You.

IF I SHOULD LOSE YOU
from the Paramount Picture ROSE OF THE RANCHO

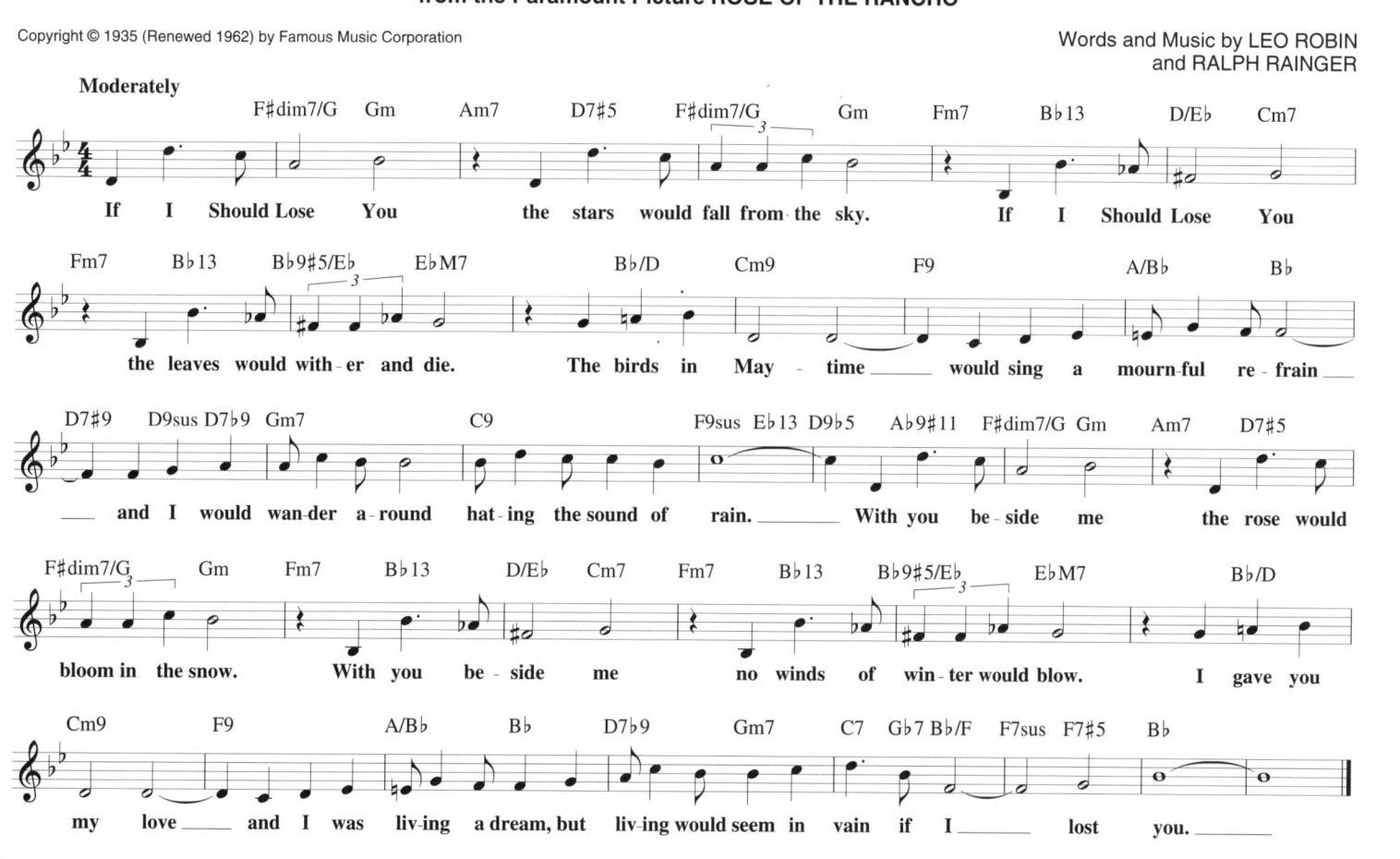

Copyright © 1935 (Renewed 1962) by Famous Music Corporation

Words and Music by LEO ROBIN
and RALPH RAINGER

Moderately

If I Should Lose You the stars would fall from the sky. If I Should Lose You the leaves would with-er and die. The birds in May-time would sing a mourn-ful re-frain and I would wan-der a-round hat-ing the sound of rain. With you be-side me the rose would bloom in the snow. With you be-side me no winds of win-ter would blow. I gave you my love and I was liv-ing a dream, but liv-ing would seem in vain if I lost you.

I TOLD YA I LOVE YA NOW GET OUT

By JOHN FRIGO, LOU CARTER and HERB ELLIS

Copyright © 1947 (Renewed 1975) Criterion Music Corp.

Moderately

I Told Ya I Love Ya, Now Get Out!

I Told Ya I Love Ya, Now Get Out!

Ev-'ry-thing's cos-y and ev-'ry-thing's gone, but let's cool it, hon-ey, time march-es on.

I Told Ya I Love Ya, Now Get Out! There may be times when I need ya, there's no doubt. Ba-by,

now you're some-thin' I can do with-out. Leave your num-ber and go on home, but don't wait with sand-wich-es by the 'phone. I Told Ya I Love Ya, Now Get Out! Ba-by,

please leave me be. You want a pup-pet and there's no strings on me. Get hep, you can leave on the five-eight-een.

Now don't go 'way say-in' I've been mean. 'Cause

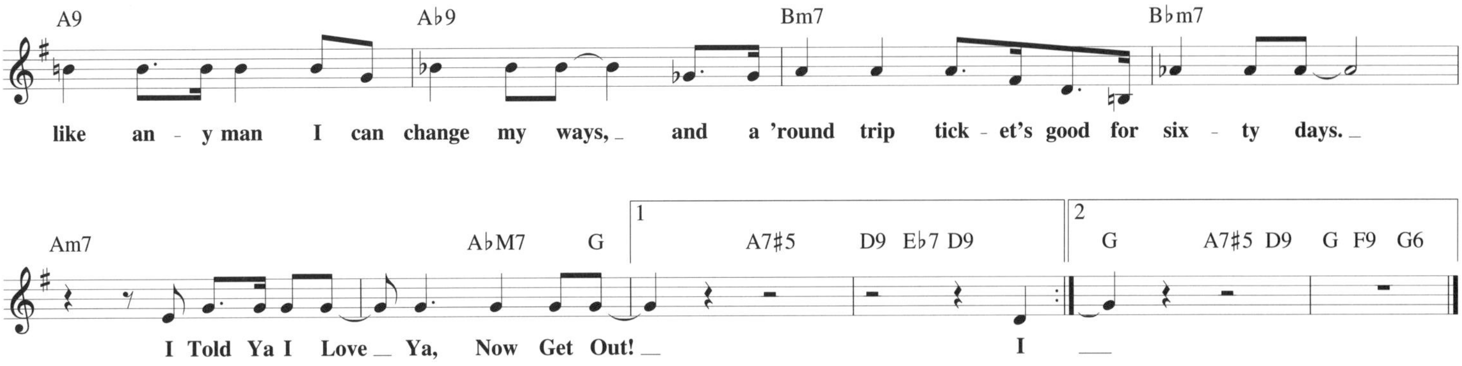
A9 Ab9 Bm7 Bbm7
like an - y man I can change my ways, and a 'round trip tick - et's good for six - ty days.
Am7 AbM7 G 1 A7#5 D9 Eb7 D9 2 G A7#5 D9 G F9 G6
I Told Ya I Love Ya, Now Get Out! I

I WATCHED HER WALK AWAY

Copyright © 1990 Songs Of PolyGram International, Inc. and Who's Hacking Music

By RUSS FREEMAN

Moderate Jazz Rock
Eb(add9) Ab(add9) Bbsus Bb Eb(add9) AbM7 Cm7 Fm7 Fm6
G7/B Fm6/C Cm Bb Ab AbM9 Bb(add9)/D Eb Cm Bb Ab
Bb(add9)/D Eb Bb(add9)/D Eb/Ab Fm7 Ab/Bb G7/B Cm
Db Eb Ab (add9) 1 Ab/Bb 2 Ab/Bb G7/B
Cm(add9) Bb AbM9 Fm7/Bb Eb/G Ab Bb
Cm(add9) Bb AbM9 Fm7/Bb Gm7 Cm7 Fm7 Fm7/Bb
Eb(add9)/G AbM7 Cm11 Bb Eb(add9)/G AbM7 Fm7 Bbsus Bb
Eb(add9)/G Ab(add9) Ab/C Bbsus Bb Eb(add9)/G Ab(add9)

I WISH I WERE IN LOVE AGAIN
from BABES IN ARMS

Copyright © 1937 by Williamson Music and The Estate Of Lorenz Hart in the United States
Copyright Renewed
All Rights on behalf of The Estate Of Lorenz Hart Administered by WB Music Corp.

Words by LORENZ HART
Music by RICHARD RODGERS

The sleep-less nights, the dai-ly fights, the quick to-bog-gan when you reach the heights; I
fur-tive sigh, the black-ened eye, the words "I'll love you till the day I die," the

miss the kiss-es and I miss the bites, I Wish I Were In Love A-gain! ___ The
self de-cep-tion that be-lieves the lie, I Wish I Were In Love A-gain! ___ When

brok-en dates, the end-less waits, the love-ly lov-ing and the hate-ful hates, the
love con-geals it soon re-veals the faint a-rom-a of per-form-ing seals, the

con-ver-sa-tion with the fly-ing plates, I Wish I Were In Love A-gain! No ___ more
dou-ble cross-ing of a pair of heels, I Wish I Were In Love A-gain! No ___ more

pain, no ___ more strain. Now ___ I'm sane, but ___ I would rath-er be
care, no de-spair. I'm ___ all there now, ___ but I'd rath-er be

ga - ga! ___ The pulled out fur of cat and cur, the fine mis-mat-ing of a
punch - drunk! ___ Be-lieve me sir, I much pre-fer the clas-sic bat-tle of a

him and her, I've learned my les-son, but I Wish I Were In Love A - gain! The
him and her, I don't like qui-et and I Wish I Were In Love A - gain!

I WISHED ON THE MOON

Copyright © 1934, 1935 (Renewed 1961, 1962) by Famous Music Corporation

Words and Music by DOROTHY PARKER
and RALPH RAINGER

I Wished On The Moon ___ for some-thing I nev-er knew, ___

wished on the moon ___ for more than I ev-er knew: ___ a

sweet-er rose, a soft-er sky, an A-pril day ___ that would not dance ___ a-

IF YOU GO

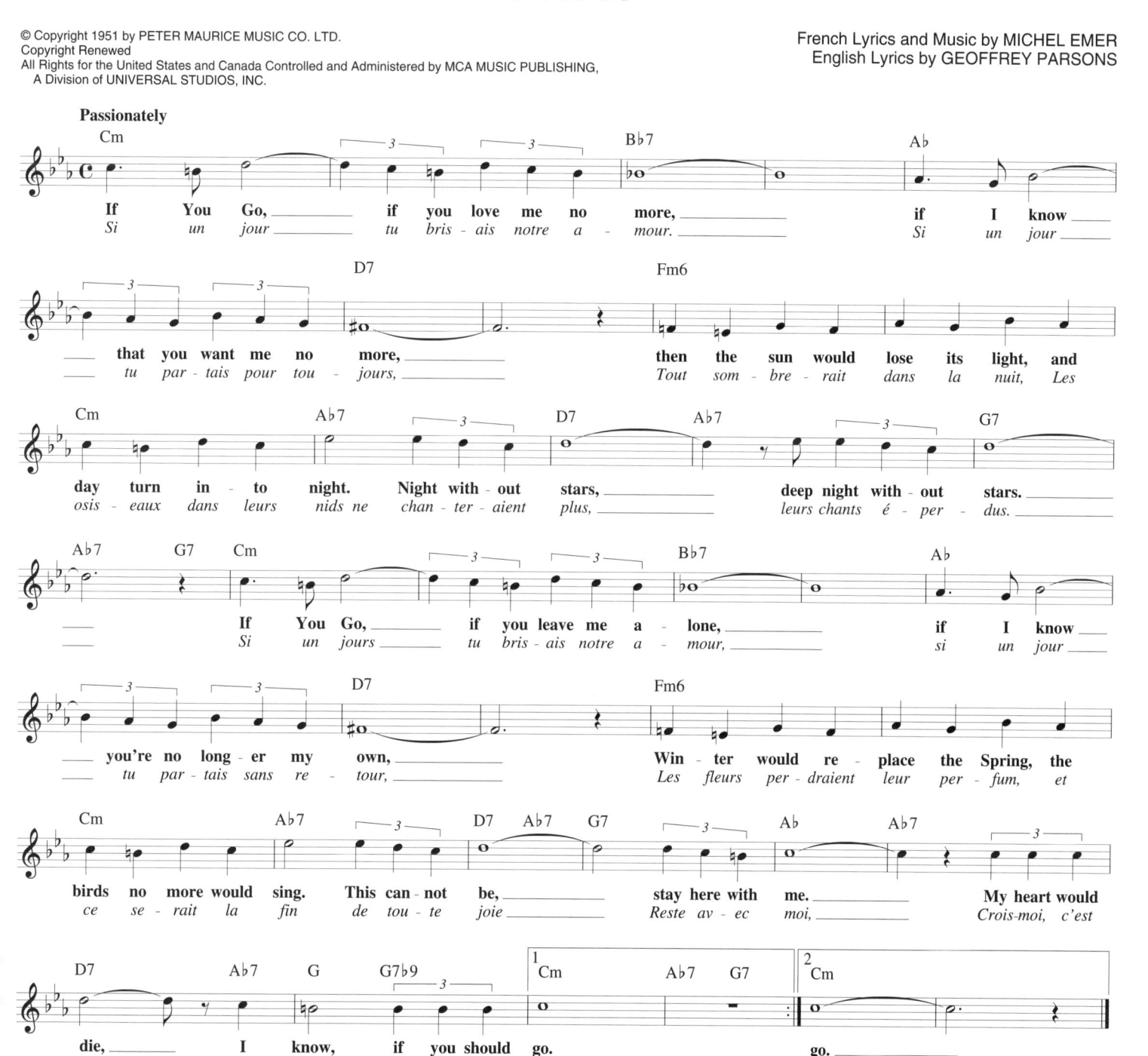

French Lyrics and Music by MICHEL EMER
English Lyrics by GEOFFREY PARSONS

© Copyright 1951 by PETER MAURICE MUSIC CO. LTD.
Copyright Renewed
All Rights for the United States and Canada Controlled and Administered by MCA MUSIC PUBLISHING,
A Division of UNIVERSAL STUDIOS, INC.

Passionately

If You Go, if you love me no more, if I know that you want me no more, then the sun would lose its light, and day turn into night. Night without stars, deep night without stars. If You Go, if you leave me alone, if I know you're no longer my own, Winter would replace the Spring, the birds no more would sing. This cannot be, stay here with me. My heart would die, I know, if you should go.

Si un jour tu brisais notre amour. Si un jour tu partais pour toujours, Tout sombrerait dans la nuit, Les oiseaux dans leurs nids ne chanteraient plus, leurs chants éperdus. Si un jours tu brisais notre amour, si un jour tu partais sans retour, Les fleurs perdraient leur parfum, et ce serait la fin de toute joie Reste avec moi, Crois-moi, c'est vrai J'en mourrais si tu partais.

IF WE MEET AGAIN, PART ONE

By AL DI MEOLA

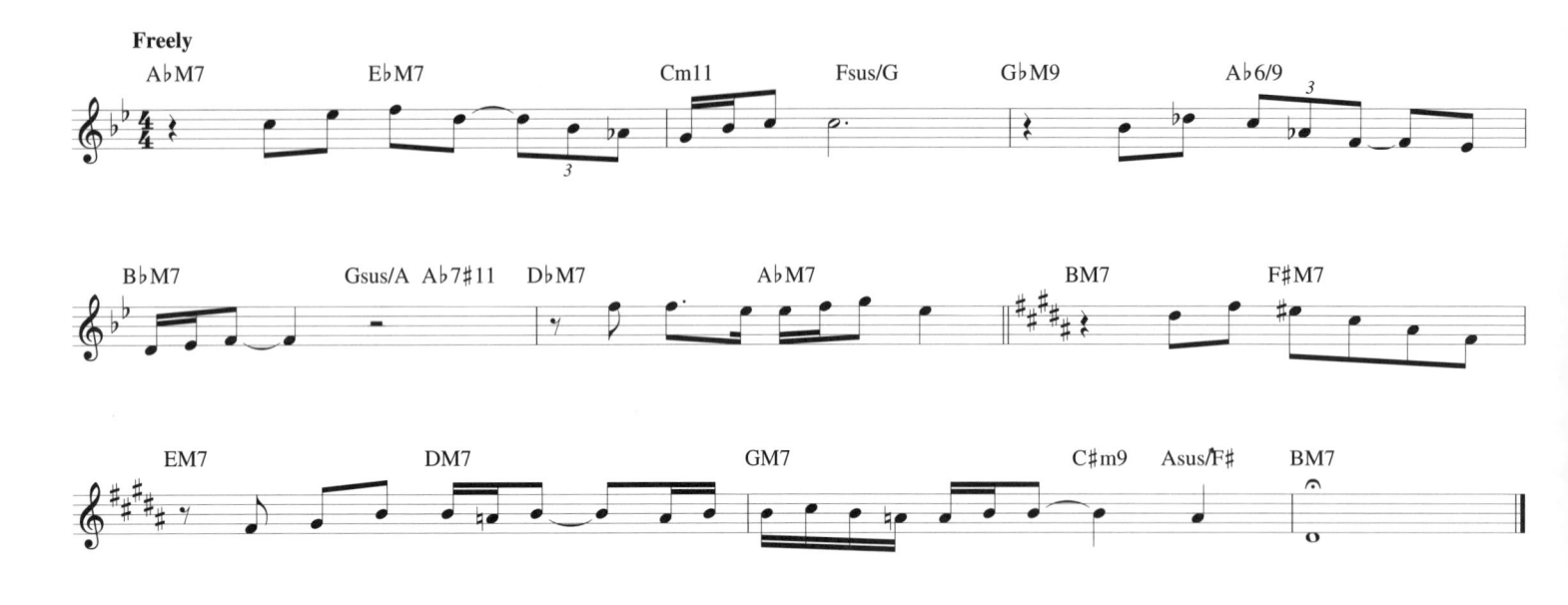

Copyright © 1994 DI MEOLA MUSIC CO.

IF YOU NEVER COME TO ME
(Inutil paisagem)

Music by ANTONIO CARLOS JOBIM
Portuguese Lyrics by ALOYSIO DE OLIVEIRA
English Lyrics by RAY GILBERT

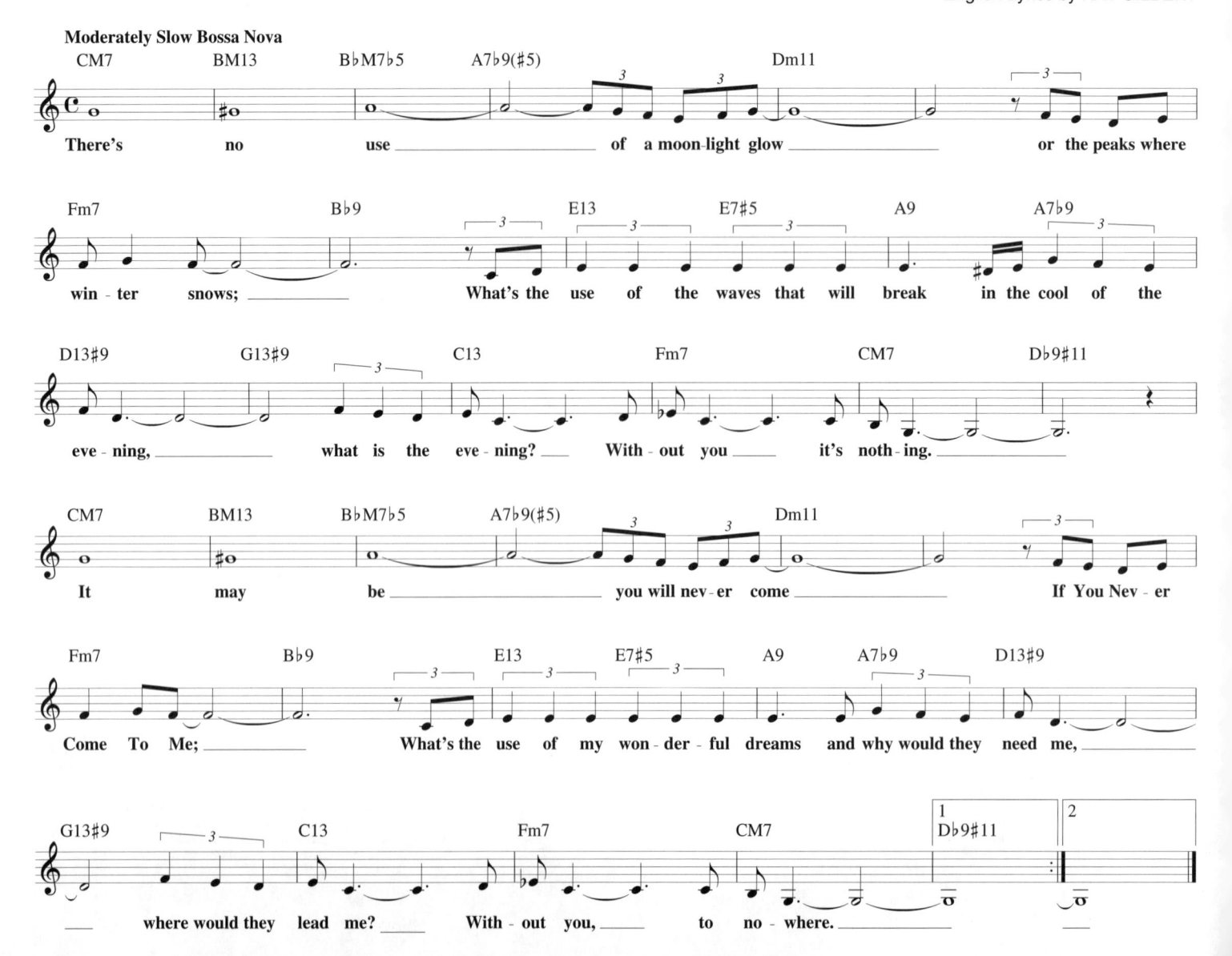

Copyright © 1965 Ipanema Music Corp.
Copyright Renewed, Assigned to Corcovado Music Corp., Ipanema Music Corp. and Aloysio de Oliveira

There's no use ___ of a moon-light glow ___ or the peaks where win-ter snows; ___ What's the use of the waves that will break in the cool of the eve-ning, ___ what is the eve-ning? ___ With-out you ___ it's noth-ing. ___ It may be ___ you will nev-er come ___ If You Nev-er Come To Me; ___ What's the use of my won-der-ful dreams and why would they need me, ___ where would they lead me? ___ With-out you, ___ to no-where.

I'LL BUILD A STAIRWAY TO PARADISE

Words by B.G. DeSYLVA and IRA GERSHWIN
Music by GEORGE GERSHWIN

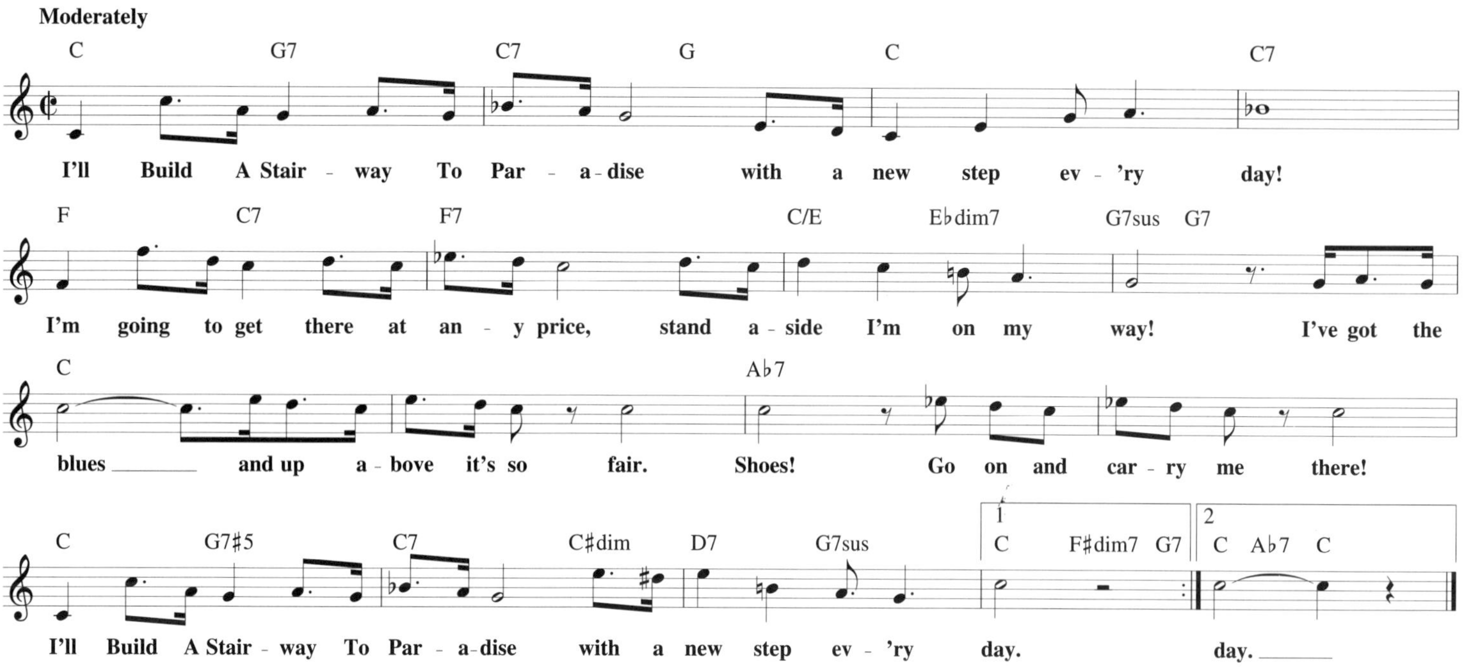

I'M A FOOL TO WANT YOU

Words and Music by JACK WOLF, JOEL HERRON and FRANK SINATRA

I'LL CLOSE MY EYES

© 1945 (Renewed 1973) COLGEMS-EMI MUSIC INC.

By BUDDY KAYE
and BILLY REID

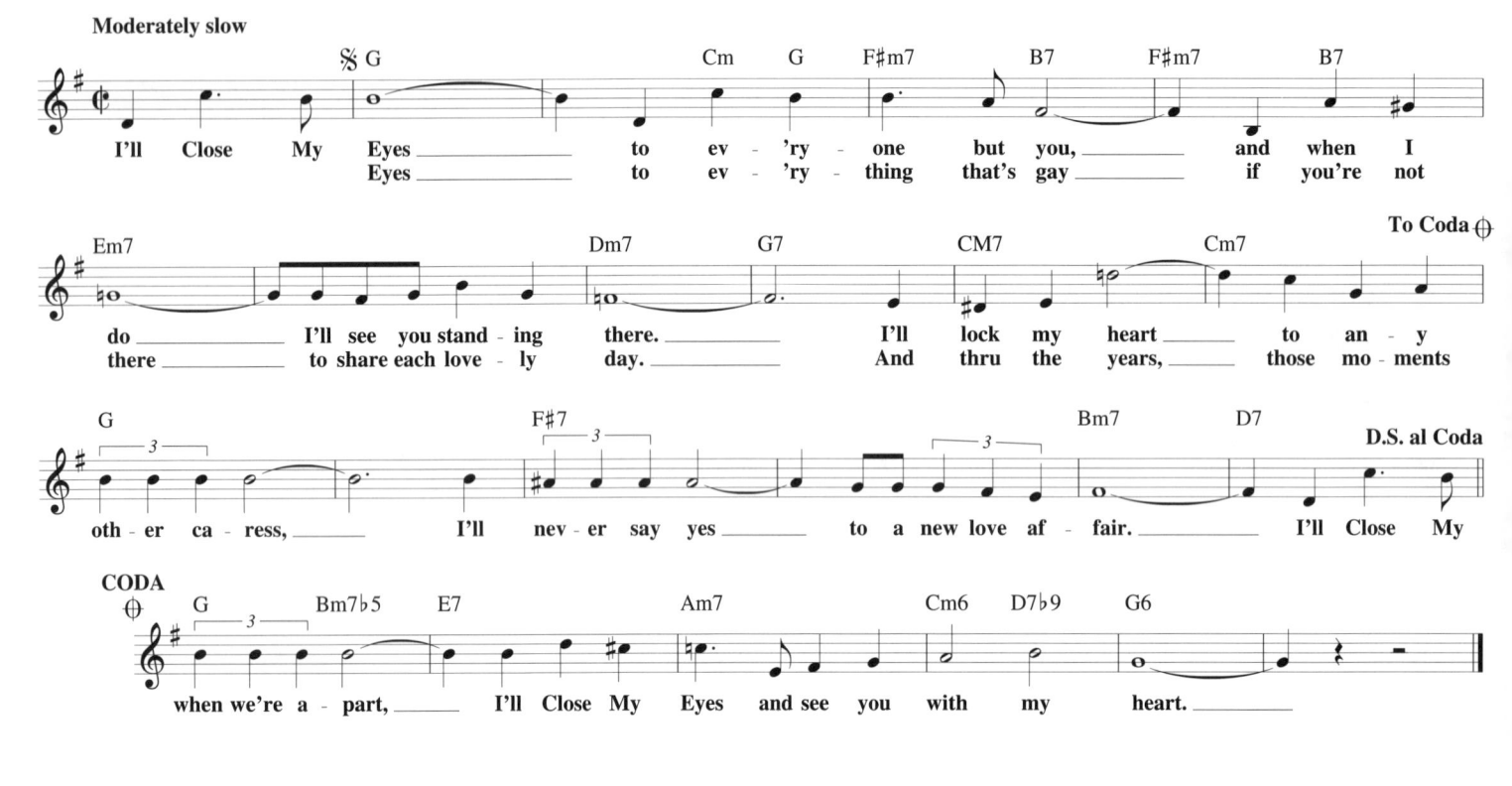

Moderately slow

I'll Close My Eyes _____ to ev-'ry-one but you, _____ and when I
Eyes _____ to ev-'ry-thing that's gay _____ if you're not

do _____ I'll see you stand-ing there. _____ I'll lock my heart _____ to an-y
there _____ to share each love-ly day. _____ And thru the years, _____ those mo-ments

oth-er ca-ress, _____ I'll nev-er say yes to a new love af-fair. I'll Close My

CODA

when we're a-part, _____ I'll Close My Eyes and see you with my heart. _____

I'M ALL SMILES
from THE YEARLING

© 1964 (Renewed) HERBERT MARTIN and MICHAEL LEONARD
All Rights Controlled by EDWIN H. MORRIS & COMPANY, A Division of MPL Communications, Inc.
and EMANUEL MUSIC CORP.

Lyric by HERBERT MARTIN
Music by MICHAEL LEONARD

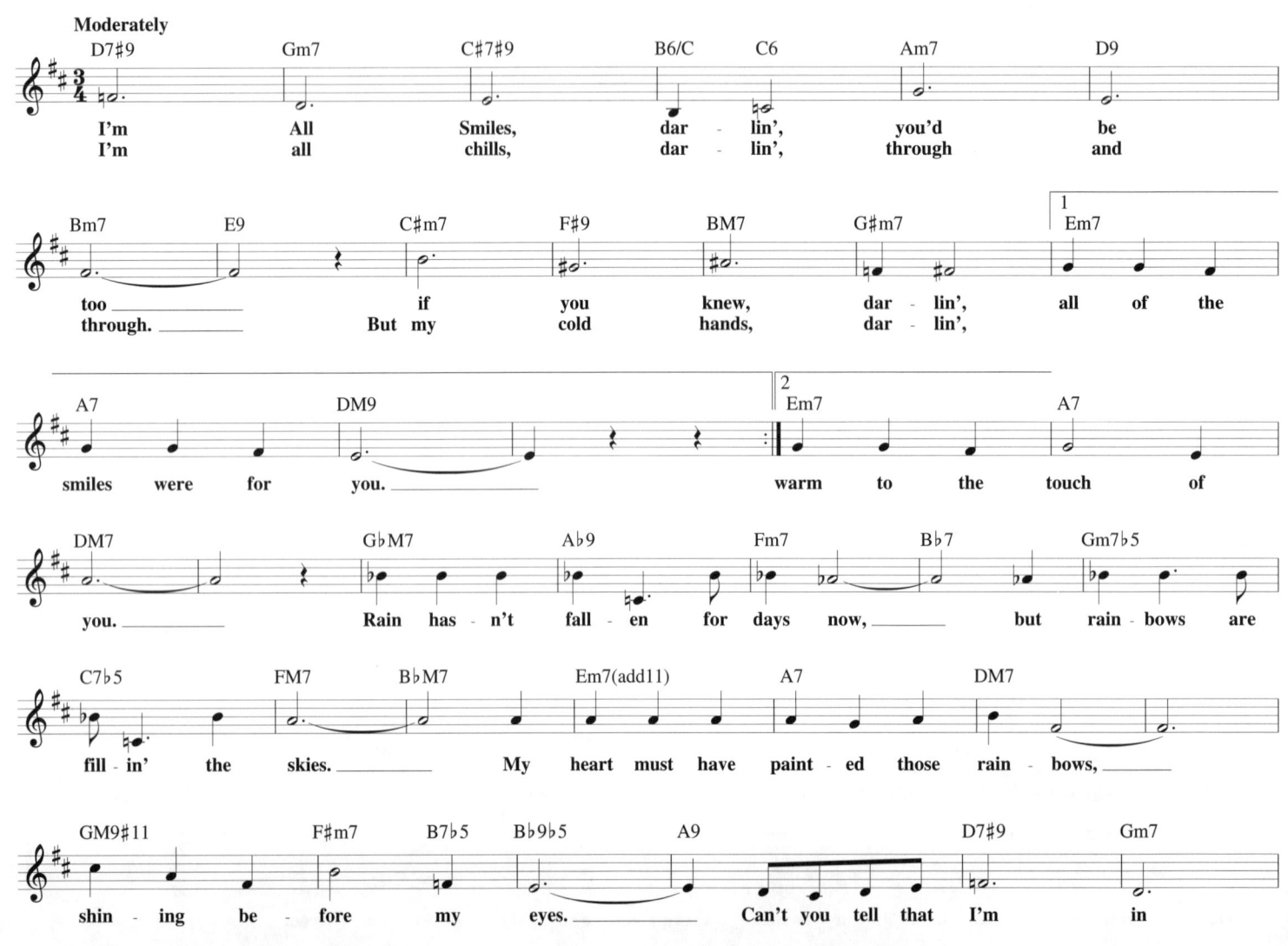

Moderately

I'm All Smiles, dar-lin', you'd be
I'm all chills, dar-lin', through and

too _____ if you knew, dar-lin', all of the
through. _____ But my cold hands, dar-lin',

smiles were for you. _____ warm to the touch of

you. _____ Rain has-n't fall-en for days now, _____ but rain-bows are

fill-in' the skies. _____ My heart must have paint-ed those rain-bows,

shin-ing be-fore my eyes. _____ Can't you tell that I'm in love, dar-lin', deep and true. _____ With guess who, dar-lin': Some-one I'd die for, beg, steal, or lie for, eat hum-ble pie for, some-one to fly to the sun, moon and sky for, some-one to live for, to laugh __ with and cry for, and that some-one is you. _____

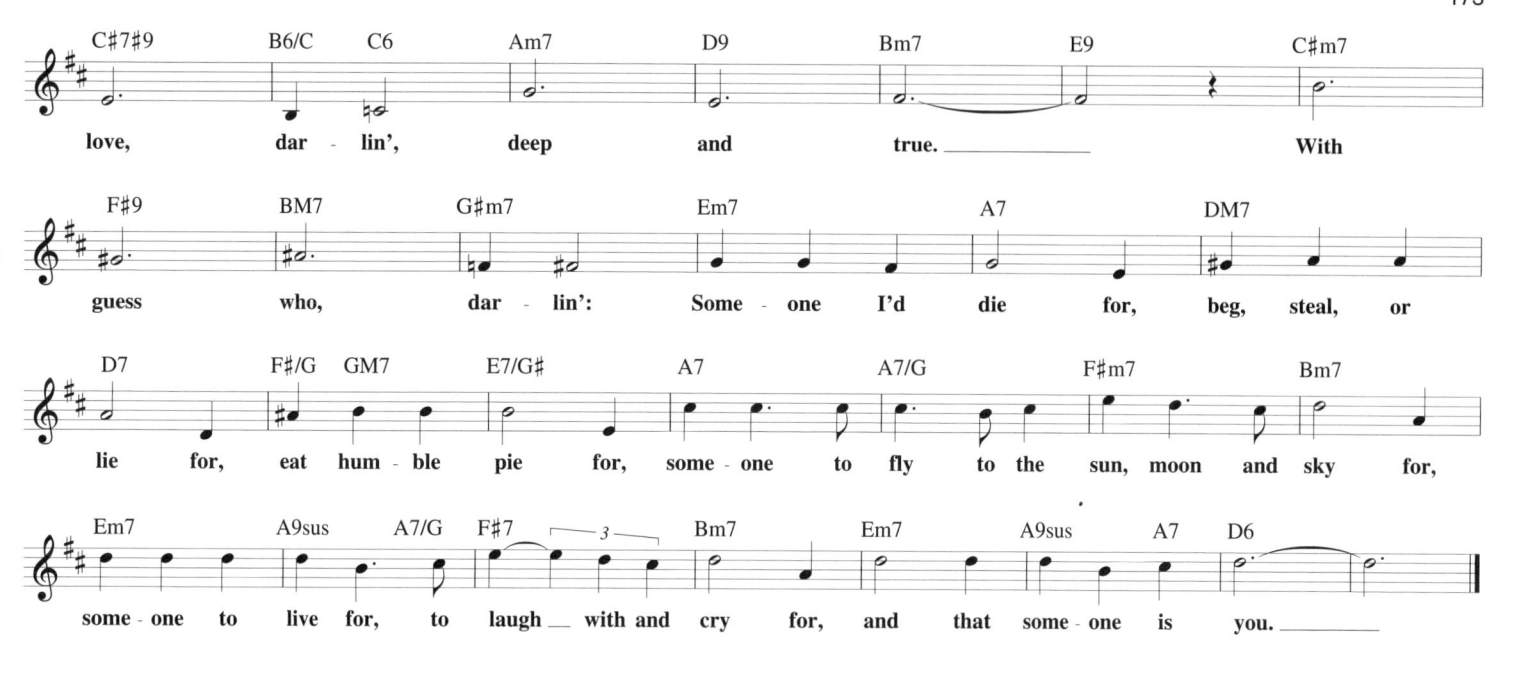

I'M JUST A LUCKY SO AND SO

Copyright © 1945 (Renewed 1973) and Assigned to Paramount Music Corporation
and PolyGram International Publishing, Inc. in the U.S.A.
Rights for the world outside the U.S.A. Controlled by Paramount Music Corporation

Words by MACK DAVID
Music by DUKE ELLINGTON

Very slow and rhythmical

As I walk down the street ___ seems ev-'ry-one I meet ___ gives me a friend-ly hel-lo. ___
___ I guess I'm Just A Luck-y So And-So. ___
The birds in ev-'ry tree ___ are all so neigh-bor-ly ___ they sing wher-ev-er I go.
I guess I'm Just A Luck-y So And-So. ___ If you should ask me the a-mount
in my bank ac-count, I'd have to con-fess ___ that I'm slip-pin'. ___ But that don't wor-ry me,
con-fi-den-tial-ly, I've got a dream that's a pip-pin'. ___ And when the day is through ___
each night I hur-ry to ___ a home where love waits, I know. ___ I guess I'm
Just A Luck-y So And-So. ___

I'M A DREAMER AREN'T WE ALL

Copyright © 1929 by Chappell & Co., Ray Henderson Music and Stephen Ballentine Music
Copyright Renewed

Words and Music by B.G. DeSYLVA,
LEW BROWN and RAY HENDERSON

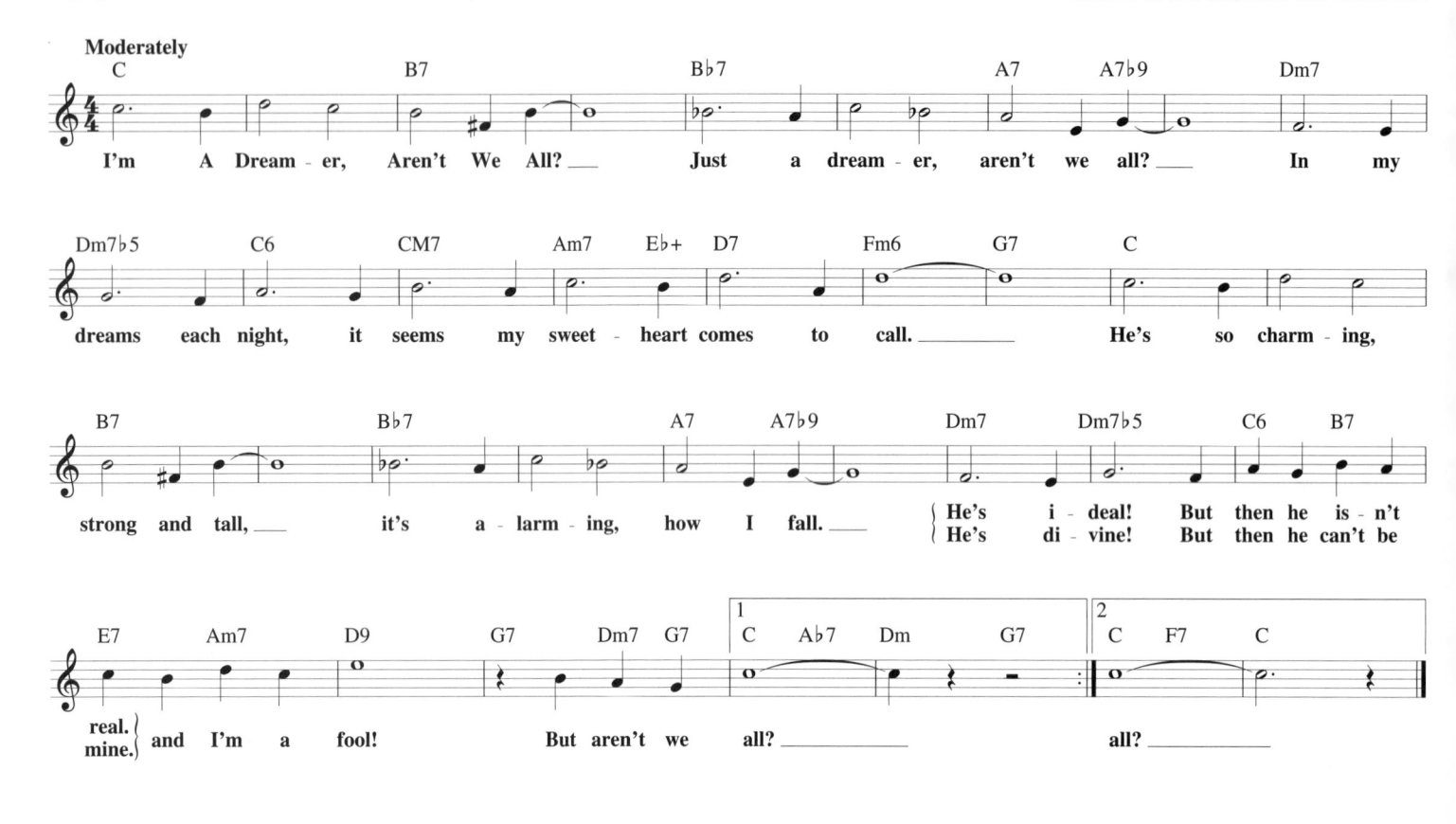

Moderately

I'm A Dreamer, Aren't We All? Just a dreamer, aren't we all? In my dreams each night, it seems my sweetheart comes to call. He's so charming, strong and tall, it's alarming, how I fall.

He's ideal! But then he isn't real. and I'm a fool! But aren't we all?
He's divine! But then he can't be mine.

I'M YOURS
from the Paramount Picture Short LEAVE IT TO LESTER

Copyright © 1930 (Renewed 1957) by Famous Music Corporation

Words by E.Y. HARBURG
Music by JOHNNY GREEN

Moderately

Ask the sky above and ask the earth below, why I'm so in love and why I love you so, couldn't tell you tho' I try, dear, just why, dear, I'm Yours.
When you went away you left a glowing spark, trying to be gay is whistling in the dark; I am only what you make me, come take me, I'm Yours. How happy I would be to beg and borrow, or sorrow with you, even tho' I knew tomorrow you'd say we were through. If we drift apart, then I'll be lost alone, though you use my heart just for a stepping stone. How can I help dreaming of you? I love you, I'm Yours. Yours.

I'M GONNA GO FISHIN'

Words and Music by DUKE ELLINGTON
and PEGGY LEE

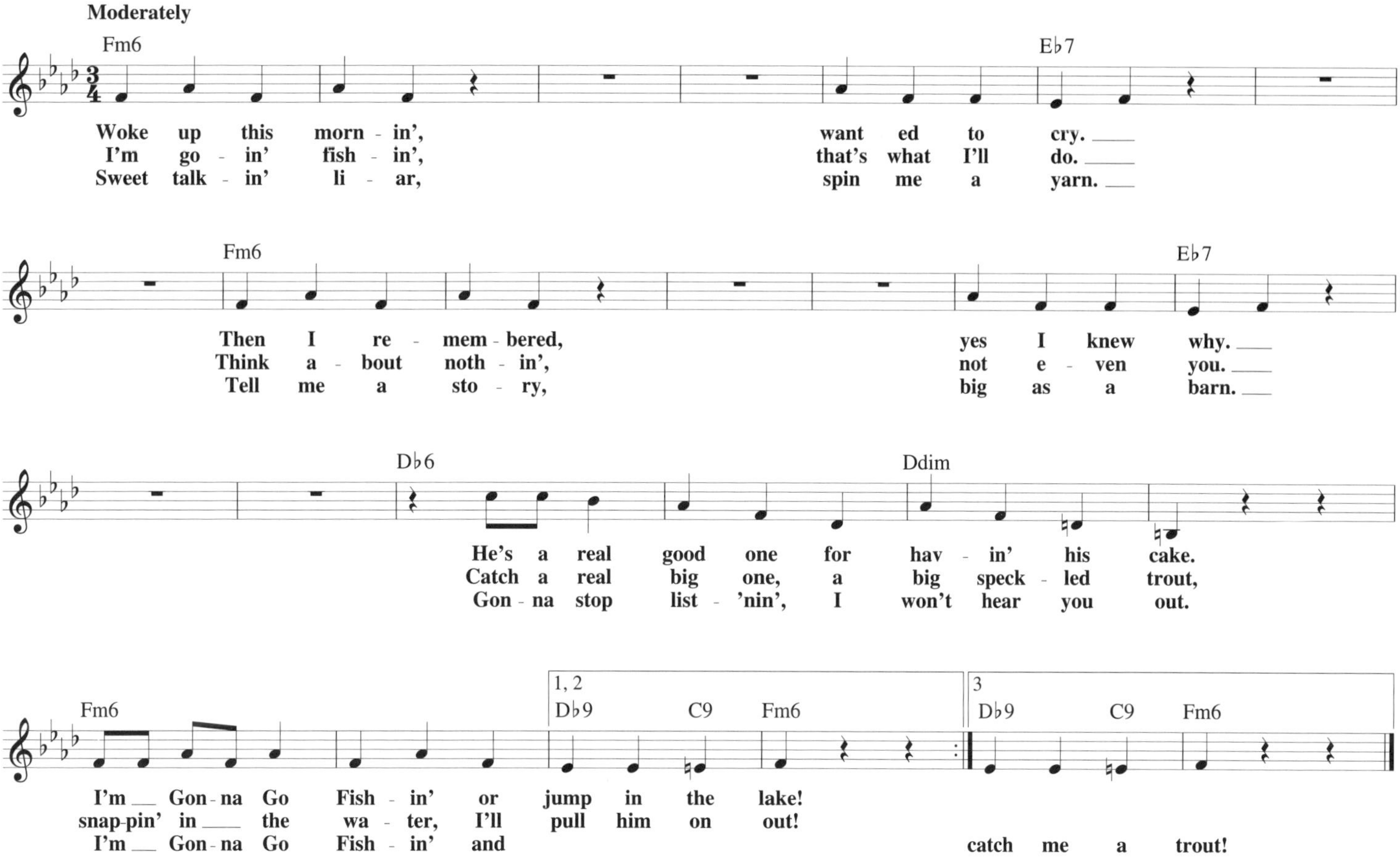

IMPRESSIONS

By JOHN COLTRANE

IN A SENTIMENTAL MOOD

Words and Music by DUKE ELLINGTON, IRVING MILLS and MANNY KURTZ

Slowly

In A Sentimental Mood I can see the stars come thru my room, while your loving attitude is like a flame that lights the gloom. On the wings of ev'ry kiss drifts a melody so strange and sweet, in this sentimental bliss you make my paradise complete. Rose petals seem to fall, it's all like a dream to call you mine. My heart's a lighter thing since you make this night a thing divine. In A Sentimental Mood I'm within a world so heavenly, for I never dreamt that you'd be loving sentimental me.

IN LOVE IN VAIN

Words by LEO ROBIN
Music by JEROME KERN

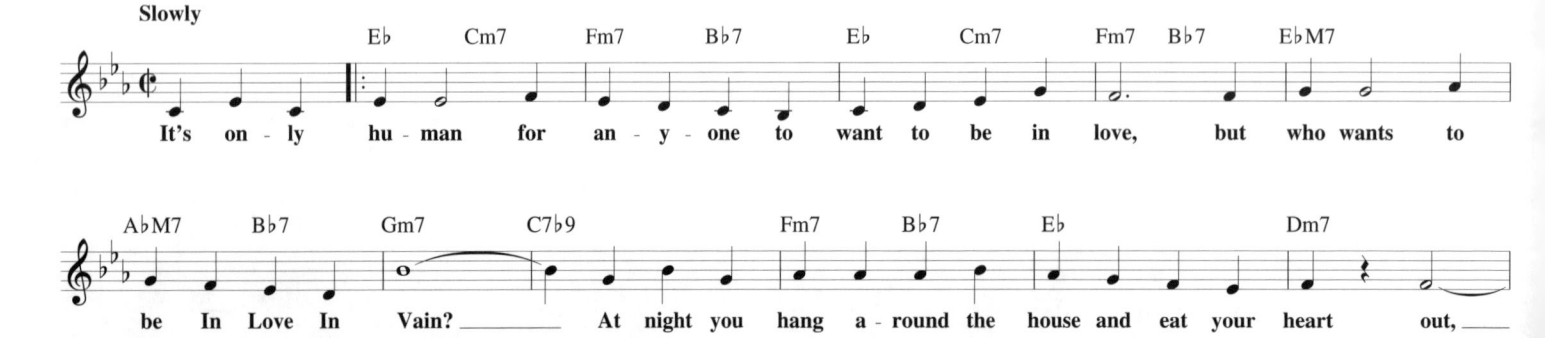

Slowly

It's only human for anyone to want to be in love, but who wants to be In Love In Vain? At night you hang around the house and eat your heart out,

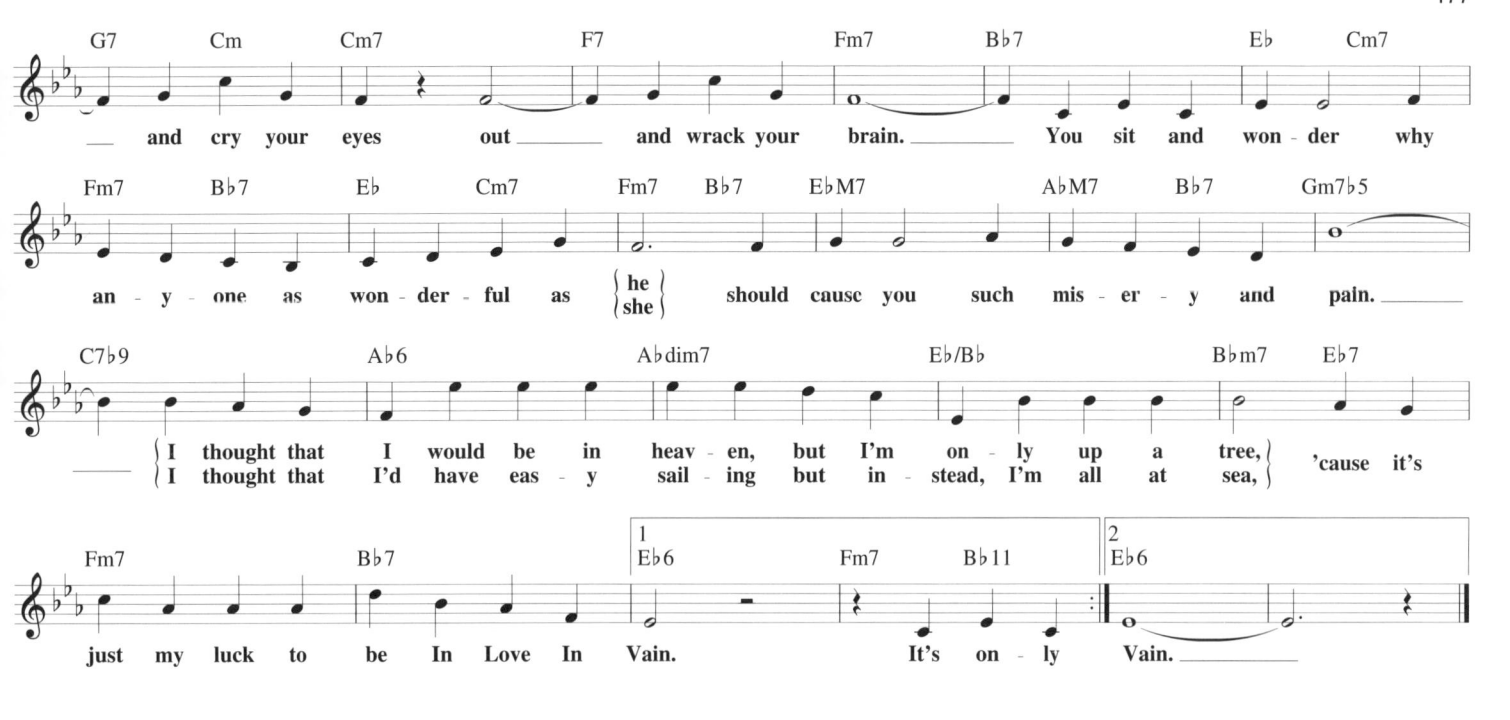

IN THE COOL, COOL, COOL OF THE EVENING
from the Paramount Picture HERE COMES THE GROOM

Words by JOHNNY MERCER
Music by HOAGY CARMICHAEL

Copyright © 1951 (Renewed 1979) by Famous Music Corporation

IN THE LAND OF EPHESUS

Written by JOE LOVANO

Copyright © 1993 LOVO MUSIC (BMI)

IN THE WEE SMALL HOURS OF THE MORNING

Words by BOB HILLIARD
Music by DAVID MANN

© 1955 REDD EVANS MUSIC CO.
© Renewed 1983 RYTVOC, INC. and BETTER HALF MUSIC

In The Wee Small Hours Of The Morn-ing, While the whole wide world is fast a-sleep, You lie a-wake and think a-bout the {girl, boy,} And nev-er ev-er think of count-ing sheep. When your lone-ly heart has learned its les-son You'd be {hers his} if on-ly {she he} would call. In the Wee Small Hours Of The Morn-ing, That's the time you miss {her him} most of all. In The time you miss {her him} most of all.

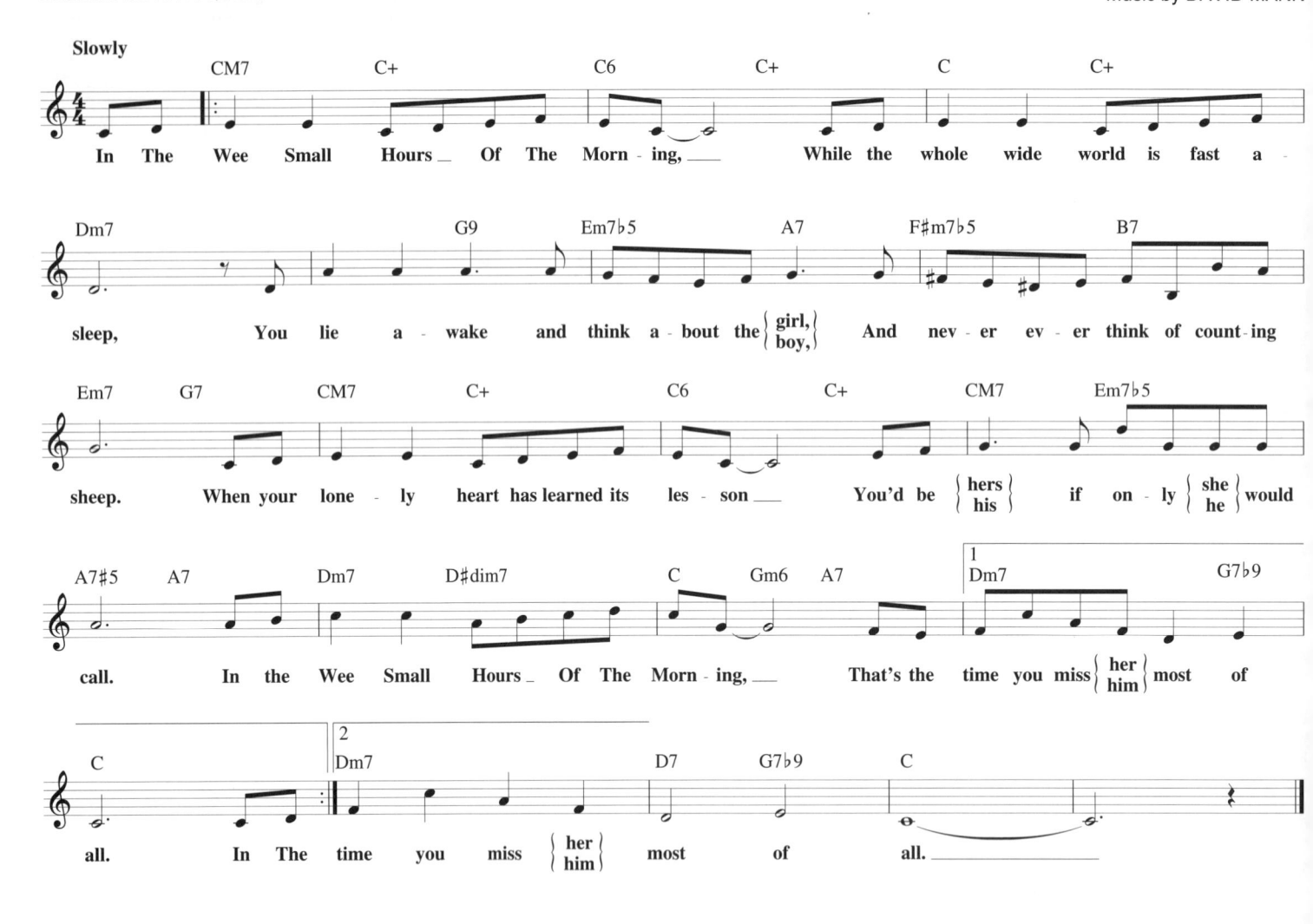

IN WALKED BUD

By THELONIOUS MONK

Copyright © 1948 (Renewed) by Embassy Music Corporation

INSIDE

Written by KEVIN EUBANKS

THE INTREPID FOX

By FREDDIE HUBBARD

INSIDE OUT

By RANDY BRECKER

INVITATION

Words by PAUL FRANCIS WEBSTER
Music by BRONISLAU KAPER

ISRAEL

By JOHN CARISI

IT DON'T MEAN A THING
(If It Ain't Got That Swing)
from SOPHISTICATED LADIES

Words and Music by DUKE ELLINGTON and IRVING MILLS

IS IT YOU?

By LEE RITENOUR, ERIC TAGG and BILL CHAMPLIN

Copyright © 1980 RIT OF HABEAS MUSIC, SYMPATHETIC MUSIC and MUSIC SALES CORP.

Moderate 2 beat

Some-one's just out-side knock-in' on my door; a stran-ger some-bod-y un-known. Some-one's in my dreams, sneak-in' round my heart? I'll get it off my mind. I'm ti-red of be-ing a-lone. Some-one's tryin' to find an eas-y way in-side. Who's that deep in-side me. Are you some-bod-y to love? Show me what you'll do and tell me who you are.

Come on, I'm right here at home, right at home.
Hey, I'm read-y for love, for love.

Is It You? Is It You?

To Coda

Is It You?

1.
Is It You, you, you?

2.
you? If it's you, come out in the o-pen, you don't need to hide your love.

If it's you, you know I'm hop-in',

'cause it's way too late to run a - way. Don't run a - way from love, ___ my ___ love. ___

D.S. al Coda

CODA

Is It You ___ knock - in' on ___ my door? ___ Is it my i - mag - i - na - tion? ___ Is It You ___ I can't ___ get off ___ my mind? ___ Is ___ It

Repeat and Fade

You, ___ you, ___ you? ___

ISN'T IT ROMANTIC?
from the Paramount Picture LOVE ME TONIGHT

Copyright © 1932 (Renewed 1959) by Famous Music Corporation

Words by LORENZ HART
Music by RICHARD RODGERS

Easy Swing

Is - n't It Ro - man - tic? Mu - sic in the night, a dream that can be heard. Isn't it Ro - man - tic? Mov - ing shad - ows write the old - est mag - ic word. I hear the breez - es play - ing in the trees a - bove. While all the world is say - ing you were meant for love. Is - n't It Ro -

Is - n't It Ro - man - tic? Mere - ly to be young on such a night as this? Isn't It Ro - man - tic? Ev - 'ry note that's sung is like a lov - er's kiss. Sweet sym - bols in the moon - light Do you mean that I will fall in love per - chance? ___ Is - n't it ro - mance? ___

IT COULD HAPPEN TO YOU
from the Paramount Picture AND THE ANGELS SING

Words by JOHNNY BURKE
Music by JAMES VAN HEUSEN

Copyright © 1944 (Renewed 1971) by Famous Music Corporation

Hide your heart from sight, lock your dreams at night, It Could Hap-pen To You.

Don't count stars or you might stum-ble, some-one drops a sigh and down you tum-ble.

Keep an eye on spring, run when church bells ring, It Could Hap-pen To You.

All I did was won-der how your arms would be, and it hap-pened to me.

IT'S A LOVELY DAY TODAY
from the Stage Production CALL ME MADAM

Words and Music by IRVING BERLIN

© Copyright 1950 by Irving Berlin
Copyright Renewed

It's A Love-ly Day To-day. So what-ev-er you've got to do, you've got a

love-ly day to do it in, that's true. And I hope what-ev-er you've got to do is

some-thing that can be done by two. For I'd real-ly like to stay. It's A

Love-ly Day To-day. And what-ev-er you've got to do, I'd be so hap-py to be

do-ing it with you. But if you've got some-thing that must be done, and

it can on-ly be done by one, there is noth-ing more to say ex-

cept it's a love-ly day for say-ing it's a love-ly day. It's A day.

IT ONLY HAPPENS WHEN I DANCE WITH YOU
from the Motion Picture Irving Berlin's EASTER PARADE

© Copyright 1947 by Irving Berlin
Copyright Renewed

Words and Music by
IRVING BERLIN

Moderately

It Only Happens When I Dance With You, that trip to heav-en 'til the dance is through. With no one else do the heav-ens seem quite so near. Why does it hap-pen, dear, on-ly with you? Two cheeks to-geth-er can be so di-vine, but on-ly when those cheeks are yours and mine. I've danced with doz-ens of oth-ers the whole night through, but the thrill that comes with spring when an-y-thing could hap-pen, that on-ly hap-pens with you. you.

IT'S EASY TO REMEMBER
from the Paramount Picture MISSISSIPPI

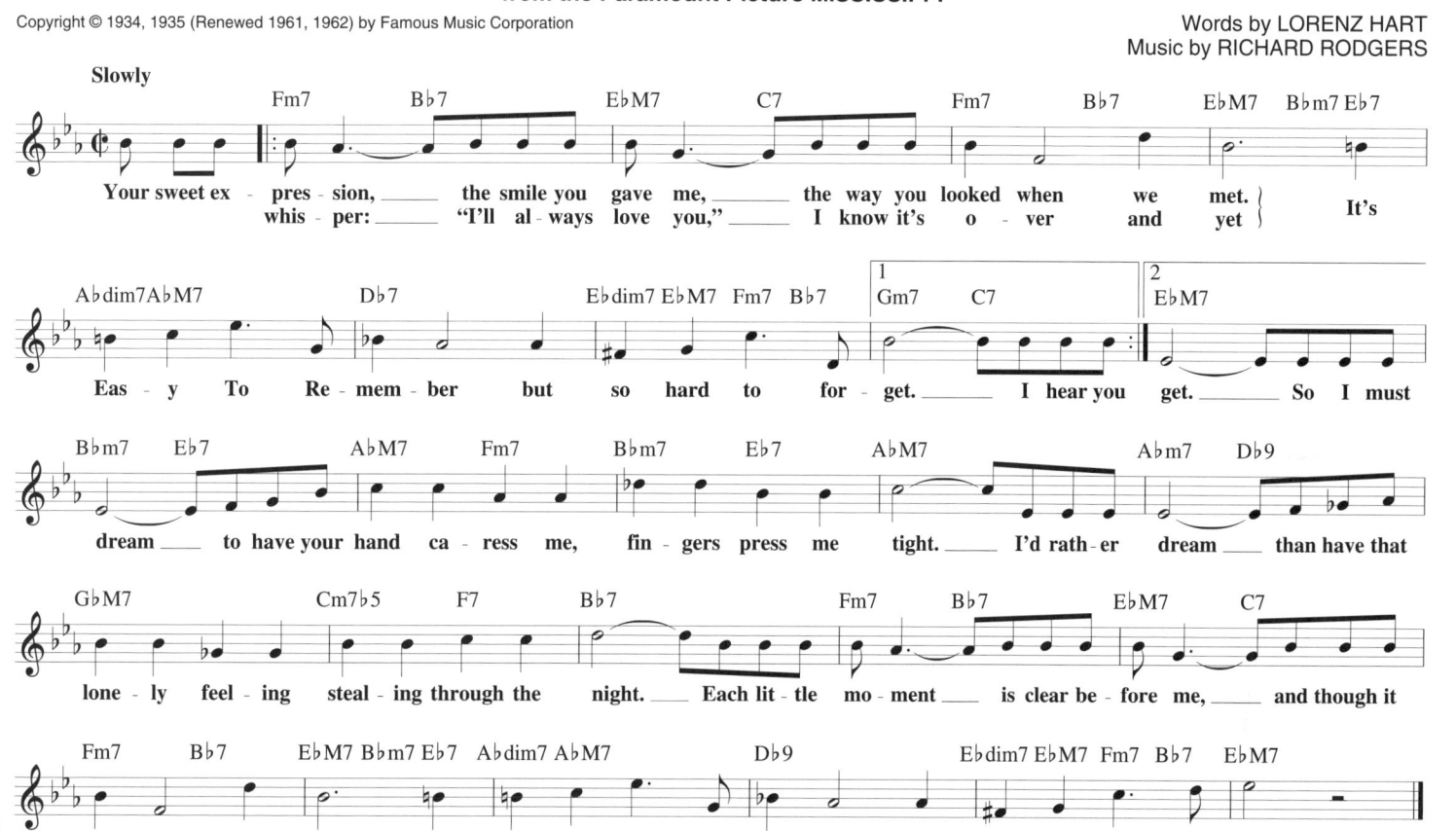

Copyright © 1934, 1935 (Renewed 1961, 1962) by Famous Music Corporation

Words by LORENZ HART
Music by RICHARD RODGERS

Slowly

Your sweet ex-pres-sion, the smile you gave me, the way you looked when we met. It's
whis-per: "I'll al-ways love you," I know it's o-ver and yet

Eas-y To Re-mem-ber but so hard to for-get. I hear you get. So I must dream to have your hand ca-ress me, fin-gers press me tight. I'd rath-er dream than have that lone-ly feel-ing steal-ing through the night. Each lit-tle mo-ment is clear be-fore me, and though it brings me re-gret, It's Eas-y To Re-mem-ber, and so hard to for-get.

IT'S YOU

Written by DAVID SANBORN

IT'S YOU OR NO ONE

from ROMANCE ON THE HIGH SEAS

Words by SAMMY CAHN
Music by JULE STYNE

I'VE FOUND A NEW BABY
(I Found A New Baby)

© Copyright 1926 by MCA MUSIC PUBLISHING, A Division of UNIVERSAL STUDIOS, INC.
Copyright Renewed

Words and Music by JACK PALMER
and SPENCER WILLIAMS

JAZZMANIA

By BILLY CHILDS

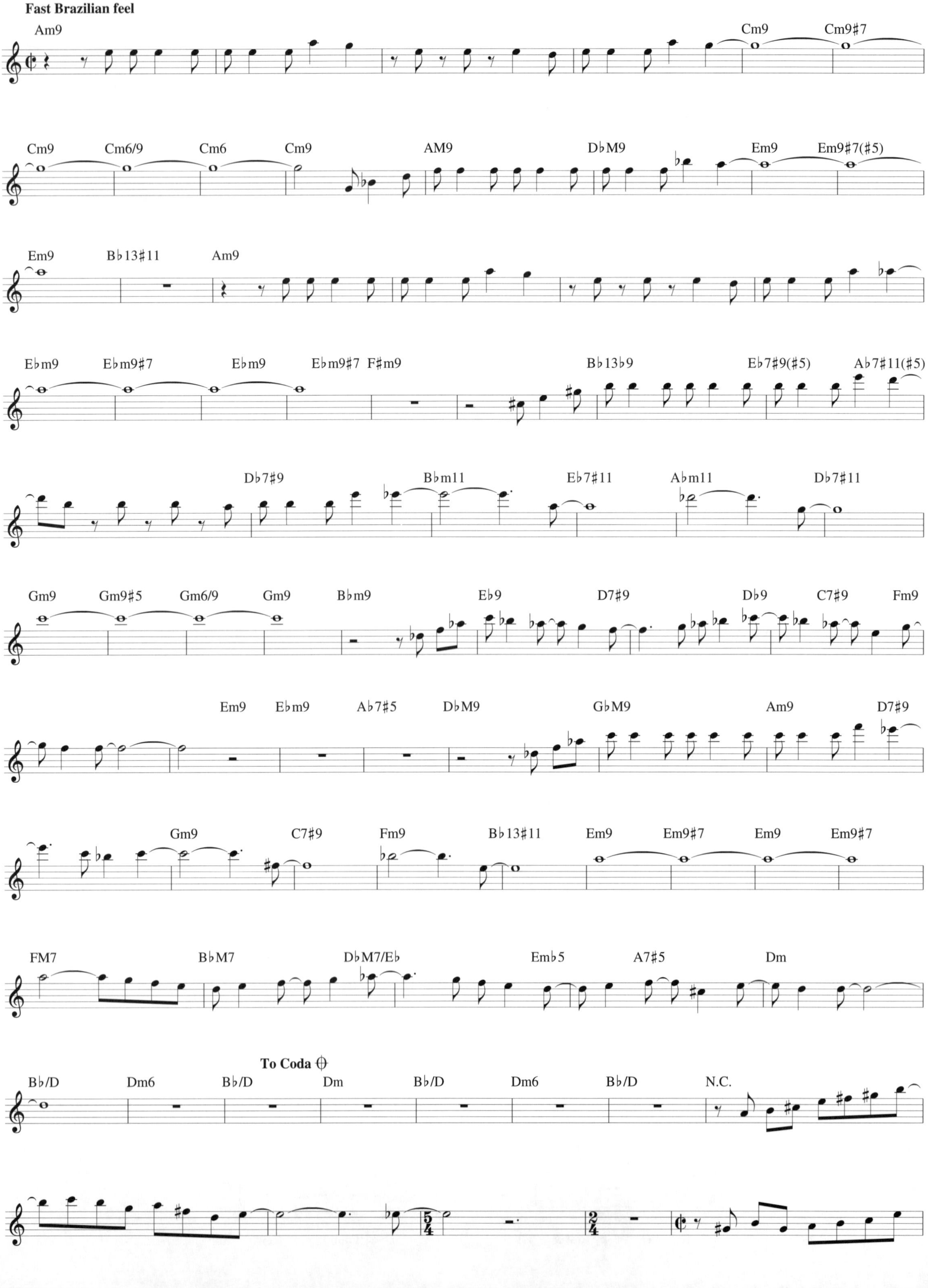

I'VE GOT MY LOVE TO KEEP ME WARM
from the 20th Century Fox Motion Picture ON THE AVENUE

© Copyright 1936, 1937 by Irving Berlin
© Arrangement Copyright 1948 by Irving Berlin
Copyright Renewed

Words and Music by
IRVING BERLIN

Bright jump tempo

The snow is snow-ing, the wind is blow-ing, but I can weath-er the storm.
can't re-mem-ber a worse De-cem-ber; just watch those i-ci-cles form.
What do I care how much it may storm?
What do I care if i-ci-cles form? I've Got My Love To Keep Me Warm.

I Off with my o-ver-coat, off with my glove.
I need no o-ver-coat, I'm burn-ing with love. My heart's on fire, the flame grows high-er. So I will weath-er the storm. What do I care how much it may storm? I've Got My Love To Keep Me Warm.

I'VE GOT THE WORLD ON A STRING

Lyric by TED KOEHLER
Music by HAROLD ARLEN

JOSIE AND ROSIE

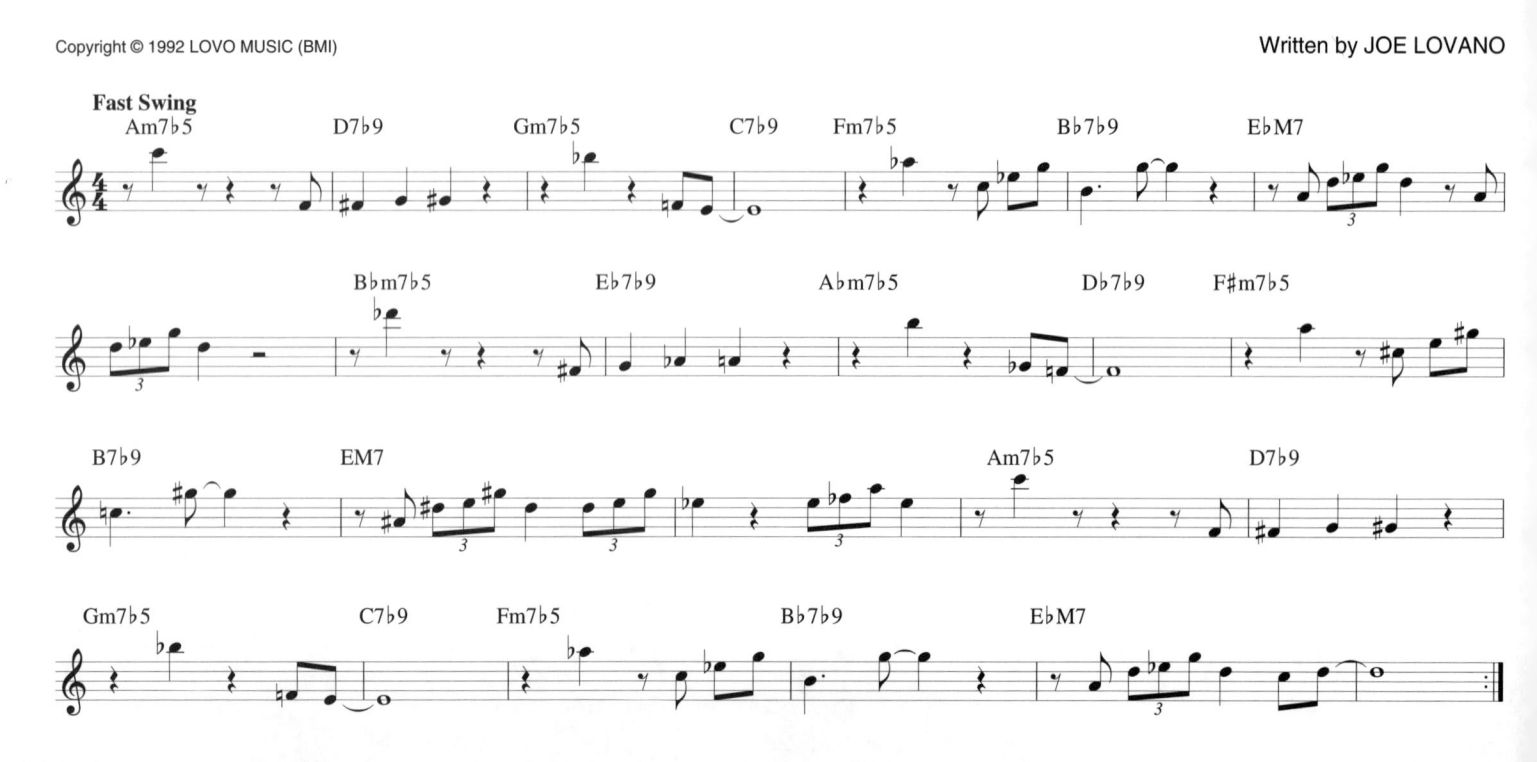

Written by JOE LOVANO

JITTERBUG WALTZ

Music by THOMAS "FATS" WALLER

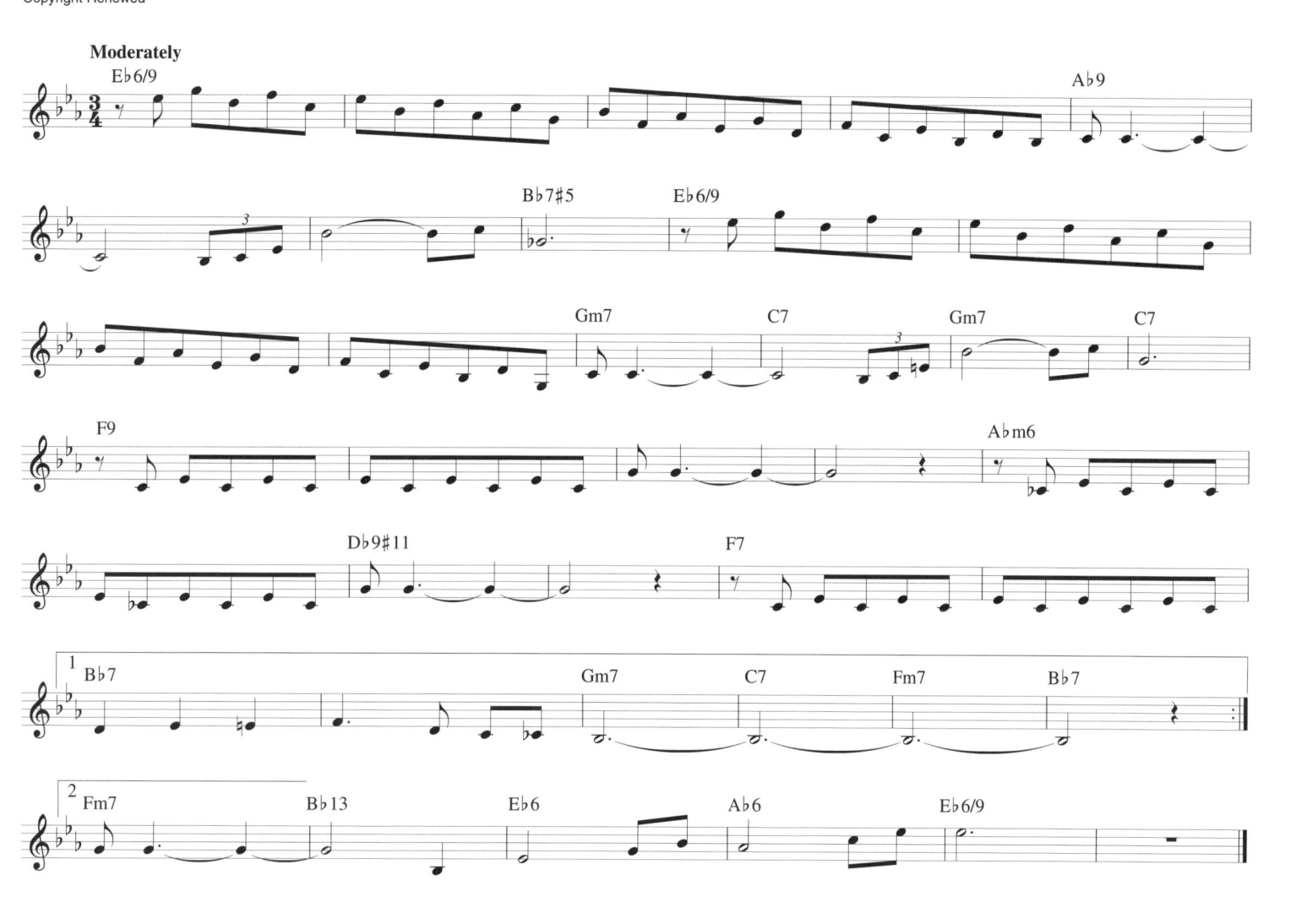

JUST A GIGOLO

Original German Text by JULIUS BRAMMER
English Words by IRVING CAESAR
Music by LEONELLO CASUCCI

Just A Gi - go - lo, ev' - ry - where I go, peo - ple know the part I'm play - ing.
Schö - ner Gi - go - lo, ar - mer Gi - go - lo, den - ke nicht mehr an die Zei - ten.

Paid for ev' - ry dance, sell - ing each ro - mance, ev' - ry night some heart be - tray - ing.
Wo du als Hu - sar, gold - ver - schnürt so - gar, koon - test durch die Stras - sen rei - ten!

There will come a day, youth will pass a - way, then what will they say a - bout ___ me. When the
U - ni - form pas - sée, Lieb - chen sagt: A - dieu! Schö - ne Welt, du gingst in Fran - sen! Wenn das

end comes I know they'll say, "Just A Gi - go - lo." As life goes on with - out me.
Herz das auch bricht, zeig' ein Ja - chen - des Ge - sicht, man zahlt und du musst tan - zen!

JULY

By AL DI MEOLA

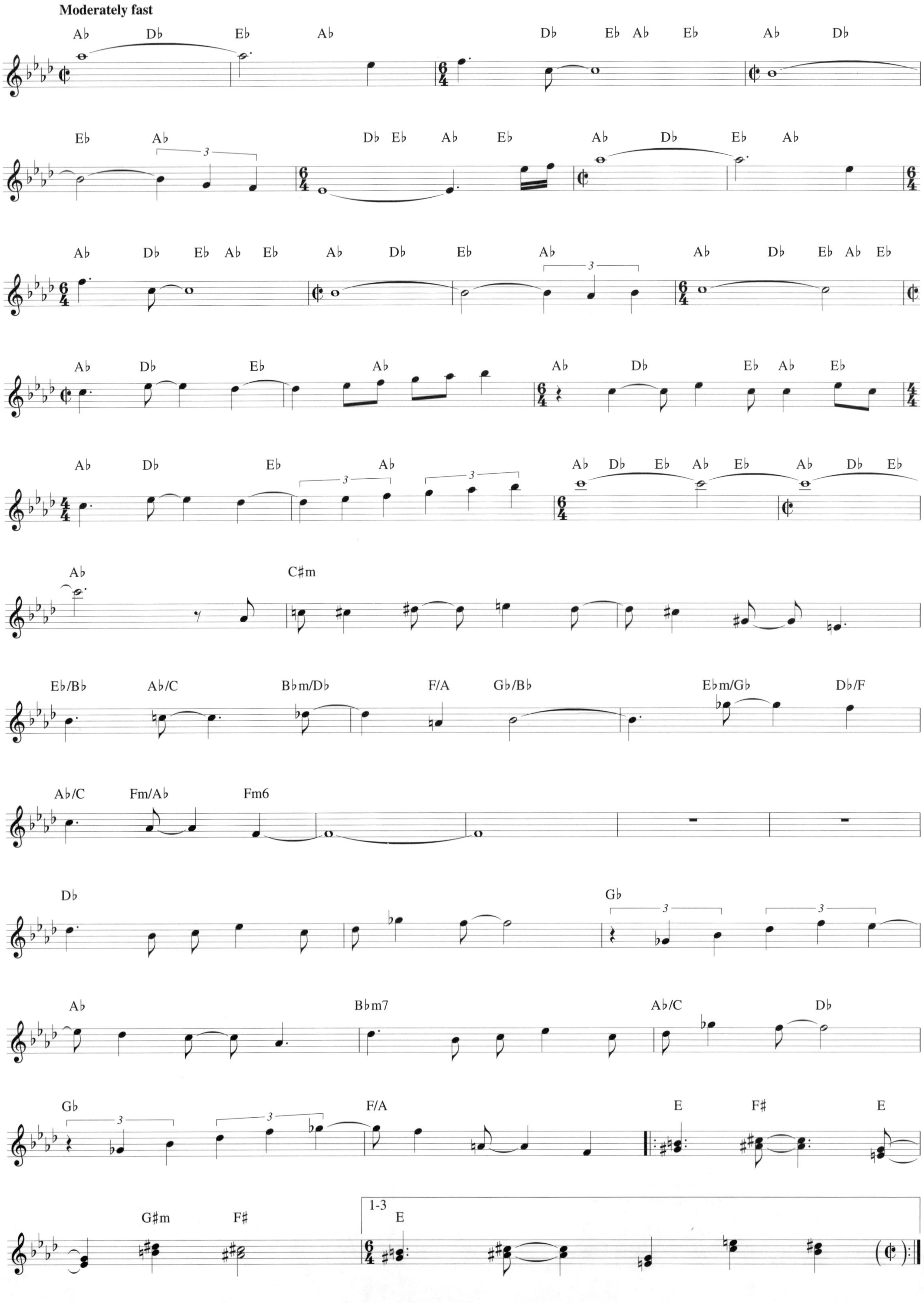

4
E/G# F#/A# E/B F#/C# Eb Ab Db Eb Ab
Db Eb Ab Eb
Play 4 times
To Coda
C F G C C F G C G
C F G C C F G C G
C F G C C F G C G C F G
C C F G C G Eb(no chord)
Ab(no chord) D(no chord) B(no chord) Eb(no chord) Gb(no chord) F(no chord)
Eb Ab/C Bbm/Db Ab Eb Ab/C Db Ab/C Bbm Ab Bbm
Fm Gb(add2) Gb G Ab
Play 4 times
D.C. al Coda
CODA
Bb Eb F Bb Bb Eb F Bb F
Bb Eb F Bb Bb Eb F Bb F
Bb Eb F Bb Bb Eb F Bb F Bb Eb F
Bb Bb Eb F Bb F Bb Eb F Bb
1-3
Bb Eb F Bb F
4
Bb Eb F Bb F Bb

JUNE BUG

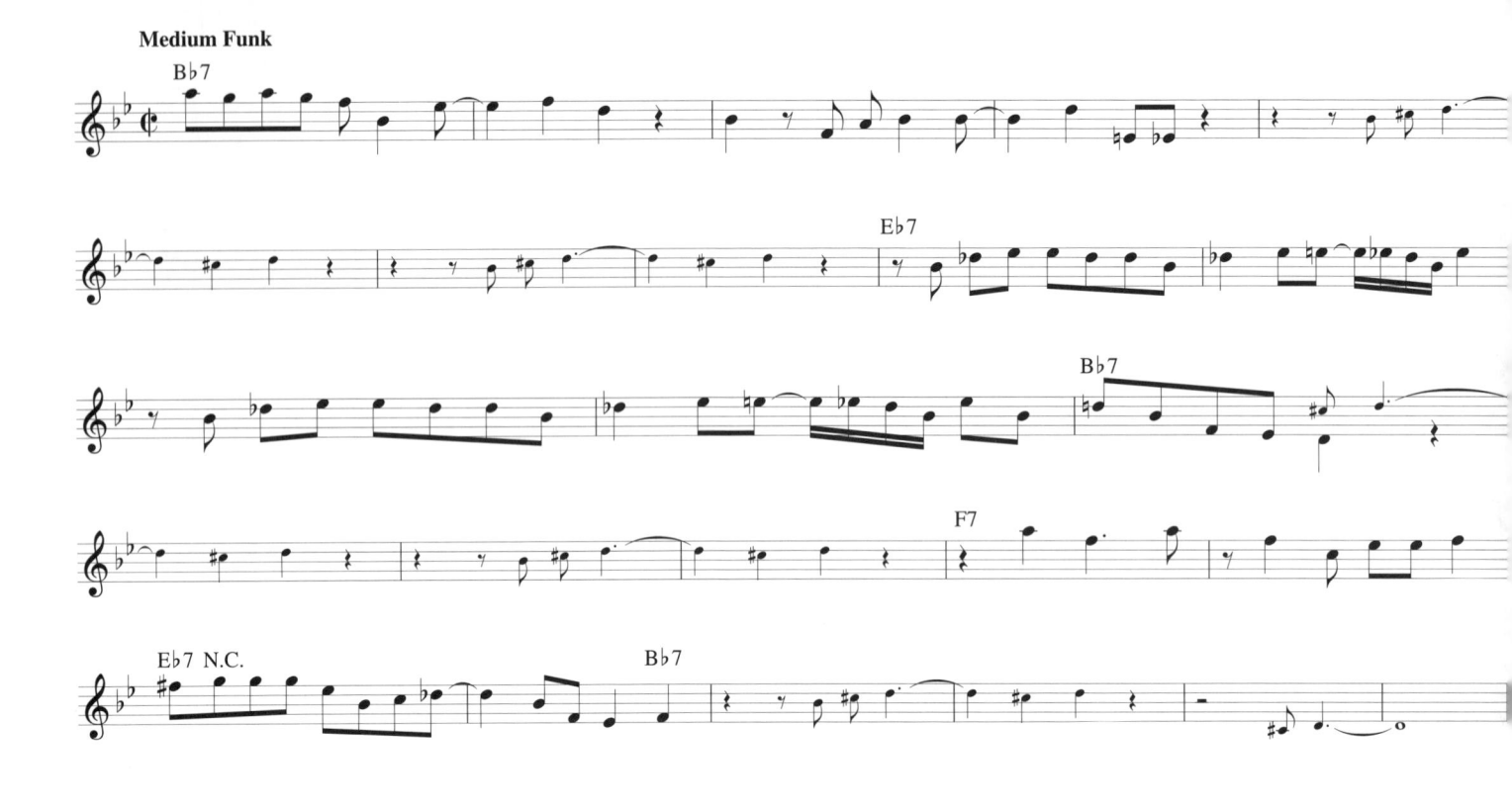

Copyright © 1994 by Laplace Music

Music by THOMAS TURRENTINE

Medium Funk

JUST ONE MORE CHANCE

Copyright © 1931 (Renewed 1958) by Famous Music Corporation

Words by SAM COSLOW
Music by ARTHUR JOHNSTON

Moderately slow

Just One More Chance, to prove it's you a-lone I care for, each night I say a lit-tle prayer for Just One More Chance. Just one more night, to taste the kiss-es that en-chant me, I'd want no oth-ers if you'd grant me Just One More Chance. I've learned the mean-ing of re-pen-tance; Now you're the ju-ry at my trial. I know that I should serve my sen-tence; Still I'm hop-ing all the while you'll give me Just one more word. I said that I was glad to start out; But now I'm back to cry my heart out for Just One More Chance.

JUNE IN JANUARY
from the Paramount Picture HERE IS MY HEART

Words and Music by LEO ROBIN
and RALPH RAINGER

JUST THE WAY WE PLANNED IT

By ERNIE WATTS
and BOB LEATHERBARROW

KEEPIN' OUT OF MISCHIEF NOW

Lyric by ANDY RAZAF
Music by THOMAS "FATS" WALLER

© 1932 EDWIN H. MORRIS & COMPANY, A Division of MPL COMMUNICATIONS, INC.
© Renewed 1960 EDWIN H. MORRIS & COMPANY, A Division of MPL COMMUNICATIONS, INC. and CHAPPELL & CO.

Keep-in' Out Of Mis-chief Now, real-ly am in love, and how! I'm through play-in' with fire, it's you whom I de-sire. All the world can plain-ly see, you're the on-ly one for me; I have told them in ad-vance, they can't break up our ro-mance. Liv-in' up to ev-'ry vow, Keep-in' Out Of Mis-chief Now.

LADY OF THE EVENING
from the 1922 Stage Production MUSIC BOX REVUE

Words and Music by IRVING BERLIN

© Copyright 1922 by Irving Berlin
© Copyright Renewed

Eve-ning, La-dy Of The Eve-ning. I can hear you call-ing me. Call-ing while the shades are fall-ing, fall-ing o-ver land and sea. You can make the cares and trou-bles that fol-lowed me through the day fold their tents just like the A-rabs and si-lent-ly steal a-way. Eve-ning, La-dy Of The Eve-ning, I hear you call-ing me. me.

KOGUN

By TOSHIKO AKIYOSHI

Deliberately

LADY SINGS THE BLUES

Words and Music by HERBERT NICHOLS and BILLIE HOLIDAY

Slow Blues

THE LADY'S IN LOVE WITH YOU
from the Paramount Picture SOME LIKE IT HOT

Copyright © 1939 (Renewed 1966) by Paramount Music Corporation

Words by FRANK LOESSER
Music by BURTON LANE

Rhythmically

If there's a gleam in her eye___ each time she straight-ens your tie,___ you'll know The La-dy's In Love___ With You. If she can dress for a date___ with-out that wait-ing you hate___ it means The La-dy's In Love With You. And when your friends ask you o-ver to join their ta-ble___ but she picks that far-a-way booth for two, well, sir, here's just how it stands,___ you've got ro-mance on your hands___ be-cause The La-dy's In Love___ With You. If there's a You.___

LAZY

© Copyright 1924 by Irving Berlin
© Copyright Renewed

Words and Music by
IRVING BERLIN

Moderately

La-zy.___ I want___ to be La-zy.___ I long___ to be out in the sun___ with no work___ to be done,___ un-der that awn-ing___ they call the sky,___ stretch-ing and yawn-ing___ and let the world___ go drift-ing by.___ I wan-na peep through the deep___ tan-gled wild-wood,___ count-ing sheep___ 'til I sleep___ like a child___ would,___ with a great big va-lise full of books to read___ where it's peace-ful, while I'm kill-ing time___ be-ing La-zy. zy.

LAST NIGHT WHEN WE WERE YOUNG

Lyric by E.Y. HARBURG
Music by HAROLD ARLEN

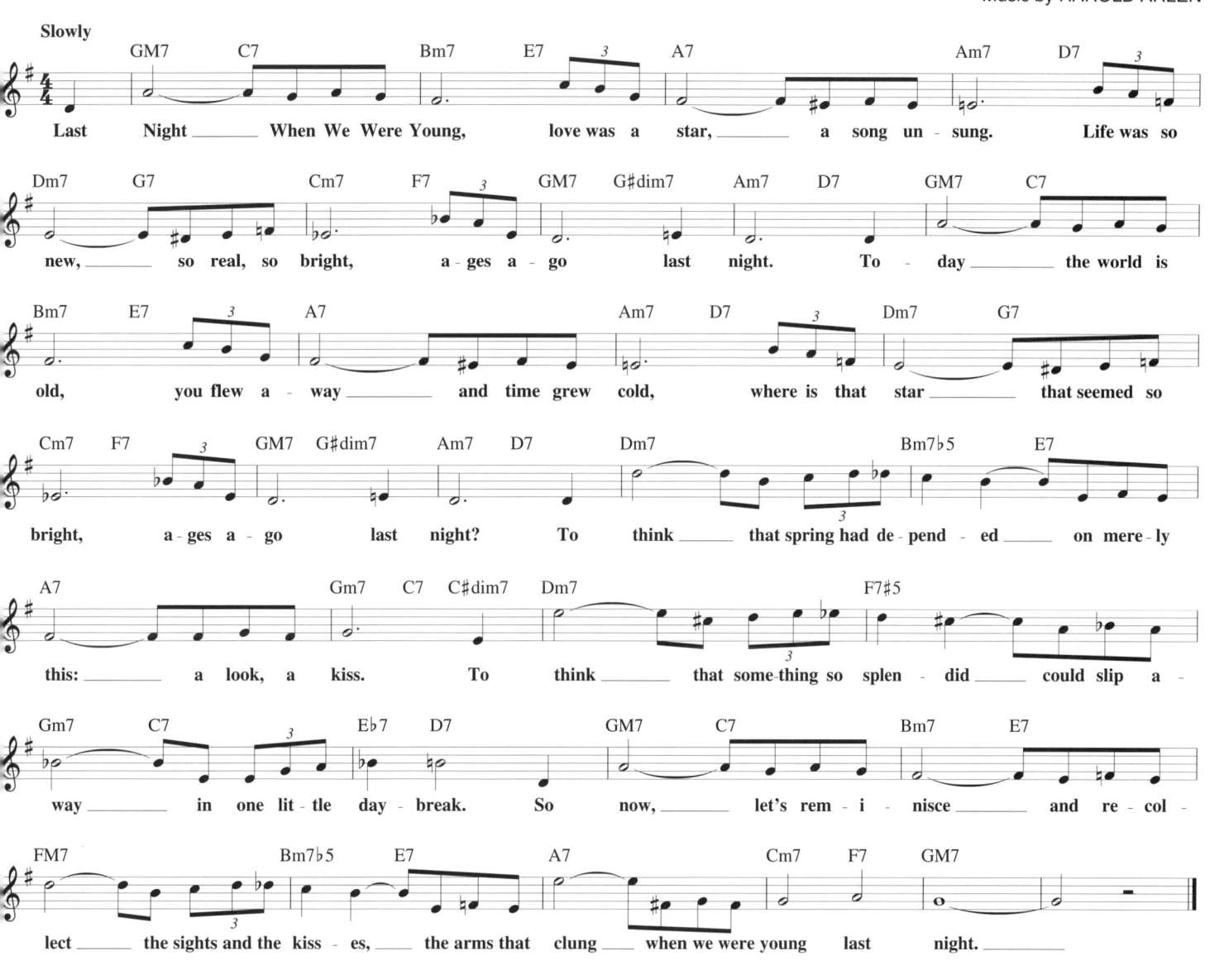

Last Night When We Were Young, love was a star, a song un-sung. Life was so new, so real, so bright, a-ges a-go last night. To-day the world is old, you flew a-way and time grew cold, where is that star that seemed so bright, a-ges a-go last night? To think that spring had de-pend-ed on mere-ly this: a look, a kiss. To think that some-thing so splen-did could slip a-way in one lit-tle day-break. So now, let's rem-i-nisce and re-col-lect the sights and the kiss-es, the arms that clung when we were young last night.

LET'S GET LOST
from the Paramount Picture HAPPY GO LUCKY

Words by FRANK LOESSER
Music by JIMMY McHUGH

Let's Get Lost, lost in each oth-er's arms, Let's Get Lost, let them send out a-larms. And though they'll think us rath-er rude, let's tell the world we're in that cra-zy mood. Let's de-frost, in a rom-an-tic mist, let's get crossed off ev-'ry bod-y's list. To cel-e-brate this night we found each oth-er, mm, Let's Get Lost.

LIVELY UP YOURSELF

Copyright © 1975 Fifty-Six Hope Road Music Ltd. and Odnil Music Ltd.
All Rights for the United States and Canada Administered by
PolyGram International Publishing, Inc.

Words and Music by
BOB MARLEY

Bright Reggae Shuffle

Oh, Live-ly Up Your-self and don't be no drag. Live-ly Up Your-self, reg-gae is an-oth-er bag. Live-ly Up Your-self and don't say no. Live-ly Up Your-self 'cause I said so. You, what you gon-na do? You rock so, you rock so, like you nev-er did be-fore. You dip so, you dip so till you dip through my door. You skank so, you skank so, oh yeah. You come so, you come so, come a-live to-day. And Live-ly Up Your-self a-lot-a, a-lot-a, a-lot-a, a-lot-a. Live-ly Up Your-self, did you know, did you know? Live-ly Up Your-self, 'cause if you don't do it, ain't no-bod-y gon-na do it for you. Live-ly Up Your-self and don't be no, don't be no, don't be no, don't be no, no drag. What you got that I don't know? I'm a-try-in' to won-der, won-der why you, won-der, won-der why you act so. And don't be no drag. Live-ly Up Your-self, for reg-gae is an-oth-er bag. You're gon-na

201

CODA

Live-ly Up Your-self, your wom-an in the morn-ing time, y'all.

Keep a Live-ly Up Your-self and when the eve-ning come and take ya, take ya, take ya, take ya.

Come on ba-by, I wan-na be live-ly my-self. Come on babe, I wan-na be live-

-ly my-self. Live-ly Up Your-self. *Repeat ad lib.*

LET'S FACE THE MUSIC AND DANCE
from the Motion Picture FOLLOW THE FLEET

© Copyright 1935, 1936 by Irving Berlin
Copyright Renewed

Words and Music by
IRVING BERLIN

Moderately

There may be trou-ble a - head. But while there's moon-light and mu-sic and love and ro-

-mance, Let's Face The Mu-sic And Dance. Be-fore the fid-dlers have

fled, be-fore they ask us to pay the bill, and while we still have the chance,

Let's Face The Mu-sic And Dance. Soon we'll be with-out the moon,

hum-ming a dif-f'rent tune, and then there may be tear-drops to shed.

So while there's moon-light and mu-sic and love and ro-mance, Let's Face The

Mu-sic And Dance, dance. Let's Face The Mu-sic And Dance.

LINES AND SPACES

LITTLE WHITE LIES

Words and Music by
WALTER DONALDSON

LOVE IS JUST AROUND THE CORNER

from the Paramount Picture HERE IS MY HEART

Words and Music by LEO ROBIN
and LEWIS E. GENSLER

LOOK TO THE SKY

By ANTONIO CARLOS JOBIM

LOVE LETTERS
Theme from the Paramount Picture LOVE LETTERS

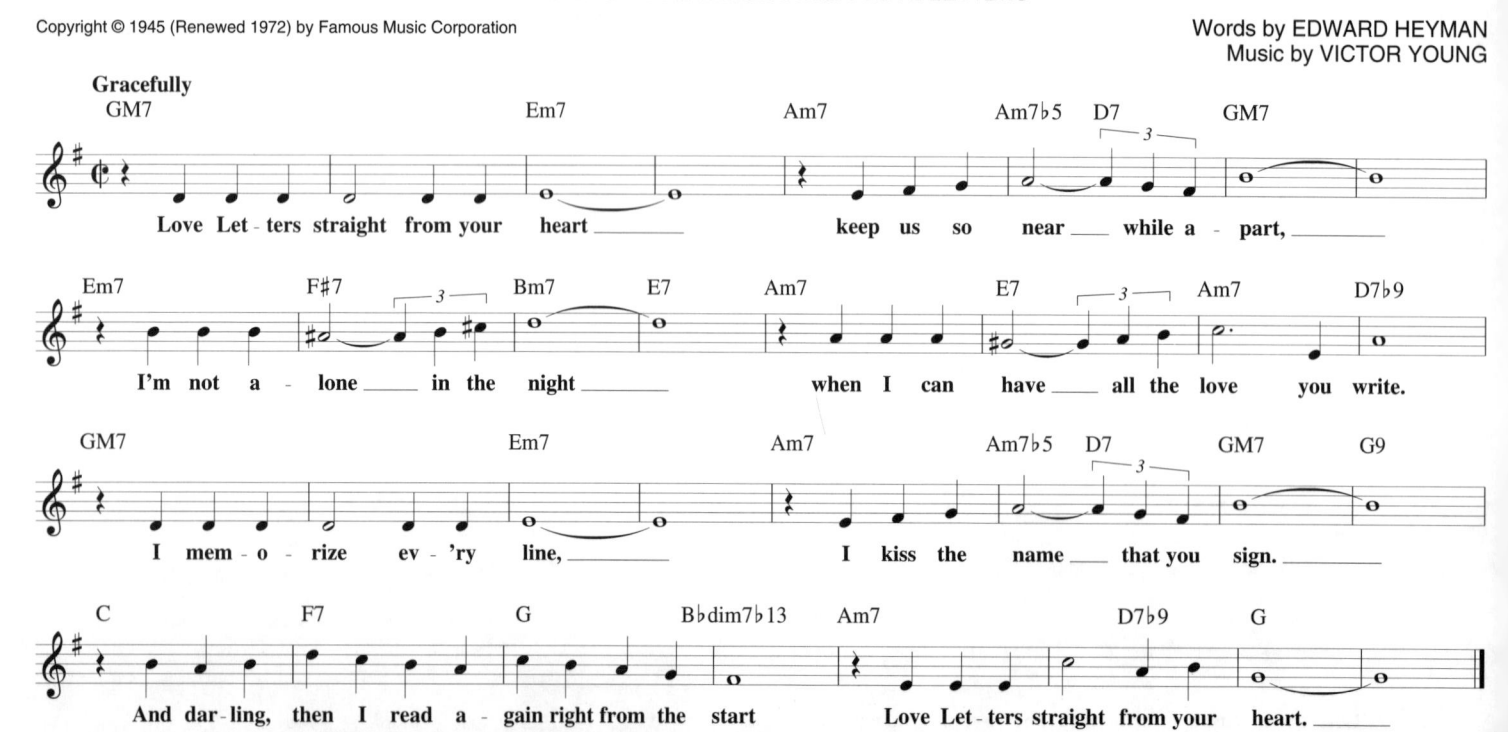

Words by EDWARD HEYMAN
Music by VICTOR YOUNG

Love Letters straight from your heart _____ keep us so near _____ while a-part,
I'm not a-lone _____ in the night _____ when I can have _____ all the love you write.
I mem-o-rize ev-'ry line, _____ I kiss the name _____ that you sign.
And dar-ling, then I read a-gain right from the start Love Let-ters straight from your heart. _____

LOVE IS THE SWEETEST THING

205

Copyright © 1932 Francis, Day & Hunter Ltd.
Copyright renewed; extended term of Copyright deriving from Ray Noble assigned and effective November 9, 1988
to Range Road Music Inc. and Quartet Music Inc.

Words and Music by
RAY NOBLE

Flowing

Love Is _____ The Sweet - est Thing. What else on earth could ev - er bring
Love Is _____ the strang - est thing. No song of birds up - on the wing

such hap - pi - ness to ev - 'ry - thing, as love's old sto - ry.
shall in our hearts more sweet - ly sing, than love's old sto - ry. sto - ry.

What - ev - er heart may de - sire, what - ev - er fate may send, this is the tale that

nev - er will tire, this is the song with - out end. Love is _____ the great - est thing, the old - est,

yet the lat - est thing, I on - ly hope that fate _____ may bring love's sto - ry to you.

A LOVELY WAY TO SPEND AN EVENING

Copyright © 1943 PolyGram International Publishing, Inc.
Copyright Renewed

Words by HAROLD ADAMSON
Music by JIMMY McHUGH

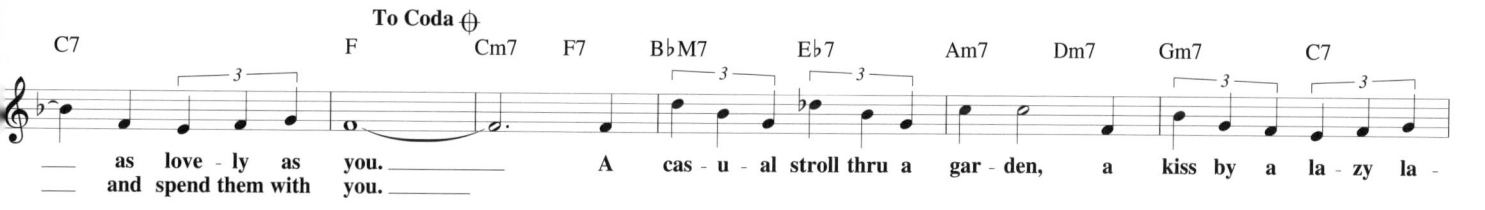

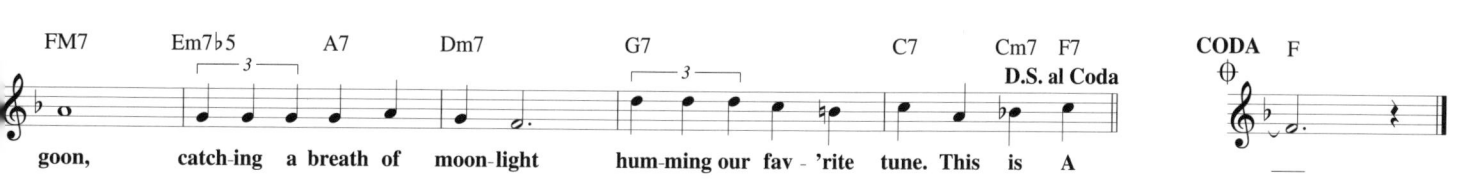

Slowly

This is A Love - ly Way _____ To Spend An Eve - ning. _____ Can't think of an - y - thing _____ I'd rath - er

do. _____ This is A Love - ly Way _____ To Spend An Eve - ning. _____ Can't think of an - y - one
Love - ly Way _____ To Spend An Eve - ning. _____ I want to save all my nights

To Coda

_____ as love - ly as you. _____ A cas - u - al stroll thru a gar - den, a kiss by a la - zy la -
_____ and spend them with you. _____

D.S. al Coda

goon, catch - ing a breath of moon - light hum - ming our fav - 'rite tune. This is A

CODA

LOVE ME OR LEAVE ME
from LOVE ME OR LEAVE ME

Copyright © 1928 (Renewed) by Donaldson Publishing Co. and Gilbert Keyes Music Co.

Lyrics by GUS KAHN
Music by WALTER DONALDSON

Medium Swing

Love Me Or Leave Me, and let me be lone-ly; You won't be-lieve me, and I love you on-ly. I'd rath-er be lone-ly, than hap-py with some-bod-y else. You
might find the night-time, and right time for kiss-ing; But night-time is my time for just rem-i-nisc-ing, re-gret-ting, in-stead of for-get-ting with some-bod-y else.

There'll be no one un-less that some-one is you, I in-tend to be in-de-pen-dent-ly blue. I want your love, but I don't want to bor-row, to have it to-day, and to give back to-mor-row; For my love is your love, there's no love for no-bod-y else!

LOVER
from the Paramount Picture LOVE ME TONIGHT

Copyright © 1932, 1933 (Renewed 1959, 1960) by Famous Music Corporation

Words by LORENZ HART
Music by RICHARD RODGERS

Brightly

Lov-er, when I'm near you and I hear you speak my name, soft-ly in my ear, you breathe a flame.

Lov-er, when we're danc-ing keep on glanc-ing in my eyes,

till love's own entrancing music dies.
All of my future is in you. Your ev'ry plan I design.
Promise you'll always continue to be mine.
Lover, please be tender, when your tender fears depart,
lover, I surrender to my heart.

LIGIA

Copyright © 1976 Antonio Carlos Jobim
Published by Corcovado Music Corp.

Words and Music by
ANTONIO CARLOS JOBIM

Moderate Latin

Eu nunca sonhei com você, nunca fui ao cinema, não gosto de
nunca quis tê-la ao meu lado. Num fim de semana. Um chope ge-
(Instrumental Solo)

samba não vou a Ipanema, não gosto de chuva nem gosto de sol.
lado em Copacabana. Andar pela praia até o Leblon.

E quando eu lhe telefonei. Desliguei foi engano. O seu nome eu não
E quando eu me apaixonei. Não passou de ilusão. O seu nome ras-
(Solo Ends) E quando você me envolver. Nos seus braços serenos. Eu vou me ren-

sei. Esqueci no piano As bobagens de amor. Que eu iria di-
guei. Fiz um samba-canção Das mentiras de amor. Que aprendi com vo-
der. Mas seus olhos morenos. Me metem mais medo. Que um raio de

zer. Não, Ligia, Ligia. Eu
cê. E, Ligia, Ligia.
sol, Ligia, Ligia.

LAST RESORT

Written by RON CARTER

LATE LAMENT

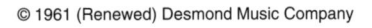

By PAUL DESMOND

LIVIN'

Written by KEVIN EUBANKS

Copyright © 1993 Nivek Publishing (BMI)

LONELY GIRL

from the Paramount Motion Picture HARLOW

Words by RAY EVANS and JAY LIVINGSTON
Music by NEAL HEFTI

LADY BIRD

By TADD DAMERON

LAMENT

By J.J. JOHNSON

La Fiesta

By CHICK COREA

© Copyright 1972 by MCA MUSIC PUBLISHING, A Division of UNIVERSAL STUDIOS, INC.

LIKE A LOVER
(O Cantador)

Copyright © 1968 by Berna Music, Inc., E.B.R.A.E., Dory Caymmi and Nelson Mota
Copyright Renewed

Music by DORY CAYMMI and NELSON MOTA
English Lyric by ALAN BERGMAN and MARILYN BERGMAN

Medium Bossa Nova

Like A Lov-er, the morn-ing sun slow-ly ris-es and kiss-es you a-wake.
Like A Lov-er, the riv-er wind sighs and rip-ples its fin-gers through your hair.

Your smile is soft and drow-sy as you let it play up-on your face.
Up-on your cheek it lin-gers, nev-er hav-ing known a sweet-er place.

Oh, how I dream I might be like the morn-ing sun to you.
Oh, how I dream I might be like the riv-er wind to you.

How I en-vy a cup that knows your lips, Let it be me, my love, And a ta-ble that feels your fin-ger-tips, Let it be me, Let me be your love, Bring an end to the end-less days and nights with-out you.

Like A Lov-er, the vel-vet moon shares your pil-low and watch-es while you sleep.

Its light ar-rives on tip-toe, gen-tly tak-ing you in its em-brace.

Oh, how I dream I might be like the vel-vet moon to you.

LAZY RIVER

Words and Music by HOAGY CARMICHAEL and SIDNEY ARODIN

Copyright © 1931 by Peermusic Ltd.
Copyright Renewed

Moderately slow

| D7 | D♭7 C7 F♯dim | G7 | G A♭9 G9 |

Up a La-zy Riv-er by the old mill run, That la-zy, la-zy riv-er in the noon-day sun,

| C7 | C6 D♭7 C7 | F | C7 Bdim F |

Lin-ger in the shade of a kind old tree; Throw a-way your trou-bles, dream a dream with me

| D7 | D♭7 C7 F♯dim | G7 | G A♭9 G9 |

Up a La-zy Riv-er where the rob-in's song A-wakes a bright new morn-ing, We can loaf a-long,

| B♭ | Bdim F E7 | E♭6 D7 G9 | C7 |

Blue skies up a-bove, ev-'ry-one's in love, Up a La-zy Riv-er, how

| F E7 D7 | G9 C7 | 1. F B♭6 F | 2. F6 |

hap-py you can be. Up a La-zy Riv-er with me. ___ me. ___

LISTEN HERE

Words and Music by DAVE FRISHBERG

© 1985 Swiftwater Music and MTM Music

Moderately slow

| D♭M7 | G♭M7 D♭M7 | G♭M7 | Cm7 | F7 |

When you're still, ___ do you hear one small voice, ___ crys-tal clear, say-ing, "Lis-ten Here, my friend, Lis-ten

| Cm7 F7♯5 | D♭M7 G♭M7 | D♭M7 | G♭M7 | Cm7 | F7 |

Here"? Well, that voice ___ is your own, and it speaks to you ___ a-lone, "You can count on me," it says, "So Lis-ten

| B♭M7 | E♭M7 B♭7sus | E♭M7 B♭7sus | E♭ | G7♯5 |

Here." This is you, this is real, this is tru-ly the way you

| Cm9 G/B | G♭/B♭ F7/A | D♭M7/A♭ Gm7♭5 | FM7 | C13 |

feel. You can run, You can hide, oh, but some time, some place, we

LEMON DROP

Composed by
GEORGE WALLINGTON

LITTLE SHOES

By MIKE STERN

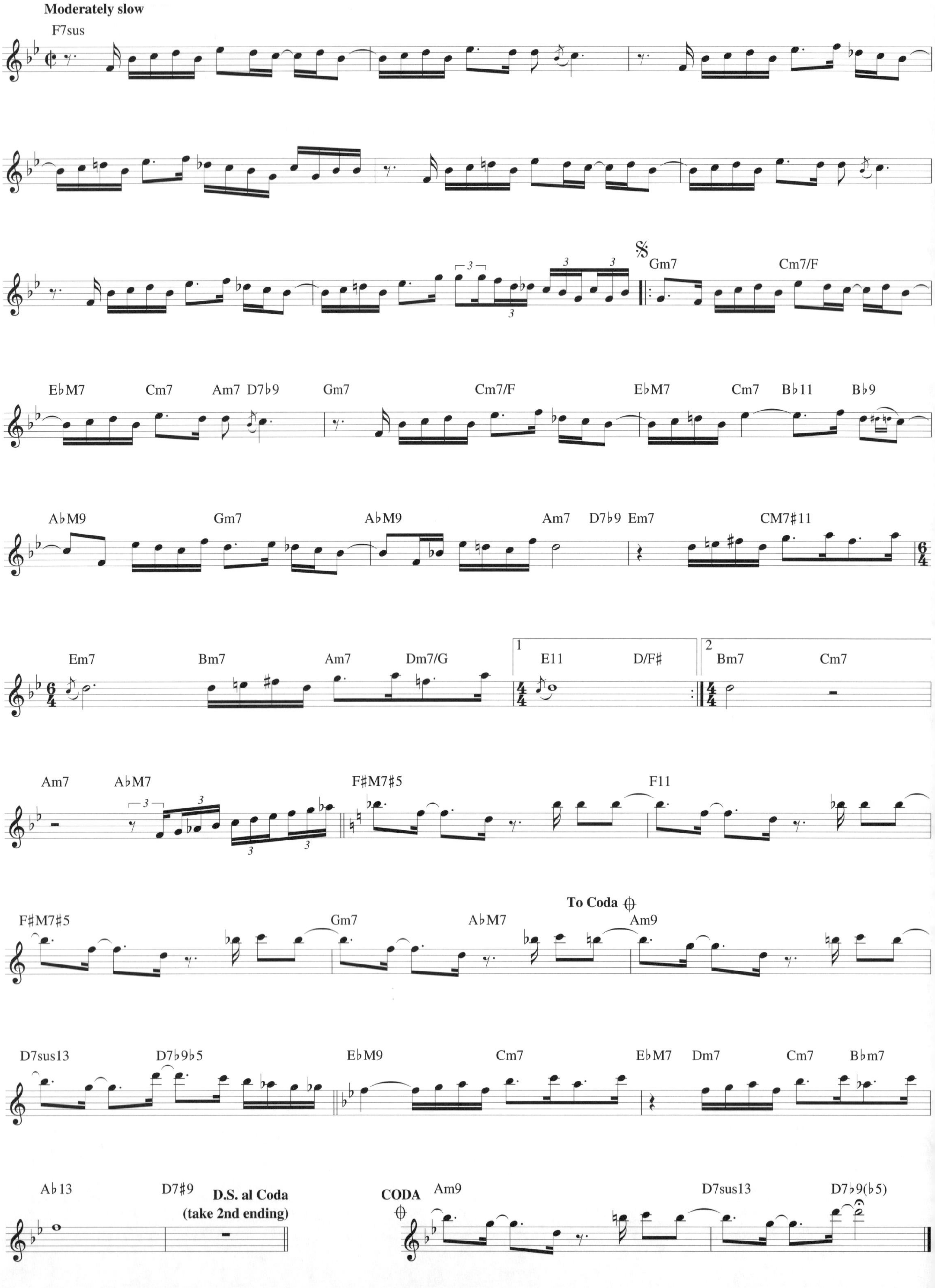

LITTLE SUNFLOWER

By FREDDIE HUBBARD

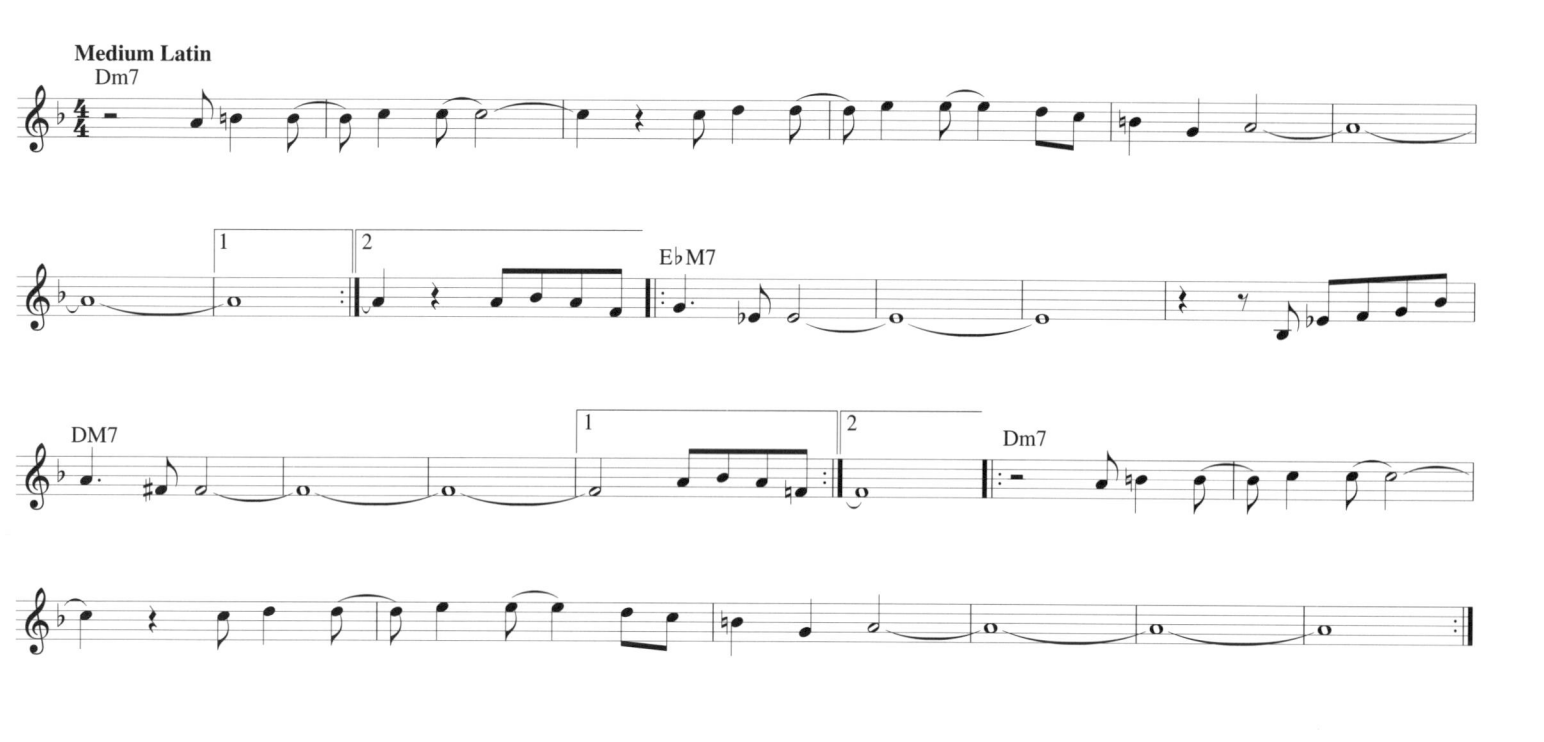

LOVE LIES

Words and Music by CARL SIGMAN, RALPH FREED and JOSEPH MEYER

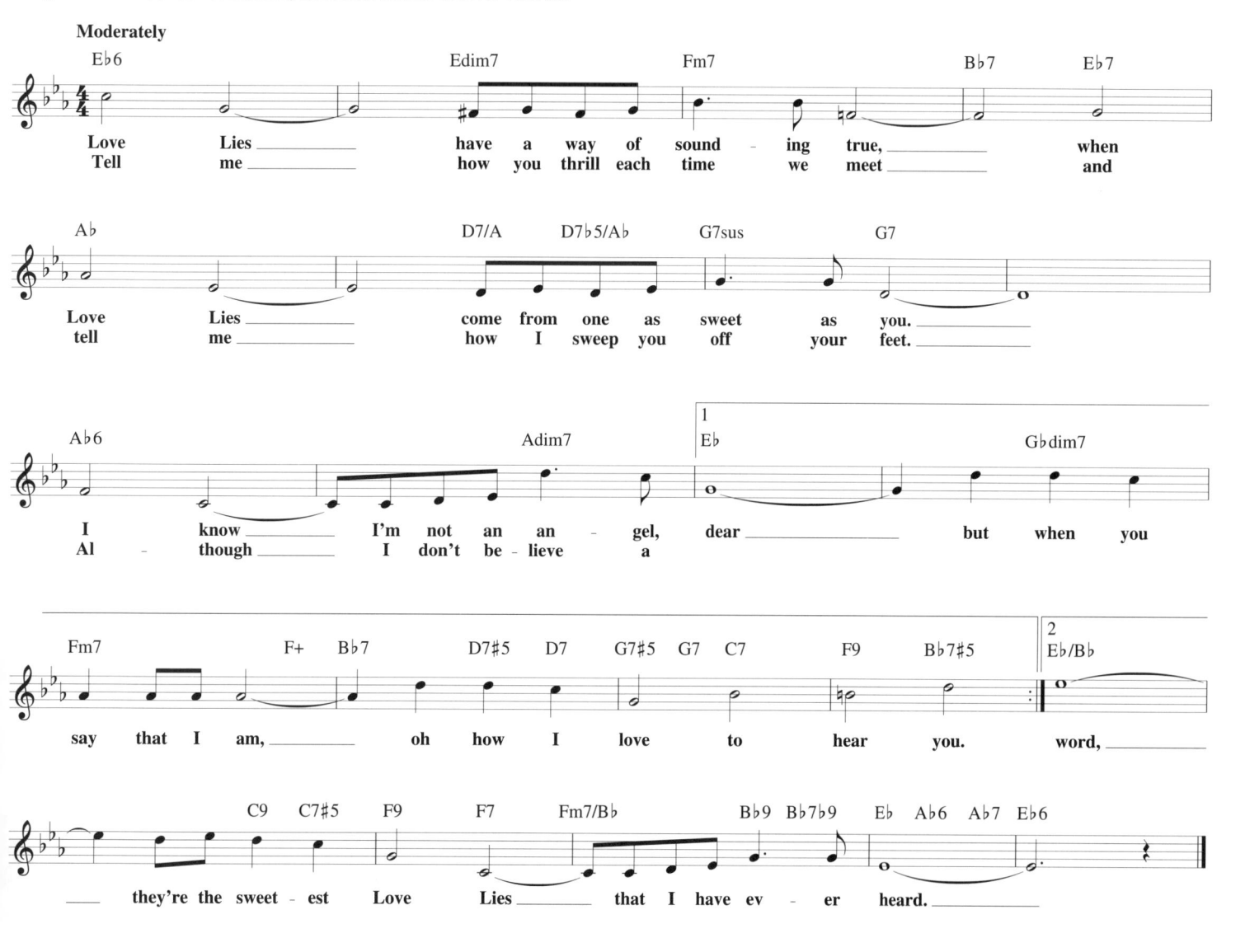

Love Lies have a way of sounding true, when
Love Lies come from one as sweet as you.
I know I'm not an angel, dear but when you
say that I am, oh how I love to hear you.
they're the sweetest Love Lies that I have ever heard.

Tell me how you thrill each time we meet and
tell me how I sweep you off your feet.
Although I don't believe a word,

LITTLE WALTZ

Written by RON CARTER

Copyright © 1977 RETRAC PRODUCTIONS, INC.

LYDIA

By JACK DeJOHNETTE

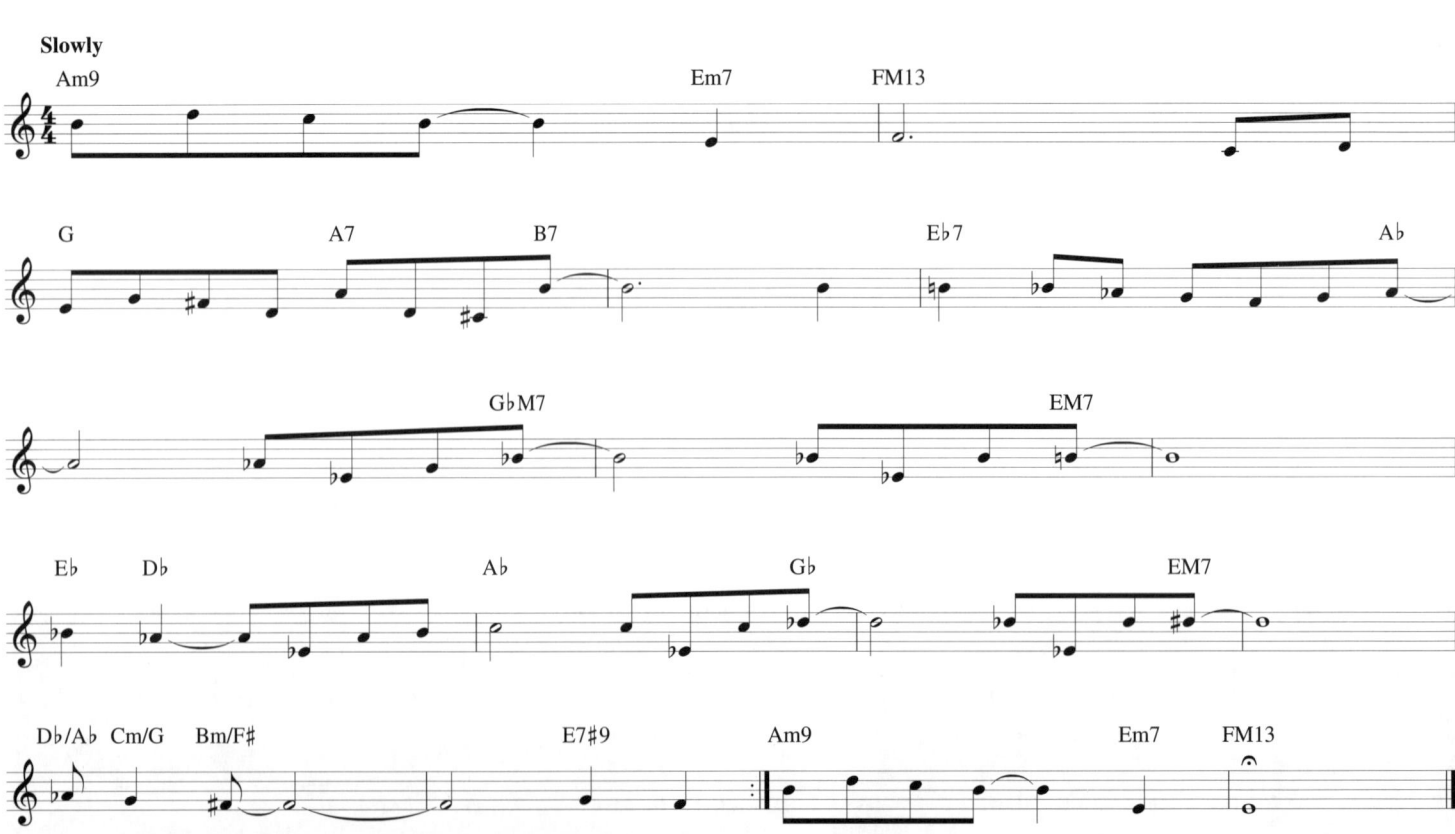

Copyright © 1971 DeJohnette Music

LOVE YOU MADLY

By DUKE ELLINGTON

MISSION: IMPOSSIBLE THEME

from the Paramount Television Series MISSION: IMPOSSIBLE

by LALO SCHIFRIN

MAKE BELIEVE
from SHOW BOAT

Copyright © 1927 PolyGram International Publishing, Inc.
Copyright Renewed

Lyrics by OSCAR HAMMERSTEIN II
Music by JEROME KERN

Moderately slow

We could Make Be-lieve I love you, on-ly Make Be-lieve that you love me. Oth-ers find peace of mind in pre-tend-ing. Could-n't you, could-n't I? Could-n't we Make Be-lieve our lips are blend-ing in a phan-tom kiss, or two, or three? Might as well Make Be-lieve I love you, for to tell the truth, I do.

MAKIN' WHOOPEE!
from WHOOPEE!

Copyright © 1928 (Renewed) by Donaldson Publishing Co. and Gilbert Keyes Music Co.

Lyrics by GUS KAHN
Music by WALTER DONALDSON

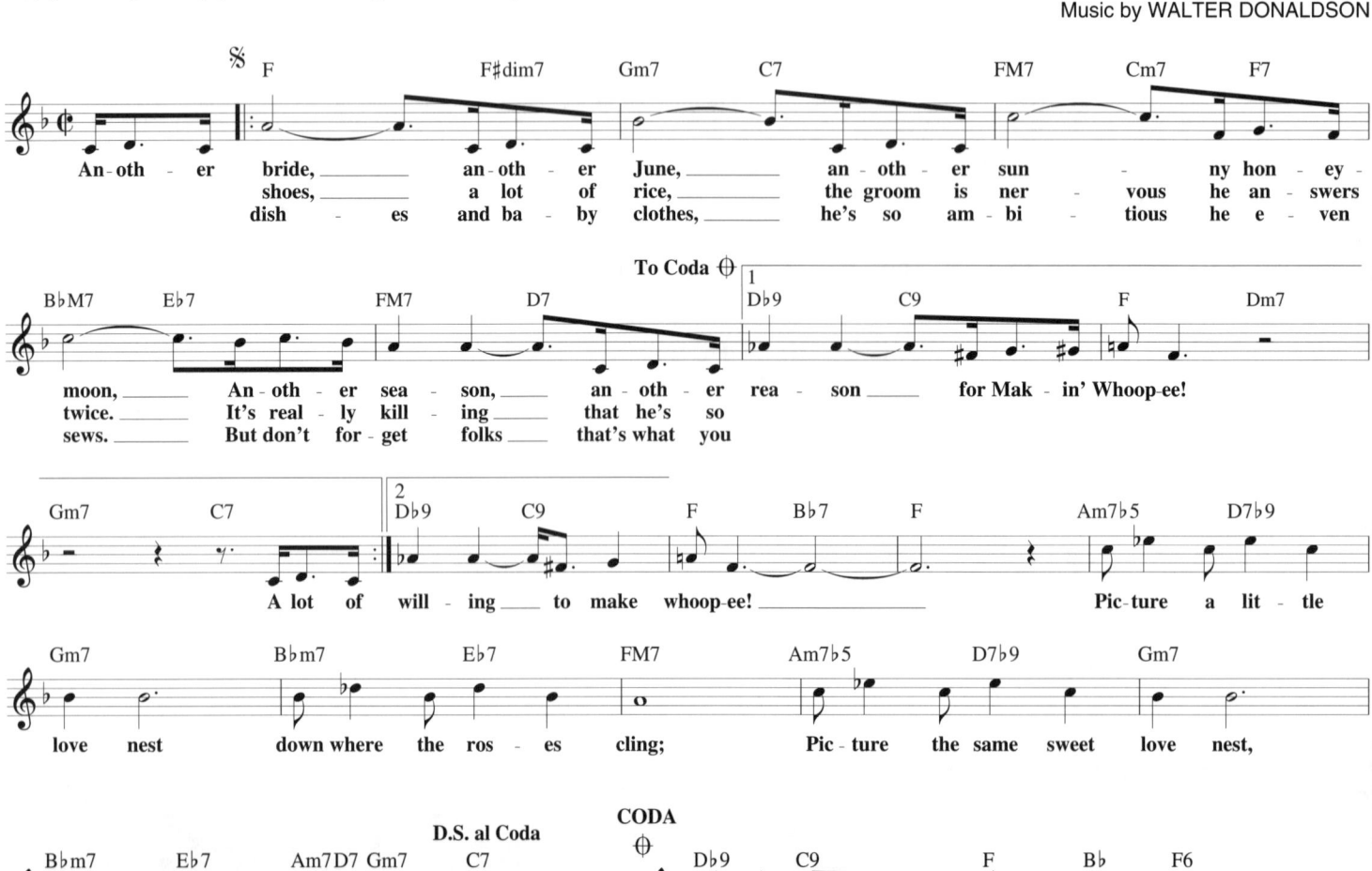

An-oth-er bride, an-oth-er June, an-oth-er sun-ny hon-ey-
shoes, a lot of rice, the groom is ner-vous he an-swers
dish-es and ba-by clothes, he's so am-bi-tious he e-ven

moon, An-oth-er sea-son, an-oth-er rea-son for Mak-in' Whoop-ee!
twice. It's real-ly kill-ing that he's so
sews. But don't for-get folks that's what you

A lot of will-ing to make whoop-ee! Pic-ture a lit-tle love nest down where the ros-es cling; Pic-ture the same sweet love nest,

D.S. al Coda
think what a year can bring. He's wash-ing

CODA
get folks for Mak-in' Whoop-ee!

MAKE A LIST
(Make a Wish)

Written by ART PEPPER

Copyright © 1981 ARTHUR PEPPER MUSIC

MANTECA

By DIZZY GILLESPIE, WALTER "GIL" FULLER
and LUCIANO POZO GONZALES

Copyright © 1948 (Renewed) by Music Sales Corporation (ASCAP)
and Luciano Pozo Gonzales Publishing Designee

ME AND MY BABY

Words and Music by
HORACE SILVER

Music © 1960 by Ecaroh Music, Inc.
Copyright Renewed 1988
Words © 1996 by Ecaroh Music, Inc.

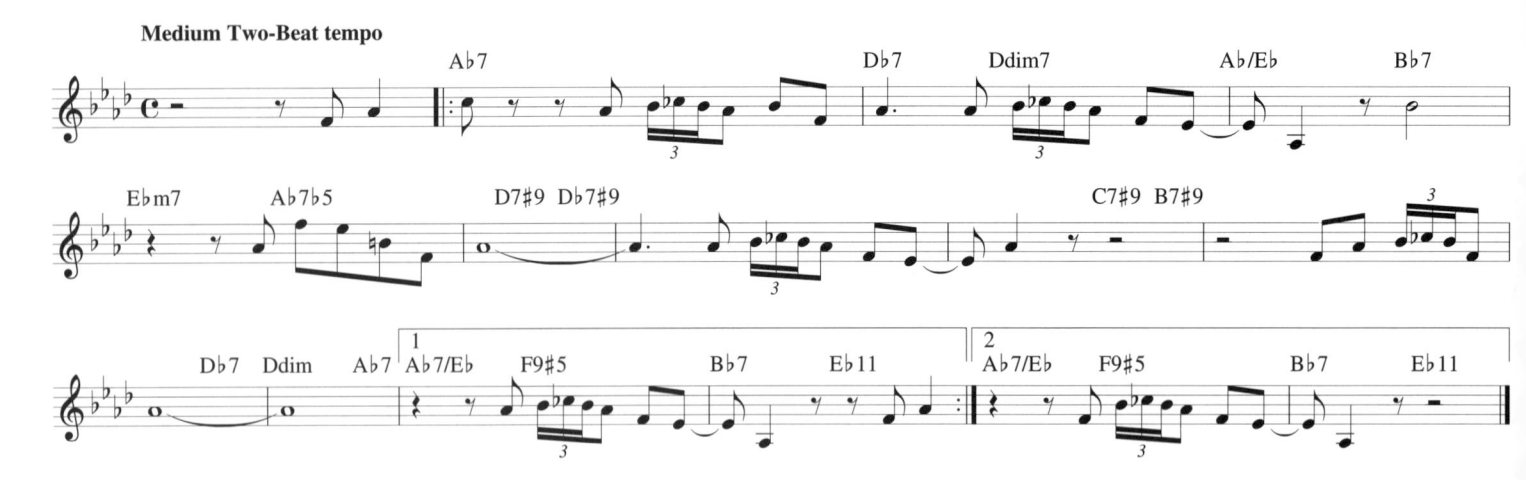

Medium Two-Beat tempo

Intro (Male)
I've been puttin' it together day by day.
I've finally worked it out.

Chorus (Male)
I got plans,
I really got some plans
For Me And My Baby.
A brand new Cadillac.
And I don't mean maybe.
They won't take it back
From Me And My Baby.

She's my spouse.
I'm gonna buy a house
For Me And My Baby.
Way out in Malibu.
And I don't mean maybe.
Plenty money too.
For Me And My Baby.

If I work
And stash a bit away
For Me And My Baby.
Now there will come a day
And I don't mean maybe.
No more dues to pay.
For Me And My Baby.

SHOUT CHORUS (Male & Female)
(To be sung twice)
We're strivin' to live the good life.
There's nothin' that we can't do.
We've got our plans in full view.
We're gonna come in on cue.
We're not about to sub-due.
We're gonna see it on through.

TAG ENDING (Male & Female)
We will get to crackin'
So there's nothin' lackin'.
We will start attackin'
Send out doubts a-packin'.
We will keep on backin'
All the plans that we have
Carefully worked out
For Me And My Baby.

FOLLOWED BY CHORUS (Female)
He's my man
I'm doin' all I can
For me and my baby.
He sure can count on me.
And I don't mean maybe.
Perfect harmony
For Me And My Baby.

There's no doubt
That things will all work out
For Me And My Baby.
Our dreams will all come true.
And I don't mean maybe.
No more feelin' blue
For Me And My Baby.

Wait and see.
There'll be a family.
For Me And My Baby.
We've planned it carefully.
And I don't mean maybe.
Blessings they will be
For Me And My Baby.

*AFTER SHOUT CHORUS GO BACK
TO INTRO AND SING THROUGH
THEN TAKE TAG ENDING OUT*

MONA LISA
from the Paramount Picture CAPTAIN CAREY, U.S.A.

Words and Music by JAY LIVINGSTON
and RAY EVANS

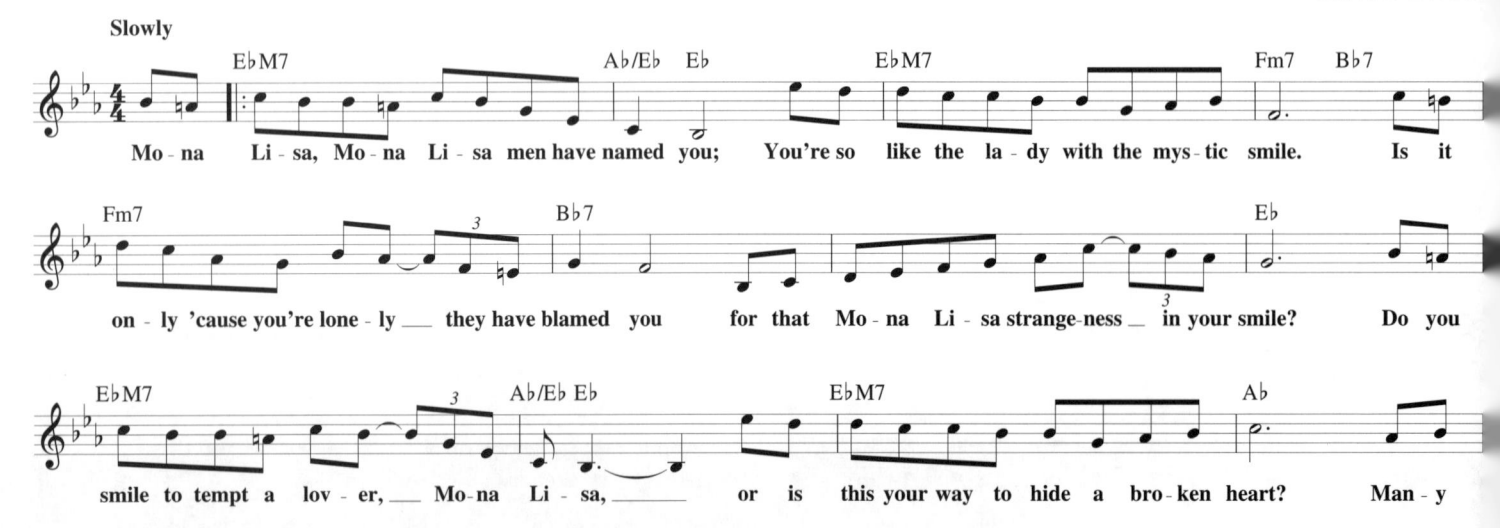

Copyright © 1949 (Renewed 1976) by Famous Music Corporation

Slowly

Mo-na Li-sa, Mo-na Li-sa men have named you; You're so like the la-dy with the mys-tic smile. Is it on-ly 'cause you're lone-ly they have blamed you for that Mo-na Li-sa strange-ness in your smile? Do you smile to tempt a lov-er, Mo-na Li-sa, or is this your way to hide a bro-ken heart? Man-y dreams have been brought to your door-step. They just lie there, and they die there. Are you warm, are you real, Mo-na Li-sa, or just a cold and lone-ly love-ly work of art? Mo-na art?

MAPUTO

© Copyright 1974 by MCA MUSIC PUBLISHING, A Division of UNIVERSAL STUDIOS, INC.
and THRILLER MILLER MUSIC
All Rights Controlled and Administered by MCA MUSIC PUBLISHING, A Division of UNIVERSAL STUDIOS, INC.

By MARCUS MILLER

Moderately slow Rock

MOROCCO

By RUSS FREEMAN

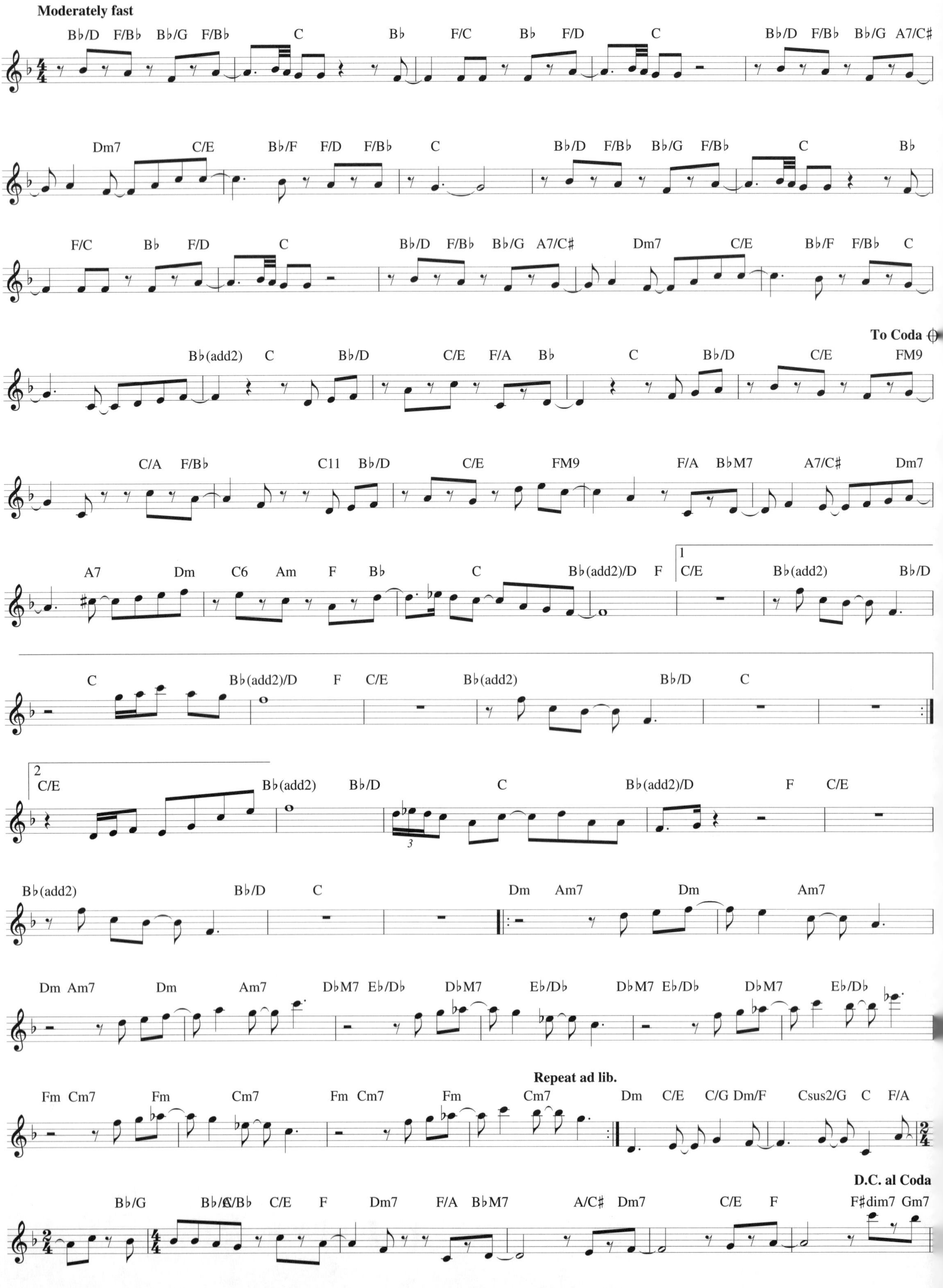

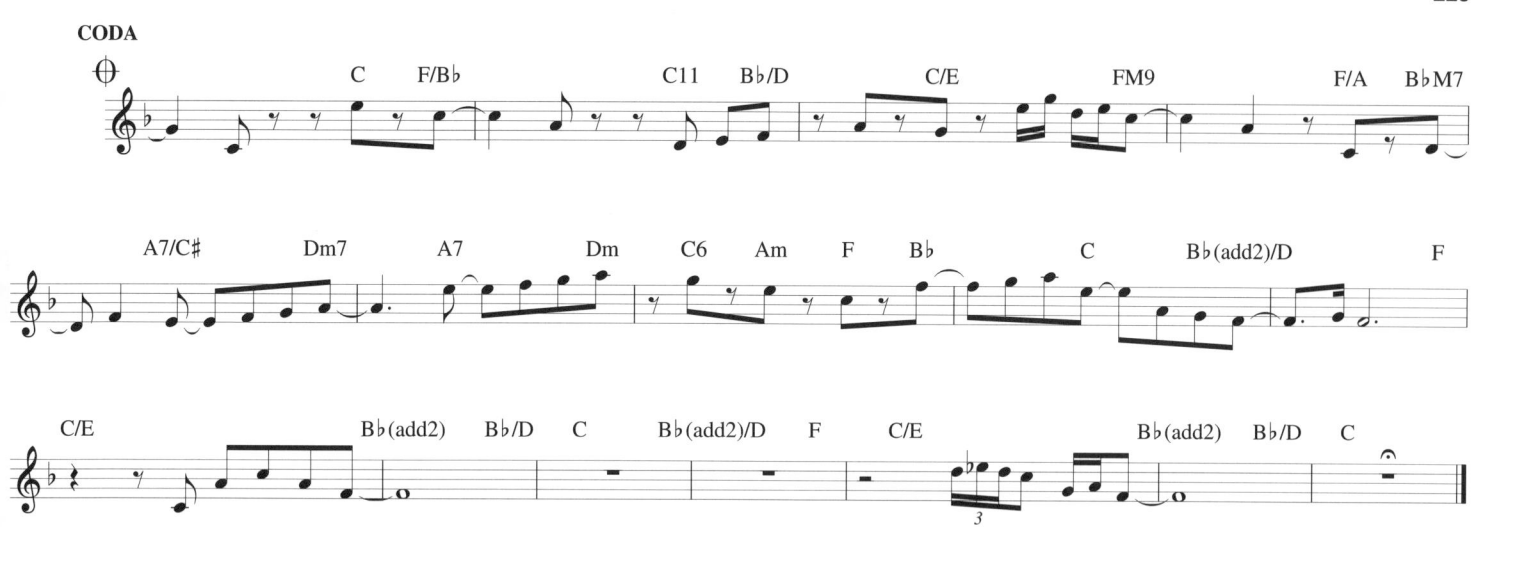

MOOD INDIGO
from SOPHISTICATED LADIES

Words and Music by DUKE ELLINGTON, IRVING MILLS and ALBANY BIGARD

Copyright © 1931 (Renewed 1958) and Assigned to Famous Music Corporation, EMI Mills Music Inc. and Indigo Mood Music c/o The Songwriters Guild Of America in the U.S.A.
Rights for the world outside the U.S.A. Controlled by EMI Mills Music Inc. and Warner Bros. Publications Inc.

Moderately slow

You ain't been blue, no, no, no, you ain't been blue, till you've had that Mood In-di-go. That feel-in' goes steal-in' down to my shoes, while I sit and sigh: "Go 'long, blues." Al-ways get that Mood In-di-go, since my ba-by said good-bye. In the eve-nin' when lights are low, I'm so lone-some I could cry, 'cause there's no-bod-y who cares a-bout me. I'm just a soul who's blu-er than blue can be, when I get that Mood In-di-go, I could lay me down and die.

DAYS OF WINE AND ROSES

Lyric by JOHNNY MERCER
Music by HENRY MANCINI

© 1962 WARNER BROS. INC. (Renewed)

Moderately

The Days Of Wine And Ros- es laugh and run a- way like a child at play, through the mead- ow- land to- ward a clos- ing door, a door marked "Nev- er- more," that was- n't there be- fore. The lone- ly night dis- clos- es just a pass- ing breeze filled with mem- o- ries of the gold- en smile that in- tro- duced me to the Days Of Wine And Ro- ses and

1. F6 | Gm7 C7
you. The

2. F | Gm7/C FM9
you.

MR. BIG FALLS HIS J.G. HAND

Written by ART PEPPER

Copyright © 1981 ARTHUR PEPPER MUSIC

Medium Blues

MY ATTORNEY BERNIE

Words and Music by
DAVE FRISHBERG

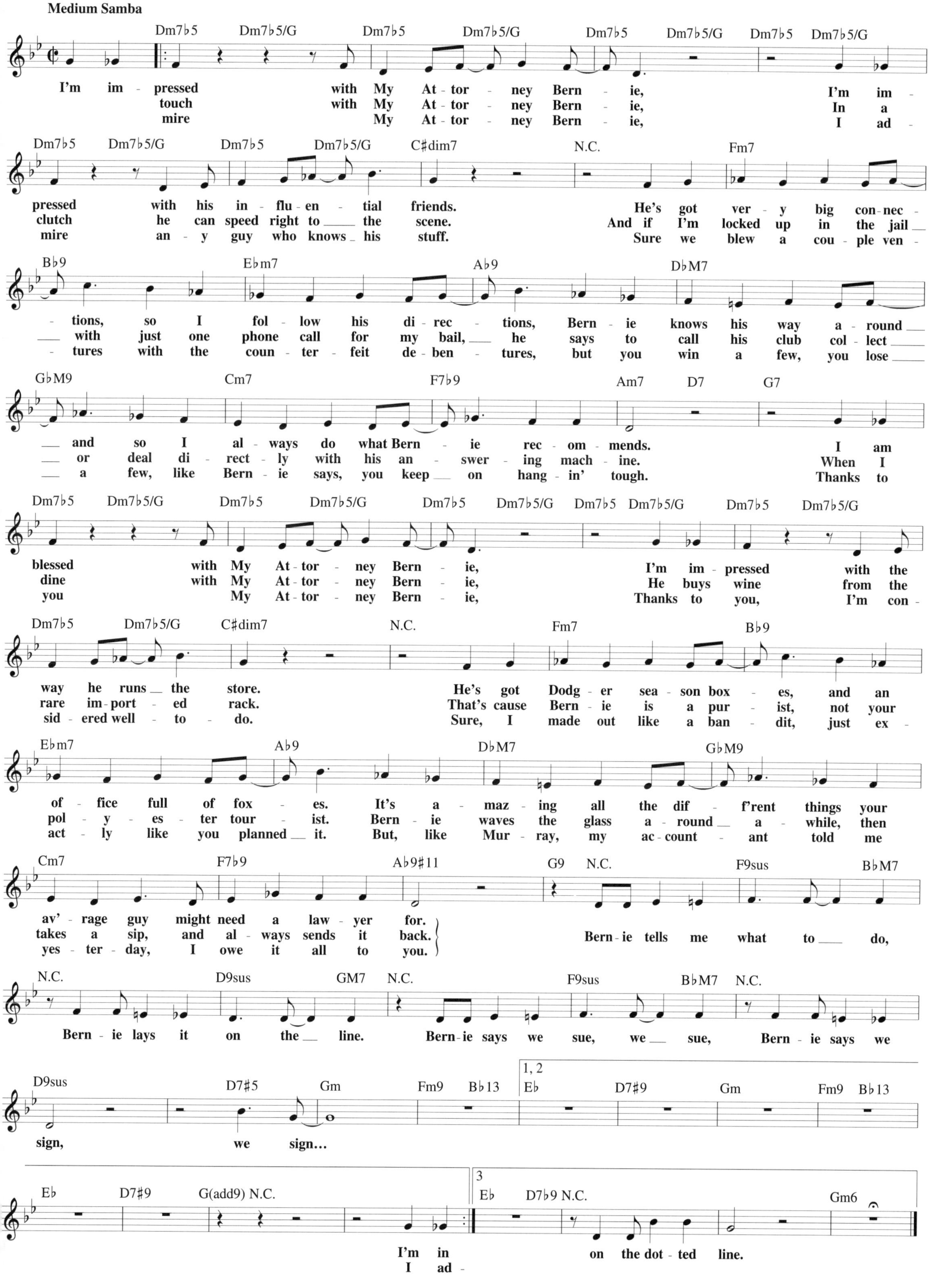

MR. GONE

Music by JOSEF ZAWINUL

MAIDEN VOYAGE

Music by HERBIE HANCOCK

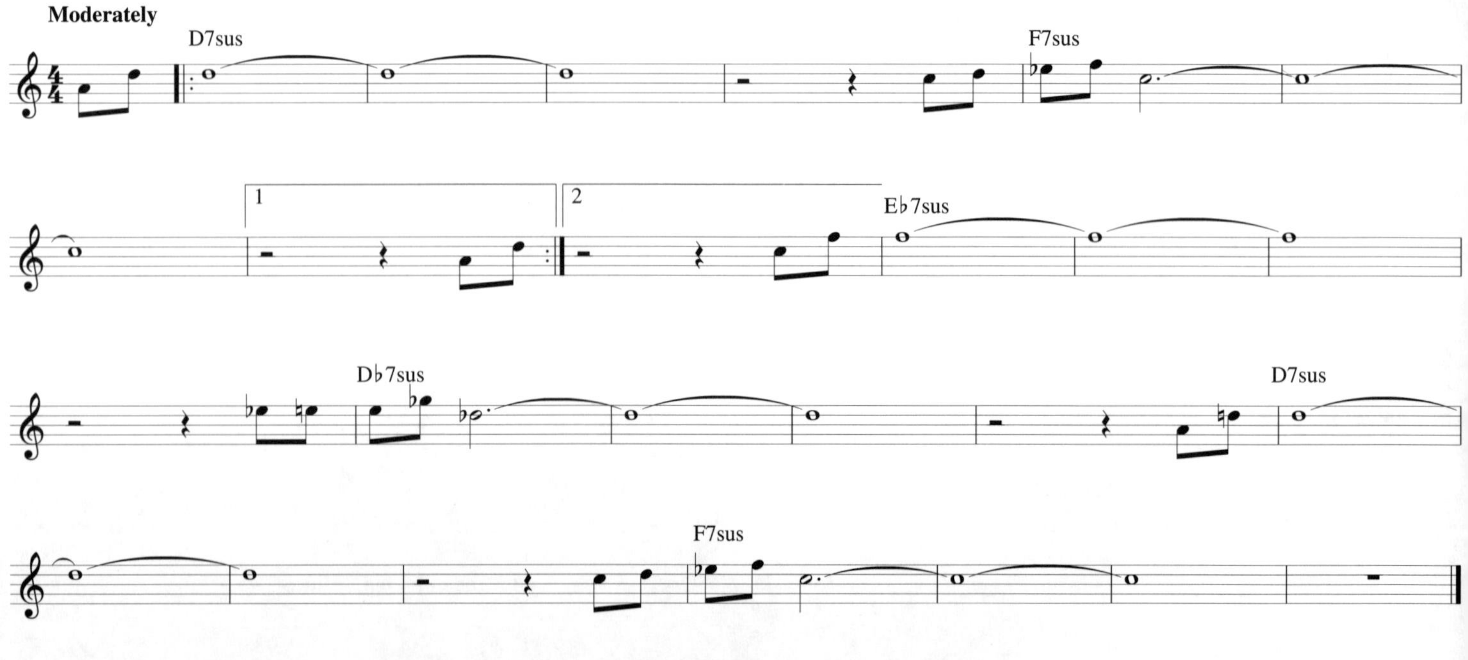

(I'm Afraid)
THE MASQUERADE IS OVER

Words by HERB MAGIDSON
Music by ALLIE WRUBEL

MORNIN'

Words and Music by AL JARREAU, JAY GRAYDON and DAVID FOSTER

© Copyright 1983 by ALJARREAU MUSIC, GARDEN RAKE MUSIC and FOSTER FREES MUSIC
All Rights for ALJARREAU MUSIC Controlled and Administered by MUSIC CORPORATION OF AMERICA, INC.

Moderate R & B Shuffle

Mornin' Mister Radio. Mornin' little Cherios. Mornin' Sister Oriole.
Mornin' Mister Shoeshine man. Shine 'em bright in white and tan. My baby said she loves me and

Did I tell you ev'rything is fine in my
need I tell you that ev'rything here is just fine, in my

mind?
mind? 'Scuse me if I

sing. My heart has found its wings; searchin' high and

low, and now at last I know.

Mornin' Mister Golden Gate. I should walk but I can't wait, I can't wait to set it straight.

I was shakin' but now I am makin' it fine here in my mind.

My heart will soar with love that's rare and real.

My smiling face will feel ev'ry cloud.

MOMENT'S NOTICE

By JOHN COLTRANE

MAMBO A LA SAVOY

Music and Lyric by WALTER "GIL" FULLER
Spanish Lyric by FRANK GRILLO (MACHITO)

Here's the lat-est dance cre-a-tion, it's not a fad but a real sen-sa-tion; Lat-ins do it, you can do it too. It was start-ed by a La-tin who brought the dance to all Man-hat-tan, and he called it Mam-bo A La Sa-voy. When the band plays clav-es and rhy-thm, you start danc-ing by hyp-no-tism. And you feel a new sen-sa-tion, it's the mam-bo with syn-co-pation. If you want some eas-y les-sons, just ask a Lat-in from Man-hat-tan and he'll teach you to Mam-bo A La Sa-voy.

MAS QUE NADA

Words and Music by
JORGE BEN

Copyright © 1963 by Peermusic Do Brasil Edic. Mus. Ltda.
Copyright Renewed
All Rights Administered by Peer International Corporation

Moderately bright

Ooo, _____ when your eyes meet _____ mine.
Ooo, _____ I could lose _____ my mind.
Ô _____ a - ri - á _____ rai - ô

_____ Pow! Pow! Pow! _____ Ow!
_____ Ow! Ow! _____
_____ ô - bá, ô - bá, ô - ba. _____ bá.

It's _____ a feel - ing that be - gins to grow an' grow an' grow in - side
Mas _____ Que Na - da sai da mi - nha fren - te que eu que - ro pa -

me _____ 'til I feel like I'm gon - na ex - plode. _____ Oh, this is
- sar, _____ Pois o sam - ba es - tá a - ni - ma - do, O que

what you do to me! _____ Are your lips say - ing things
eu que - ro e sam - bar. Es - se sam - ba Que é mix -

_____ that you feel in your heart? If your heart is beat - ing
- to de ma - ra - ca - tú E sam - ba de pre - to

mad - ly, _____ Then _____ let the mu - sic start. _____ Hold _____ me, hold
vel - ho, _____ Sam - ba de pre - to tú. _____ Mas _____ Que Na -

_____ me! It's heav - en ooo it's heav - en when you hold me; _____ I
- da, _____ Um sam - ba co - mo es - se ta - o le - gal, _____ Vo -

want you night and day. Ooo I want you here _____ to stay. _____
cê nao vai que - rer que eu che - gue no _____ fi - nal.

D.C. al Coda

CODA

Ow! _____
bá! _____

LAURA

© 1945 (Renewed 1973) by TWENTIETH CENTURY MUSIC CORPORATION
All Rights Controlled by EMI ROBBINS CATALOG INC. (Publishing) and
WARNER BROS. PUBLICATIONS U.S. INC. (Print)

Lyric by JOHNNY MERCER
Music by DAVID RAKSIN

Slowly

Lau - ra is the face in the mist - y light, foot - steps that you hear down the hall. The laugh that floats on a sum - mer night, that you can nev - er quite re - call. And you see Lau - ra on the train that is pass - ing thru, those eyes, how fa - mil - iar they seem. She gave your ver - y first kiss to you, that was Lau - ra but she's on - ly a dream.

MANOIR DE MES REVES
(Django's Castle)

Copyright © 1945 (Renewed) by Publications Francis Day S.A.
All Rights in the U.S.A. and Canada Controlled by Jewel Music Publishing Co., Inc.

By DJANGO REINHARDT

Moderately

MIMOSA

By GEORGE BENSON

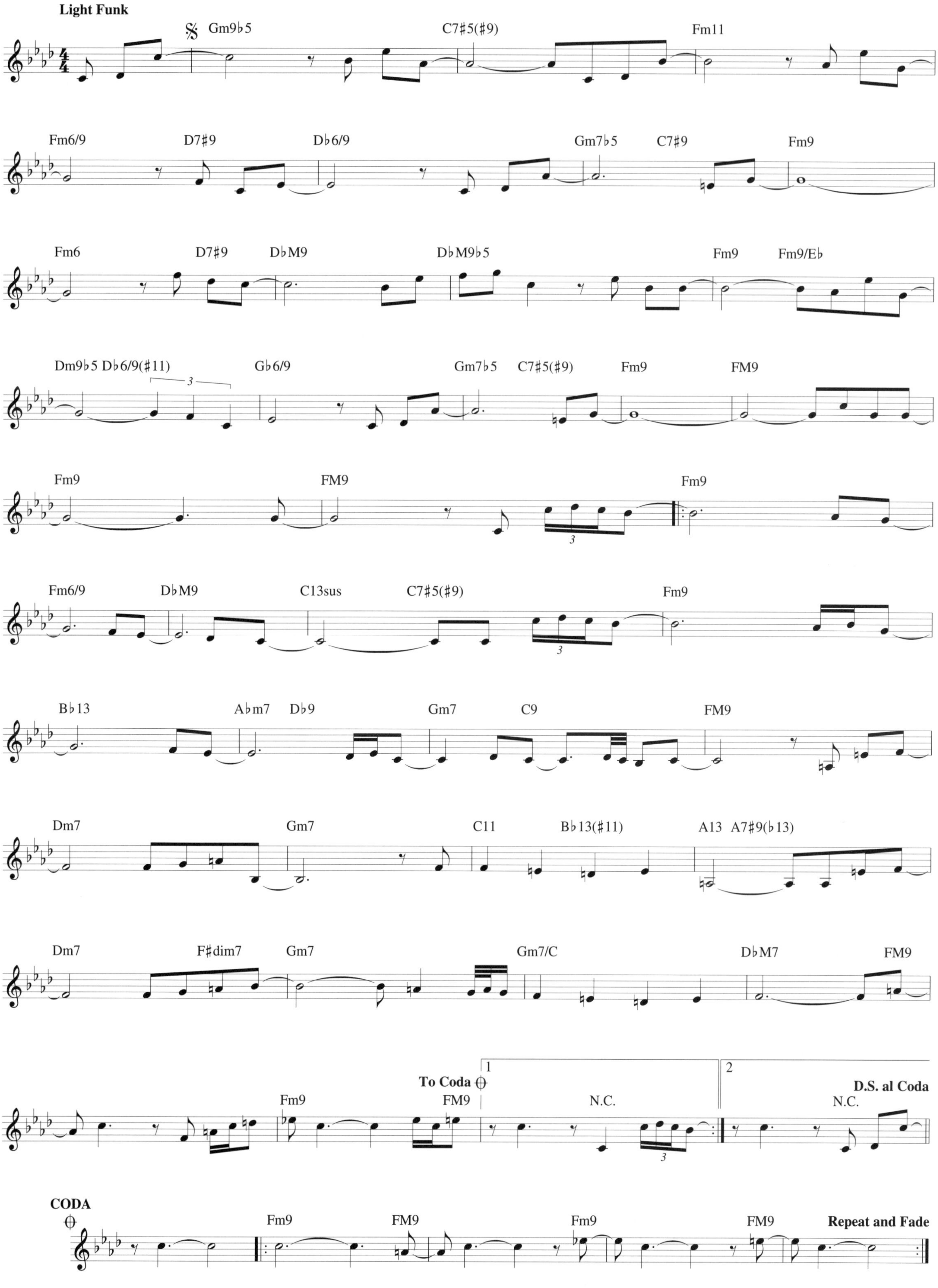

Mandy Make Up Your Mind

Words and Music by GRANT CLARKE,
ROY TURK, GEORGE MEYER and ARTHUR JOHNSTON

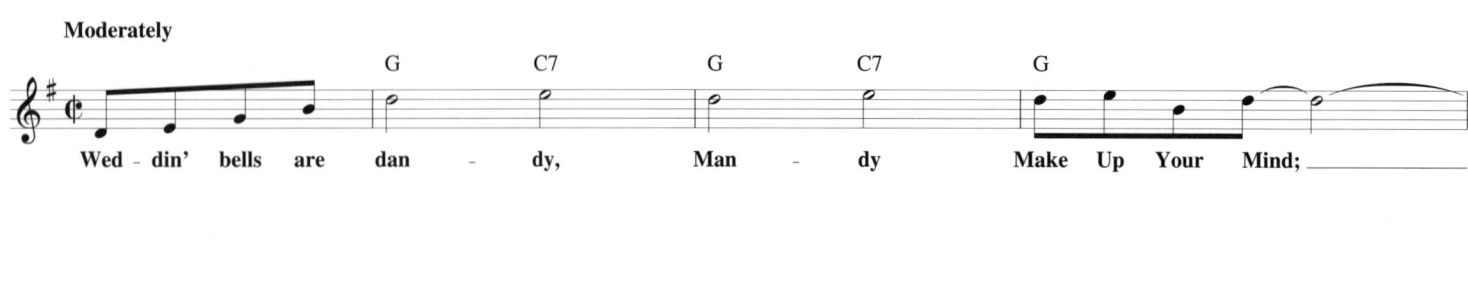

Copyright © 1924 Sony/ATV Tunes LLC and Bourne Co.
Copyright Renewed
All Rights on behalf of Sony/ATV Tunes LLC Administered by Sony/ATV Music Publishing,
8 Music Square West, Nashville, TN 37203

Moderately

Wed-din' bells are dan-dy, Man-dy Make Up Your Mind; preach-er man is han-dy, Man-dy, eas-y to find. March-ing down the isle, your style will make 'em all stare with a lit-tle black-eyed Su-san stuck in your hair. Gee, but you're the can-dy, Man-dy, won't you de-cide; ev-'ry thing is dan-dy, Man-dy, once you're a bride. In a year or two, there may be three of a kind; lis-ten to me Man-dy, Make Up Your Mind.

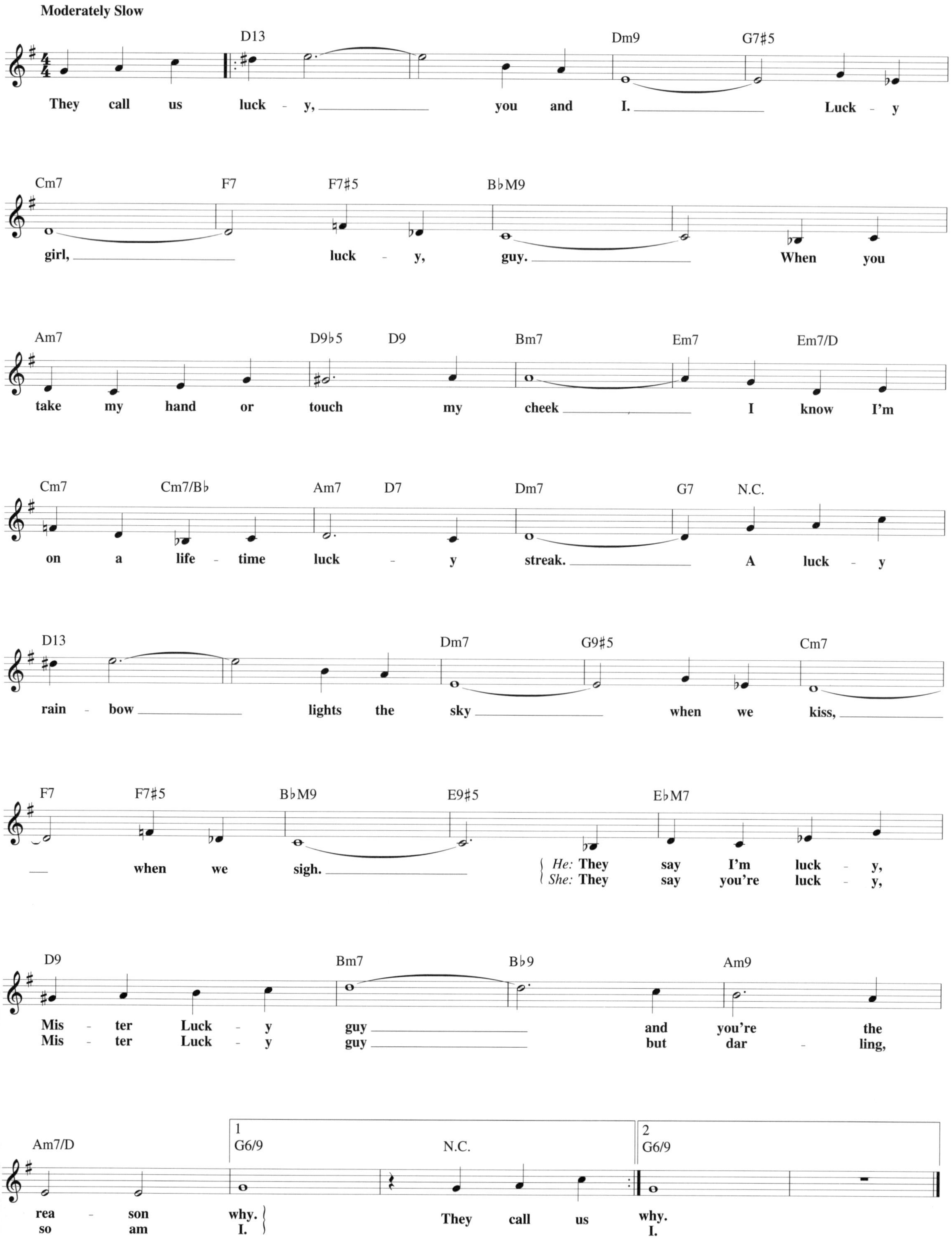

MR. JELLY-LORD

By FERDINAND "JELLY ROLL" MORTON

© 1923, 1927 (Renewed) EDWIN H. MORRIS & COMPANY, A Division of MPL Communications, Inc.

MR. WONDERFUL

Copyright © 1956 by The Herald Square Music Co.
Copyright Renewed and Assigned to Range Road Music Inc., Quartet Music Inc.,
Abilene Music, Inc. and Jerry Bock Enterprises
All Rights on behalf of Abilene Music, Inc. Administered by The Songwriters Guild Of America

Words and Music by JERRY BOCK,
LARRY HOLOFCENER and GEORGE DAVID WEISS

Moderately

Why this feel - ing? Why this glow? Why the
trem - bling when you speak?
thrill when you say "Hel - lo"? It's a strange and ten - der
joy when you touch my cheek? I must tell you what my
mag - ic you do. Mis - ter Won - der - ful, that's
heart knows is true:
you! Why this Won - der - ful, that's you! And why this
long - ing to know your charms; to spend for - ev - er here in your
arms! Oh! There's much more I could say, but the
words keep slip - ping a - way. And I'm left with on - ly
one point of view: Mis - ter Won - der - ful, that's you!
One more thing, then I'm through; Mis - ter Won - der - ful. Mis - ter
Won - der - ful, Mis - ter Won - der - ful, I love you!

THE MOOCH

By DUKE ELLINGTON and IRVING MILLS

MOON RIVER
from the Paramount Picture BREAKFAST AT TIFFANY'S

Words by JOHNNY MERCER
Music by HENRY MANCINI

Slowly

| CM7 | Am7 | F7#11 | C/E | F7#11 |

Moon Riv-er, wid-er than a mile, I'm cross-in' you in

| C/E | Bm7b5 | E7 | Am7 | C7/G |

style some day. Old dream-mak-er, you

| FM7 | Bb9#11 | Am | Am7/G | F#m7b5 | B7 |

heart-break-er, wher-ev-er you're go-in', I'm

| Em7 | A7 | Dm7 | G9 | CM7 | Am7 | F7#11 |

go-in' your way. Two drift-ers, off to see the

| C/E | F7#11 | C/E | Bm7b5 | E7 |

world. There's such a lot of world to see. We're

| Am7 | Am/G | F#m7b5 | F13 | C/E | F7#11 |

af-ter the same rain-bow's end, wait-in' 'round the

| C/E | F7#11 | C/E | Am7 | Dm7 |

bend, my Huck-le-ber-ry friend, Moon Riv-er

| G9 | 1. CM7 | 2. AbM7 | DbM7 | CM7 |

and me. me.

MACK THE KNIFE
from THE THREEPENNY OPERA

Music by KURT WEILL
English Words by MARC BLITZSTEIN
Original German Words by BERT BRECHT

© 1928 UNIVERSAL EDITION
© 1955 WEILL-BRECHT-HARMS CO., INC.
Renewal Rights Assigned to the KURT WEILL FOUNDATION FOR MUSIC, BERT BRECHT
and EDWARD and JOSEPHINE DAVIS, as Executors of the ESTATE OF MARC BLITZSTEIN

Moderately

Oh, the shark has pretty teeth, dear and he shows them pearly white. Just a jackknife has Macheath, dear and he keeps it out of sight. When the shark bites with his teeth, dear scarlet billows start to spread. Fancy gloves, though, wears Macheath, dear so there's not a trace of red. On the sidewalk Sunday morning lies a body oozing life; someone's sneaking 'round the corner. Is the someone Mack The Knife? From a tugboat by the river a cement bag's dropping down; the cement's just for the weight, dear. Mackie's back in town. Louie

Miller disappeared, dear after drawing out his cash; and Macheath spends like a sailor. Did our boy do something rash? Sukey Tawdry, Jenny Diver, Polly Peachum, Lucy Brown, oh, the line forms on the right, dear now that Mackie's back in town.

MORE I CANNOT WISH YOU
from GUYS AND DOLLS

By FRANK LOESSER

© 1949, 1950 (Renewed) FRANK MUSIC CORP.

Slowly

Vel - vet I can wish you for the col - lar of your coat, and for - tune smil - ing all a - long your way. But More I Can - not Wish You than to wish you find your love. Your own true love this day. Man - sions I can wish you, sev - en foot - men all in red and call - ing cards u - pon a sil - ver tray. But More I Can - not Wish You than to wish you find your love, your own true love, this day. Stand - ing there gaz - ing at you, full of the bloom of youth. Stand - ing there gaz - ing at you with the sheep's eye and the

Mu - sic I can wish you, mer - ry mu - sic while you're young. And wis - dom when your hair has turned to gray.

D.C. al Coda

lick - er - ish tooth.

CODA

day. With the sheep's eye and the lick - er - ish tooth and the strong arms to car - ry you a - way.

MOON OVER MIAMI

Lyric by EDGAR LESLIE
Music by JOE BURKE

Copyright © 1935 (Renewed 1963) Fred Ahlert Music Corporation and Edgar Leslie
All Rights for Edgar Leslie Administered by Herald Square Music Inc.

Slowly

Moon O-ver Mi-a-mi, Shine on my love and me, So we can stroll be-side the
Moon O-ver Mi-a-mi, Shine on as we be-gin, a dream or two that may come

roll of the roll-ing sea.
true, When the tide comes in. Hark to the song of the smil-ing trou-ba-dours,

Hark to the throb-bing gui-tars hear how the waves of-fer thun-der-ous ap-plause,

Af-ter each song to the stars. Moon O-ver Mi-a-mi, You know we're wait-ing

for, a lit-tle love, a lit-tle kiss on Mi-a-mi shore.

MOONLIGHT BECOMES YOU
from the Paramount Picture ROAD TO MOROCCO

Words by JOHNNY BURKE
Music by JAMES VAN HEUSEN

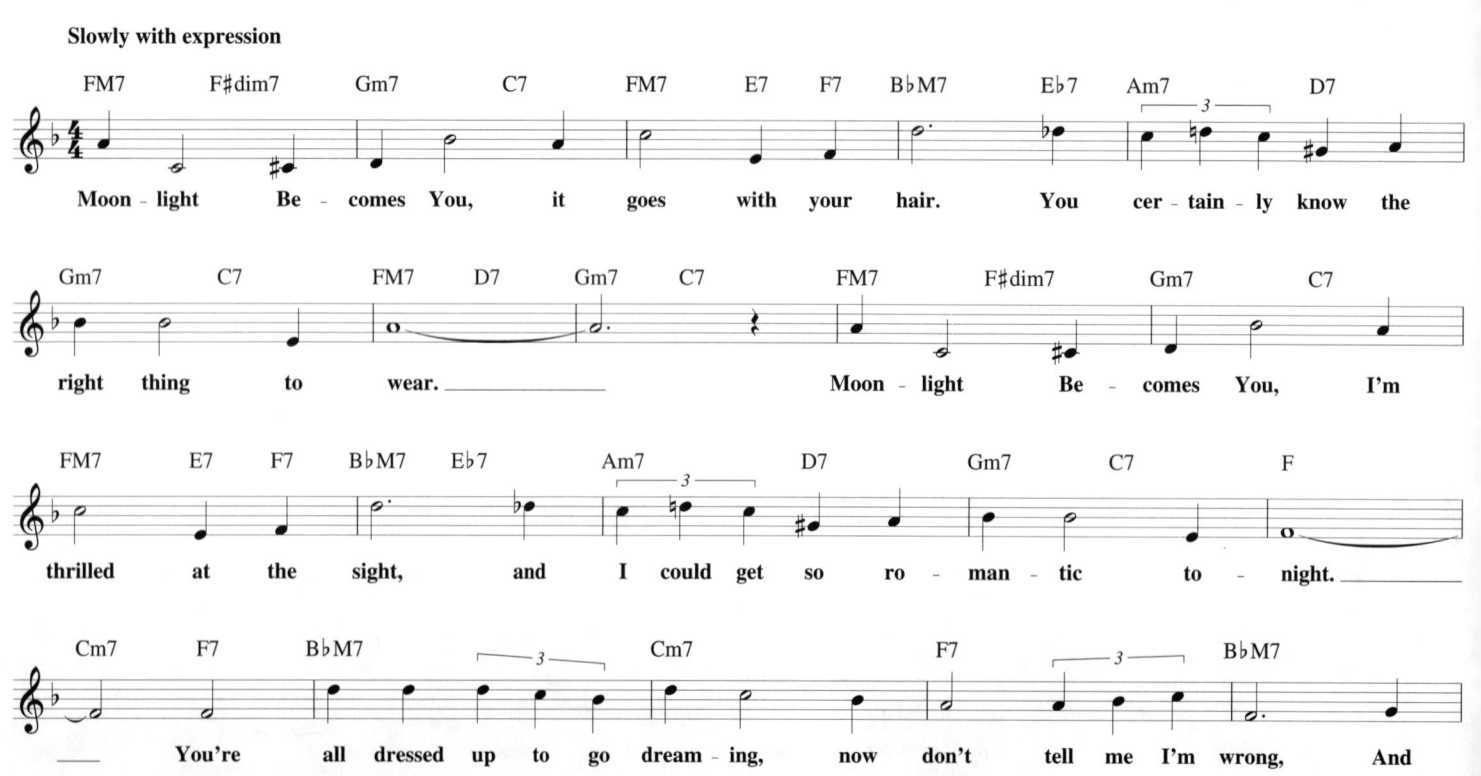

Copyright © 1942 (Renewed 1970) by Famous Music Corporation

Slowly with expression

Moon-light Be-comes You, it goes with your hair. You cer-tain-ly know the

right thing to wear. Moon-light Be-comes You, I'm

thrilled at the sight, and I could get so ro-man-tic to-night.

You're all dressed up to go dream-ing, now don't tell me I'm wrong, And

245

what a night to go dream-ing, mind if I tag a-long? If I say I love you, I want you to know it's not just be-cause there's moon-light, al - though Moon-light Be-comes You so.

(There Ought to Be A) MOONLIGHT SAVING TIME

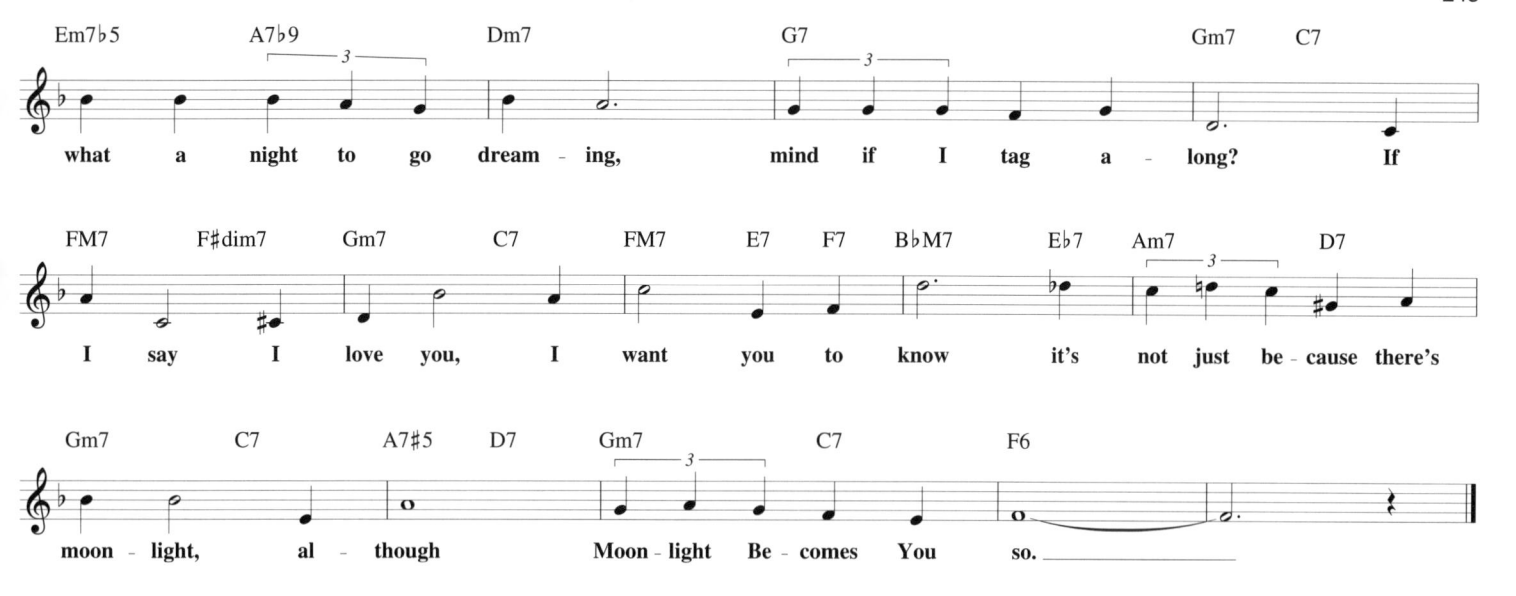

Copyright © 1931 (Renewed 1958) The New Irving Kahal Music Company and Fisher Music Co.
All rights administered by Fred Ahlert Music Corporation on behalf of The New Irving Kahal Music Company

Lyric and Music by IRVING KAHAL and HARRY RICHMAN

Moderately

There ought to be a Moon-light Sav-ing Time, So I could love that girl of mine, Un-til the bird-ies wake and chime, "Good morn-ing." There ought to be a law in clo-ver time, To keep that moon out o-ver time, To keep each lov-er's lane in rhyme till dawn-ing. You'd bet-ter hur-ry up, hur-ry up, hur-ry up, get bus-y to-day. You'd bet-ter croon a tune, croon a tune to the man up in the moon And here's what I'd say; There ought to be a Moon-light Sav-ing Time, So I could love that girl of mine, Un-til the bird-ies wake and chime, "Good morn-ing." There ing."

LULLABY OF BIRDLAND

Words by GEORGE DAVID WEISS
Music by GEORGE SHEARING

MORNING DANCE

By JAY BECKENSTEIN

MY BABY JUST CARES FOR ME

Lyrics by GUS KAHN
Music by WALTER DONALDSON

Medium Swing

My ba-by don't care for shows, my ba-by don't care for clothes,
My ba-by don't care for rings, or oth-er ex-pen-sive things,

My Ba-by Just Cares For Me! My ba-by don't care for

furs and la-ces, my ba-by don't care for high-toned pla-ces.

CODA

she's sen-si-ble as can be.

My ba-by don't care who knows it, My Ba-by Just Cares For Me!

MOST GENTLEMEN DON'T LIKE LOVE
from LEAVE IT TO ME!

Words and Music by
COLE PORTER

Copyright © 1938 by Chappell & Co.
Copyright Renewed, Assigned to John F. Wharton, Trustee of the Cole Porter Musical and Literary Property Trusts

Additional Lyrics

2. Most Gentlemen Don't Like Love,
They just like to kick it around,
Most Gentlemen Don't Like Love,
'Cause most gentlemen can't be profound.
So just remember when you get that glance,
A romp and a quickie
Is all little Dickie means
When he mentions romance,
For Most Gentlemen Don't Like Love,
They just like to kick it around.

3. Most Gentlemen Don't Like Love,
They just like to kick it around,
Most Gentlemen Don't Like Love,
'Cause most gentlemen can't be profound.
In ev'ry land, children, they're all the same,
A pounce in the clover
And then when it's over
"So long and what is your name?"
'Cause Most Gentlemen Don't Like Love,
They just like to kick it around.

4. Most Gentlemen Don't Like Love,
They just like to kick it around,
Most Gentlemen Don't Like Love,
'Cause most gentlemen can't be profound.
So if your boy friend, some fine night,
Should say he'll love you forever
And part from you never,
Just push him out of the hay, (way)
'Cause Most Gentlemen Don't Like Love,
They just like to kick it around.

MY HEART STOOD STILL

Words by LORENZ HART
Music by RICHARD RODGERS

Copyright © 1927 by Williamson Music and The Estate Of Lorenz Hart in the United States
Copyright Renewed
All Rights on behalf of The Estate Of Lorenz Hart Administered by WB Music Corp.

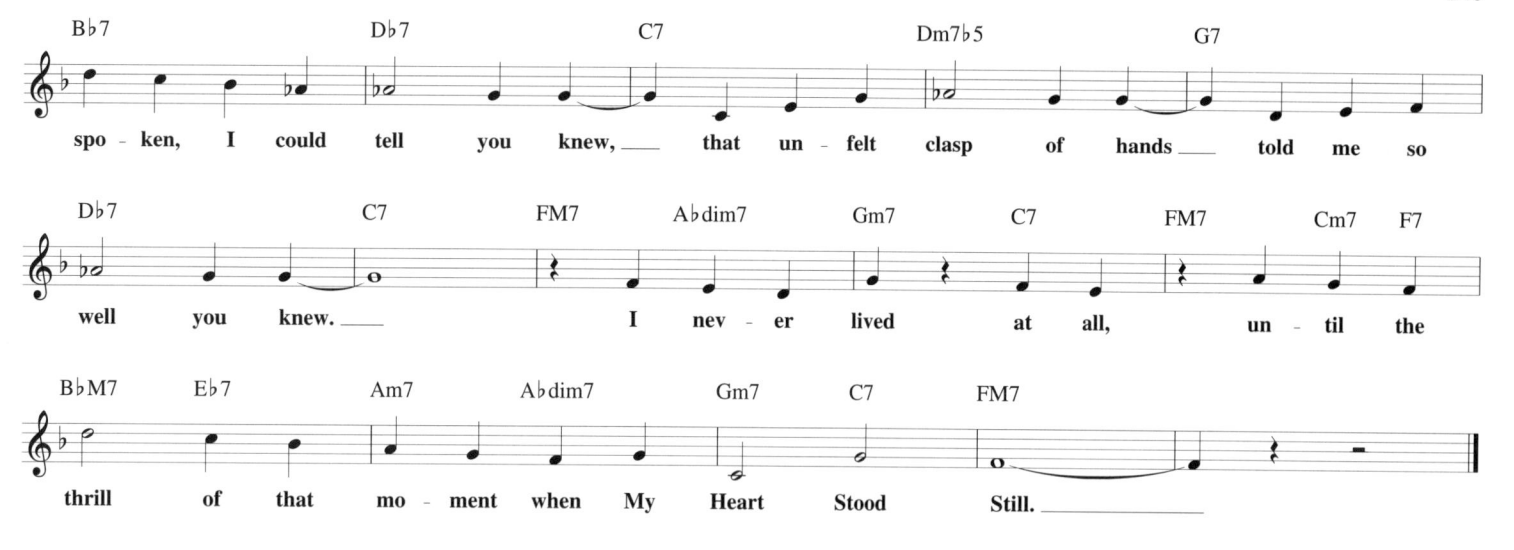

spo-ken, I could tell you knew, that un-felt clasp of hands told me so well you knew. I nev-er lived at all, un-til the thrill of that mo-ment when My Heart Stood Still.

MOUNTAIN GREENERY
from the Broadway Musical THE GARRICK GAIETIES

Copyright © 1926 by Williamson Music and The Estate Of Lorenz Hart in the United States
Copyright Renewed
All Rights on behalf of The Estate Of Lorenz Hart Administered by WB Music Corp.

Words by LORENZ HART
Music by RICHARD RODGERS

Moderately

In a Moun-tain Green-er-y, where God paints the scen-er-y, just two cra-zy peo-ple to-geth-er; ___

While you love your lov-er, let blue skies be your cov-er-let, when it rains, we'll laugh at the weath-er. And if you're good I'll search for wood, so you can cook while I stand look-ing.

How we love se-ques-ter-ing where no pests are pest-er-ing, no, dear, ma-ma holds us in teth-er! Mos-qui-tos here won't bite you, dear; I'll let them sting me on the fin-ger.

Beans could get no keen-er re-cep-tion in a bean-er-y,
We could find no clean-er re-treat from life's ma-chin-er-y,

bless our Moun-tain Green-er-y home!
than our Moun-tain Green-er-y home!

MY GIRL

Words and Music by WILLIAM "SMOKEY" ROBINSON and RONALD WHITE

I've got sun-shine on a cloud-y day; When it's cold out-side, I've got the month of May. I guess you say, what can make me feel this way? My Girl, talk-ing 'bout My Girl. I've got so much hon-ey, the bees en-vy me; I've got a sweet-er song than the birds in the tree. Well, I guess you say, what can make me feel this way? My Girl, talk-ing 'bout My Girl. I don't need no mon-ey, for-tune or fame. I've got all the rich-es, ba-by, one man can claim. Well, I guess you say, what can make me feel this way? My Girl, talk-ing 'bout My Girl. I've got sun-shine on a cloud-y day with My Girl; I've ev-en got the month of May with My Girl. Talk-ing 'bout, talk-ing 'bout, talk-ing 'bout My Girl. Woo! My Girl. That's all I can talk a-bout, is My Girl.

© 1964 (Renewed 1992), 1972, 1973, 1977 JOBETE MUSIC CO., INC.
All Rights Controlled and Administered by EMI APRIL MUSIC INC.

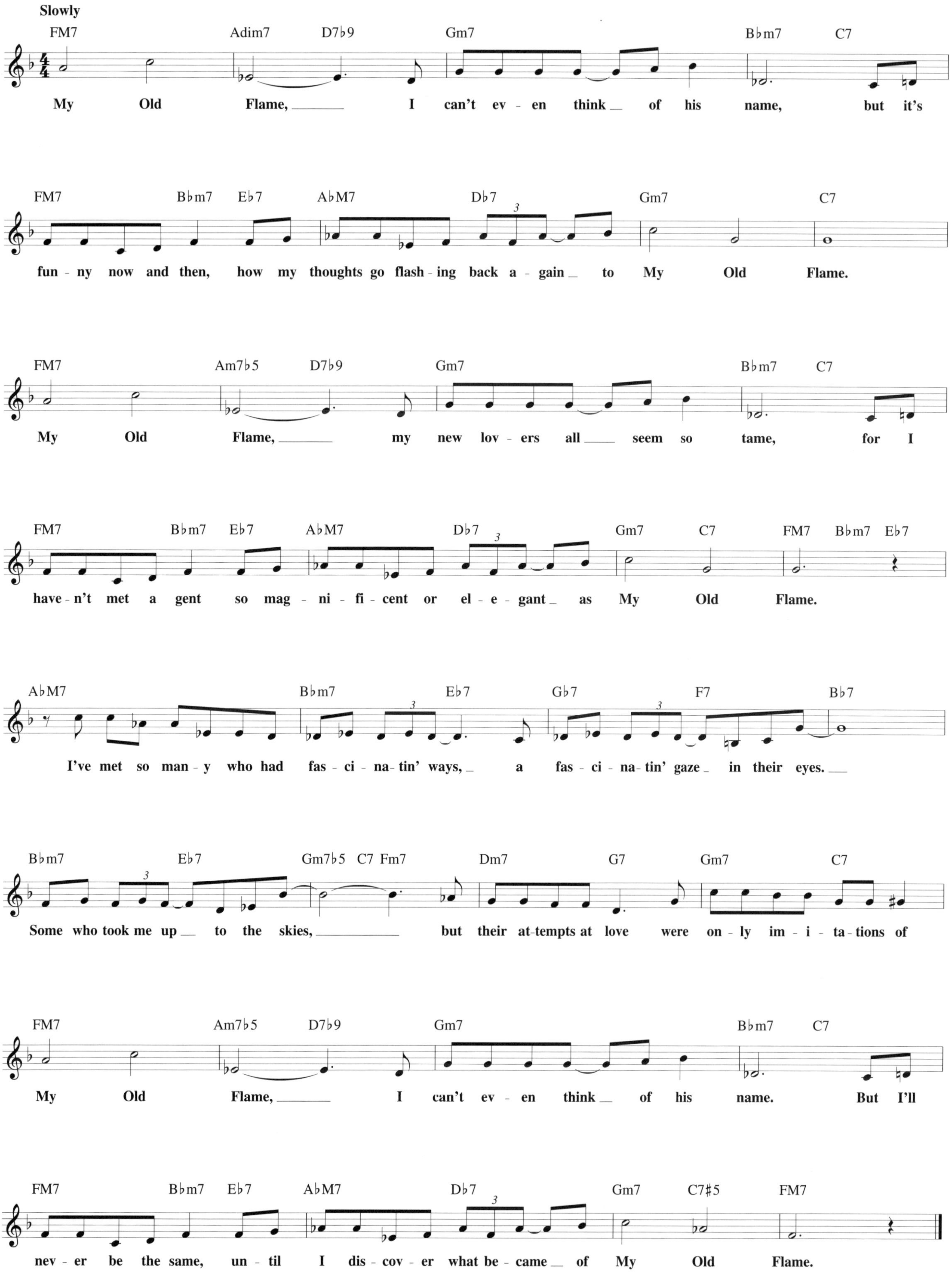

MY SILENT LOVE

Words by EDWARD HEYMAN
Music by DANA SUESSE

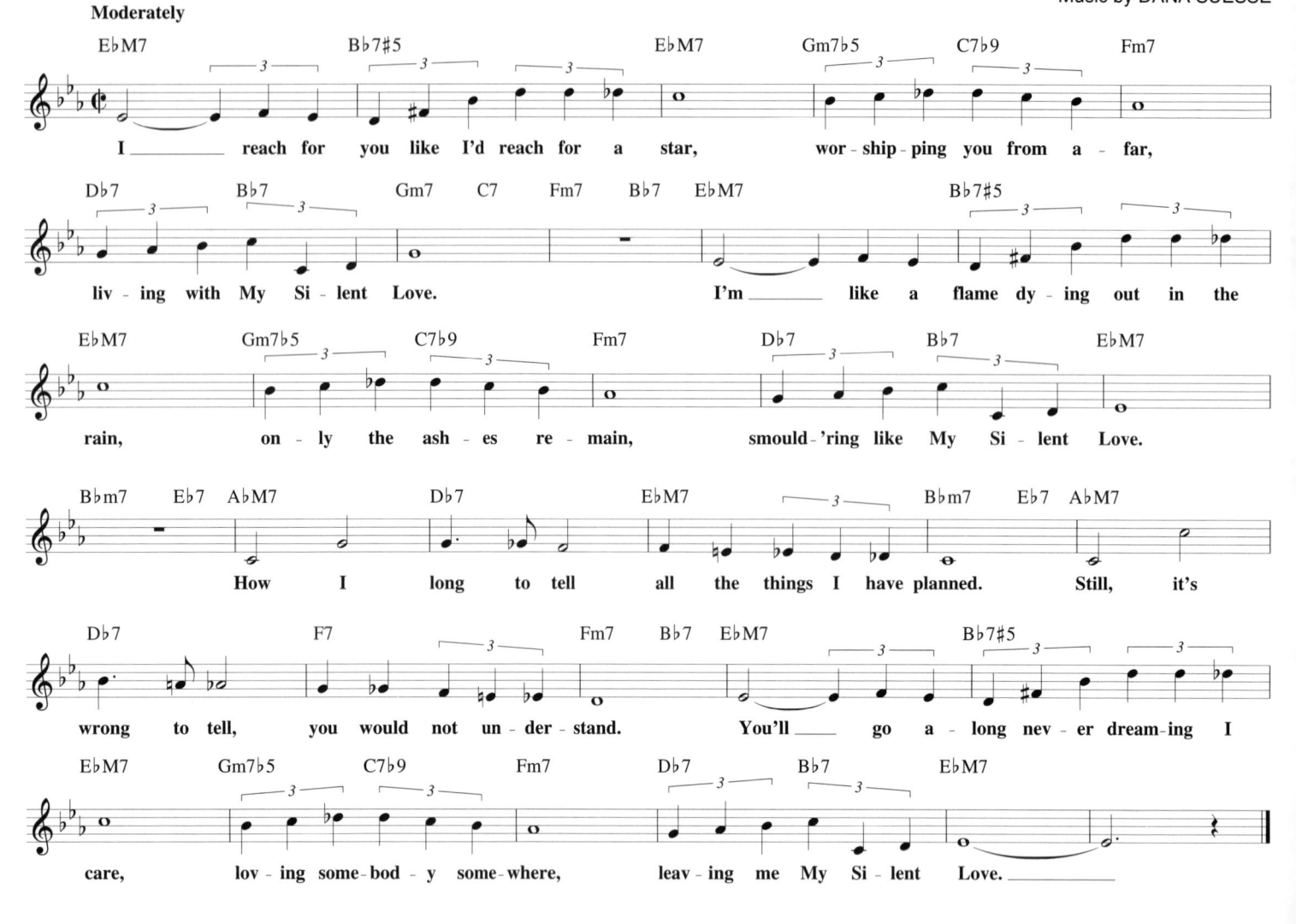

I _____ reach for you like I'd reach for a star, wor-ship-ping you from a-far, liv-ing with My Si-lent Love. I'm _____ like a flame dy-ing out in the rain, on-ly the ash-es re-main, smould-'ring like My Si-lent Love. How I long to tell all the things I have planned. Still, it's wrong to tell, you would not un-der-stand. You'll _____ go a-long nev-er dream-ing I care, lov-ing some-bod-y some-where, leav-ing me My Si-lent Love. _____

MY IDEAL

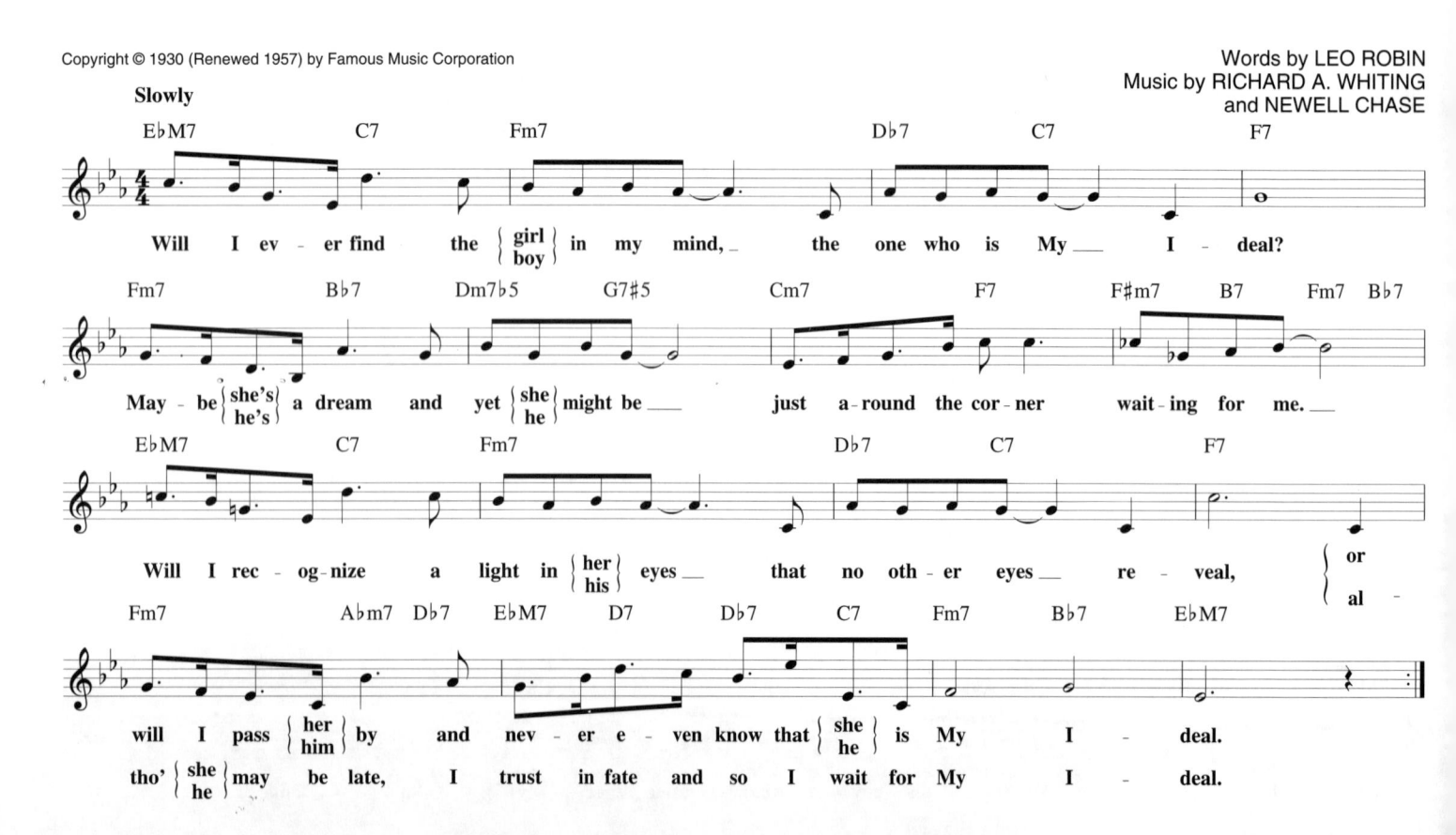

Words by LEO ROBIN
Music by RICHARD A. WHITING
and NEWELL CHASE

Will I ev-er find the {girl/boy} in my mind, _____ the one who is My _____ I-deal? May-be {she's/he's} a dream and yet {she/he} might be _____ just a-round the cor-ner wait-ing for me. Will I rec-og-nize a light in {her/his} eyes _____ that no oth-er eyes _____ re-veal, {or/al-} will I pass {her/him} by and nev-er e-ven know that {she/he} is My I-deal. tho' {she/he} may be late, I trust in fate and so I wait for My I-deal.

NAIMA
(Niema)

By JOHN COLTRANE

Copyright © 1973 JOWCOL MUSIC

NATURE BOY

Words and Music by EDEN AHBEZ

Copyright © 1948 by Eden Ahbez
Copyright Renewed 1975 by Golden World

There was a boy. A very strange, enchanted boy; They say he wandered very far, very far, over land and sea. A little shy and sad of eye, but very wise was he. And then one day, one magic day, he passed my way, and as we spoke of many things, fools and kings, this he said to me: "The greatest thing you'll ever learn is just to love and be loved in return. there just to love and be loved in return."

THE NEARNESS OF YOU
from the Paramount Picture ROMANCE IN THE DARK

Words by NED WASHINGTON
Music by HOAGY CARMICHAEL

Slowly

It's not the pale moon that ex-cites me, that thrills and de-lights me. Oh,
no, it's just The Near-ness Of You. It is-n't
your sweet con-ver-sa-tion that brings this sen-sa-tion. Oh,
no, it's just The Near-ness Of You. When you're in my
arms and I feel you so close to me all my
wild-est dreams come true. I need no
soft lights to en-chant me if you'll on-ly grant me the
right to hold you ev-er so tight and to feel in the
night The Near-ness Of You.

NEARLY

Written by RON CARTER

NEVER LET ME GO

from the Paramount Picture THE SCARLET HOUR

Words and Music by JAY LIVINGSTON and RAY EVANS

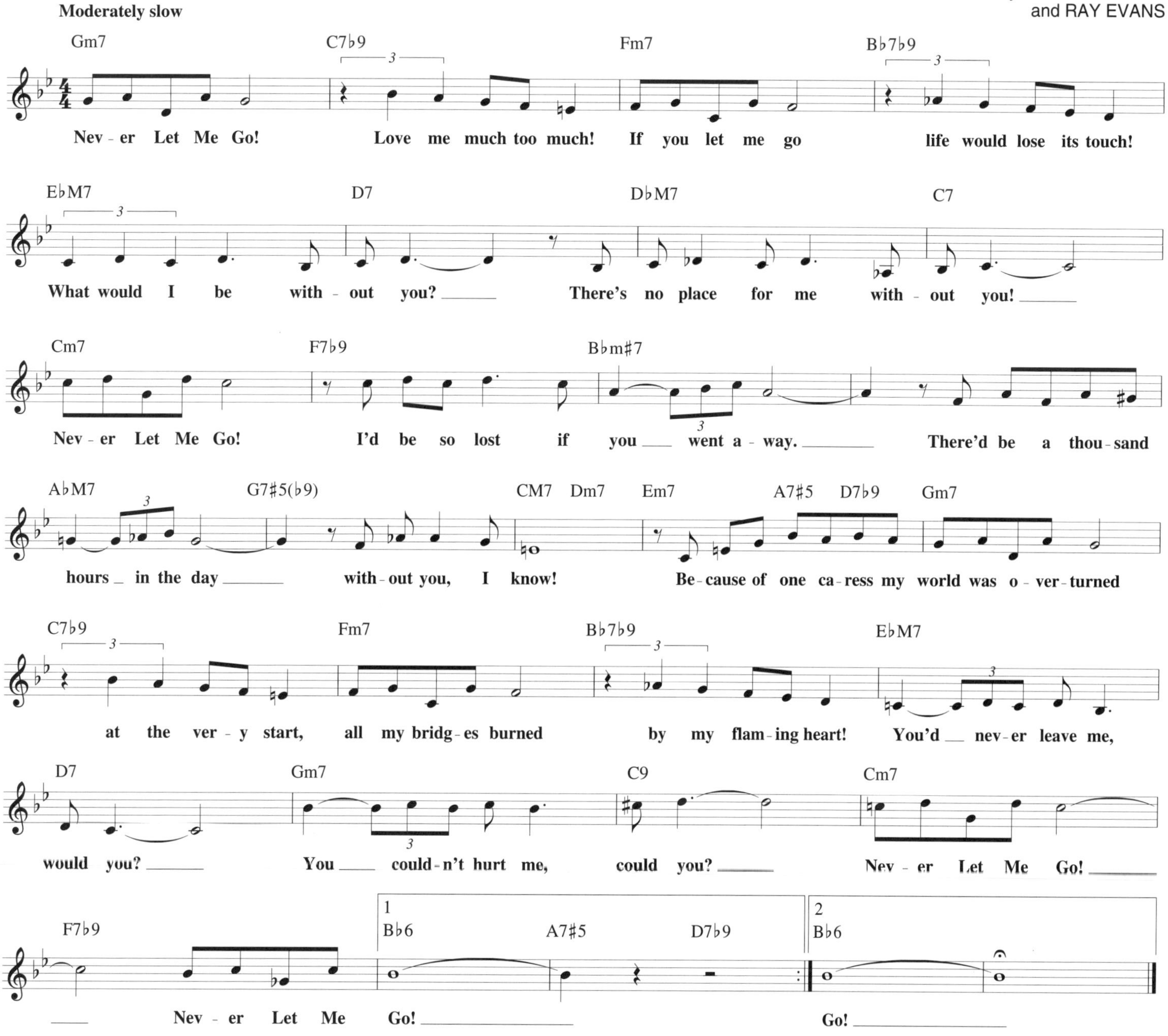

NEW ORLEANS BLUES

By FERDINAND "JELLY ROLL" MORTON

© 1925 (Renewed) EDWIN H. MORRIS & COMPANY, A Division of MPL Communications, Inc.

YOU GOTTA PAY THE BAND

Copyright © 1990 Moseka Music
All Rights Administered by Embassy Music Corp.

Words and Music by
ABBEY LINCOLN

Medium Swing, half-time feel

Oh, it really isn't easy just to let the good times roll. Ev'rything is measured at a cost. Ev'rybody living pays their share of dues, and sometimes what you think you got you lost. So, ring a ding ding do your thing, but remember darling, when you give a dance You Gotta Pay The Band, the band that played your song the whole night through. When you give a dance it's better if you plan to pay the piper what the piper's due.

{The moves were free and easy as we danced across the floor. The turns and the exchanges being what the music's for. But, when the ball is over and the revelry is done, You Gotta Pay The Band that played your song.

{The music brought the magic and we found each other's arms. We danced until the morning, and we knew each other's charms. But, when the party's over and the people are all gone, You Gotta Pay The Band that played your song.

You Gotta Pay The Band that played your song.

THE NEXT TIME IT HAPPENS
from PIPE DREAM

Lyrics by OSCAR HAMMERSTEIN II
Music by RICHARD RODGERS

Copyright © 1955 by Richard Rodgers and Oscar Hammerstein II
Copyright Renewed
WILLIAMSON MUSIC owner of publication and allied rights throughout the world

Brightly

The Next Time It Hap-pens _____ I'll be wise e-nough to know _____ not to trust my eye-sight when my eyes be-gin to glow. _____ The next time I'm in love _____ with an-y-one like you, _____ my heart will sing no love song till I know the words are true. "The Next Time It Hap-pens," _____ what a fool-ish thing to say! _____ Who ex-pects a mi-ra-cle to hap-pen ev-'ry day? _____ It is-n't in the cards _____ as far as I can see _____ that a thing so beau-ti-ful and won-der-ful could hap-pen more than once _____ to me.

me. _____

NIGHT TRAIN

Words by OSCAR WASHINGTON
and LEWIS C. SIMPKINS
Music by JIMMY FORREST

NICE PANTS

By BENNY GREEN

Copyright © 1994 Benny Green Music (BMI)

Moderately slow Blues

THE NIGHT HAS A THOUSAND EYES
Theme from the Paramount Picture THE NIGHT HAS A THOUSAND EYES

Words by BUDDY BERNIER
Music by JERRY BRAININ

Copyright © 1948 (Renewed 1975) by Paramount Music Corporation

Moderately

Don't whis-per things to me you don't mean, for my
ro-mance may have called in the past my

words deep down in-side can be seen by the night. The Night
love for you will be ev-er-last-ing and bright. As bright

NOBODY KNOWS YOU WHEN YOU'RE DOWN AND OUT

© Copyright 1923, 1929, 1950, 1959, 1963 by MCA MUSIC PUBLISHING,
A Division of UNIVERSAL STUDIOS, INC.
Copyright Renewed

Words and Music by
JIMMIE COX

NOBODY'S HEART
from BY JUPITER

Words by LORENZ HART
Music by RICHARD RODGERS

NORWEGIAN WOOD
(This Bird Has Flown)

Words and Music by JOHN LENNON
and PAUL McCARTNEY

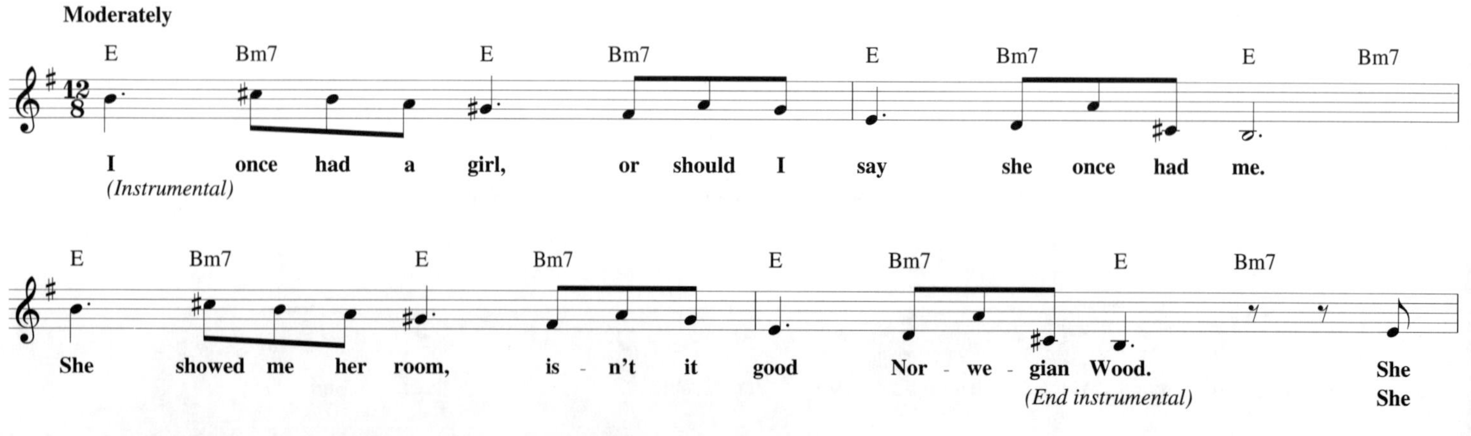

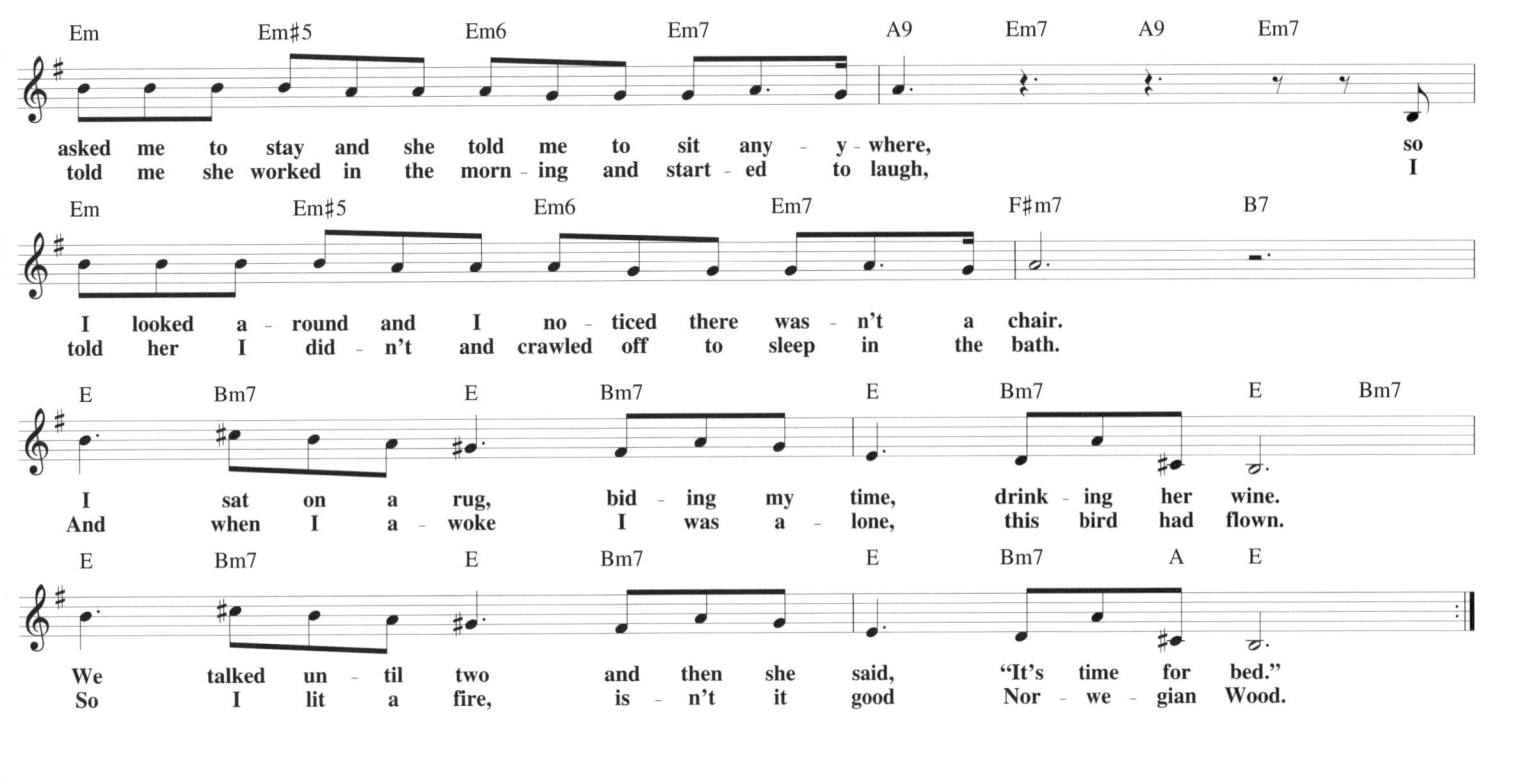

asked me to stay and she told me to sit any-y-where, so I
told me she worked in the morn-ing and start-ed to laugh, I

I looked a-round and I no-ticed there was-n't a chair.
told her I did-n't and crawled off to sleep in the bath.

I sat on a rug, bid-ing my time, drink-ing her wine.
And when I a-woke I was a-lone, this bird had flown.

We talked un-til two and then she said, "It's time for bed."
So I lit a fire, is-n't it good Nor-we-gian Wood.

NOW IT CAN BE TOLD
from ALEXANDER'S RAGTIME BAND

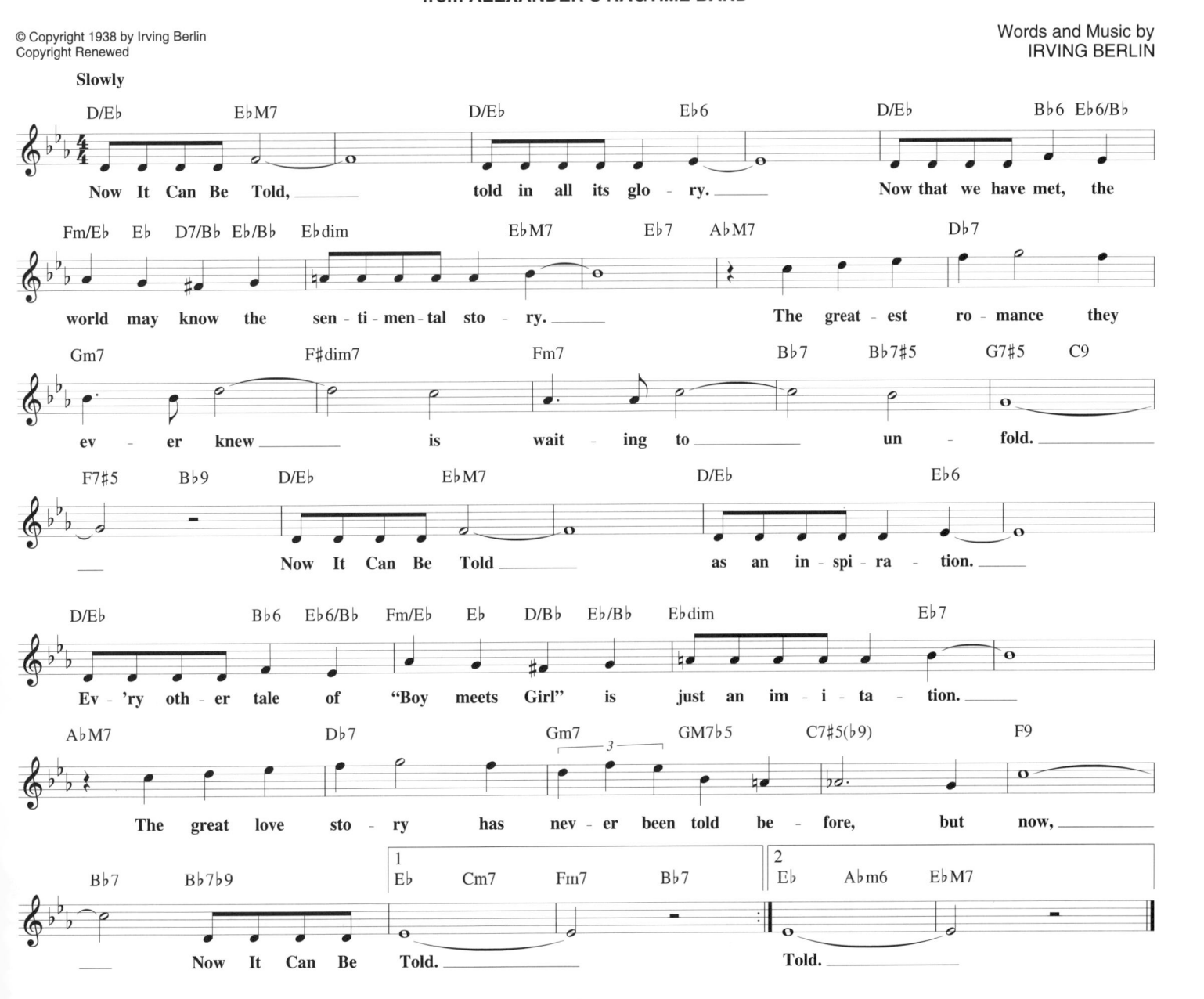

© Copyright 1938 by Irving Berlin
Copyright Renewed

Words and Music by
IRVING BERLIN

Slowly

Now It Can Be Told, told in all its glo-ry. Now that we have met, the
world may know the sen-ti-men-tal sto-ry. The great-est ro-mance they
ev-er knew is wait-ing to un-fold.
Now It Can Be Told as an in-spi-ra-tion.
Ev-'ry oth-er tale of "Boy meets Girl" is just an im-i-ta-tion.
The great love sto-ry has nev-er been told be-fore, but now,

1. Now It Can Be Told.
2. Told.

NUAGES

By DJANGO REINHARDT and JACQUES LARUE

© 1980 PETER MAURICE MUSIC LTD.
All Rights for the U.S. and Canada Controlled and Administered by
by COLGEMS-EMI MUSIC INC.

O MORRO NÃO TEM VEZ
(Favela)
(Somewhere in the Hills)

Words and Music by ANTONIO CARLOS JOBIM and VINICIUS DE MORAES

Copyright © 1963 Corcovado Music Corp. and VM Enterprises, Inc.
Copyright Renewed

O Morro Não Tem Vez E o que e le fez já foi de mais
um é dois, é três É cem, é mil a ba tu car

Mas o lhem bem vo cês Quan do de rem vez ao mor ro To da a
O Mor ro Não Tem Vez Mas se de rem vez ao mor ro To da a

cida-de vai can tar Mor ro pe de pas-sa-gem Mor ro quer se mo-strar
cida-de vai can tar

A bram a las pro mor ro Tam bo rim vai fa lar É

OFF MINOR

By THELONIOUS MONK

ON BROADWAY

Words and Music by BARRY MANN, CYNTHIA WEIL,
MIKE STOLLER and JERRY LEIBER

ONCE I LOVED
(Amor Em Paz)
(Love in Peace)

Music by ANTONIO CARLOS JOBIM
Portuguese Lyrics by VINICIUS DE MORAES
English Lyrics by RAY GILBERT

ONE FINGER SNAP

By HERBIE HANCOCK

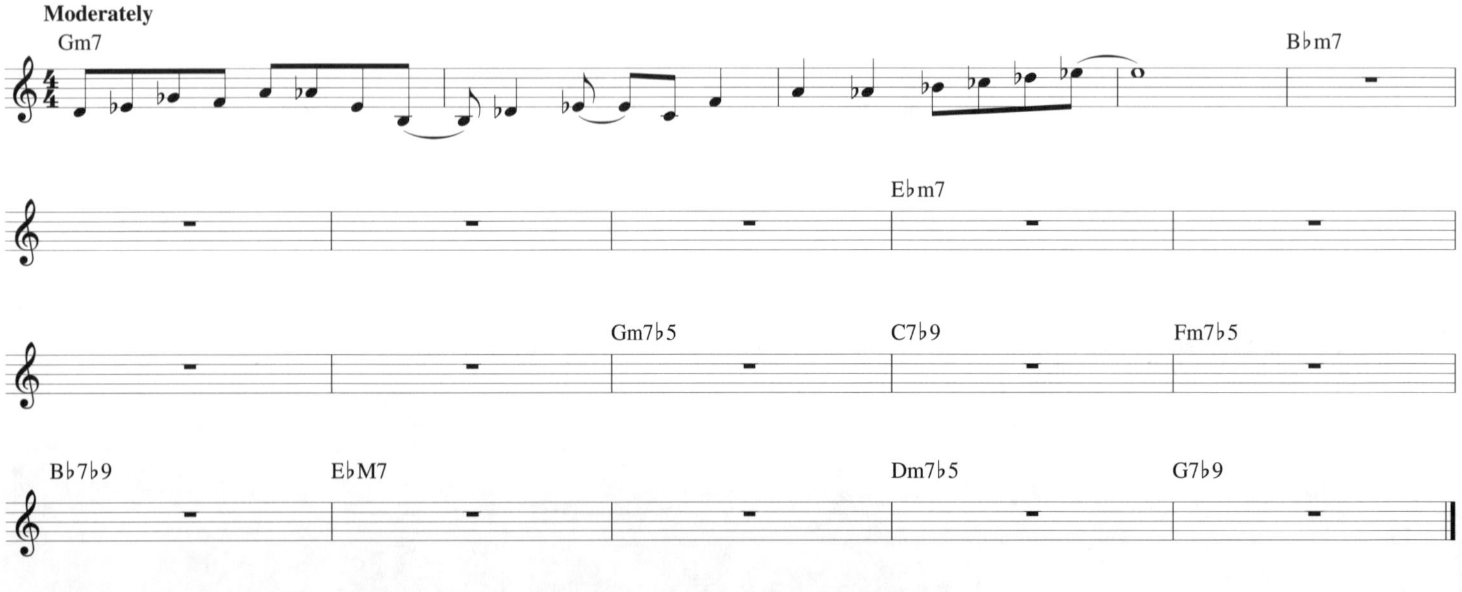

ONE FOR MY BABY
(And One More for the Road)
from the Motion Picture THE SKY'S THE LIMIT

Lyric by JOHNNY MERCER
Music by HAROLD ARLEN

© 1943 (Renewed) HARWIN MUSIC CO.

It's quarter to three, there's no one in the place except you and me. So set 'em up, Joe, I've got a little story you oughta know. We're drinking, my friend, to the end of a brief episode, make it One For My Baby and one more for the road. I got the routine, so drop another nickel in the machine. I'm feelin' so bad, I wish you'd make the music dreamy and sad. Could tell you a lot, but you've got to be true to your code, make it One For My Baby and one more for the road. You'd never know it, but buddy, I'm a kind of poet and I've gotta lotta things to say. And when I'm gloomy you simply gotta listen to me until it's talked away. Well, that's how it goes and Joe, I know you're getting anxious to close. So, thanks for the cheer, I hope you didn't mind my bending your ear. This torch that I've found must be drowned or it soon might explode, make it One For My Baby and one more for the road.

ON GREEN DOLPHIN STREET

Lyrics by NED WASHINGTON
Music by BRONISLAU KAPER

© 1947 (Renewed 1975) METRO-GOLDWYN-MAYER, INC.
All Rights Controlled by EMI FEIST CATALOG INC. (Publishing) and
WARNER BROS. PUBLICATIONS U.S. INC. (Print)

Moderate Latin

Lov - er, one love - ly day. Love came, plan - ning to stay. Green Dol - phin Street sup - plied the set - ting, the set - ting for nights be - yond for - get - ting. And through these mo - ments a - part, mem - 'ries live in my heart. When I re - call the love I found on, I could kiss the ground On Green Dol - phin Street. Street.

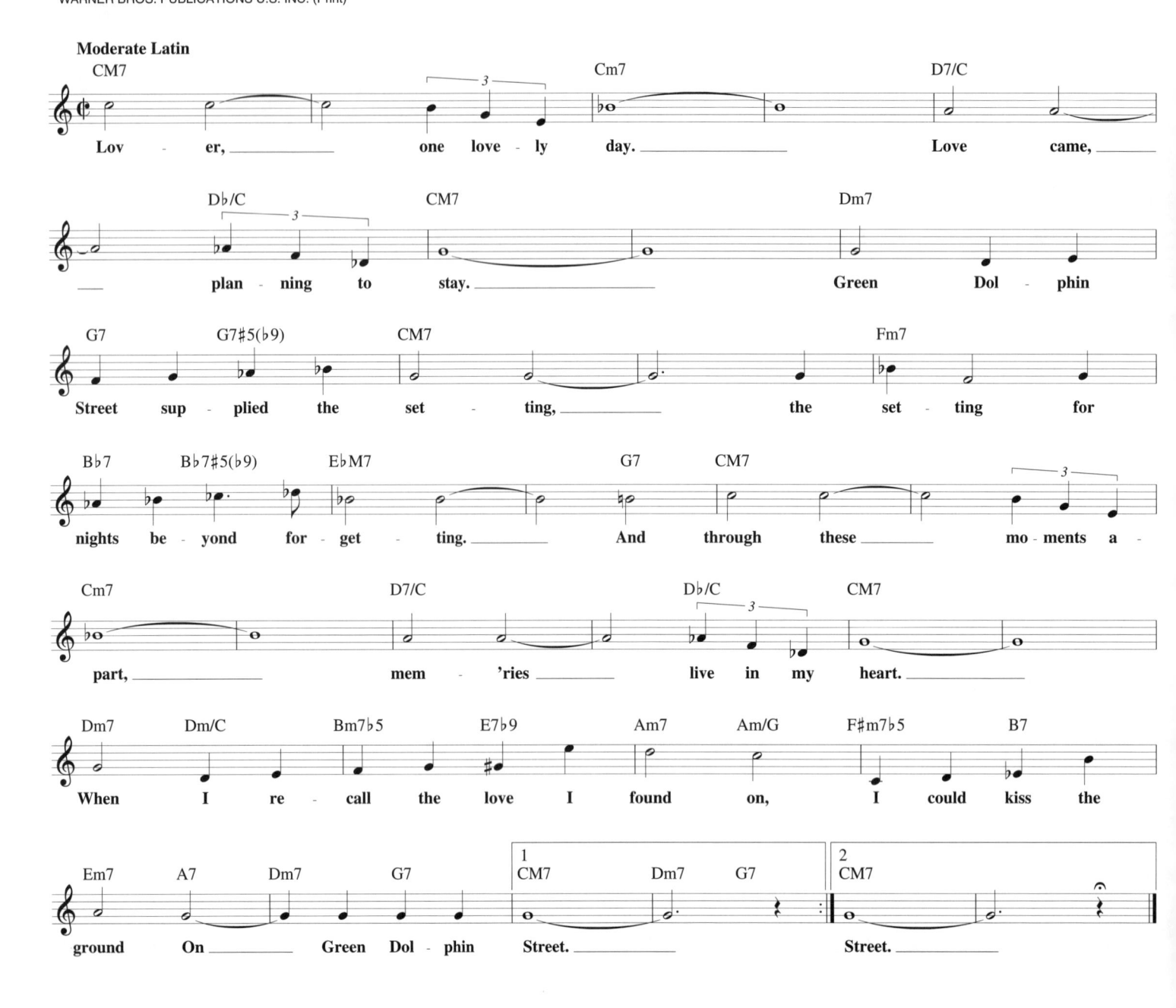

ON THE BORDER

By ERNIE WATTS

© 1988 URBAN RENEWAL MUSIC/Administered by BUG

Moderate Latin

THE ONE I LOVE
(Belongs to Somebody Else)

Words by GUS KAHN
Music by ISHAM JONES

Copyright © 1924 by GILBERT KEYES MUSIC and BANTAM MUSIC
Copyright Renewed
All Rights Administered by THE SONGWRITERS GUILD OF AMERICA

The One I Love belongs to somebody else, she means her tender songs for somebody else. And even when I have my arms around her, I know her thoughts are strong for somebody else. The hands I hold belong to somebody else, I'll bet they're not so cold to somebody else. It's tough to be alone on the shelf, it's worse to fall in love by yourself, The One I Love belongs to somebody else.

ORIGINAL RAYS

By MICHAEL BRECKER, DON GROLNICK and MICHAEL STERN

Copyright © 1987 Grand Street Music (BMI), Carmine Street Music (BMI) and Little Shoes Music (ASCAP)

PASSION DANCE

By McCOY TYNER

Copyright © 1974 Aisha Music Company

OUT OF NOWHERE
from the Paramount Picture DUDE RANCH

Words by EDWARD HEYMAN
Music by JOHNNY GREEN

Copyright © 1931 (Renewed 1958) by Famous Music Corporation

Lyrics:
You came to me from Out Of No-where, you took my heart and found it free. Won-der-ful dreams, won-der-ful schemes from no-where made ev-'ry hour sweet as a flow-er for me. If you should go back to your no-where, leav-ing me with a mem-o-ry, I'll al-ways wait for your re-turn Out Of No-where; hop-ing you'll bring your love to me.

PARKING LOT BLUES

By RAY BROWN

Copyright © 1975 Probe Music

PASSION FLOWER

Words by MILTON RASKIN
Music by BILLY STRAYHORN

PEACE

Words and Music by
HORACE SILVER

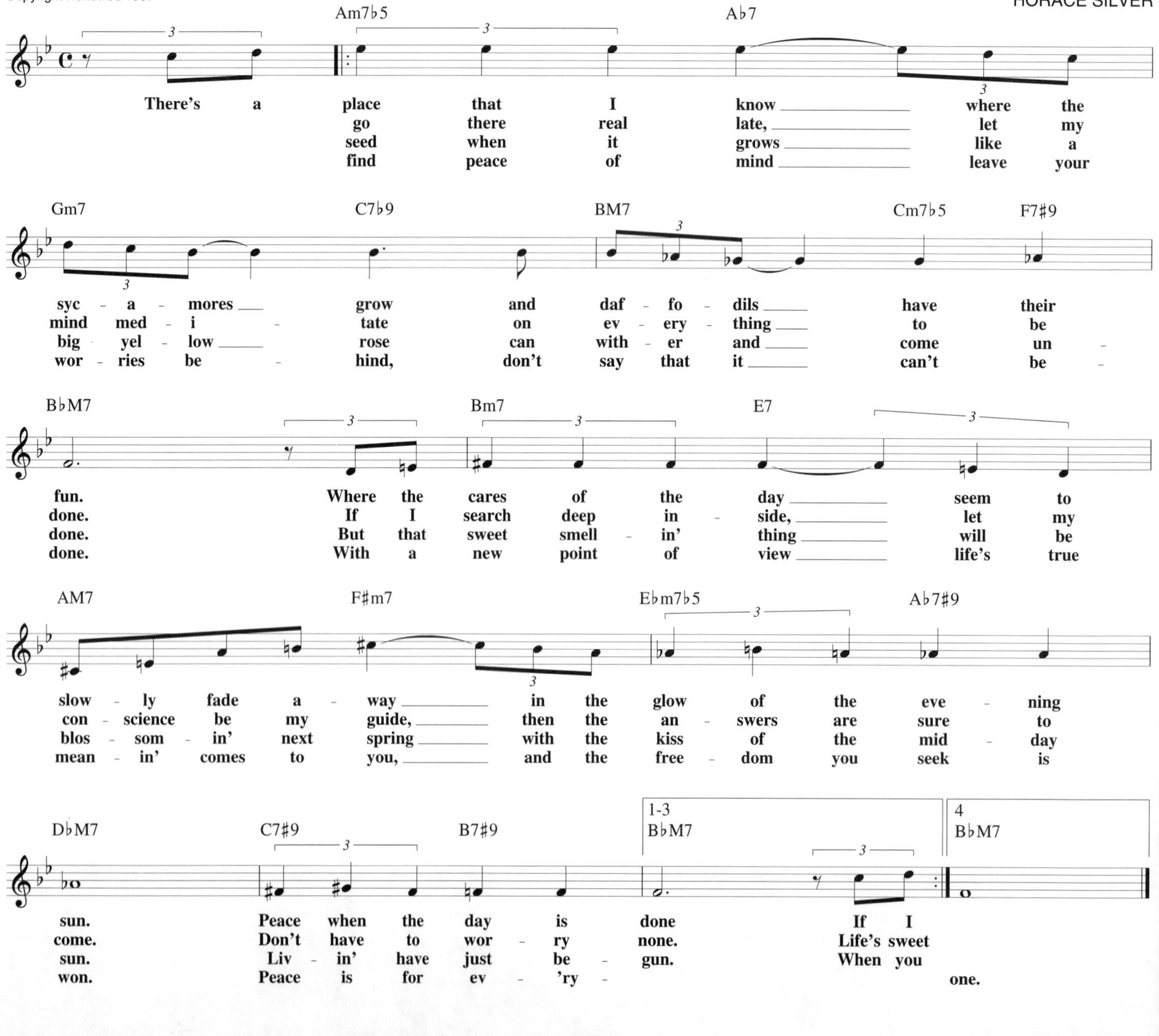

Penthouse Serenade

273

Copyright © 1931 by Famous Music Corporation
Copyright Renewed; extended term of Copyright deriving from Val Burton and Will Jason
assigned and effective July 13, 1987 to Range Road Music Inc. and Quartet Music Inc.
All Rights Administered in the U.S. by Range Road Music Inc.

Words and Music by WILL JASON
and VAL BURTON

Moderately

Pic-ture a pent-house way up in the sky, with hing-es on chim-neys for stars to go by, a sweet slice of heav-en for just you and I when we're a-lone. From all of so-ci-e-ty we'll stay a-loof, and live in pro-pri-e-ty there on the roof, two heav-en-ly her-mits we will be in truth when we're a-lone. We'll see life's mad pat-tern as we view old Man-hat-tan, then we can thank our luck-y stars that we're liv-ing as we are. In our lit-tle pent-house, we'll al-ways con-trive to keep love and ro-mance for-ev-er a-live, in view of the Hud-son just o-ver the Drive, when we're a-lone. Just lone.

PEOPLE IN ME

Words and Music by
ABBEY LINCOLN

Copyright © 1973 Moseka Music
All Rights Administered by Embassy Music Corp.

Some say the world is cold and that it's hard to find a friend, but ev-'ry time we're down and out some-bod-y takes us in. Some-times some-bod-y's wick-ed, and some-times some-bod-y's true, but there will al-ways be some-bod-y stick-in' with you and me. Be-cause the peo-ple we know are the peo-ple who say

1. I got some In-dian in me, I got some I-rish in me, I got some Ha-wai-ian blood, I got some Peo-ple In Me. I got some Peo-ple In Me. I got some Peo-ple In Me. I got the whole of Af-ri-can-us turn-in' in me. I've got some turn-in' in me.

2. - 7. *(See additional lyrics)*

Additional Lyrics

2. I got some Chinese in me,
   Some German in me,
   I got some Japanese blood,
   And blood from Vietnamese,

   I got Some People In Me,
   I Got Some People In Me,
   I got the whole of Asianus
   Turning in me,

3. I got some Jewish in me,
   Some Arab in me,
   I am Mexican rose,
   I got some Russian in me,

   I Got Some People In Me,
   I Got some people in me,
   I got the whole of Europaeus
   Turning in me,

4. I got some lessons in me,
   I got some learning in me,
   I got whatever people know right now,
   Inside of me,

   I got some children in me,
   I got some children in me,
   I got the whole of Americanus
   Turning in me,

5. I got some Guinee in me,
   Some Ghana in me,
   Some Zairewah blood,
   I Got Some People In Me,

   Dahomey in me,
   Uganda in me,
   Some Algerian blood,
   I Got Some People In Me,

6. I got some French blood in me,
   Sierra Leone in me,
   Mozambique in me,
   Some Egyptian blood,
   I Got Some People In Me,

7. I Got Some People In Me,
   I Got Some People In Me,
   I got the whole wide world...
   (he hit me - she hit me - he hit me -
   you started it - take your hands off of me -
   you must be crazy - na na na na na na)
   ...Turning in me.

PERFIDIA

Words and Music by
ALBERTO DOMINGUEZ

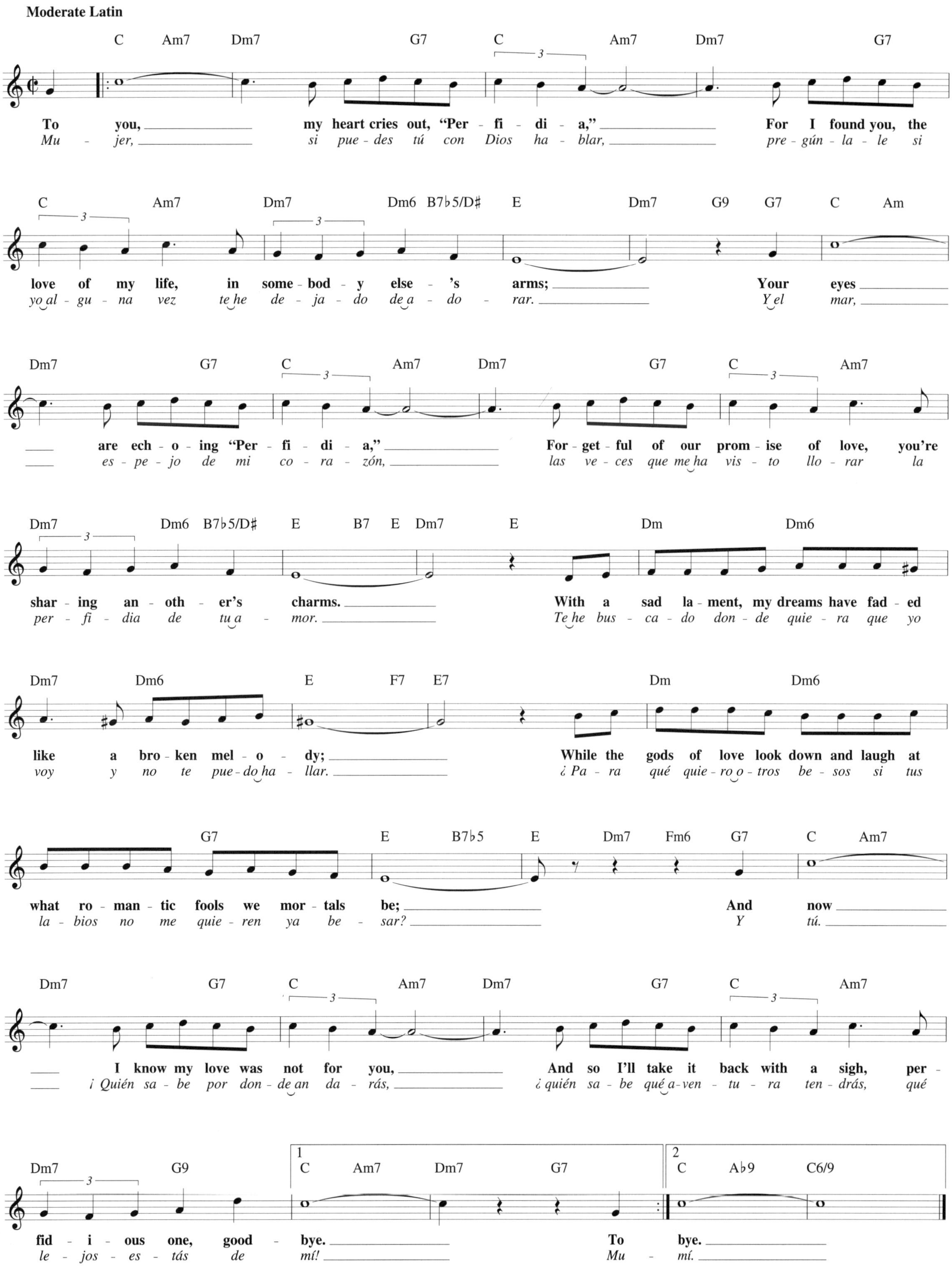

PERI'S SCOPE

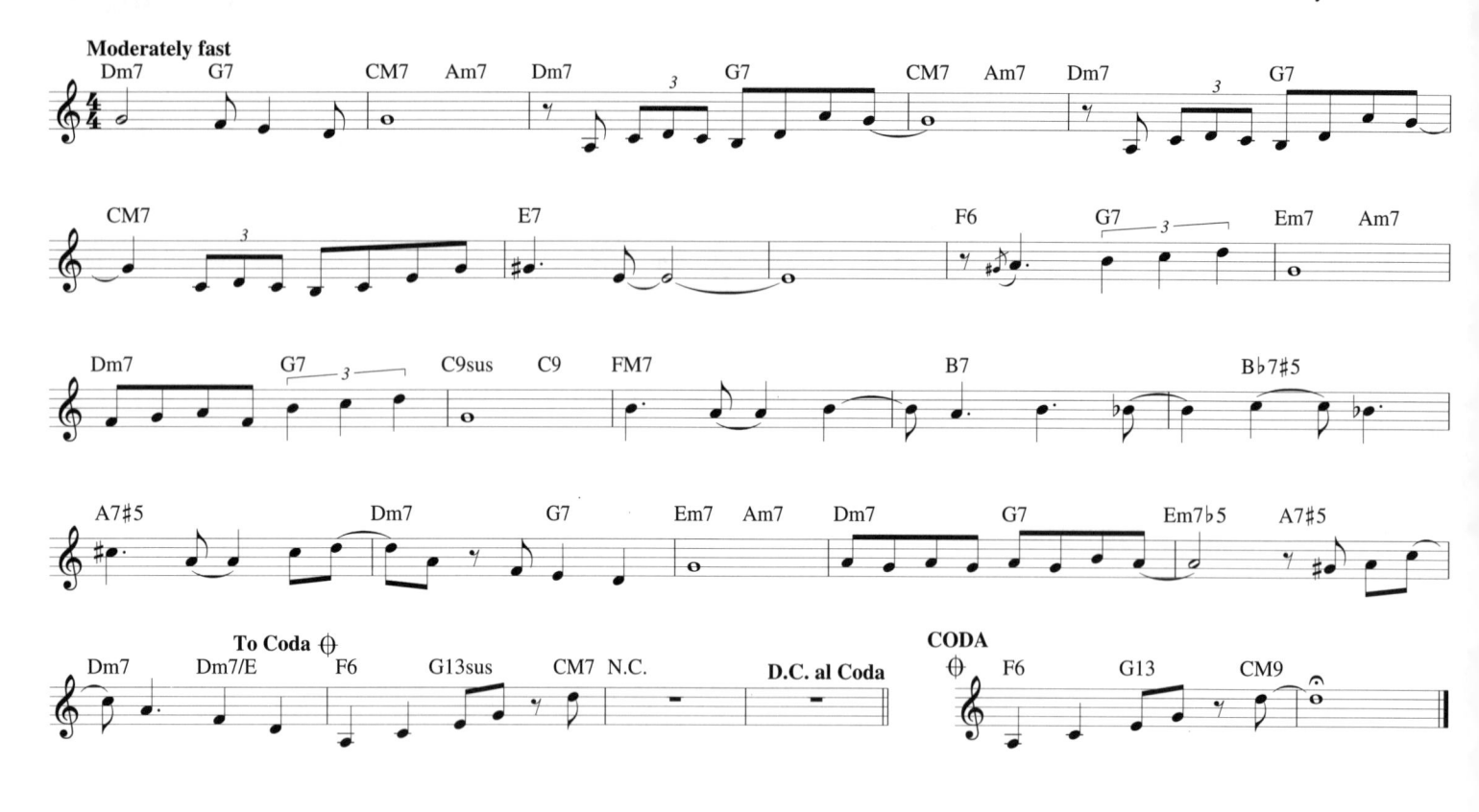

PHOEBE'S SAMBA

THE PLACE TO BE

By BENNY GREEN

PLEASE
from the Paramount Picture THE BIG BROADCAST OF 1933

Words by LEO ROBIN
Music by RALPH RAINGER

Moderately slow

Please lend your lit-tle ear to my pleas. Lend a ray of cheer to my pleas. Tell me that you love me too. Please let me hold you tight in my arms, I could find de-light in your charms ev-'ry night my whole life through. Your eyes re-veal that you have the soul of { an an-gel, white as snow; / the nic-est man I've met; } but how long must I play the role of { a gloom-y Ro-me-o? / a tear-ful Ju-li-et? } Oh! Please say you're not in-tend-ing to tease, speed the hap-py end-ing and Please tell me that you love me too. too.

PLEASE SEND ME SOMEONE TO LOVE

Words and Music by
PERCY MAYFIELD

POTATO HEAD BLUES

By LOUIS ARMSTRONG

© Copyright 1927, 1947 by MCA MUSIC PUBLISHING,
A Division of UNIVERSAL STUDIOS, INC.
Copyright Renewed

PURE IMAGINATION
from the film WILLY WONKA AND THE CHOCOLATE FACTORY

281

Copyright © 1970, 1971 Taradam Music, Inc.

Words and Music by LESLIE BRICUSSE
and ANTHONY NEWLEY

Moderately slow

Come with me and you'll be in a world of Pure I- mag- i- na- tion! Take a look and you'll see in- to your i- mag- i- na- tion!
find in your mind there's a world of end- less fas- ci- na- tion. No more fun place to be than in your i- mag- i- na- tion!

We'll be- gin with a spin trav- 'ling in the world of my cre- a- tion! What we'll see will de- fy ex- pla- na- tion!
You can dream an- y dream, you can sa- vour ev- 'ry sit- u- a- tion! Life in there's a sen- sa- tion- al sen- sa- tion!

If you want to view par- a- dise, sim- ply look a- round and view it! An- y- thing you want to, do it! Want to change the world? There's noth- ing to it!
If you want to see mag- ic lands, close your eyes and you will see one! Wan- na be a dream- er? Be one! An- y- time you please and please save me one!

There is no life I know to com- pare with Pure I- mag- i- na- tion! Liv- ing there, you'll be free if you tru- ly wish to be!
There is no place to go to com- pare with your i- mag- i- na- tion! So go there to be free if you tru- ly

You will wish to be!

POOR BUTTERFLY

Words by JOHN L. GOLDEN
Music by RAYMOND HUBBELL

Poor But - ter - fly, 'neath the blos - soms wait - ing, Poor But - ter - fly _____ for she loved him so. _____ The mo - ments pass in - to hours, _____ the hours _____ pass in - to years, _____ and as she smiles through her tears, _____ she mur - murs low, _____ "The moon and I _____ know that he be faith - ful. _____ I'm sure he come _____ to me bye and bye. _____ But if he don't come back, _____ then I nev - er sigh or ____ cry, _____ I just mus' die." _____ Poor __ But - ter - fly.

PRELUDE TO A KISS

Words by IRVING GORDON and IRVING MILLS
Music by DUKE ELLINGTON

If you hear a song in blue _____ like a flow - er cry - ing for the dew, _____ that was my heart ser - e - nad - ing you, _____ my Pre - lude To _____ A Kiss. _____ If you hear a song the grows _____ from my ten - der sen - ti - men - tal woes, _____ *that was my heart try-ing to com-pose a Pre-lude To A Kiss.*

Though it's just a sim-ple mel-o-dy with noth-ing fan-cy, noth-ing much,

you could turn it to a sym-phon-y, a Schu-bert tune with a Gersh-win touch. Oh,

how my love song gen-tly cries for the ten-der-ness with-in your eyes, my

love is a pre-lude that nev-er dies, a Pre-lude To A Kiss.

PURPLE ORCHIDS

Copyright © 1991 DI MEOLA MUSIC CO.

By AL DI MEOLA

Moderately slow

PRETEND

Copyright © 1952, 1953 (Renewed) by Music Sales Corporation (ASCAP)

Words and Music by LEW DOUGLAS, CLIFF PARMAN and FRANK LaVERE

Moderately slow

Pre-tend you're hap-py when you're blue. It is-n't ver-y hard to do, and you'll find hap-pi-ness with-out an end, when-ev-er you Pre-tend. Re-mem-ber, an-y-one can dream, and noth-ing's bad as it may seem. The lit-tle things you have-n't got, could be a lot, if you'd Pre-tend. You'll find a love you can share, one you can call all your own. Just close your eyes, {she'll / he'll} be there. You'll nev-er be a-lone, And if you sing this mel-o-dy, you'll be pre-tend-ing, just like me. The world is mine, it can be yours, my friend, so why don't you Pre-tend. Pre-tend you're hap-py when you're tend.

P.S. I LOVE YOU

Words by JOHNNY MERCER
Music by GORDON JENKINS

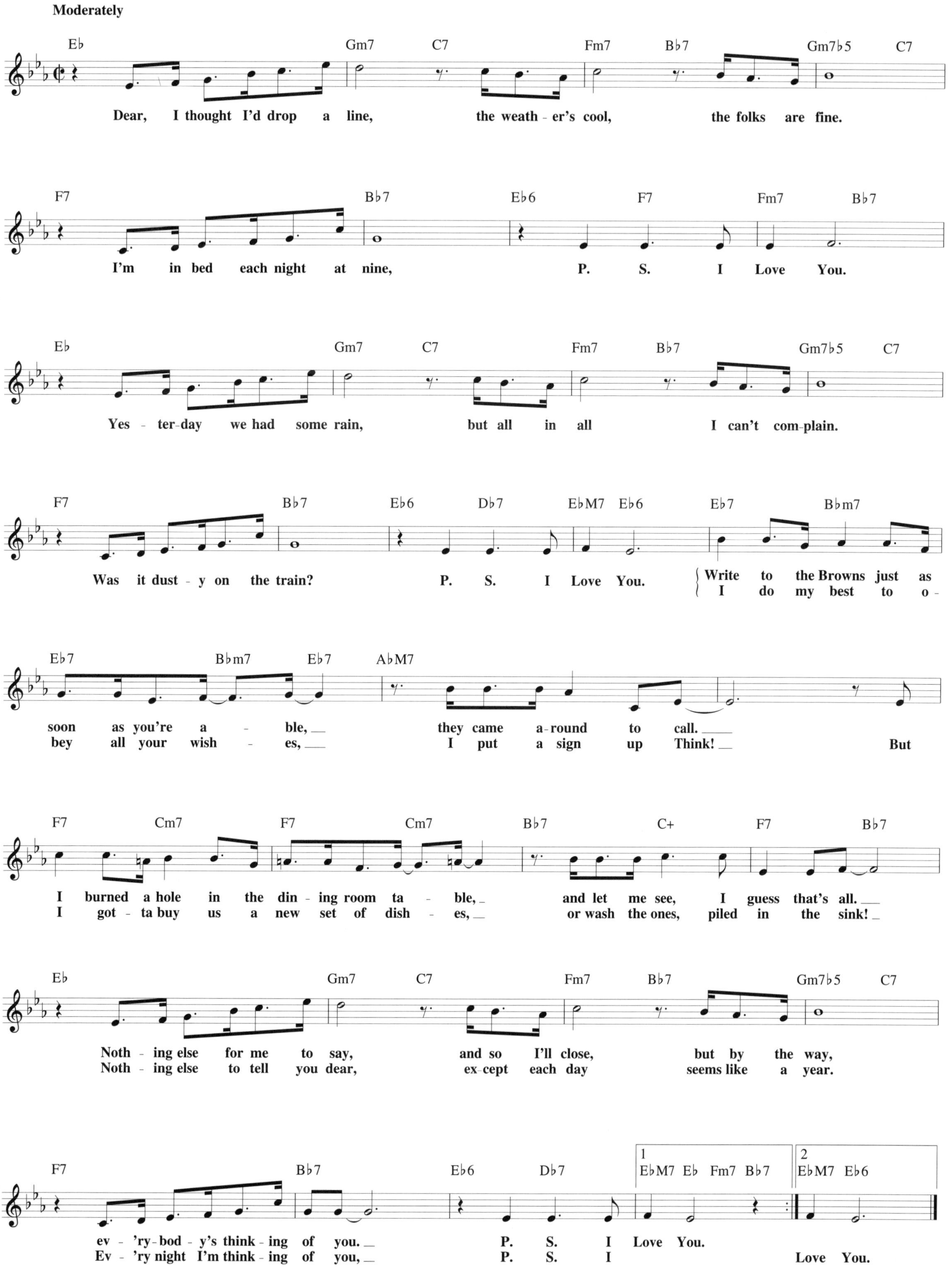

THE RAINBOW CONNECTION
from THE MUPPET MOVIE

By PAUL WILLIAMS
and KENNETH L. ASCHER

Copyright © 1979 Jim Henson Productions, Inc.
All Rights Administered by Sony/ATV Music Publishing,
8 Music Square West, Nashville, TN 37203

Flowing Waltz tempo

Why are there so many songs about rainbows, and what's on the other side? Rainbows are visions, but only illusions, And rainbows have nothing to hide. So we've been told, and some choose to believe it; I know they're wrong; wait and see. Someday we'll find it, The Rainbow Connection; The lovers, the dreamers and me.

Who said that ev'ry wish would be heard and answered when wished on the morning star? Somebody thought of that, and someone believed it; Look what it's done so far. What's so amazing that keeps us stargazing, And what do we think we might see? Someday we'll find it, The Rainbow Connection; The lovers, the dreamers and me.

All of us under its spell; we know that it's prob-a-bly magic.

Have you been half asleep, and have you heard voices? I've heard them calling my name. Is this the sweet sound that calls the young sailors? The voice might be one and the same. I've heard it too many times to ignore it. It's something that I'm s'posed to be.

La da da dee da da do la la da da da de da do.

RE: PERSON I KNEW

Music by BILL EVANS

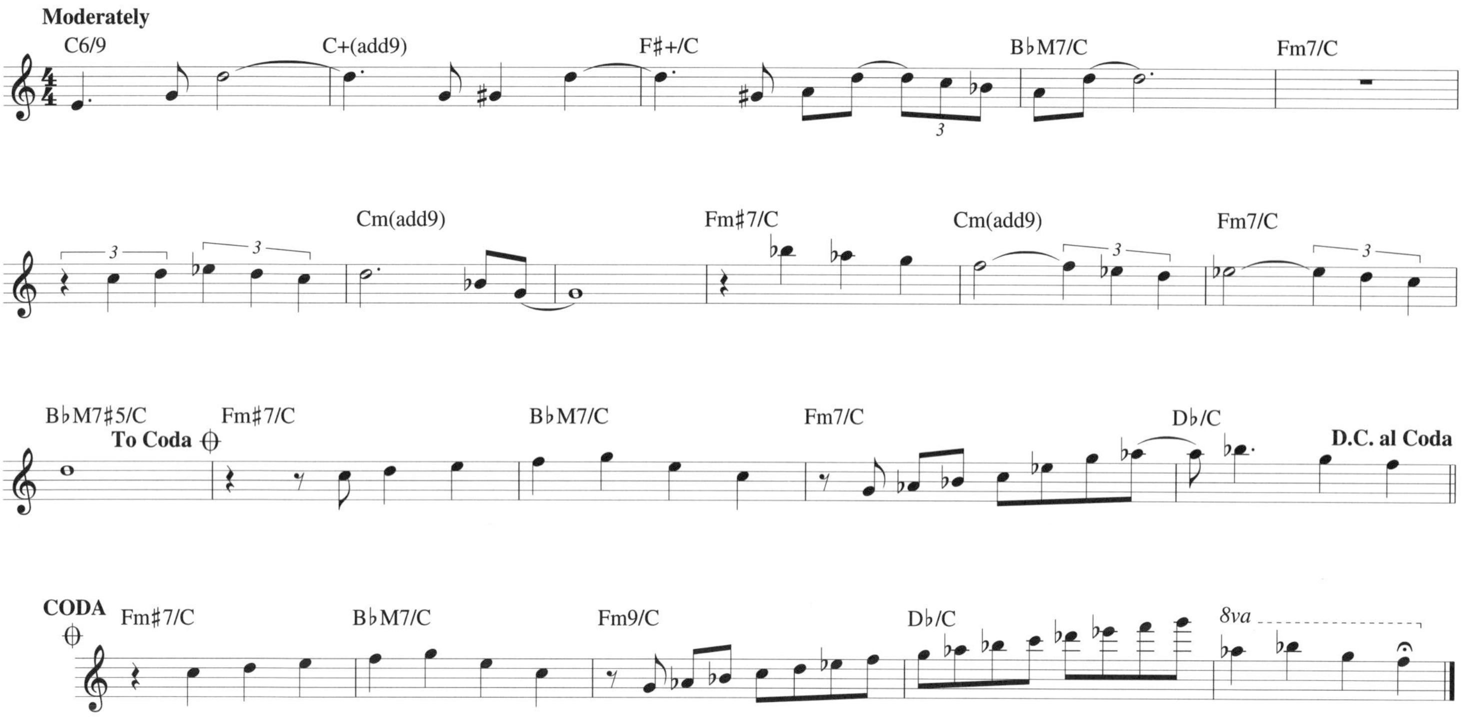

RED CLAY

By FREDDIE HUBBARD

A REMARK YOU MADE

Music by JOSEF ZAWINUL

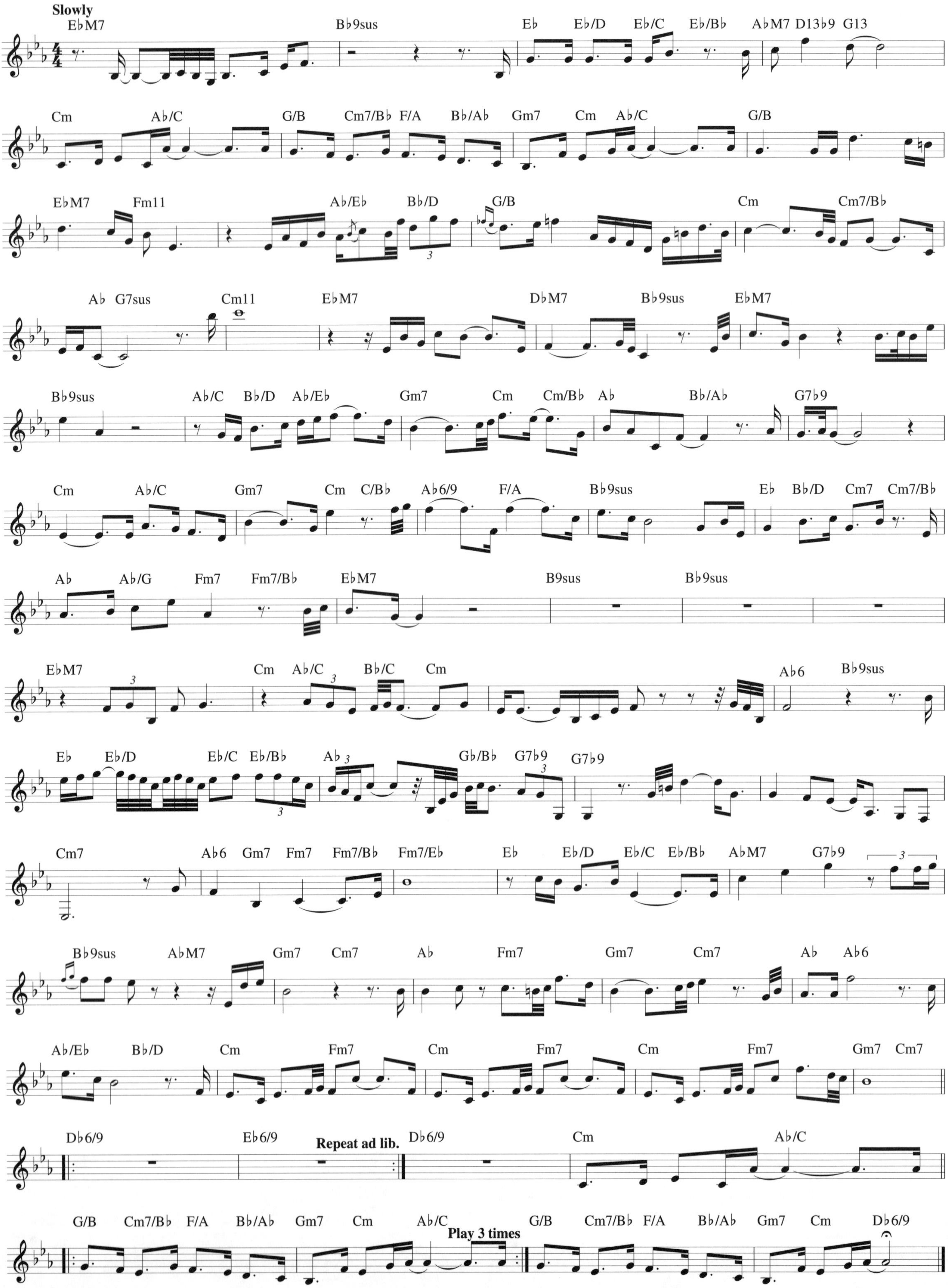

REMIND ME

Words and Music by DOROTHY FIELDS
and JEROME KERN

Moderately

Re - mind Me _____ not to find you so at - trac - tive, _____ Re -
mind Me _____ not to men - tion that I love you. _____ Re -

mind Me _____ that the world is full of men. _____ When I start to
mind Me _____ to be sor - ry that we met. _____ Al - though I a -

miss you, to touch your hand, to kiss you, Re - mind Me _____ to count to ten! _____
dore you, Re - mind Me to ig - nore you, you're one thing _____ I will re - gret!

_____ I had a feel - ing when I met you _____ you'd drive me cra - zy, if I'd let you,
_____ So when your charm be - gins to blind me, I'll sim - ply tie my hands be - hind me.

_____ But all my ef - forts to for - get you _____ Re - mind Me, I'm in love a - gain. _____ I get my
_____ Don't let me kiss you, please Re - mind Me, _____ un - less, my dar - ling you for -

heart well in hand, and I'm cer - tain that I can take you or leave you a - lone. _____ Then you "Be -

gin that Be - guine" a - gain, and boom! I give in a - gain. I have a will _____ made of

steel, my friend, _____ but when it seems a - bout to bend, Re -   get. _____

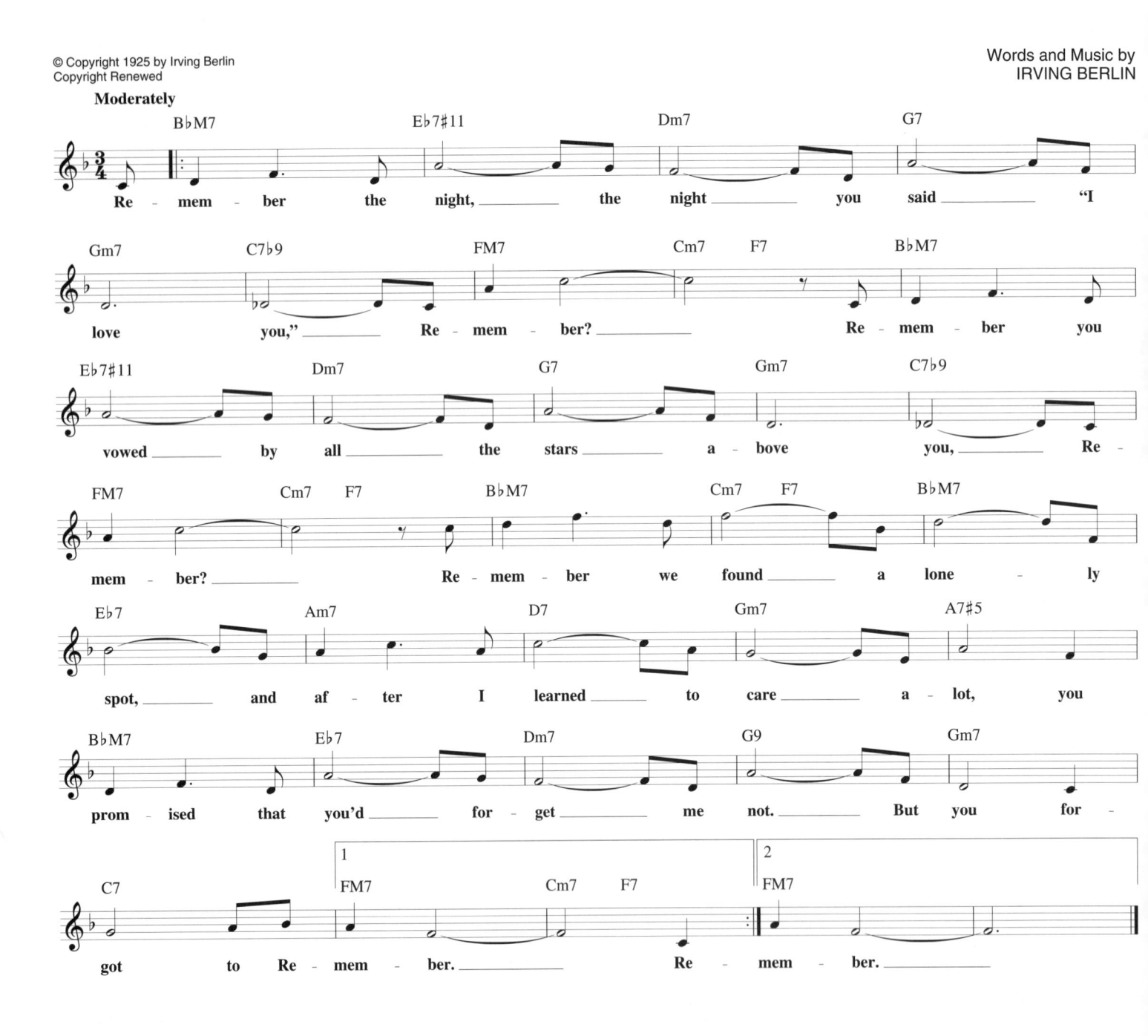

REMEMBER

© Copyright 1925 by Irving Berlin
Copyright Renewed

Words and Music by
IRVING BERLIN

Moderately

Re - mem - ber the night, the night you said "I love you," Re - mem - ber? Re - mem - ber you vowed by all the stars a - bove you, Re - mem - ber? Re - mem - ber we found a lone - ly spot, and af - ter I learned to care a - lot, you prom - ised that you'd for - get me not. But you for got to Re - mem - ber. Re - mem - ber.

RESEMBLANCE

© 1994 PALMAS FLORIBE/Administered by BUG

Written by EDDIE PALMIERI

Fast Latin

RIDIN' HIGH
from RED, HOT AND BLUE!

Copyright © 1936 by Chappell & Co.
Copyright Renewed, Assigned to John F. Wharton, Trustee of the Cole Porter Musical and Literary Property Trusts
Chappell & Co. owner of publication and allied rights throughout the world

Words and Music by
COLE PORTER

Moderately fast

Life's great, _ life's grand, _ future _ all planned. No more _ clouds in _ the sky, how'm I _ rid - in? _ I'm Rid - in' High. _

Some - one _ I love, _ mad for _ my love, so long, _ Jo - nah, _ good - bye. How'm I _ rid - in? _ I'm Rid - in' High. _

ring bells, _ sing songs, _ blow horns. _ beat gongs, _ our love _ nev - er will die. How'm I _

Float - ing _ on a star - lit ceil - ing, dot - ing _ on the cards I'm deal - ing, gloat - ing, _ be - cause I'm feel - ing so hap - hap - hap - py. I'm slap hap - py.

D.S. al Coda

CODA

So rid - in? _ I'm Rid - in' High. _

RIFFTIDE

By COLEMAN HAWKINS and STEVE GRAHAM

Copyright © 1977 Michael H. Goldsen, Inc.

RITMO DE LA NOCHE

By AL DI MEOLA

Copyright © 1982 DI MEOLA MUSIC CO.

RIGHT AS THE RAIN
from BLOOMER GIRL

Copyright © 1944 by Chappell & Co.
Copyright Renewed

Words by E.Y. Harburg
Music by HAROLD ARLEN

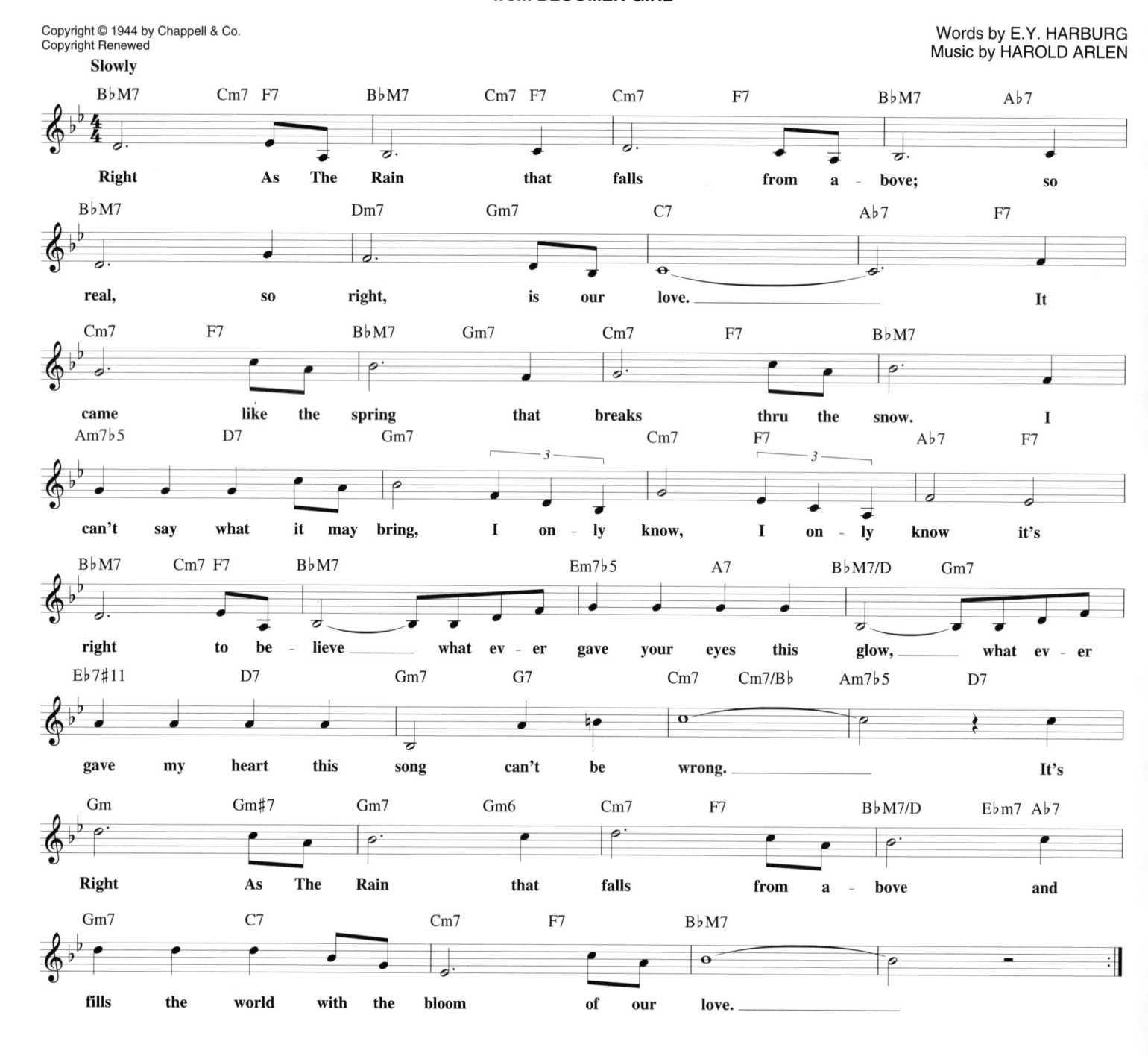

Slowly

Right As The Rain that falls from a-bove; so real, so right, is our love. It came like the spring that breaks thru the snow. I can't say what it may bring, I on-ly know, I on-ly know it's right to be-lieve what ev-er gave your eyes this glow, what ev-er gave my heart this song can't be wrong. It's Right As The Rain that falls from a-bove and fills the world with the bloom of our love.

RING DEM BELLS

Copyright © 1930 (Renewed 1957) and Assigned to Famous Music Corporation and Warner Bros. Inc. in the U.S.A.
Rights for the world outside the U.S.A. Controlled by Tempo Music, Inc. c/o Music Sales Corporation and Warner Bros. Inc.

Words and Music by DUKE ELLINGTON and IRVING MILLS

Moderately

Good time train is leav-in', Ring Dem Bells. Ain't no time for griev-in', Ring Dem Bells. Got my round-trip tick-et, I'm read-y to ride to that land of hon - ey, Ring Dem Bells.

I'm a one man wom - an, Ring Dem Bells.

Go - in' bride and groom - in', Ring Dem Bells.

Filled with wild e - la - tion, it's eas - y to tell

love's our des - ti - na - tion, Ring Dem Bells.

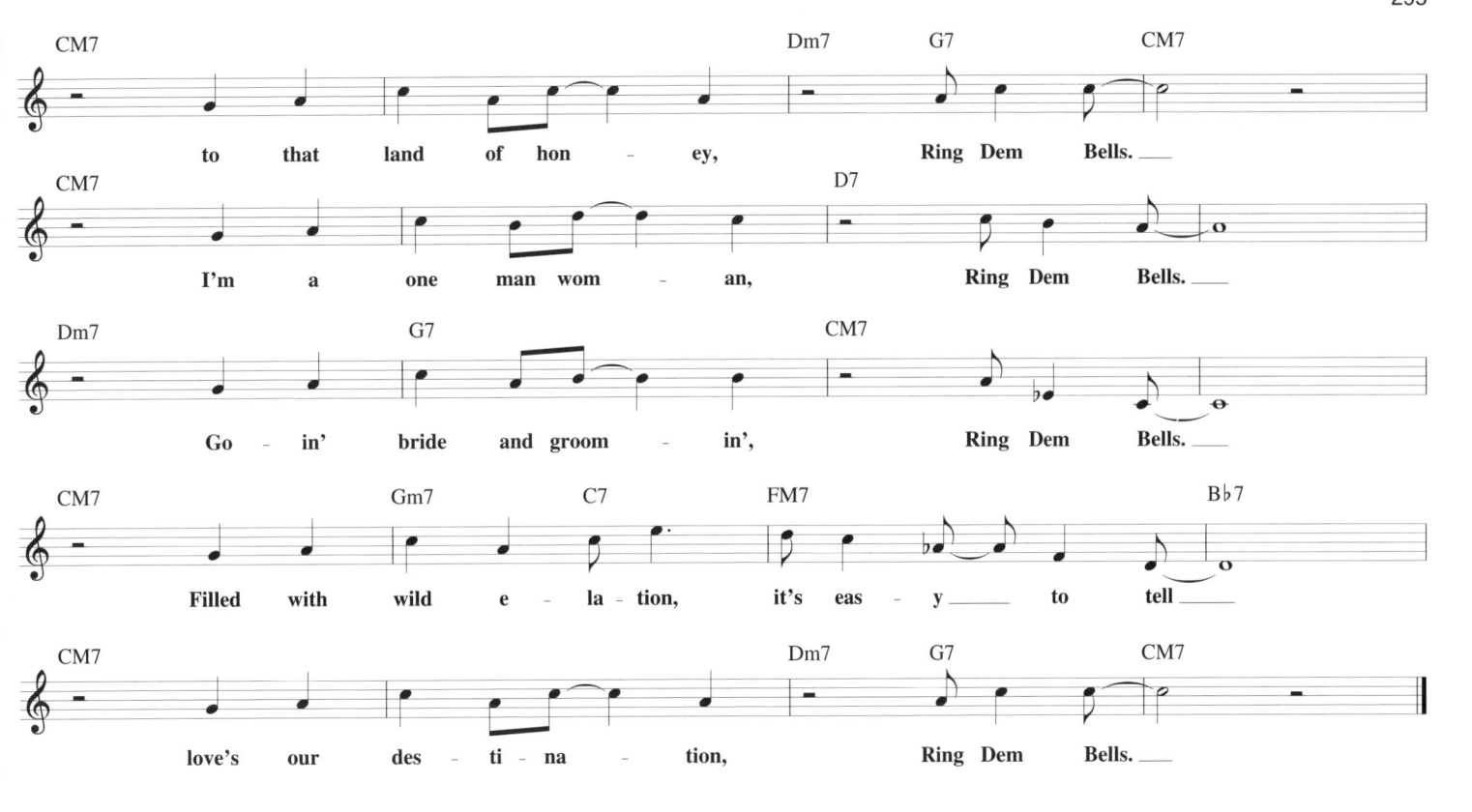

RIVERBOAT SHUFFLE

Copyright © 1939 (Renewed 1967) Hoagy Publishing Company,
EMI Mills Music, Inc. and Everbright Music Co.
All Rights for Everbright Music Co. Controlled and Administered by EMI Mills Music, Inc.

Words and Music by HOAGY CARMICHAEL, MITCHELL PARISH, IRVING MILLS and DICK VOYNOW

Moderately

Good peo - ple, you're in - vit - ed to - night to the Riv - er - boat Shuf - fle! Good peo - ple, we got rhy - thm to - night at the Riv - er - boat Shuf - fle! They tell me that slide - pipe toot - er is grand, best in Loo - si - an - na; So bring your freight - er, come and al - li - gat - or that band. Mis - ter Hawk - ins on the ten - or! Good peo - ple, you'll hear Mil - en - berg Joys in a spe - cial orch - es - tra - tion! E - ven Mam - ma Din - ah will be there to strut for the boys in a room full of noise. She'll teach you to shuf - fle it right, so, bring your ba - by. I'll be see - in' you at the Riv - er - boat Shuf - fle to - night!

ROCKIN' IN RHYTHM

By DUKE ELLINGTON, IRVING MILLS
and HARRY CARNEY

ST. LOUIS BLUES
from BIRTH OF THE BLUES

Words and Music by
W. C. HANDY

ROCKER
(Rock Salt)

By GERRY MULLIGAN

Copyright © 1953 (Renewed 1981), 1988 by JERUVIAN MUSIC

SAMBA CANTINA

By PAUL DESMOND

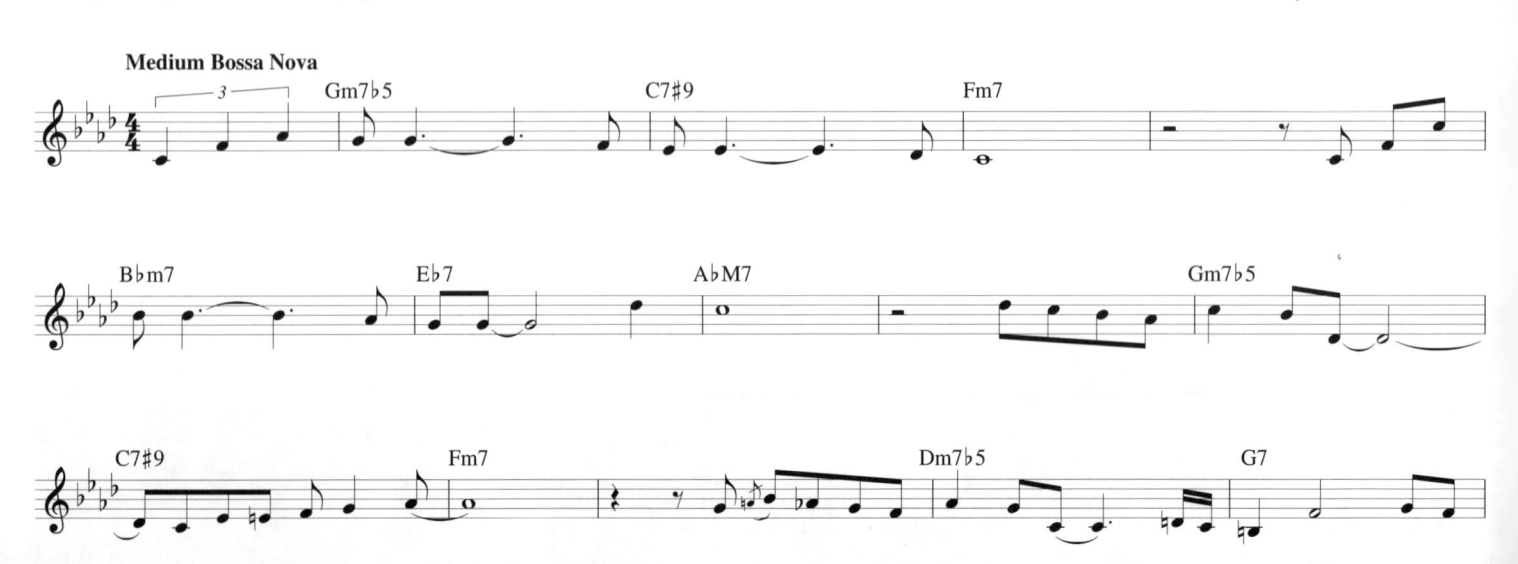

© 1965 (Renewed) Desmond Music Company

SAY IT ISN'T SO

© Copyright 1932 by Irving Berlin
© Arrangement Copyright 1948 by Irving Berlin
Copyright Renewed

Words and Music by
IRVING BERLIN

Moderately

Say It Isn't So, ____ Say It Isn't So. ____
Ev - 'ry - one is say - ing you don't love me, Say It Isn't So. ____
E - 'ry - where I go, ____ ev - 'ry - one I know ____
whis - pers that you're grow - ing tired ____ of me, Say It Isn't So.
Peo - ple say that you ____ found some - bod - y new, ____
and it won't be long be - fore you leave me, say it isn't true. ____
Say that ev - 'ry - thing is still o - kay, that's all I want to know, ____ and what they're
say - ing, ____ Say It Isn't So. ____

SEARCHING, FINDING

By JOHN PATITUCCI

SEÑOR CARLOS

By McCOY TYNER

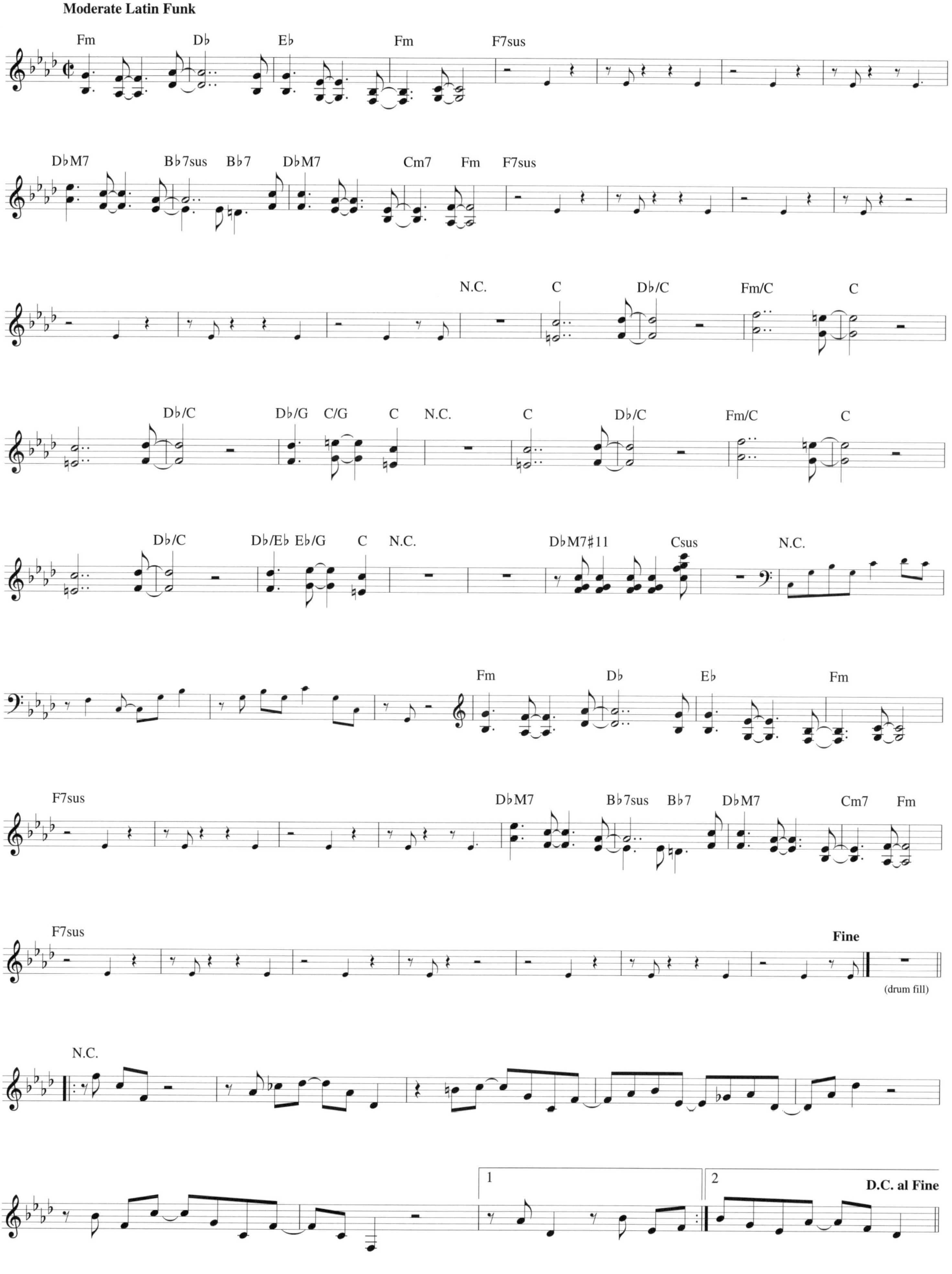

SEEMS LIKE OLD TIMES

Lyric and Music by JOHN JACOB LOEB
and CARMEN LOMBARDO

SERENGETI WALK
(Slippin' in the Back Door)

Words and Music by DAVE GRUSIN,
LOUIE JOHNSON and HARVEY MASON

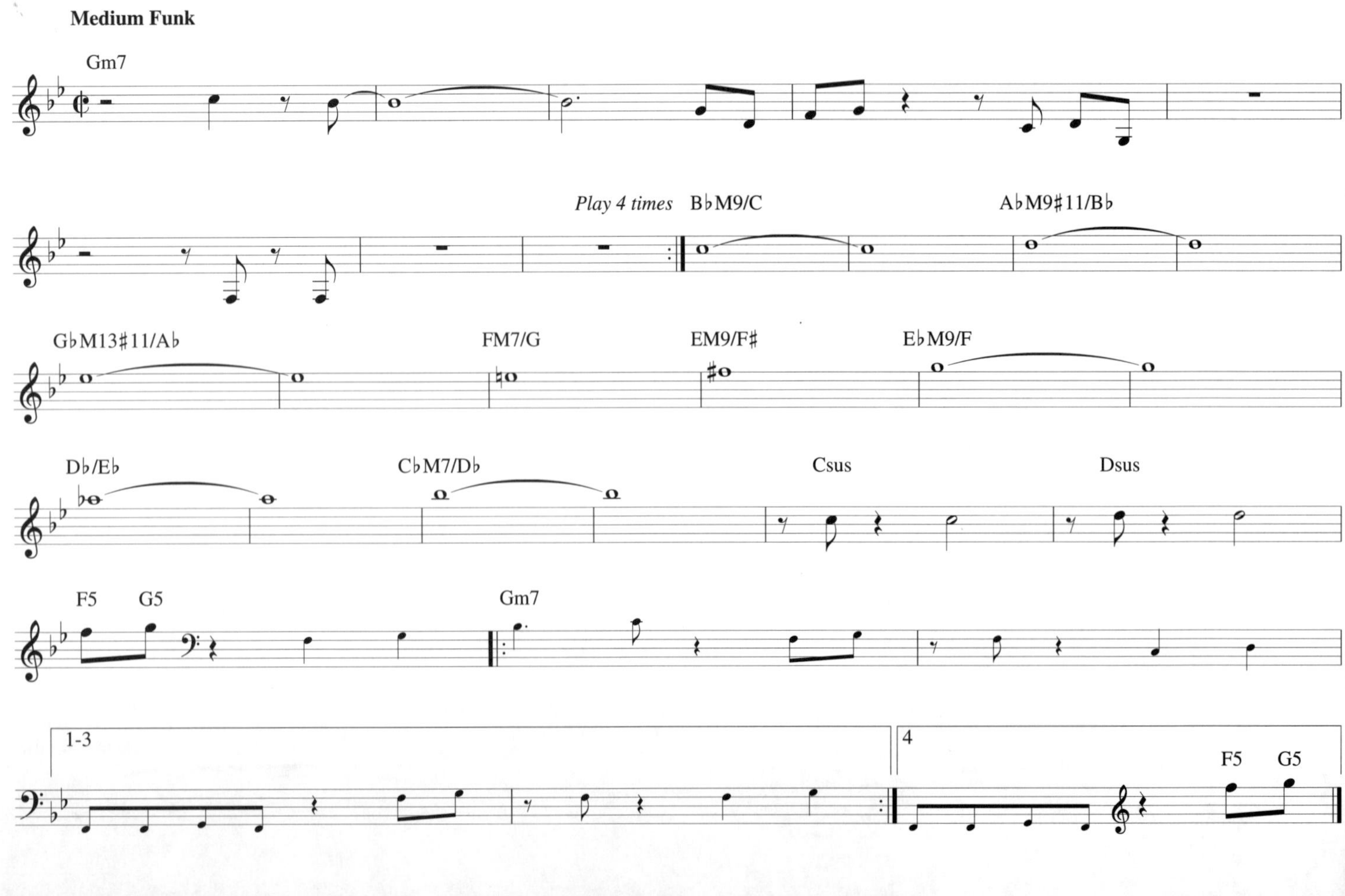

Señor Mouse

By CHICK COREA

SHAKER SONG

By JAY BECKENSTEIN

© 1977 Harlem Music, Inc. and Crosseyed Bear Music (BMI)
Administered by Harlem Music, Inc., 1762 Main Street, Buffalo, NY 14208

Medium Samba

CM7 · FM7 · CM7 · FM7
1. The fool screams, "No more." He grabs his shirt and hits the door. What she
2.-4. *(See additional lyrics)*

CM7 · FM7 · CM7 · FM7
needs from him he ig-nores, it's a bore, oh it's a bore, oh it's a bore, oh it's a bore, oh it's a...

A♭M7/B♭ · E♭M7 · G♭M7/A♭ · D♭M7
Blast the rad-i-o, the hits just come and go. Black out what he

A♭M7/B♭ · E♭M7 · G9sus
knows that he has blown, that he has blown. 2. The

FM7 · E7#9 · Am7 · Gm7 · C9sus
He can shake the blues, but you know he still can get con-fused, it seems like

FM7 · G9sus · CM7 · C13sus · C9
such a waste, 'cause he can't shake her, shake her.

FM7 · E7#9 · Am7 · Gm7 · C9sus
He can shake his tail, but you know his moves are get-ting stale, he's on the make, but

To Coda
FM7 · G9sus · CM7 · C6 · F/G · G9
oh, his heart can't fake. He can't shake her, shake her, he can't

CM7 · C6 · F/G · G9 · CM7 · C6 · F/G · G9
shake her, no, he can't shake her.

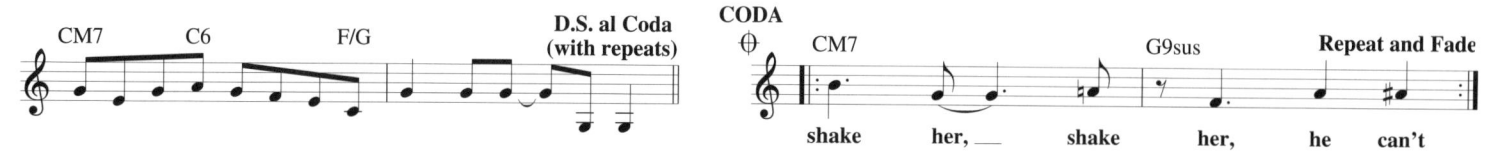

Additional Lyrics

2. The night hangs its head
   As the fool crawls into bed,
   Still his hungry heart begs to be fed
   All the words she once, that she said, that she said,
   So then he grabs his Chevrolet
   In one more attempt to get away
   But thoughts of all the crimes of passion lay,
   Lay in his way.

3. Romance falls like rain
   But all the motives are insane
   Every time that he plays the game he feels the pain,
   He feels the pain, who is to blame, who is to blame, who is to blame?
   And then he finds a joint that's jive,
   Guys are spinning girls like 45's,
   All of the live bait sinks for his lines,
   They are so high.

4. He knows he is beat
   As his heart puts on the heat,
   Run from the street that don't even fit his feet,
   Don't fit his feet, now he can see, now he can really see, now he can...
   Tell him where's a telephone,
   He can beg to let the fool come home,
   He tells her that his life's a drag alone,
   Can't be alone.

THE SHADOW OF YOUR SMILE
Love Theme from THE SANDPIPER

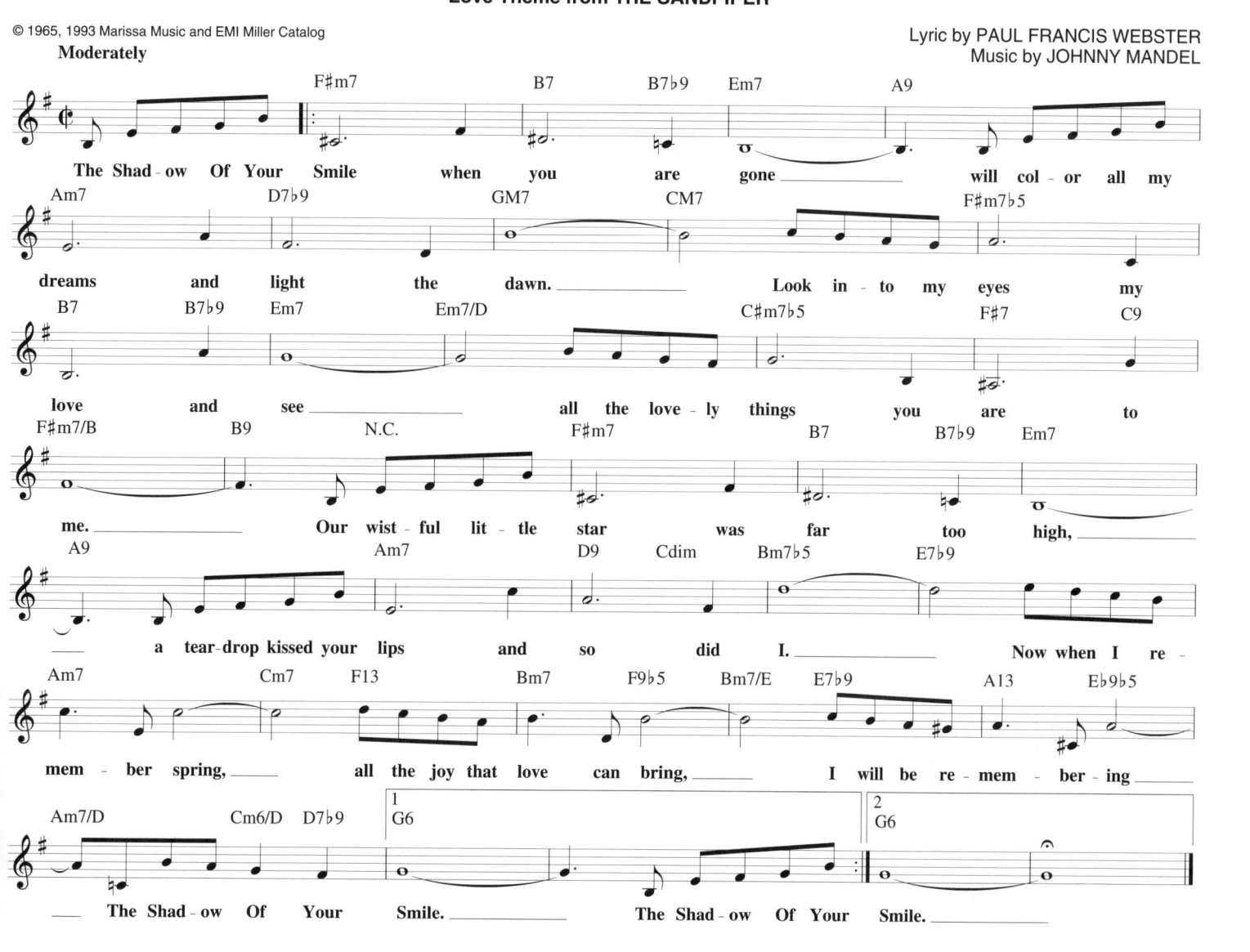

© 1965, 1993 Marissa Music and EMI Miller Catalog

Lyric by PAUL FRANCIS WEBSTER
Music by JOHNNY MANDEL

A SHIP WITHOUT A SAIL

Words by LORENZ HART
Music by RICHARD RODGERS

Moderately slow

All alone, all at sea! Why does nobody care for me, when there's no love to hold ___ my love? Why is my heart ___ so frail, like A Ship Without A Sail? ___ Out on the ocean, sailors can use a chart; ___ I'm on the ocean guided by just a lonely heart. Still alone, still at sea! Still there's no one to care for me when there's no hand to hold ___ my hand. Life is a loveless tale for A Ship Without A Sail. ___

SILVER HOLLOW

By JACK DeJOHNETTE

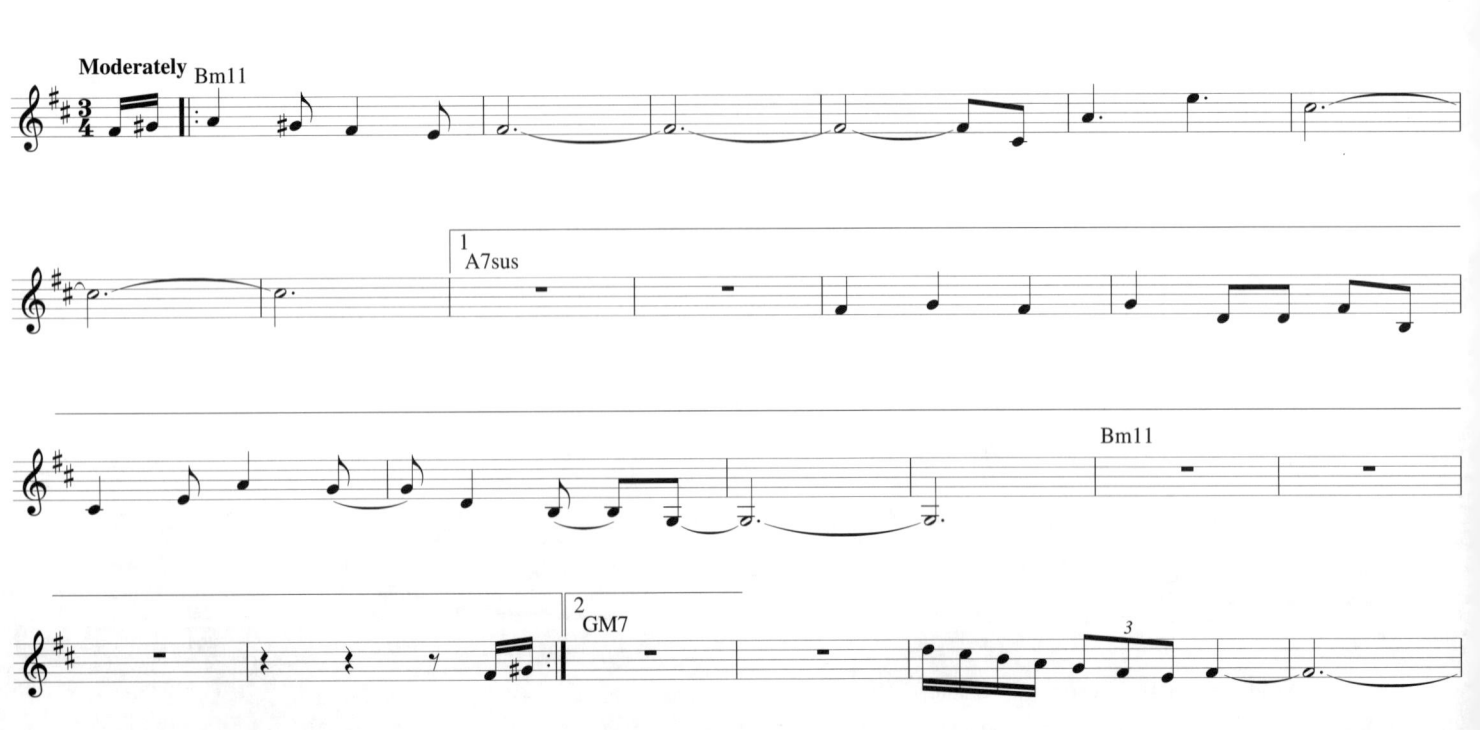

Moderately

SILHOUETTE

© 1988 EMI BLACKWOOD MUSIC INC., KUZU MUSIC, KENNY G MUSIC and HIGH TECH MUSIC
All Rights for KUZU MUSIC Controlled and Administered by EMI BLACKWOOD MUSIC INC.

By KENNY G

SIMPLE SAMBA

By JAMES S. HALL

Copyright © 1971 Janhall Music

A SLEEPIN' BEE
from HOUSE OF FLOWERS

© 1954 (Renewed) HAROLD ARLEN and TRUMAN CAPOTE
All Rights Controlled by HARWIN MUSIC CO.

Lyric by TRUMAN CAPOTE and HAROLD ARLEN
Music by HAROLD ARLEN

When a bee lies sleep-in' in the palm o' your hand, you're be-witch'd and deep in love's long look'd af-ter land. Where you'll see a sun-up sky with a morn-in' new, and where the days go laugh-in' by as love comes a-call-in' on you. Sleep on, Bee, don't wak-en, can't be-lieve what just passed. He's mine for the tak-in'. I'm so hap-py at last. May-be I dreams, but he seems sweet gold-en as a crown, A Sleep-in' Bee done told me, I'll walks with my feet off the groun' when my one true love I has foun'.

THE SINGLE PETAL OF A ROSE
from QUEEN'S SUITE

By DUKE ELLINGTON

SIPPIN' AT BELLS

© 1948 (Renewed 1975) SCREEN GEMS-EMI MUSIC INC.

By MILES DAVIS

SO EASY

Copyright © 1949 by Denton & Haskins Corp.
Copyright Renewed

By TADD DAMERON
and ARTIE SHAW

SLAUGHTER ON TENTH AVENUE
from ON YOUR TOES

By RICHARD RODGERS

SO IN LOVE
from KISS ME, KATE

Copyright © 1948 by Cole Porter
Copyright Renewed, Assigned to John F. Wharton,
 Trustee of the Cole Porter Musical and Literary Property Trusts
Chappell & Co. owner of publication and allied rights throughout the world

Words and Music by
COLE PORTER

SMILE FROM A STRANGER

By AL DI MEOLA

Copyright © 1987 NOONZIO PRODUCTIONS INC.

Moderately slow

SO YOU SAY

By JOHN SCOFIELD

Copyright © 1987 Scoway Music

SOFT LIGHTS AND SWEET MUSIC
from the Stage Production FACE THE MUSIC

© Copyright 1931 by Irving Berlin
Copyright Renewed

Words and Music by
IRVING BERLIN

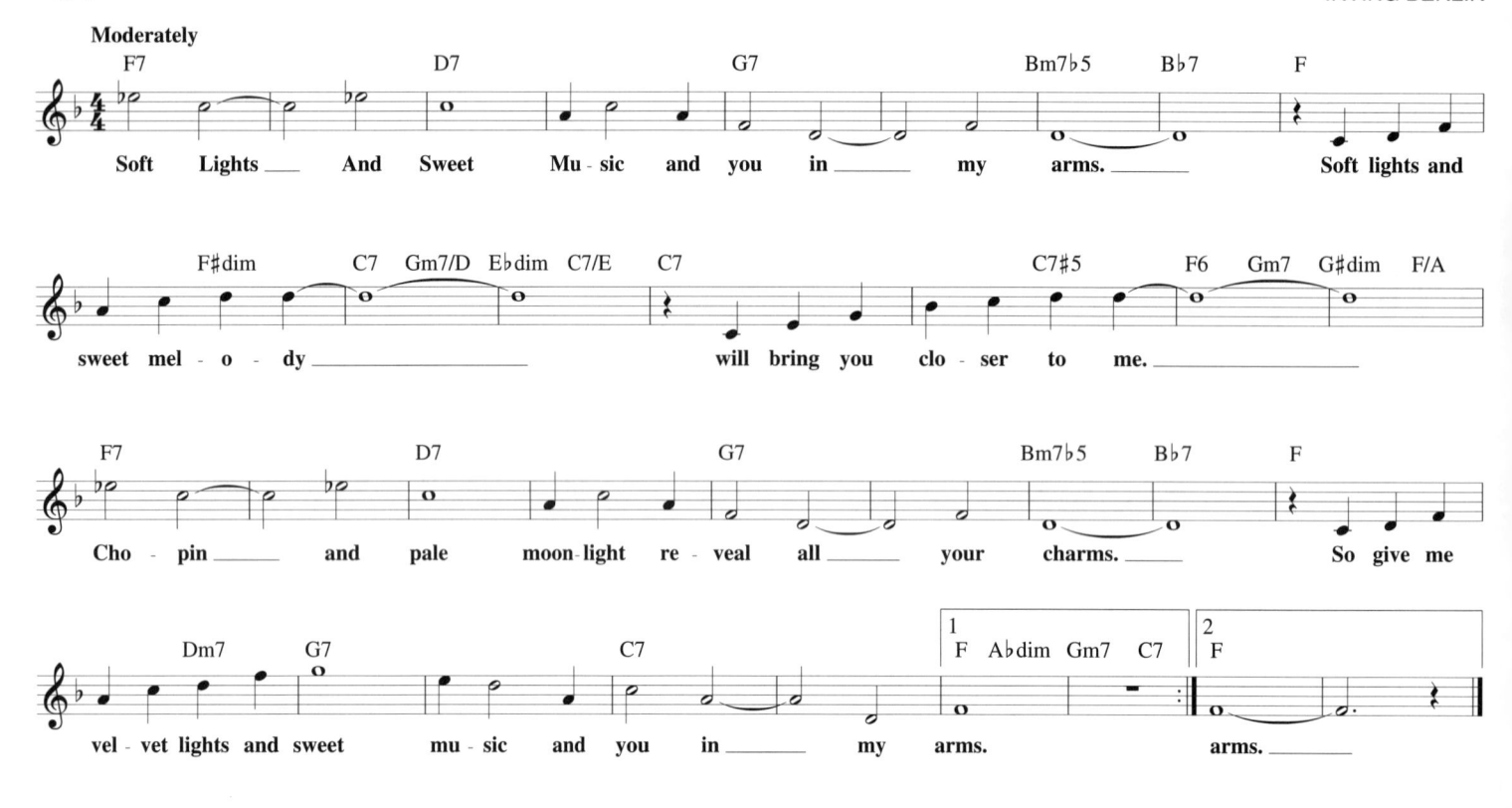

Soft Lights And Sweet Music and you in my arms. Soft lights and sweet melody will bring you closer to me. Chopin and pale moonlight reveal all your charms. So give me velvet lights and sweet music and you in my arms. arms.

SOFTLY AS IN A MORNING SUNRISE
from THE NEW MOON

Copyright © 1928 by Bambalina Music Publishing Co. and
Warner Bros. Inc. in the United States
Copyright Renewed
All Rights on behalf of Bambalina Music Publishing Co.
Administered by Williamson Music

Lyric by OSCAR HAMMERSTEIN II
Music by SIGMUND ROMBERG

Softly, As In A Morning Sunrise, the light of love comes stealing into a new born day. Oh, flaming with all the glow of sunrise, a burning kiss is stealing the vow that all betray. For the passions that thrill love, and lift you high to heaven, are the passions that kill love, and let you fall to hell! So ends each story, softly, as in an evening sunset, the light that gave you glory will take it all away.

SOME SKUNK FUNK

By RANDY BRECKER

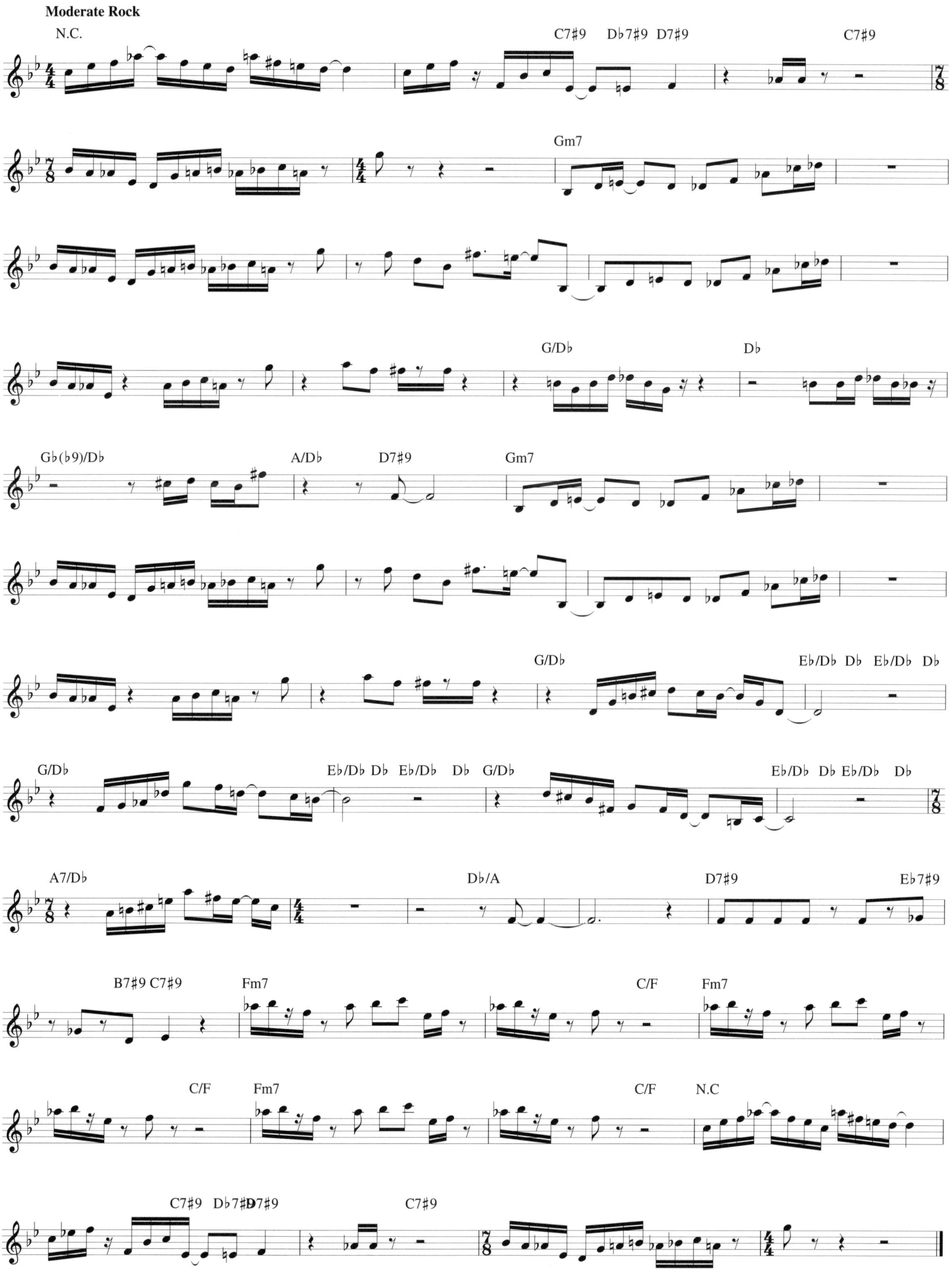

SOLEA

Written by GIL EVANS

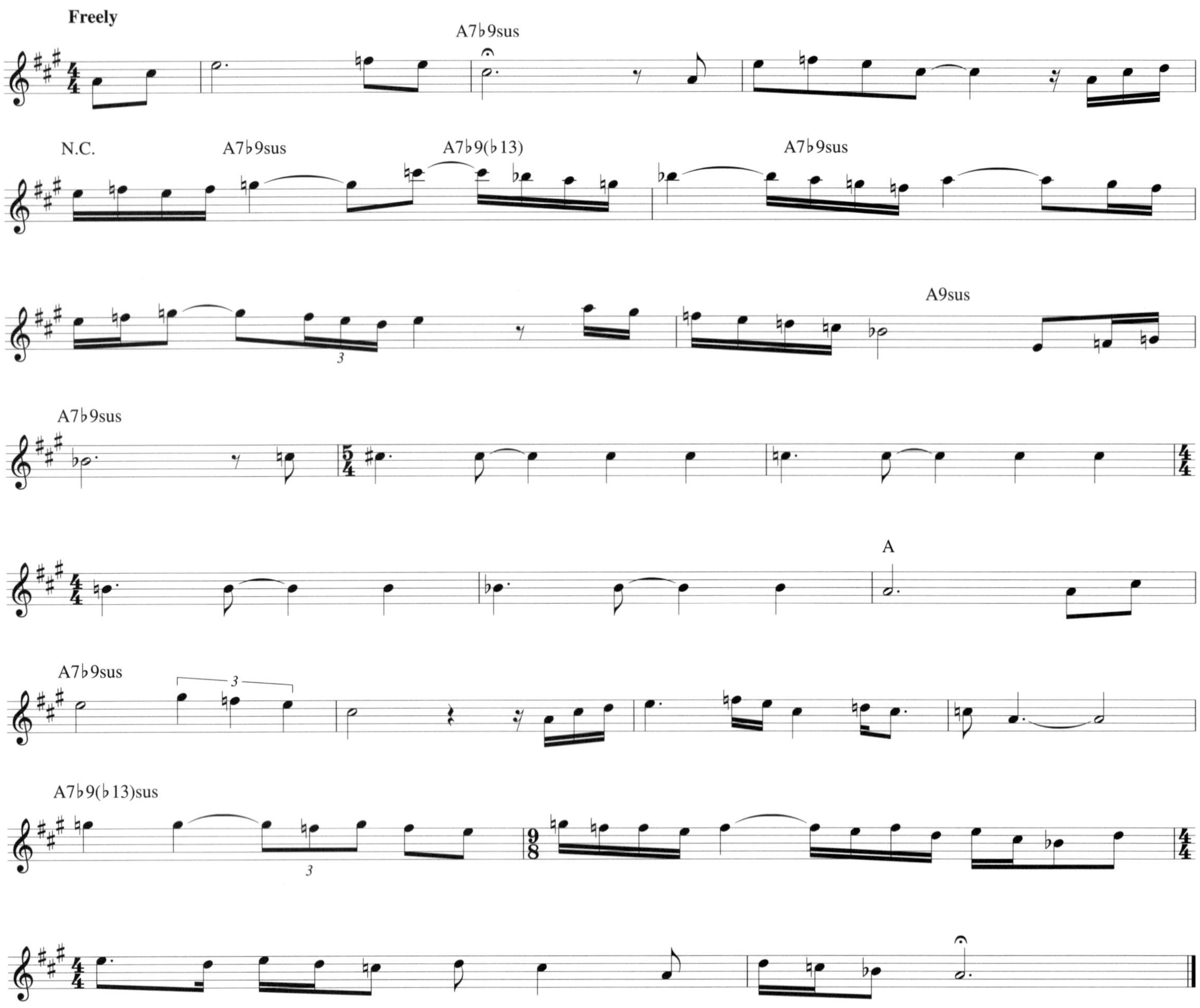

SOMEBODY LOVES ME
from SHE LOVES ME

Words by B.G. DeSYLVA and BALLARD MACDONALD
Music by GEORGE GERSHWIN
French Version by EMELIA RENAUD

who can she be wor - ries me. _____ For ev - 'ry
girl who pas - ses me I shout, "Hey, may - be
you were meant to be my lov - ing ba - by."
Some - bod - y Loves Me, I won - der who,
may - be it's you. _____

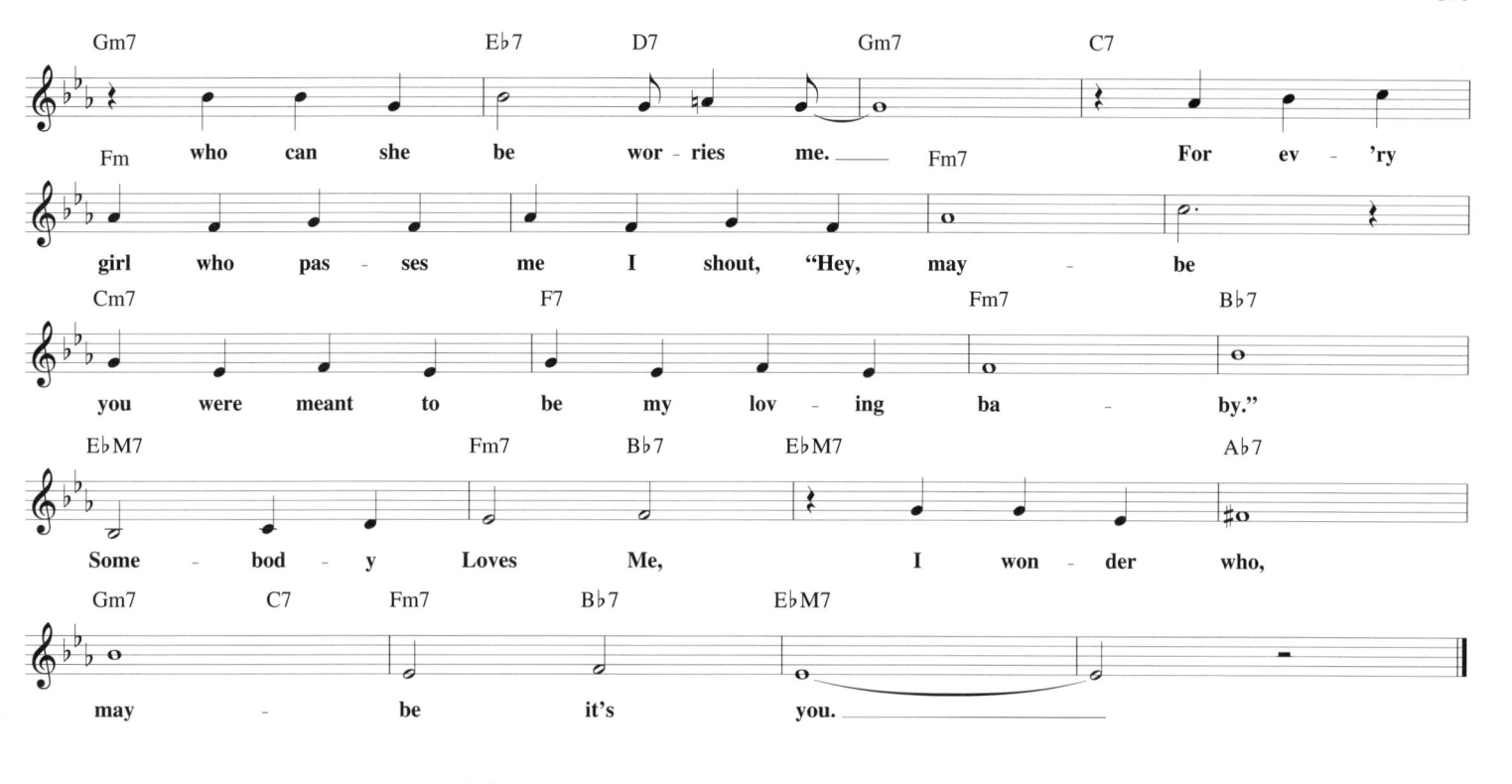

SOMETHING I DREAMED LAST NIGHT

Copyright © 1940 by Fain Music Co., Magidson Music Co., Inc. and
Jack Yellen Publishing Designee
Copyright Renewed

Words and Music by SAMMY FAIN,
HERBERT MAGIDSON and JACK YELLEN

Slowly

I can't be - lieve that you're not here with me, to have a laugh or share a tear with me.
It's all so wrong, it can't be right! _____ It must have been Some - thing _____ I Dreamed Last Night.
To nev - er see your fun - ny face a - gain! To nev - er thrill to your em - brace a - gain!
Oh, it's so wrong, it can't be right! _____ It must have been Some - thing _____ I Dreamed Last Night.
Those mid - night sup - pers for two, our "corn - y" du - ets at dawn,
those cra - zy mo - ments with you, don't tell me that they are gone!
To nev - er look in - to those eyes a - gain! The sun just might as well not rise a - gain!
Oh, no, no, no! It can't be right! _____ It must have been Some - thing _____ I Dreamed Last Night!

SOMEWHERE ALONG THE WAY

Words by SAMMY GALLOP
Music by KURT ADAMS

Copyright © 1952 (Renewed 1980) Sammy Gallop Music Company
and Music Sales Corporation (ASCAP)

Slowly

I used to walk with you a-long the av-en-ue, our hearts were care-free and gay. How could I know I'd lose you, Some-where A-long The Way. The friends we used to know, would al-ways smile, "Hel-lo." No love like our love, they'd say. Then love slipped thru our fin-gers, Some-where A-long The Way. I should for-get, but with the lone-li-ness of night, I start re-mem-ber-ing ev-'ry-thing. You're gone, and yet there's still a feel-ing deep in-side that you will al-ways be, part of me. So now I look for you a-long the av-en-ue, and as I wan-der I pray that some-day soon I'll find you, Some-where A-long The Way. Some-where A-long The Way.

SONG FOR LORRAINE

By JAY BECKENSTEIN

© 1979 Harlem Music, Inc. and Crosseyed Bear Music (BMI)
Administered by Harlem Music, Inc., 1762 Main Street, Buffalo, NY 14208

Samba

THE SONG IS ENDED
(But the Melody Lingers On)

© Copyright 1927 by Irving Berlin
© Arrangement Copyright 1951 by Irving Berlin
Copyright Renewed

Words and Music by
IRVING BERLIN

Moderately

The Song Is End-ed, but the mel-o-dy lin-gers on. You and the song are gone, but the mel-o-dy lin-gers on. The night was splen-did and the mel-o-dy seemed to say, "Sum-mer will pass a-way: take your hap-pi-ness while you may." There 'neath the light of the moon we sang a love song that end-ed too soon. The moon de-scend-ed, and I found with the break of dawn, you and the song had gone. But the mel-o-dy lin-gers on. The on.

SONG FROM M*A*S*H
(Suicide Is Painless)

© 1970 WB MUSIC CORP.

Words and Music by MIKE ALTMAN and JOHNNY MANDEL

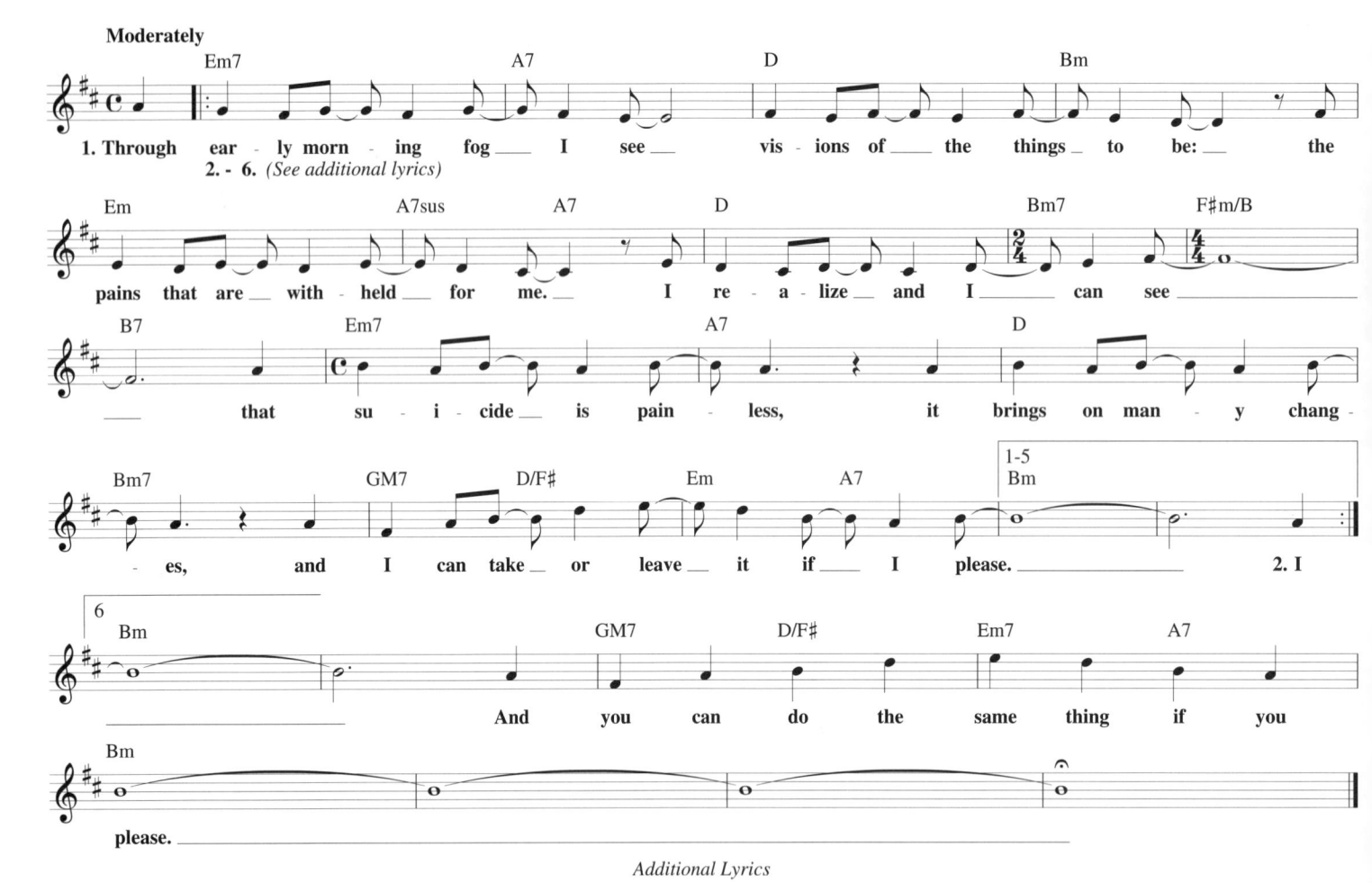

Moderately

1. Through early morning fog I see visions of the things to be: the pains that are withheld for me. I realize and I can see that suicide is painless, it brings on many changes, and I can take or leave it if I please.

2.-6. (See additional lyrics)

And you can do the same thing if you please.

Additional Lyrics

2. I try to find a way to make
   All our little joys relate
   Without that ever-present hate
   But now I know that it's too late.

3. The game of life is hard to play,
   I'm going to lose it anyway,
   The losing card I'll someday lay,
   So this is all I have to say.

4. The only way to win is cheat
   And lay it down before I'm beat,
   And to another give a seat
   For that's the only painless feat.

5. The sword of time will pierce our skins,
   It doesn't hurt when it begins
   But as it works it's way on in,
   The pain grows stronger, watch it grin.

6. A brave man once requested me
   To answer questions that are key,
   Is it to be or not to be
   And I replied; "Oh, why ask me."

SONG FOR STRAYHORN

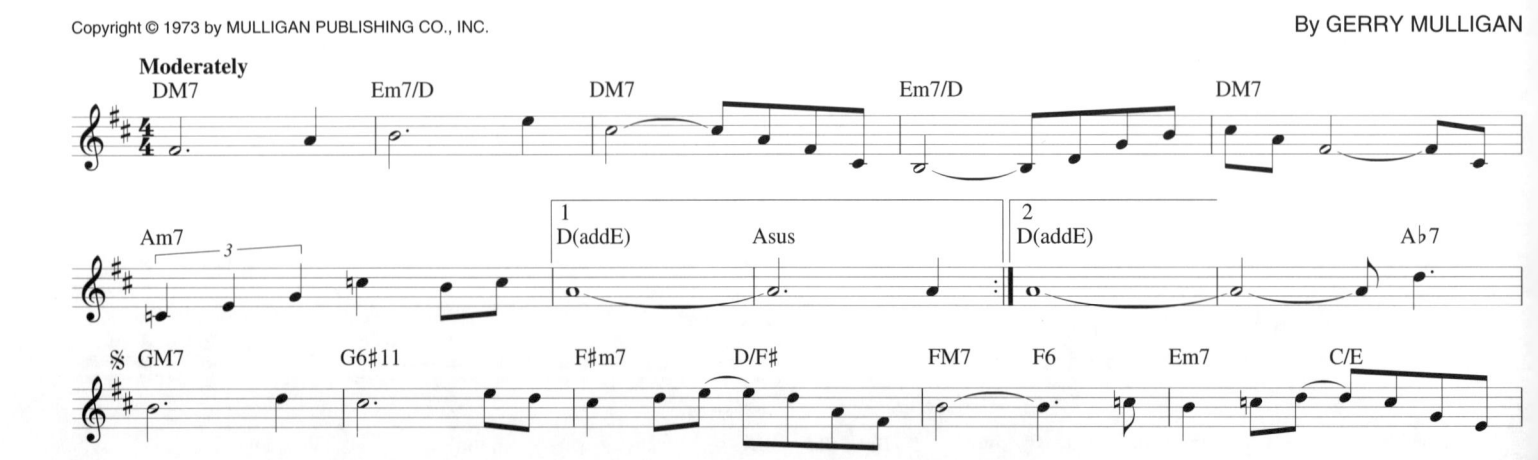

Copyright © 1973 by MULLIGAN PUBLISHING CO., INC.

By GERRY MULLIGAN

Moderately

SONGBIRD

By KENNY G

© 1986 EMI BLACKWOOD MUSIC INC., KUZU MUSIC, KENNY G MUSIC and HIGH TECH MUSIC
All Rights for KUZU MUSIC Controlled and Administered by EMI BLACKWOOD MUSIC INC.

STABLEMATES

By BENNY GOLSON

SOPHISTICATED LADY
from SOPHISTICATED LADIES

Words and Music by DUKE ELLINGTON, IRVING MILLS and MITCHELL PARISH

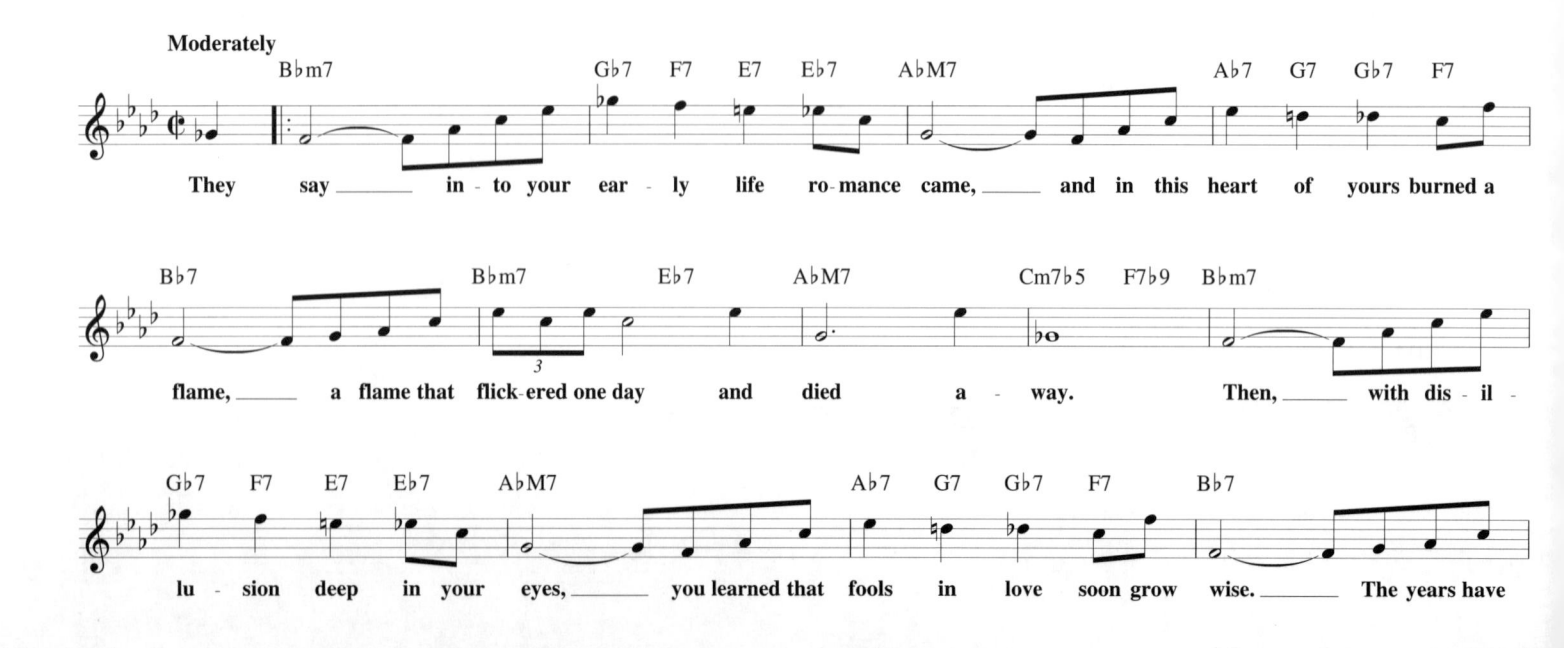

They say___ in-to your ear-ly life ro-mance came,___ and in this heart of yours burned a flame,___ a flame that flick-ered one day and died a way. Then,___ with dis-il-lu-sion deep in your eyes,___ you learned that fools in love soon grow wise.___ The years have

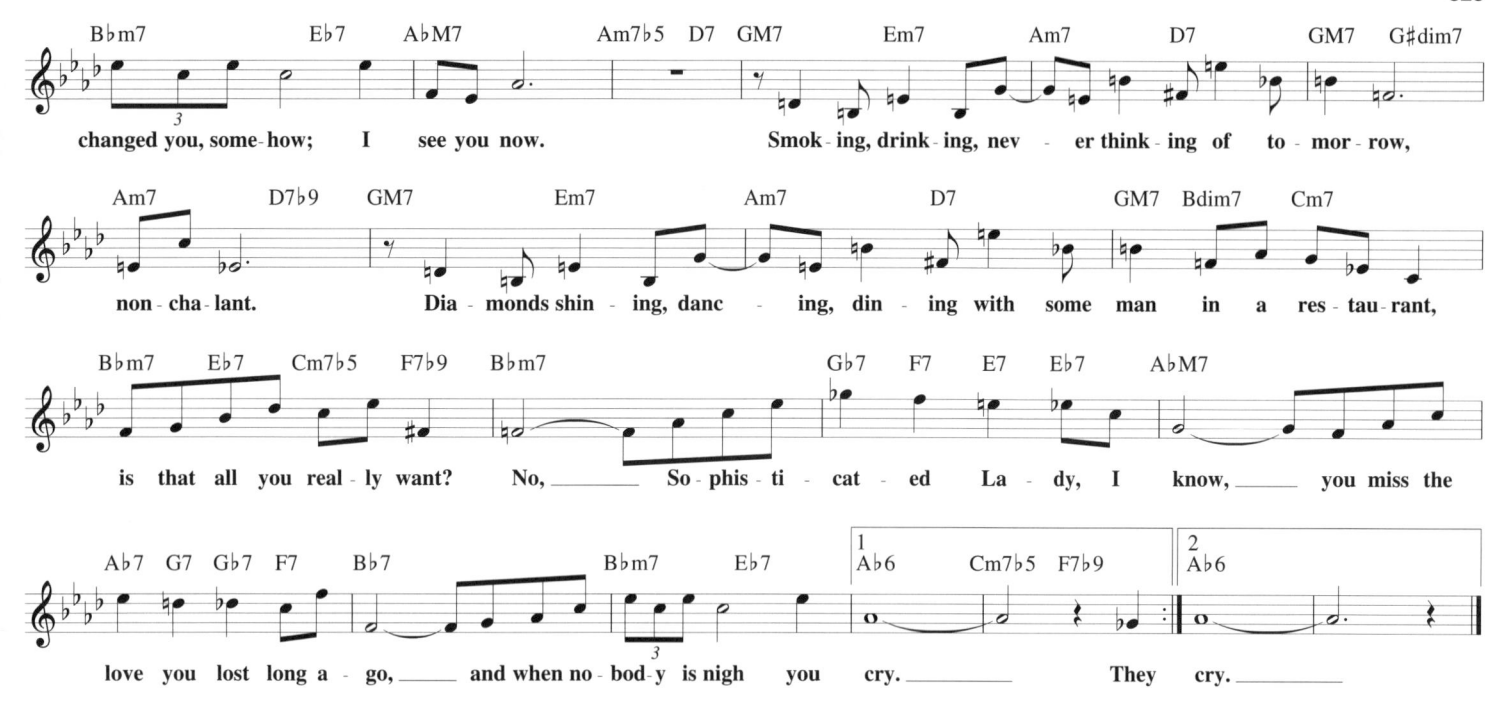

STAIRWAY TO THE STARS

Copyright © 1935 by PARMIT MUSIC and EMI ROBBINS CATALOG INC.
Copyright Renewed
All Rights for PARMIT MUSIC Administered by THE SONGWRITERS GUILD OF AMERICA

Words by MITCHELL PARISH
Music by MATT MALNECK and FRANK SIGNORELLI

SOMEONE TO LIGHT UP MY LIFE
(Se Todos Fossem Iguais a Voce)

English Lyric by GENE LEES
Original Text by VINICIUS DE MORAES
Music by ANTONIO CARLOS JOBIM

© Copyright 1958 (Renewed), 1964 (Renewed) and 1965 (Renewed)
Edicoes Euterpe Ltda., Rio de Janeiro, Brazil
TRO - Hollis Music, Inc., New York, NY, Corcovado Music Corp., New York, NY
and VM Enterprises, New York, NY control all publication rights for the U.S.A.
All Rights for Canada controlled by Hollis Music, Inc., New York, NY

Medium Samba

Where shall I look for the love to replace you? Someone To Light Up My Life. Someone with strange little ways, eyes like a blue autumn haze, Someone with your laughing style and a smile that I know will keep haunting me endlessly. Sometimes in stars or the swift flight of seabirds I catch a moment of you. That's why I walk all alone, searching for something unknown, searching for something or Someone To Light Up My Life.

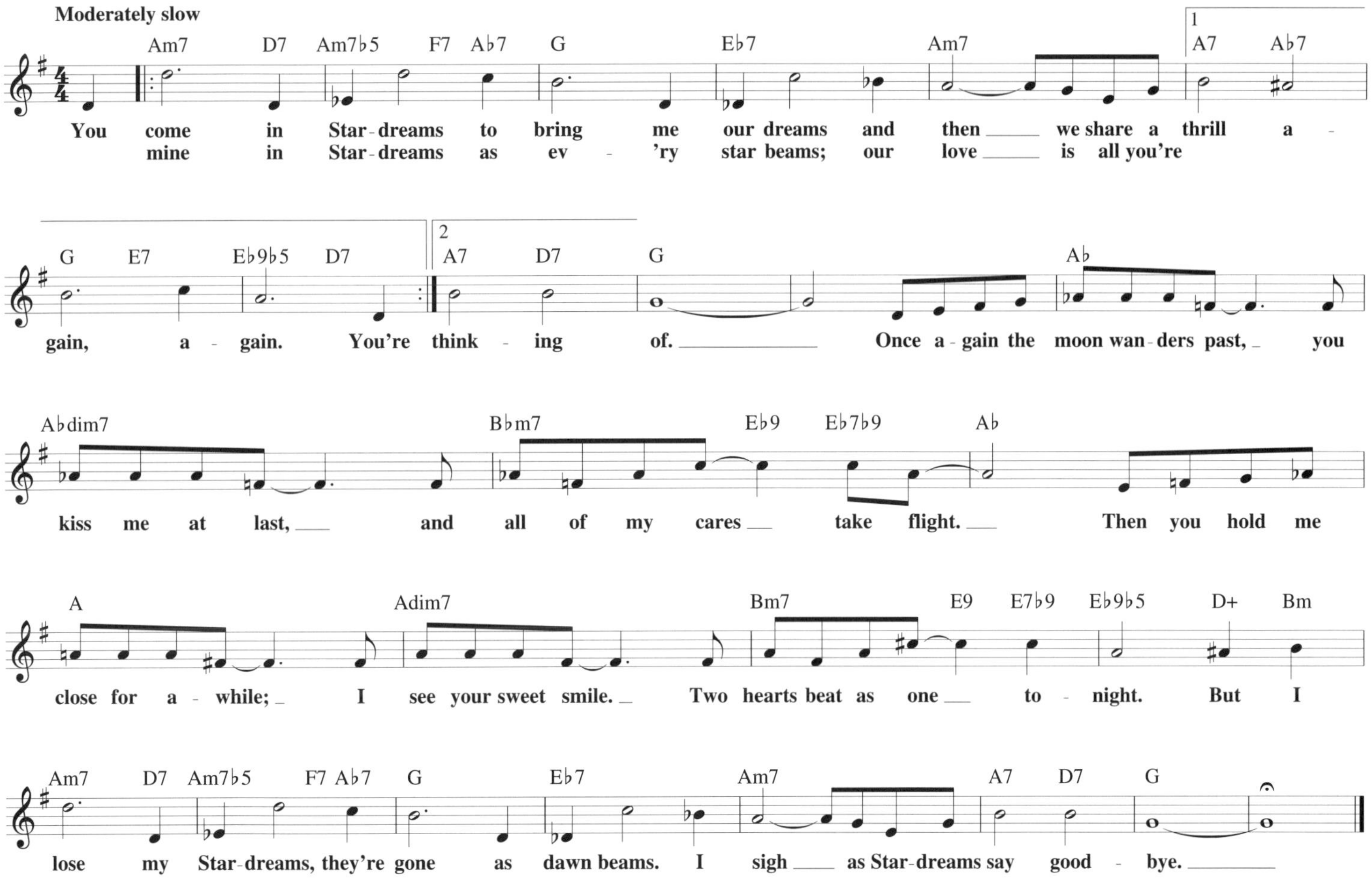

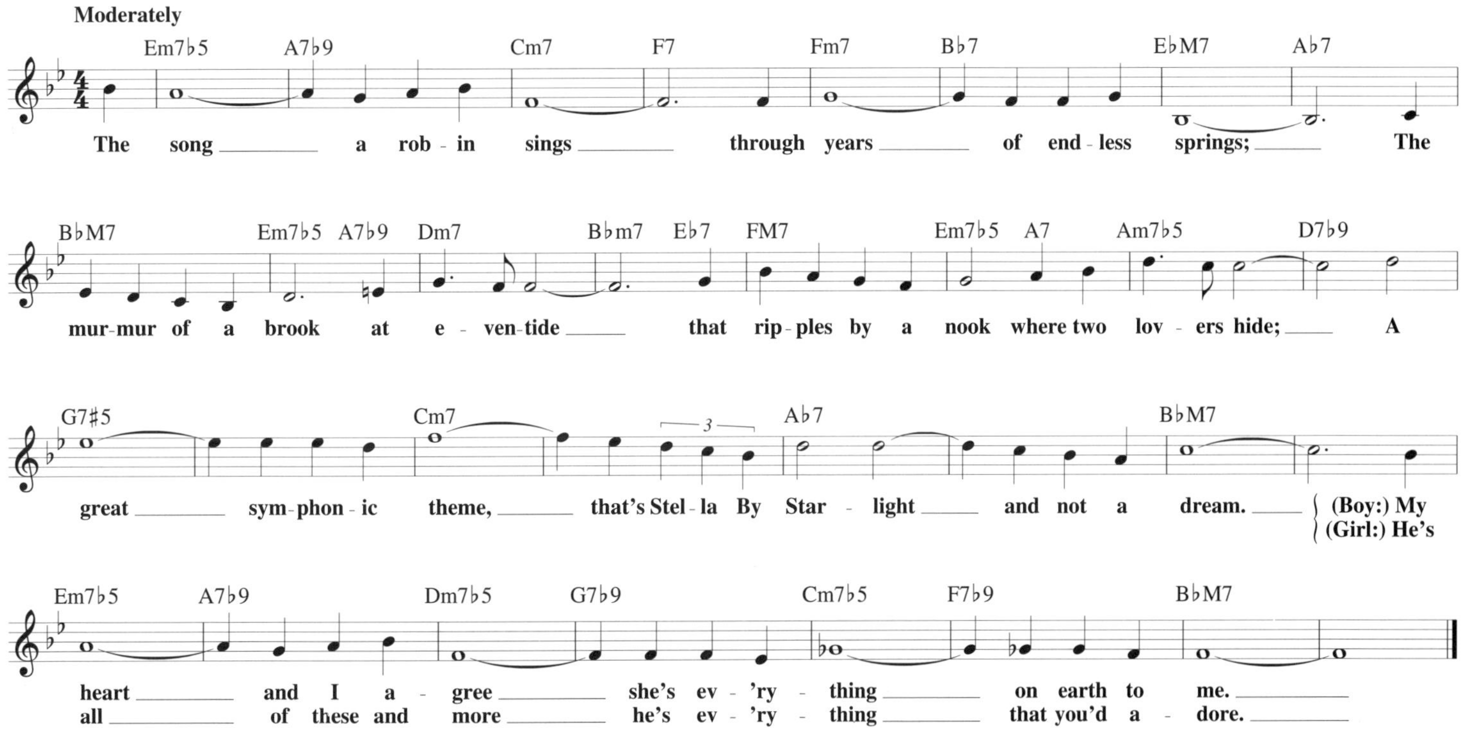

Star Dust

Words by MITCHELL PARISH
Music by HOAGY CARMICHAEL

And now the purple dusk of twilight time steals across the meadows of my heart.
High up in the sky the little stars climb, always reminding me that we're apart.
You wandered down the lane and far away, leaving me a song that will not die.
Love is now the Star Dust of yesterday, the music of the years gone by. Sometimes I
wonder why I spend the lonely night dreaming of a song. The melody
haunts my reverie, and I am once again with you, when our love was new,
and each kiss an inspiration. But that was long ago, now
my consolation is in the Star Dust of a song. Beside a garden
wall, when stars are bright, you are in my arms. The nightingale tells his fairy tale
of paradise where roses grew. Though I dream in vain, in my heart it will re-
main: my Star Dust melody, the memory of love's refrain.

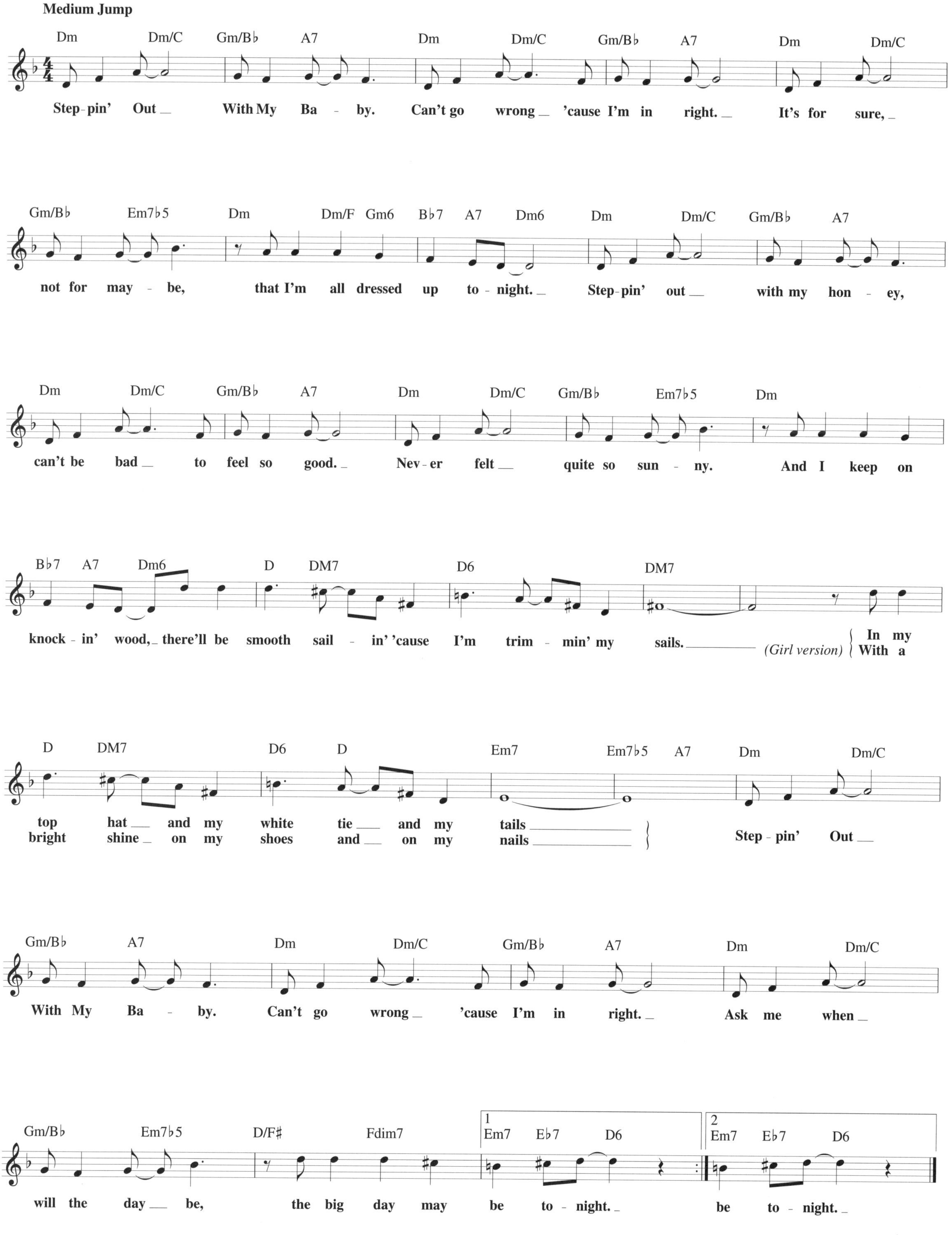

STILL WARM

By JOHN SCOFIELD

STOLEN MOMENTS

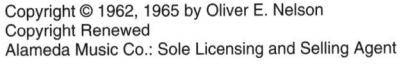

Words and Music by OLIVER NELSON

Stereophonic

331

Copyright © 1954 (Renewed) by Embassy Music Corporation (BMI)

By ERNEST B. WILKINS

Moderately

Story Of My Father

Copyright © 1980 Moseka Music
All Rights Administered by Embassy Music Corp.

Words and Music by
ABBEY LINCOLN

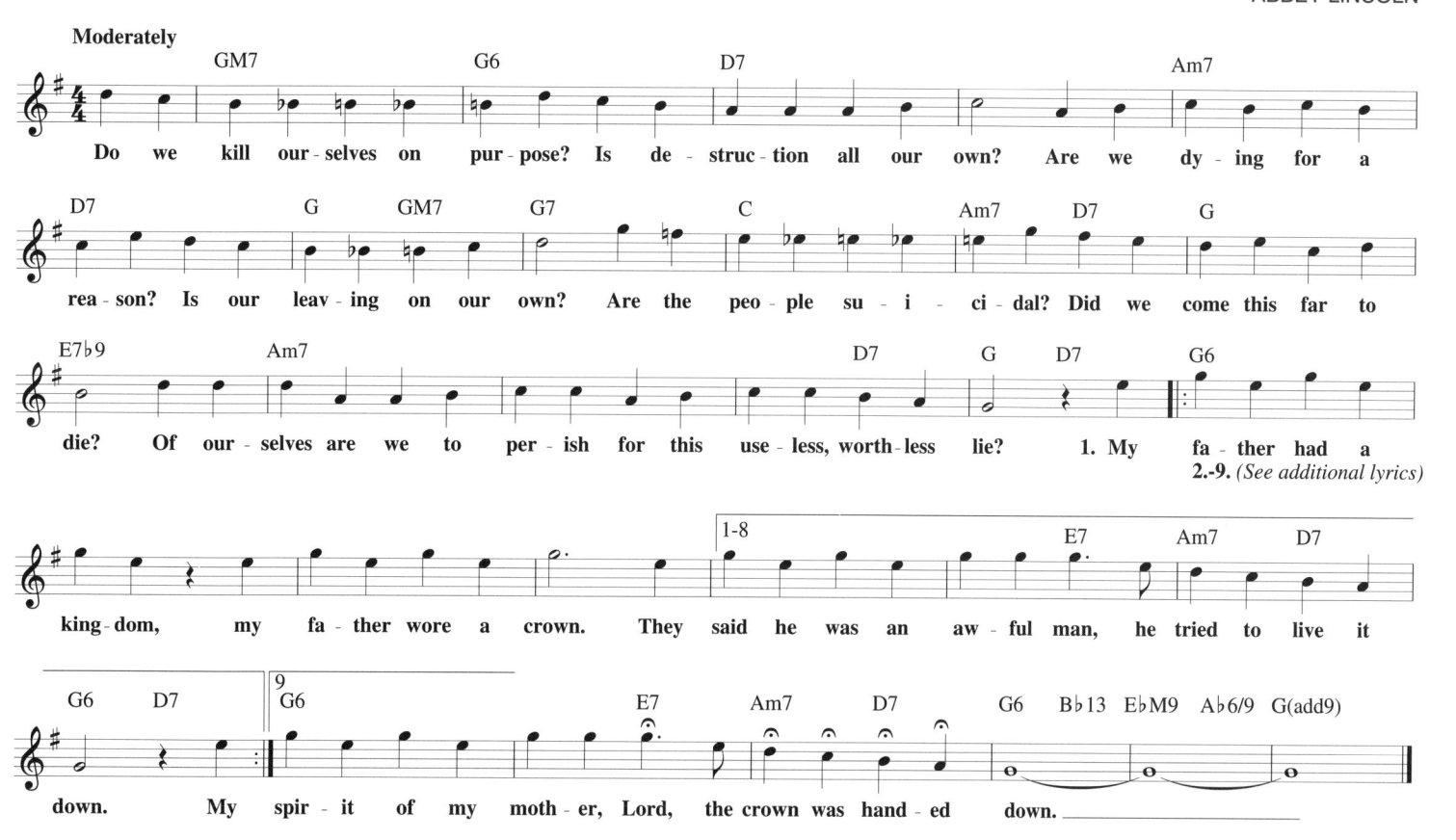

Moderately

Do we kill our-selves on pur-pose? Is de-struc-tion all our own? Are we dy-ing for a rea-son? Is our leav-ing on our own? Are the peo-ple su-i-ci-dal? Did we come this far to die? Of our-selves are we to per-ish for this use-less, worth-less lie? 1. My fa-ther had a

2.-9. (See additional lyrics)

king-dom, my fa-ther wore a crown. They said he was an aw-ful man, he tried to live it down. My spir-it of my moth-er, Lord, the crown was hand-ed down.

Additional Lyrics

2. My father built us houses,
   And he kept his folks inside,
   His images were stolen,
   And his beauty was denied,

3. My brothers are unhappy,
   My sisters they are too,
   My mother prays for glory,
   And my father stands accused,

4. My father, yes my father,
   A brace and skillful man,
   He fed and served his people,
   With the magic of his hand,

5. My father, yes my father,
   His soul was sorely tried,
   'Cause his images were stolen,
   And his beauty was denied,

6. Sometimes the river's calling
   Sometimes the shadows fall,
   That's when he's like a mountain,
   Rising master over all,

7. This Story Of My Father,
   Is the one I tell and give,
   It's the power and the glory,
   Of the life I make and live,

8. My father has a kingdom,
   My father wears a crown,
   And he lives within the people,
   In the lives he handed down.

9. My father has a kingdom,
   My father wears a crown,
   And through the spirit of my mother, Lord,
   The crown was handed down.

STRAIGHT LIFE

Written by ART PEPPER

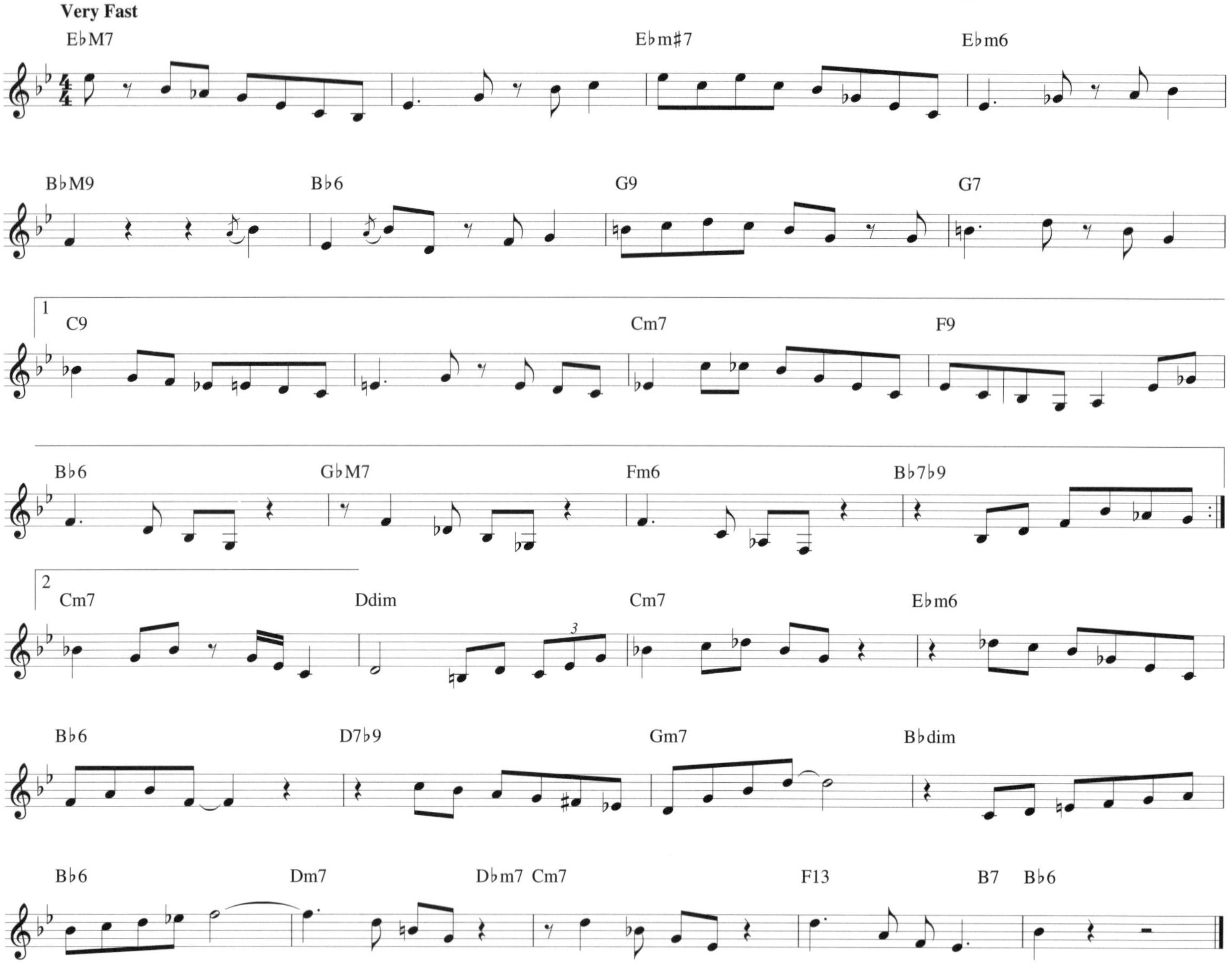

STRAPHANGIN'

By MICHAEL BRECKER

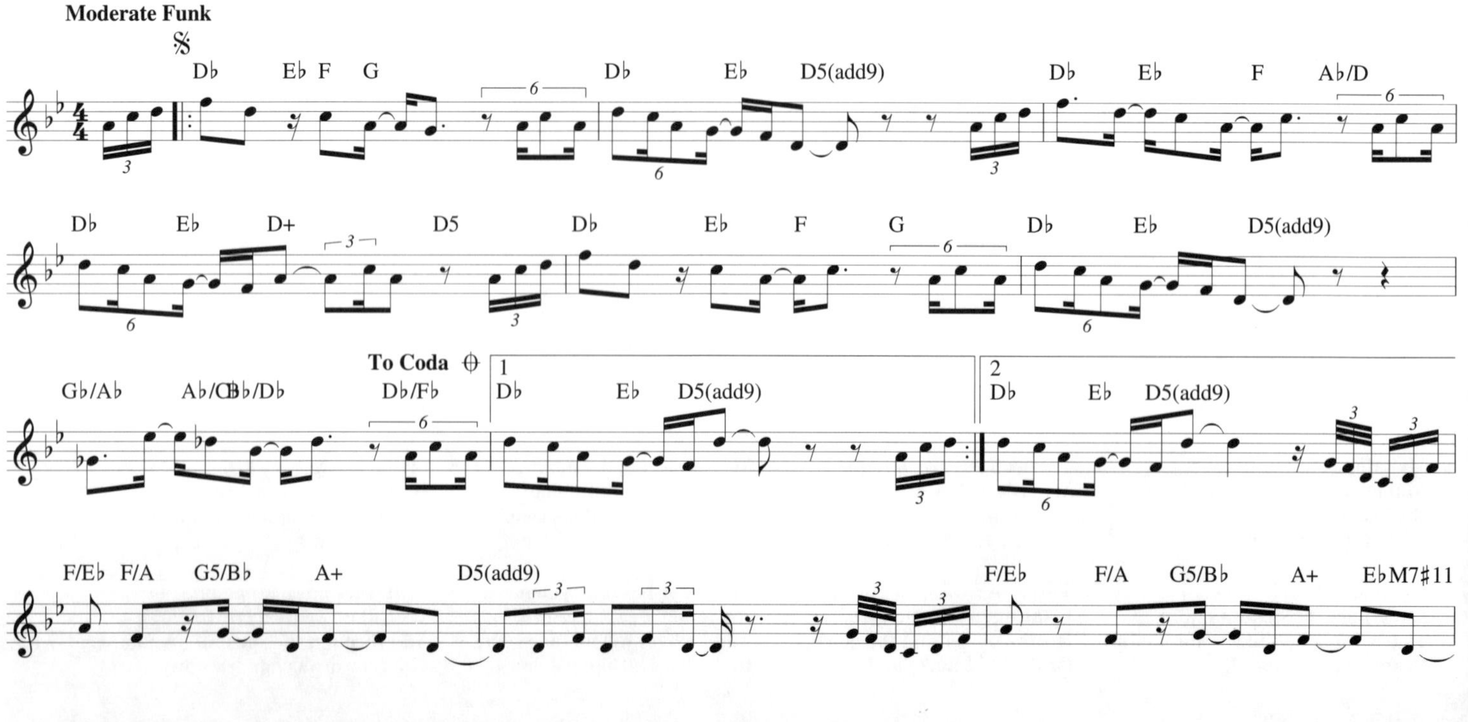

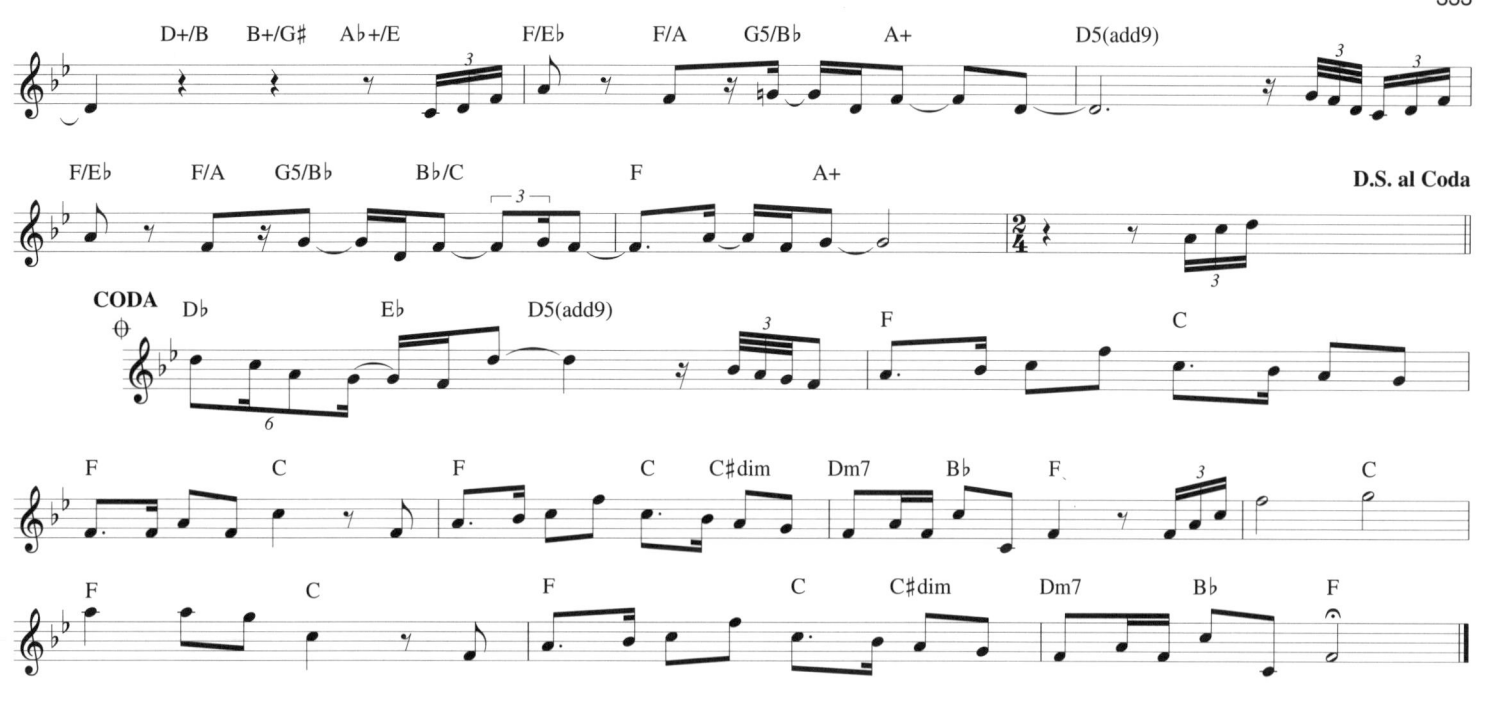

STROLLIN'

Words and Music by
HORACE SILVER

Music © 1960 by Ecaroh Music, Inc.
Copyright Renewed 1988
Words © 1994 by Ecaroh Music, Inc.

Moderately

I saw her Stroll-in' down the prom-e-nade.
She turned and smiled at me to my sur-prise.
I took one look and I said, "Oh, my God." Please help
I la-ter found out she had great big eyes. It all
me to win her. She's all that I need.
Dear Lord a-bove me please help me suc-ceed.
goes to prove that your dreams can come true, don't you see.

To Coda

I'm just as hap-py as I can be. She's Stroll-in' a-long with me.

CODA

be. Sweet-ie and me, ba-by makes three, Stroll-in'.

SUDDENLY IT'S SPRING
from the Paramount Motion Picture LADY IN THE DARK

Words by JOHNNY BURKE
Music by JAMES VAN HEUSEN

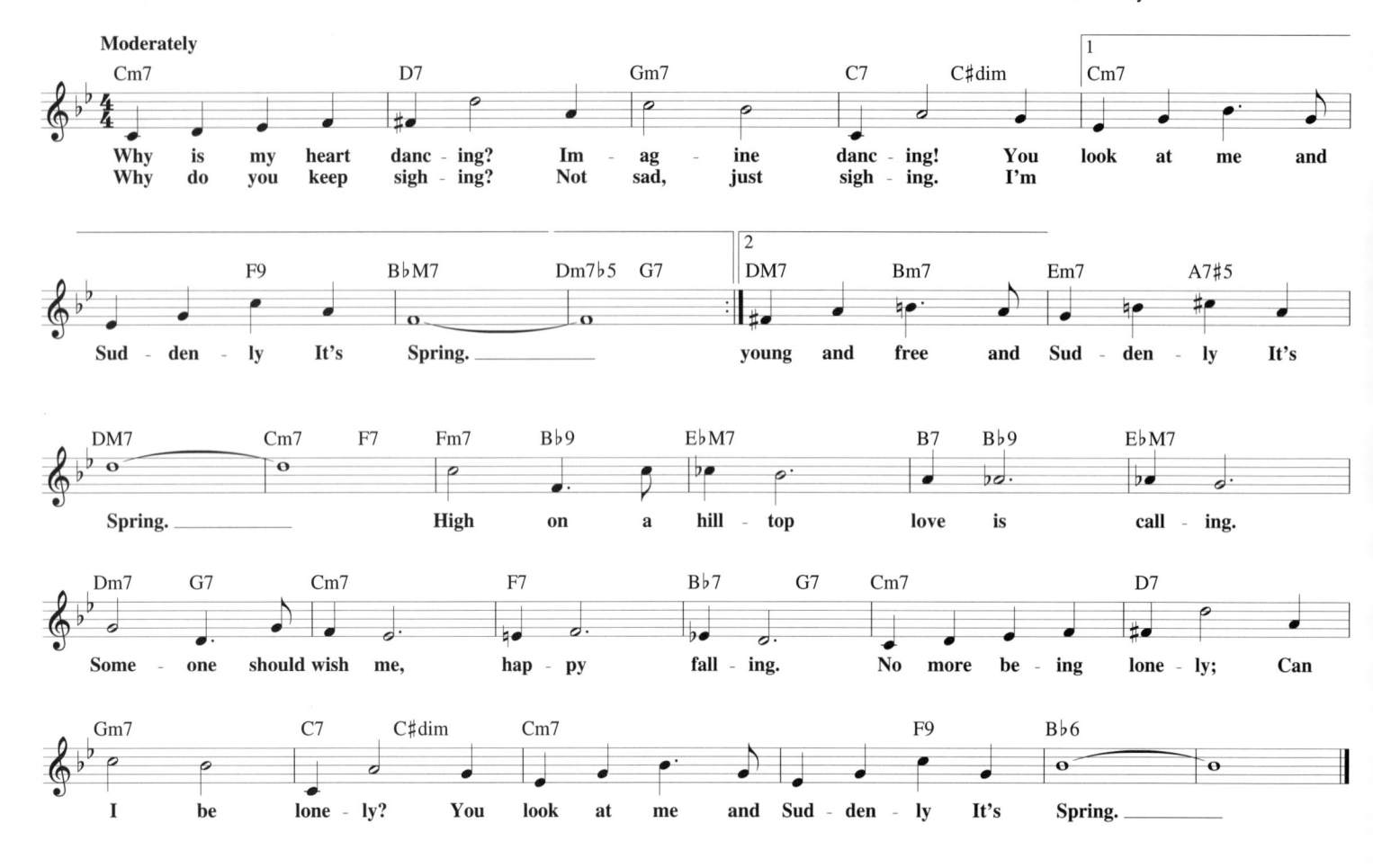

Copyright © 1943 (Renewed 1970) by Famous Music Corporation

Why is my heart danc-ing? Im-ag-ine danc-ing! You look at me and Sud-den-ly It's Spring. ____ young and free and Sud-den-ly It's Spring. ____ High on a hill-top love is call-ing. Some-one should wish me, hap-py fall-ing. No more be-ing lone-ly; Can I be lone-ly? You look at me and Sud-den-ly It's Spring. ____

Why do you keep sigh-ing? Not sad, just sigh-ing. I'm

SUN

Copyright © 1995 Nivek Publishing (BMI)

Written by KEVIN EUBANKS

D.S. al Fine
(with repeats)

SWAY
(Quien Sera)

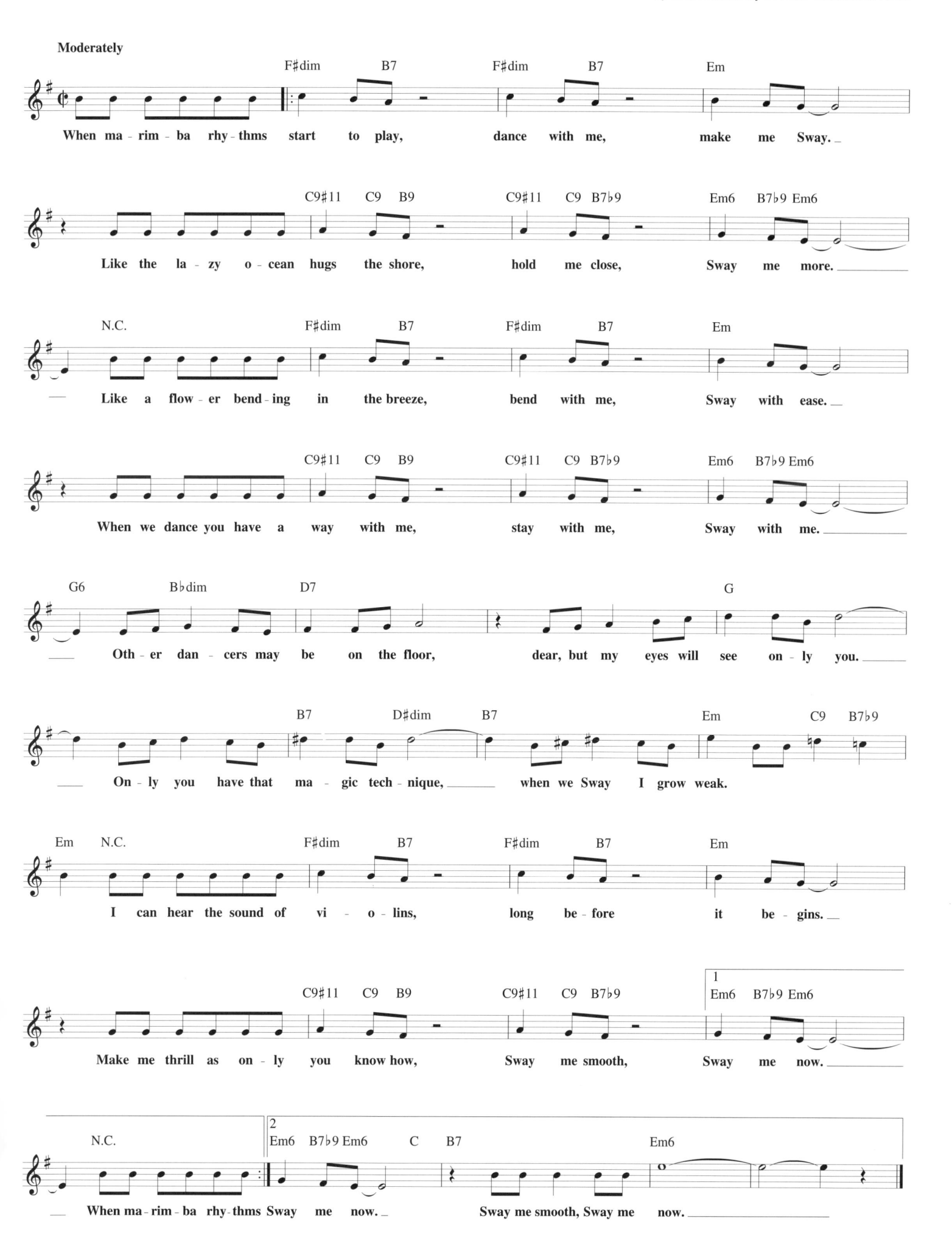

335

Copyright © 1954 by Peer International Corporation
Copyright Renewed

English Words and Music by NORMAN GIMBEL
Spanish Words by PABLO BELTRAN RUIZ

Moderately

When ma-rim-ba rhy-thms start to play, dance with me, make me Sway.
(F#dim B7 F#dim B7 Em)

Like the la-zy o-cean hugs the shore, hold me close, Sway me more.
(C9#11 C9 B9 C9#11 C9 B7b9 Em6 B7b9 Em6)

Like a flow-er bend-ing in the breeze, bend with me, Sway with ease.
(N.C. F#dim B7 F#dim B7 Em)

When we dance you have a way with me, stay with me, Sway with me.
(C9#11 C9 B9 C9#11 C9 B7b9 Em6 B7b9 Em6)

Oth-er dan-cers may be on the floor, dear, but my eyes will see on-ly you.
(G6 Bbdim D7 G)

On-ly you have that ma-gic tech-nique, when we Sway I grow weak.
(B7 D#dim B7 Em C9 B7b9)

I can hear the sound of vi-o-lins, long be-fore it be-gins.
(Em N.C. F#dim B7 F#dim B7 Em)

Make me thrill as on-ly you know how, Sway me smooth, Sway me now.
(C9#11 C9 B9 C9#11 C9 B7b9)
[1. Em6 B7b9 Em6]

[2. Em6 B7b9 Em6 C B7 Em6]
When ma-rim-ba rhy-thms Sway me now. Sway me smooth, Sway me now.
(N.C.)

SUNDAY IN NEW YORK

Words and Music by PETER NERO

Copyright © 1963 by Bermar Publishing
Copyright Renewed

Moderately

New York on Sunday, big city taking a nap!
If you've got troubles, just take them out for a walk.
Two hearts stop beating, you're both too breathless to speak!

Slow down, it's Sunday! Life's a ball, let it fall right in your lap!
They'll burst like bubbles in the fun of a Sunday In New
Love smiles her

York! You can spend time without spending a dime watching people watch people pass!

Later you pause, and in one of the stores there's that face next to yours in the glass!

D.C. al Coda

CODA

greeting, then the dream that has seen you thru the week

comes true on Sunday In New York!

SURF RIDE

Written by ART PEPPER

Copyright © 1957 Herman Lubinsky
Copyright Renewed 1985 Arthur Pepper Music

Very fast

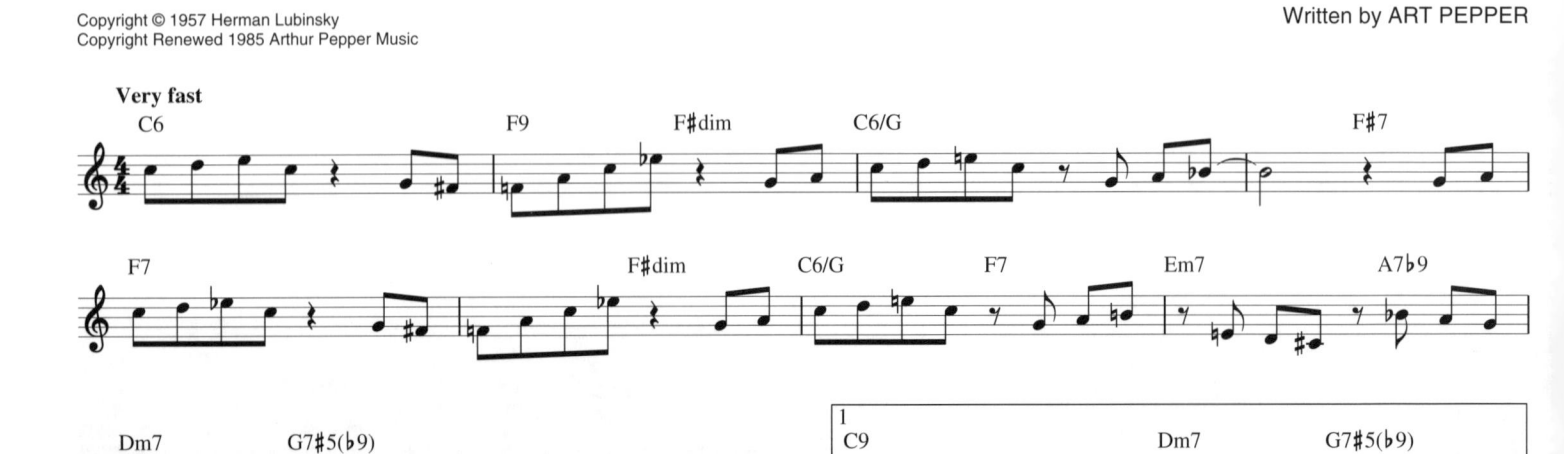

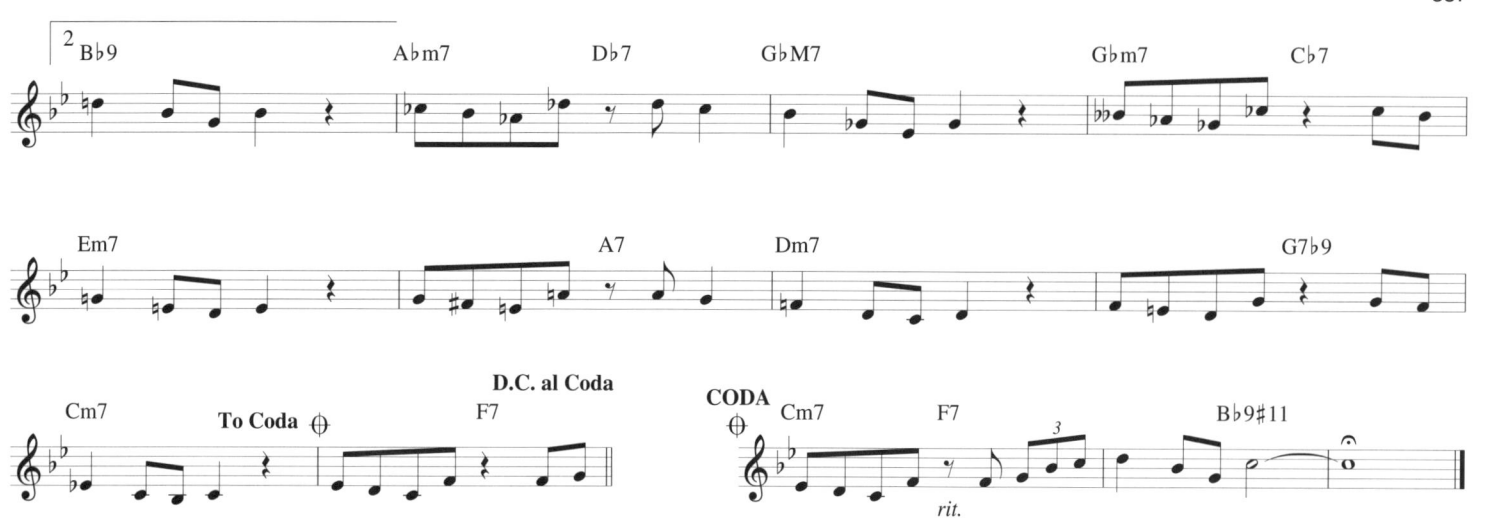

TAKE A WALK

By MICHAEL BRECKER

Copyright © 1982 Grand Street Music (BMI)

Swing 41

By DJANGO REINHARDT

Copyright © 1941 (Renewed) by Publications Francis Day S.A.
All Rights in the U.S.A. and Canada Controlled by Jewel Music Publishing Co., Inc.

[Sheet music: Swing tempo, key of G. Chord progression includes G6, C6, C#dim7, D7, G, C7, G, G#dim, Am7, D7, G6, C, C#dim7, D7, G6.]

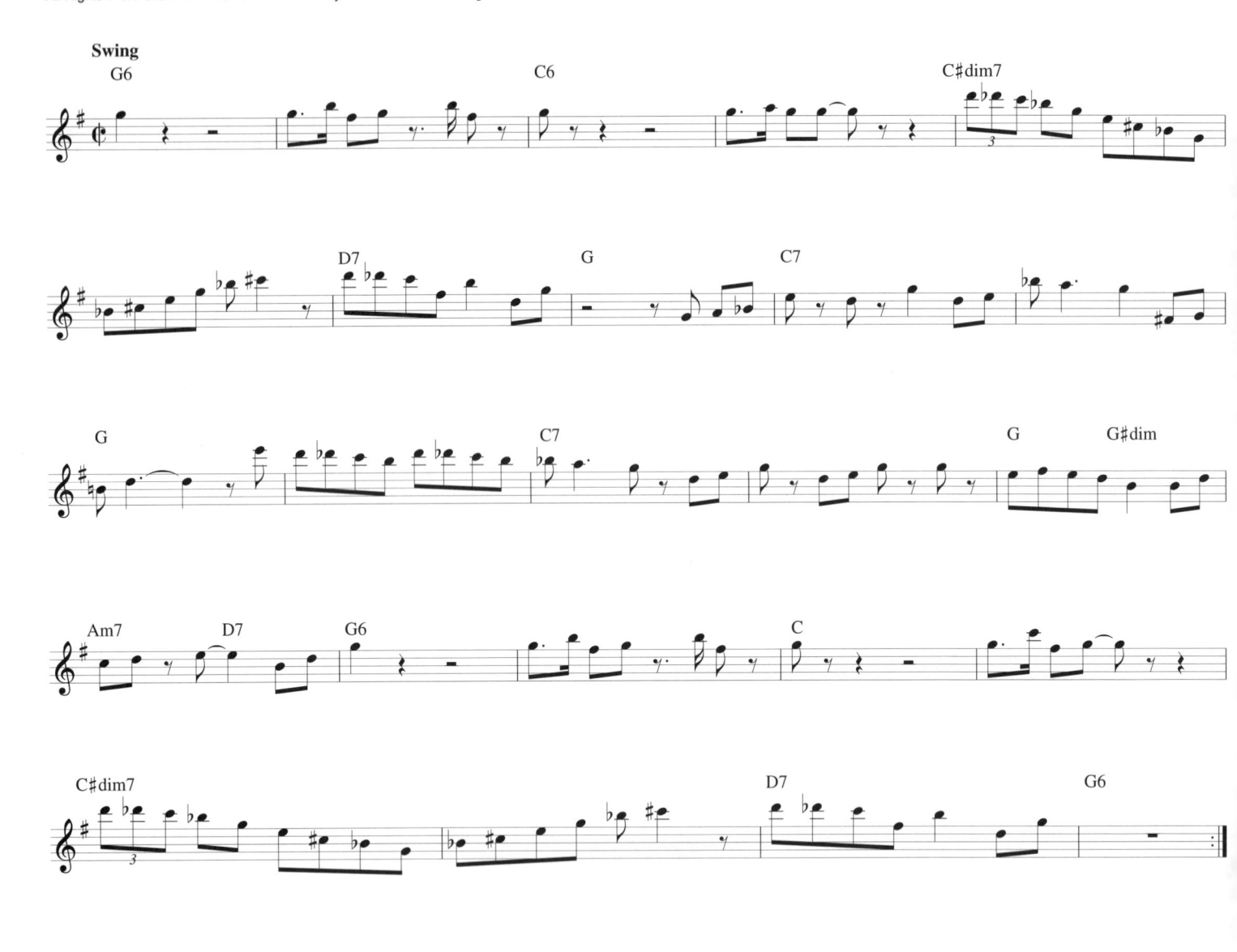

Tangerine
from the Paramount Picture THE FLEET'S IN

Words by JOHNNY MERCER
Music by VICTOR SCHERTZINGER

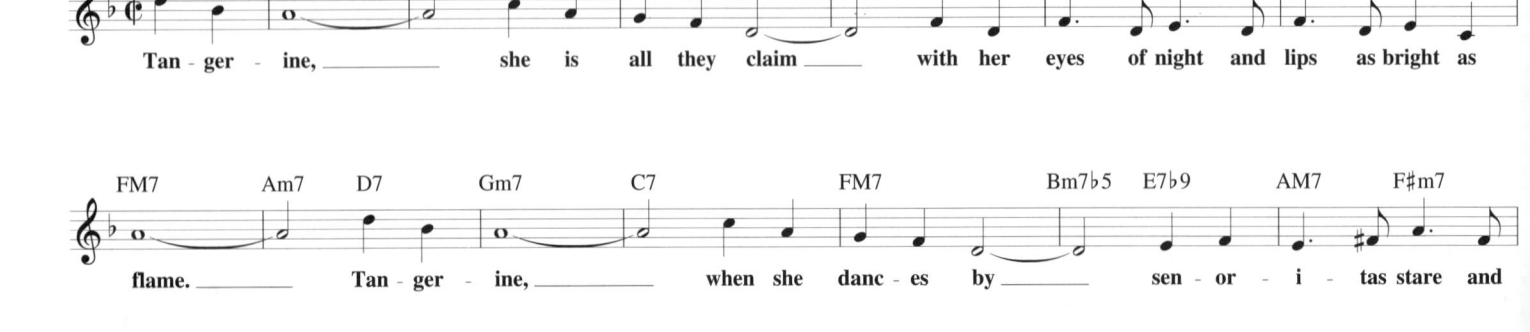

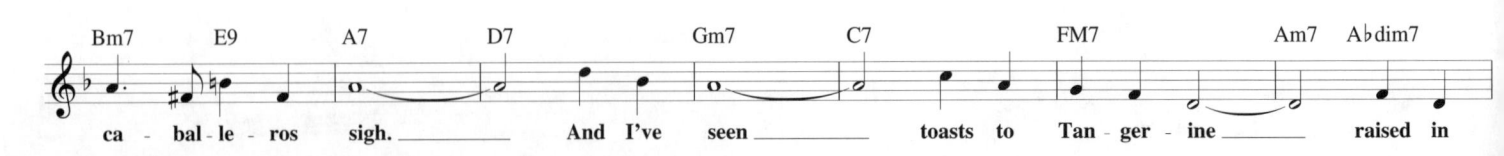

Copyright © 1942 (Renewed 1969) by Famous Music Corporation

[Sheet music: Easy Swing, key of F.]

Tan-ger-ine,____ she is all they claim____ with her eyes of night and lips as bright as flame.____ Tan-ger-ine,____ when she danc-es by____ sen-or-i-tas stare and ca-bal-le-ros sigh.____ And I've seen toasts to Tan-ger-ine____ raised in

TEACH ME TONIGHT

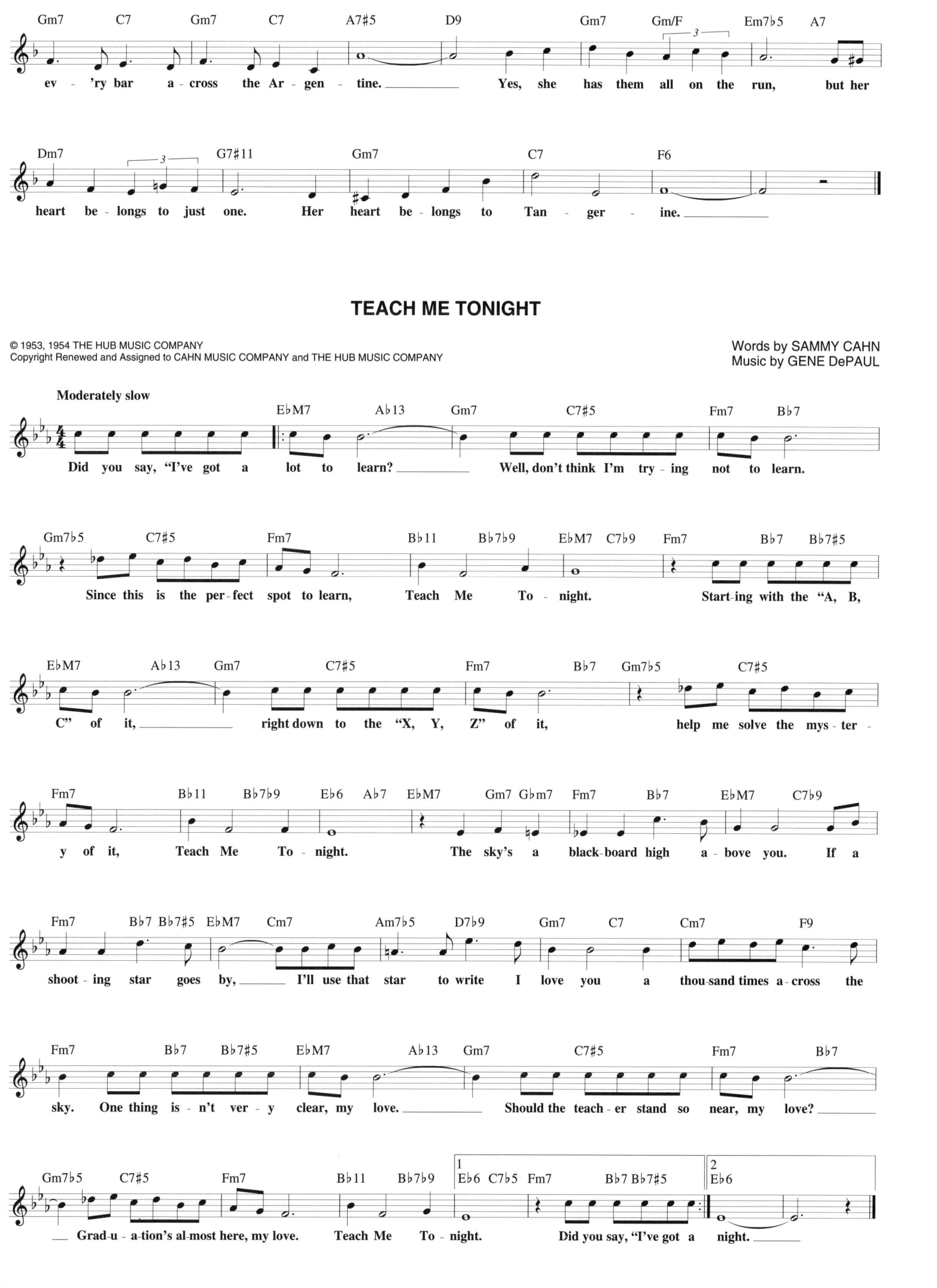

© 1953, 1954 THE HUB MUSIC COMPANY
Copyright Renewed and Assigned to CAHN MUSIC COMPANY and THE HUB MUSIC COMPANY

Words by SAMMY CAHN
Music by GENE DePAUL

Moderately slow

Did you say, "I've got a lot to learn?" Well, don't think I'm trying not to learn. Since this is the perfect spot to learn, Teach Me Tonight. Starting with the "A, B, C" of it, right down to the "X, Y, Z" of it, help me solve the mystery of it, Teach Me Tonight. The sky's a blackboard high above you. If a shooting star goes by, I'll use that star to write I love you a thousand times across the sky. One thing isn't very clear, my love. Should the teacher stand so near, my love? Graduation's almost here, my love. Teach Me Tonight. Did you say, "I've got a night."

TAKE FIVE

By PAUL DESMOND

© 1960 (Renewed 1988) Desmond Music Company
All Rights outside the USA Controlled by Derry Music Company

TAKE TEN

By PAUL DESMOND

© 1963 (Renewed) Desmond Music Company

TANGA

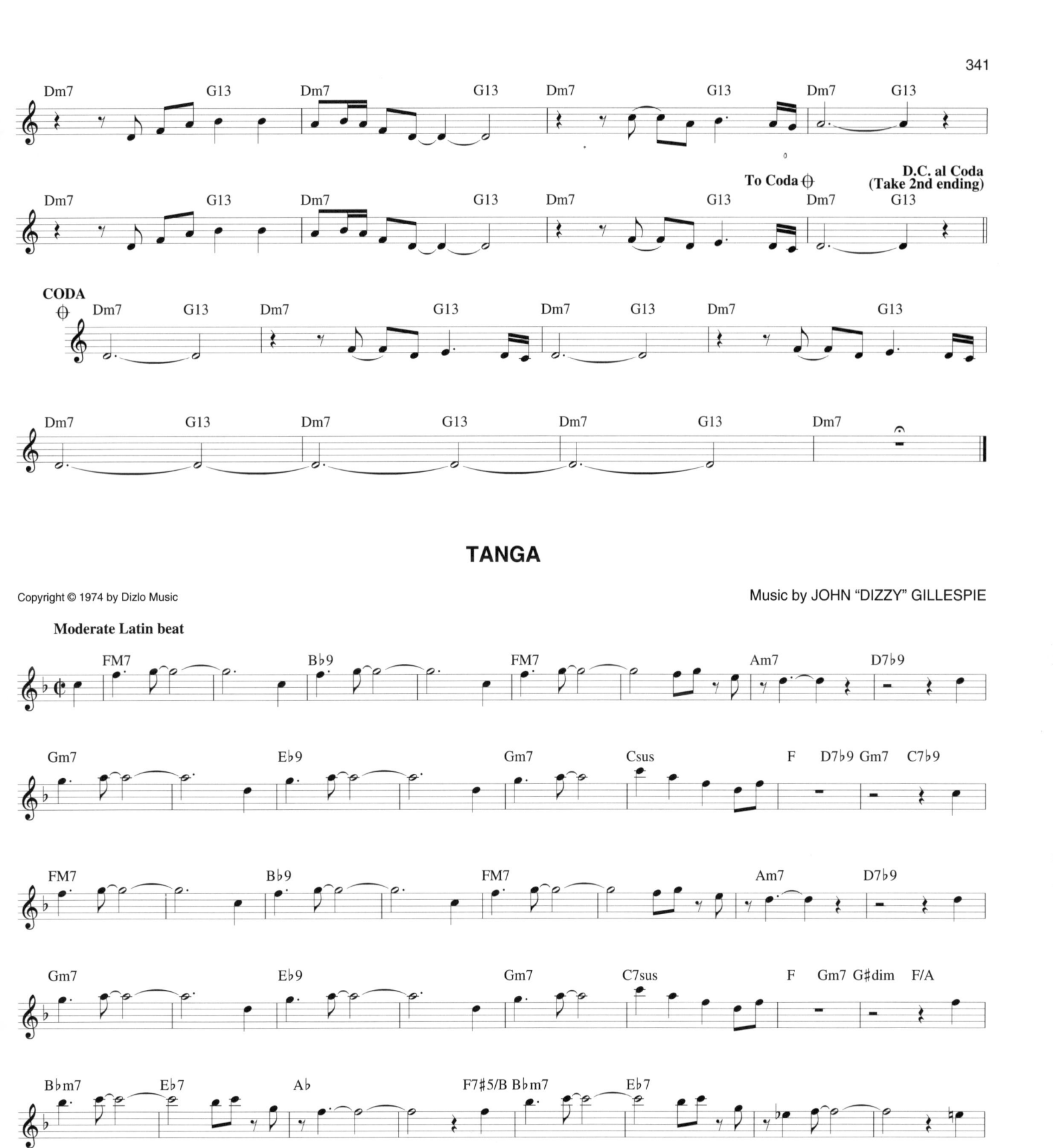

Music by JOHN "DIZZY" GILLESPIE

Copyright © 1974 by Dizlo Music

TELL ME A BEDTIME STORY

By HERBIE HANCOCK

Copyright © 1973 by Hancock Music Co.

THERE'S A MINGUS AMONK US

By RANDY BRECKER

Copyright © 1986 Bowery Music (BMI)

THINGS AIN'T WHAT THEY USED TO BE

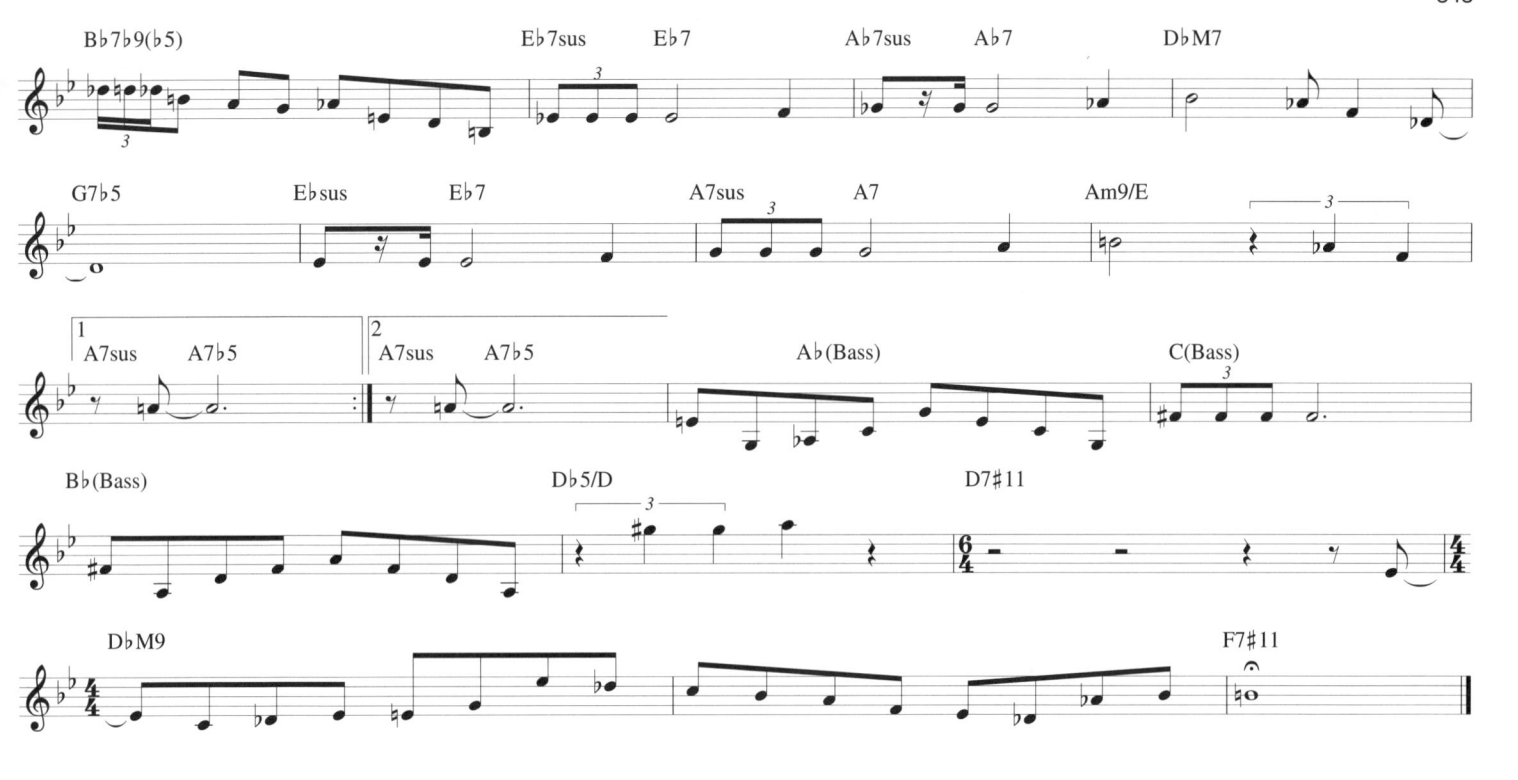

By MERCER ELLINGTON

Copyright © 1942, 1964 (Renewed) by Tempo Music, Inc. and Music Sales Corporation (ASCAP)
All Rights Administered by Music Sales Corporation

Moderately

Got so wear-y of be-in' noth-in', felt so drear-y just do-in' noth-in', did-n't care ev-er get-tin' noth-in', felt so low. Now my eyes on the far ho-ri-zon can see a glow an-noun-cin' Things Ain't What They Used To Be. Look at that ar-my fight-in' to be free. It does-n't bar me! Shows me how to go with my head up; eyes ain't look-in' low. Don't feel fed up, that's how come I see a vic-to-ry; be-lieve me Things Ain't What They Used To Be.

No use be-in' a doubt-in' Thom-as, no ig-nor-in' that ros-y prom-ise; now I know there's a hap-py sto-ry yet to come. It's the dawn of the day of glo-ry: mil-len-ni-um. I tell you Things Ain't What They Used To Be.

THANKS FOR THE MEMORY
from the Paramount Picture BIG BROADCAST OF 1938

Words and Music by LEO ROBIN
and RALPH RAINGER

Copyright © 1937 (Renewed 1964) by Paramount Music Corporation

Moderately

Thanks For The Mem-o-ry of can-dle-light and wine, cas-tles on the Rhine, the
Thanks For The Mem-o-ry of sen-ti-men-tal verse, noth-ing in my purse, and

Par-the-non and mo-ments on the Hud-son Riv-er Line. How love-ly it was! Thanks For The
chuck-les when the preach-er said, "For bet-ter or for worse." How love-ly it was! Thanks For The

Mem-o-ry of rain-y af-ter-noons, swing-y Har-lem tunes, and mo-tor trips and burn-ing lips and
Mem-o-ry of lin-ge-rie with lace, Pils-ner by the case, and how I jumped the day you trumped my

burn-ing toast and prunes. How love-ly it was! Man-y's the time that we
one and on-ly ace. How love-ly it was! We said good-bye with a

feast-ed and man-y's the time that we fast-ed. Oh, well, it was swell while it
high-ball; then I got as "high" as a stee-ple. But we were in-tel-li-gent

last-ed; we did have fun and no harm done. And Thanks For The Mem-o-ry of
peo-ple; no tears, no fuss, Hur-ray for us. So Thanks For The Mem-o-ry and

sun-burns at the shore, nights in Sing-a-pore. You might have been a head-ache but you
strict-ly en-tre-nous, dar-ling, how are you? And how are all the lit-tle dreams that

1. nev-er were a bore, so thank you so much.
2. nev-er did come true?

Awf-'ly glad I met you, chee-ri-o and too-dle-oo and thank you so much!

THAT OLD BLACK MAGIC

from the Paramount Picture STAR SPANGLED RHYTHM

Words by JOHNNY MERCER
Music by HAROLD ARLEN

THAT'S RIGHT

By BENNY GREEN

THINGS TO COME

By DIZZY GILLESPIE and GIL FULLER

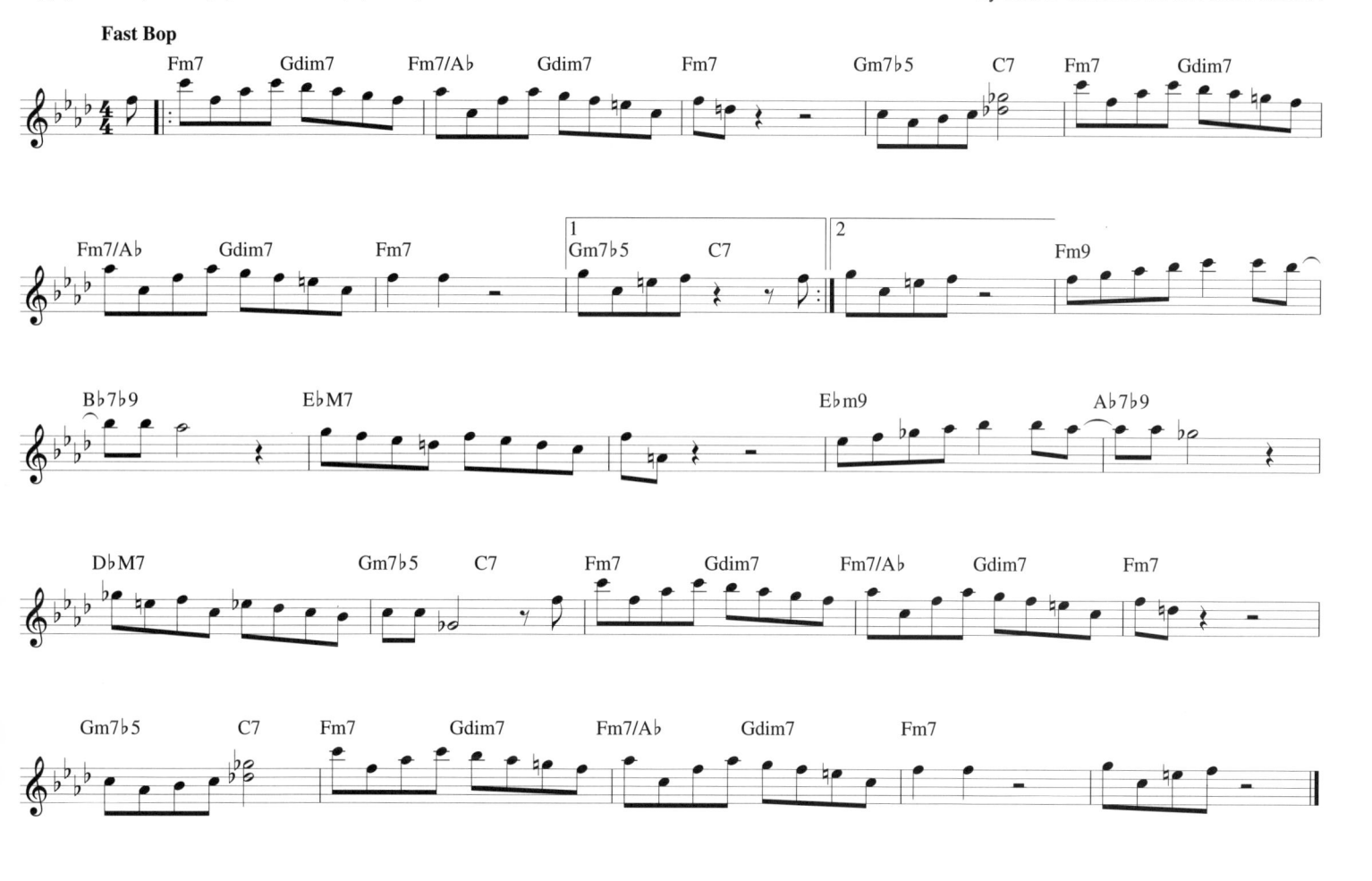

THE THIRD PLANE

Written by RON CARTER

THIS IS ALL I ASK
(Beautiful Girls Walk a Little Slower)

Words and Music by
GORDON JENKINS

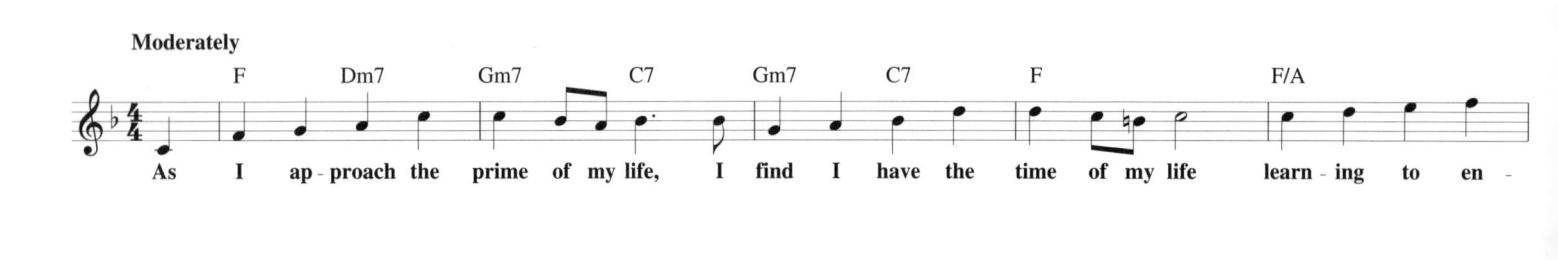

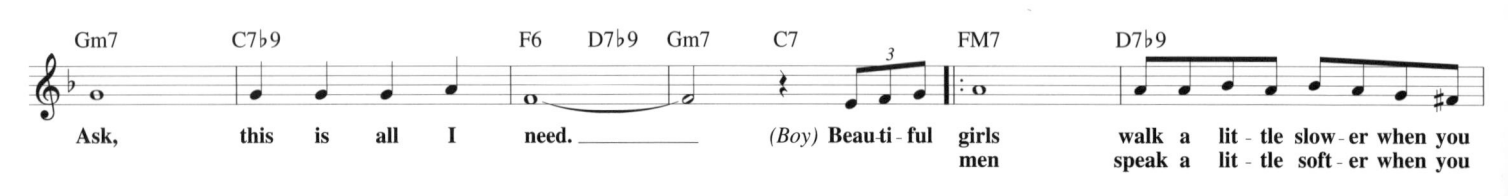

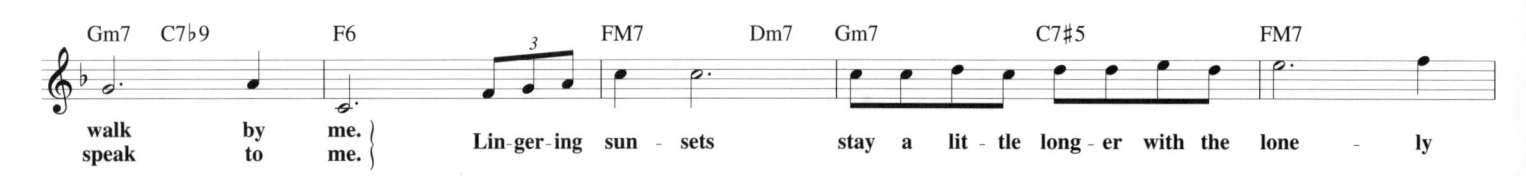

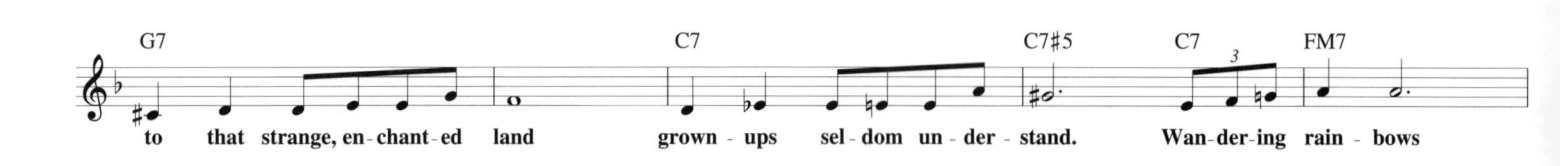

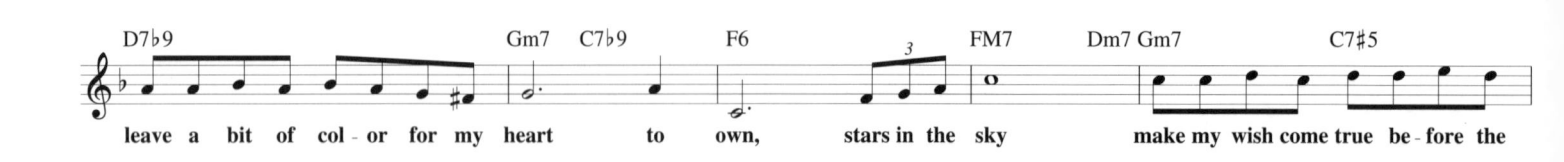

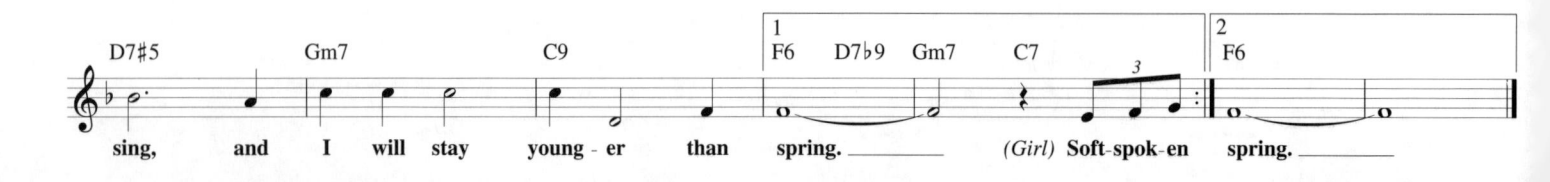

Copyright © 1958 by Chappell & Co. and Robbins Music Corp.
Copyright Renewed

Moderately

As I approach the prime of my life, I find I have the time of my life learning to enjoy at my leisure all the simple pleasures. And so I happily concede, This Is All I Ask, this is all I need.

(Boy) Beautiful girls walk a little slower when you walk by me.
men speak a little softer when you speak to me.

Lingering sunsets stay a little longer with the lonely sea. Children ev-'ry-where, when you shoot at bad men, shoot at me. Take me to that strange, enchanted land grown-ups seldom understand. Wandering rainbows leave a bit of color for my heart to own, stars in the sky make my wish come true before the night has flown. And let the music play as long as there's a song to sing, and I will stay younger than spring.

(Girl) Soft-spoken spring.

THIS YEAR'S KISSES
from the 20th Century Fox Motion Picture ON THE AVENUE

© Copyright 1937 by Irving Berlin
Copyright Renewed

Words and Music by
IRVING BERLIN

Slowly

This year's crop of kiss-es don't seem as sweet to me.

This year's crop just miss-es what kiss-es used to be.

This year's new ro-mance does-n't seem to have a chance, e-ven helped by

Mis-ter Moon a-bove. This year's crop of kiss-es is not for me,

1. for I'm still wear-ing last year's love.
2. love.

THREE LITTLE WORDS
from the Motion Picture CHECK AND DOUBLE CHECK

© 1930 WARNER BROS., INC.
© Renewed 1958 EDWIN H. MORRIS & COMPANY, A Division of MPL Communications, Inc. and HARRY RUBY MUSIC
All Rights for HARRY RUBY MUSIC Administered by THE SONGWRITERS GUILD OF AMERICA

Lyric by BERT KALMAR
Music by HARRY RUBY

Moderately fast

Three Lit-tle Words, oh, what I'd give for that won-der-ful phrase. To hear those

Three Lit-tle Words, that's all I'd live for the rest of my days. And what I

feel in my heart they tell sin-cere-ly, no oth-er words can tell it half so clear-ly.

Three Lit-tle Words, eight lit-tle let-ters which sim-ply mean, "I love you."

THIS MASQUERADE

Copyright © 1972, 1973 by Embassy Music Corporation and Stuck On Music

Words and Music by
LEON RUSSELL

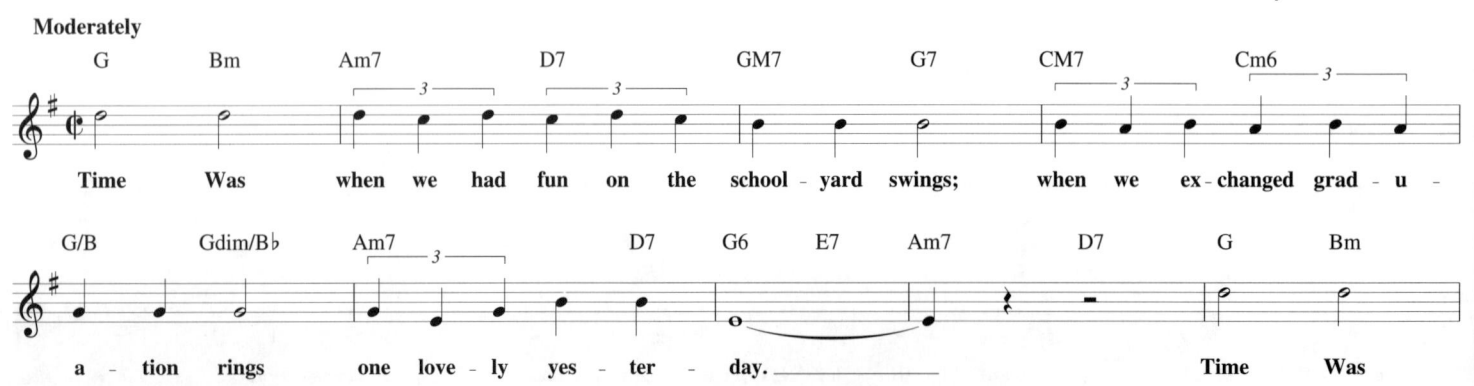

Moderately slow

Are we really happy here with this lonely game we play,
Thoughts of leaving disappear ev'ry time I see your eyes

Looking for words to say?
no matter how hard I try.

Searching but not finding understanding any way,
To understand the reasons that we carry on this way,

we're lost in a masquerade.

Both afraid to say we're just too far away from being close together from the start. We tried to talk it over, but the words got in the way. We're lost inside this lonely game we play.

TIME WAS

Copyright © 1936 by Southern Music Pub. Co. Inc.
Copyright Renewed

English Words by S.K. RUSSELL
Music by MIGUEL PRADO

Moderately

Time Was when we had fun on the schoolyard swings; when we exchanged graduation rings one lovely yesterday. Time Was

[Lyrics, first song continued:]

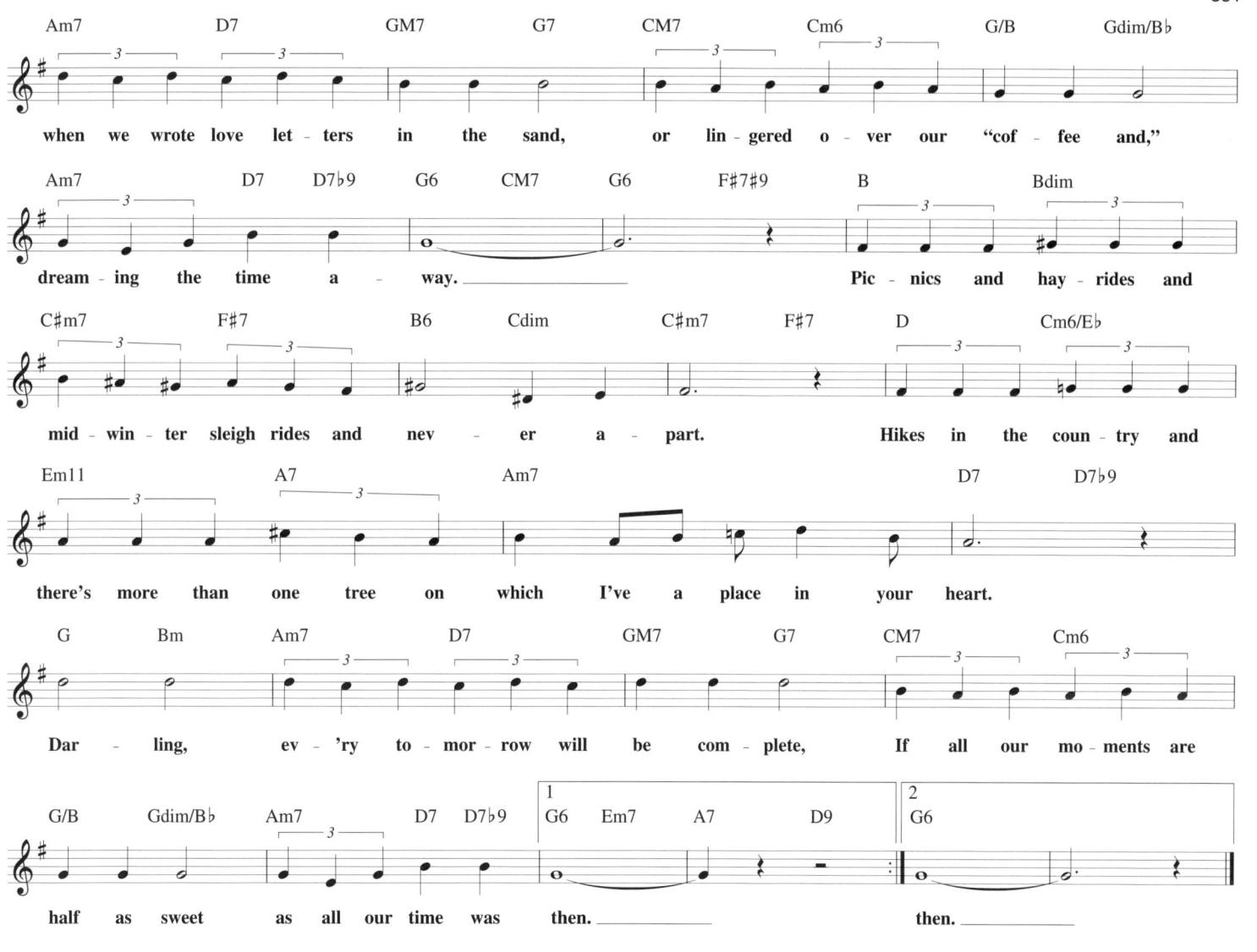

...when we wrote love letters in the sand, or lingered over our "coffee and," dreaming the time away. Picnics and hayrides and midwinter sleigh rides and never apart. Hikes in the country and there's more than one tree on which I've a place in your heart. Darling, ev'ry tomorrow will be complete, If all our moments are half as sweet as all our time was then. then.

TILL THE CLOUDS ROLL BY
from OH BOY!

Copyright © 1998 by HAL LEONARD CORPORATION

Words by P.G. WODEHOUSE
Music by JEROME KERN

Moderately

Oh, the rain comes a-pitter, patter, and I'd like to be safe in bed. Skies are weeping, while the world is sleeping, trouble heaping on our head. It is vain to remain and chatter, and to wait for a clearer sky. Helter skelter I must fly for shelter till The Clouds Roll By. Oh, the By.

TO EACH HIS OWN
from the Paramount Picture THE CONVERSATION

Copyright © 1946 (Renewed 1973) by Paramount Music Corporation

Words and Music by JAY LIVINGSTON
and RAY EVANS

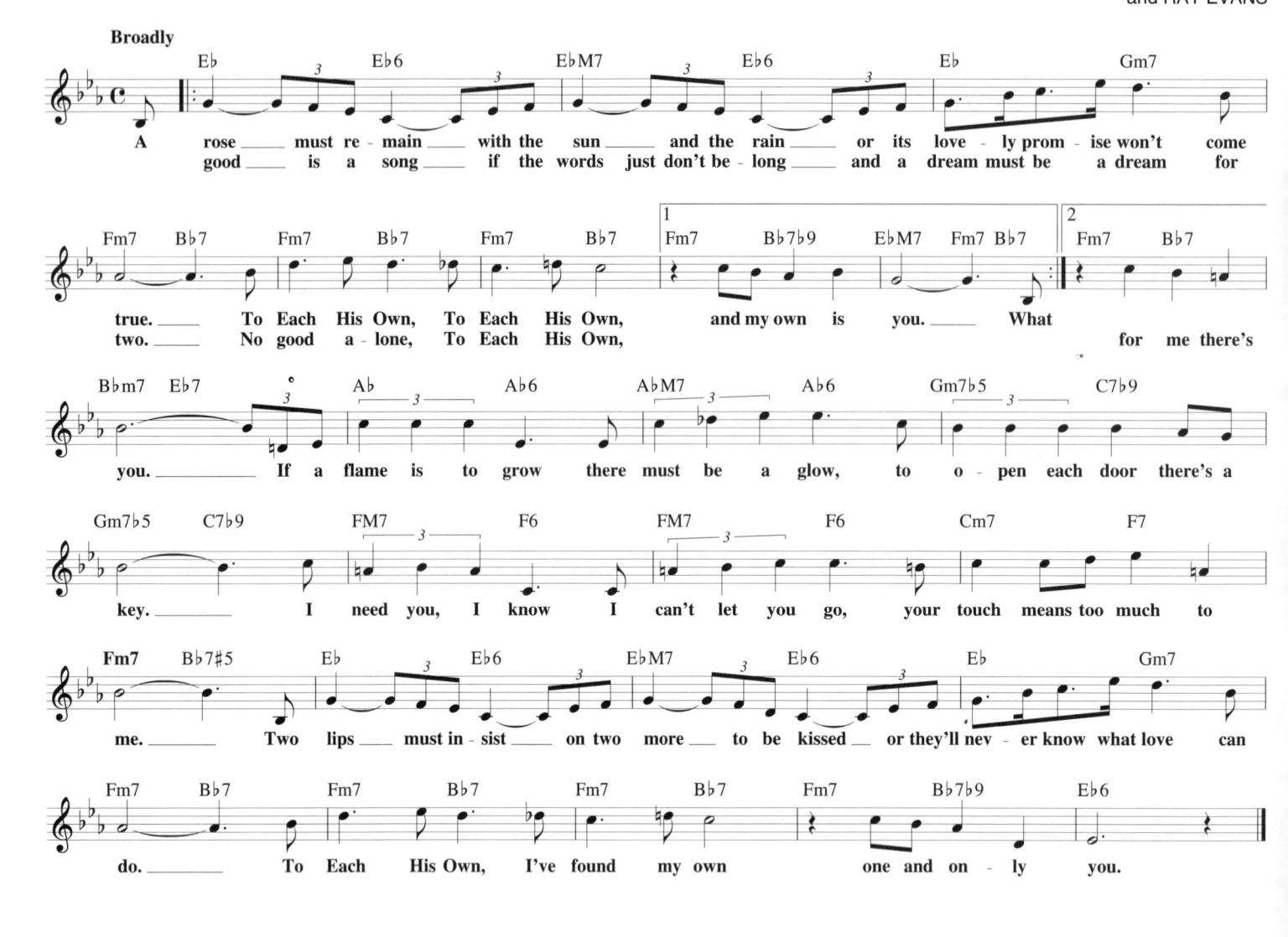

Broadly

A rose must remain with the sun and the rain or its lovely promise won't come true. To Each His Own, To Each His Own, and my own is you. What you. If a flame is to grow there must be a glow, to open each door there's a key. I need you, I know I can't let you go, your touch means too much to me. Two lips must insist on two more to be kissed or they'll never know what love can do. To Each His Own, I've found my own one and only you.

good is a song if the words just don't belong and a dream must be a dream for two. No good alone, To Each His Own, for me there's

TOKU-DO

© 1978 Buster Williams Productions, Inc. (SESAC)
All Rights Administered by Soroka Music Ltd.

By BUSTER WILLIAMS

Moderately

TOO CLOSE FOR COMFORT

from the Musical MR. WONDERFUL

Words and Music by JERRY BOCK,
LARRY HOLOFCENER and GEORGE WEISS

TOPSY

Written by EDGAR BATTLE
and EDDIE DURHAM

TOURIST IN PARADISE

By RUSS FREEMAN

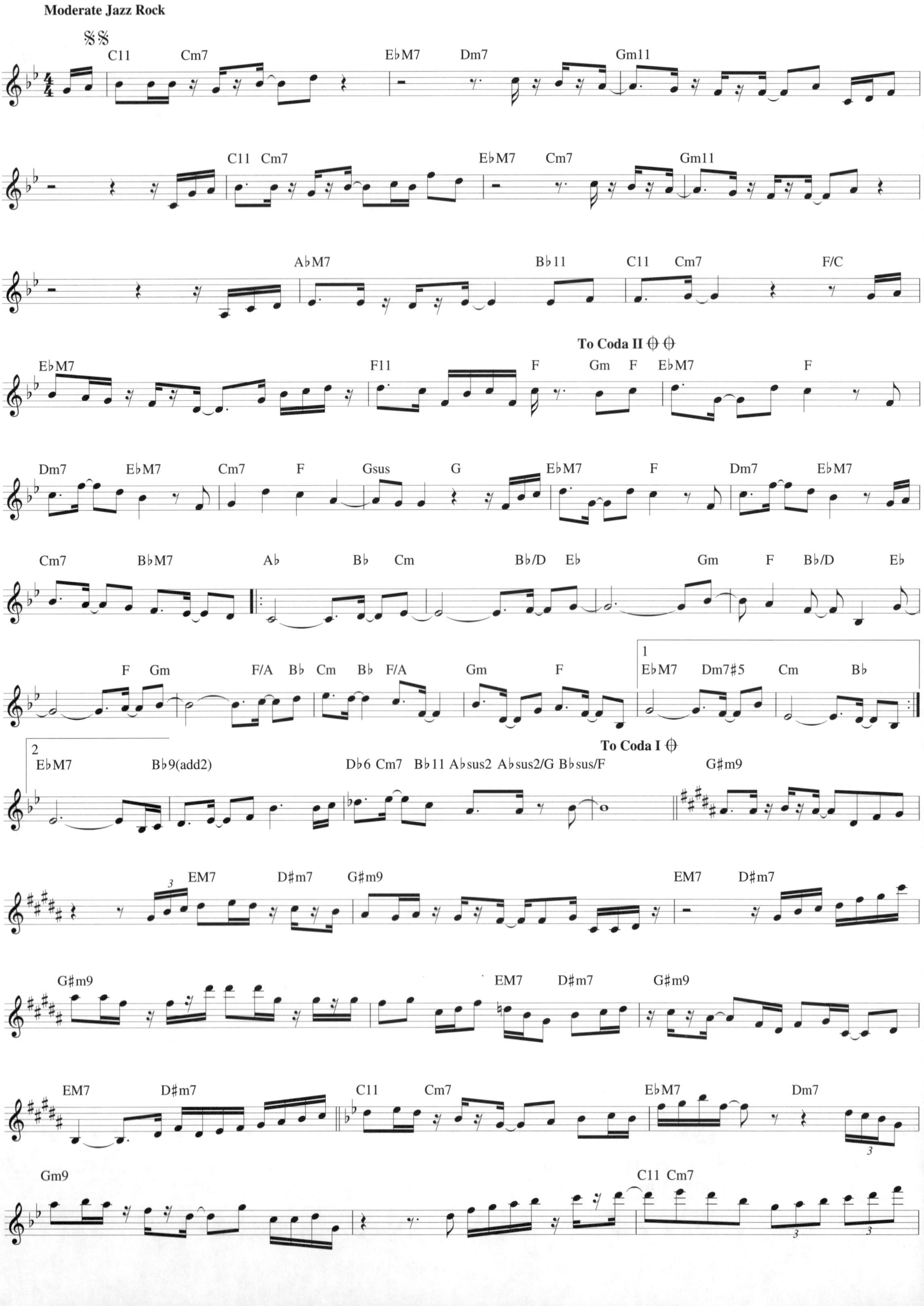

TWO OF A MIND

© 1962 (Renewed) Desmond Music Company

By PAUL DESMOND

TRISTE

By ANTONIO CARLOS JOBIM

Copyright © 1967, 1968 Antonio Carlos Jobim
Copyright Renewed
Published by Corcovado Music Corp.

Sad is to live in sol-i-tude far from your tran-quil al-ti-tude. Sad is to know that no one ev-er can live on a dream that nev-er can be, will nev-er be. Dream-er a-wake, wake up and see. Your beau-ty is an aer-o-plane so high, my heart can't bear the strain. A heart that stops when you pass by on-ly to cause me pain. Sad is to live in sol-i-tude.

ULTRAFOX

By DJANGO REINHARDT

Copyright © 1938 (Renewed) by Publications Francis Day S.A.
All Rights in the U.S.A. and Canada Controlled by Jewel Music Publishing Co., Inc.

Moderately

The Very Thought Of You

Words and Music by RAY NOBLE

Copyright © 1934 Campbell Connelly Inc. and Warner Bros. Inc.
Copyright renewed; extended term of Copyright deriving from Ray Noble assigned and effective April 16, 1990 to Range Road Music Inc. and Quartet Music Inc.

With a slow, easy swing

The Ver-y Thought Of You, and I for-get to do the lit-tle or-di-nar-y things that ev-'ry-one ought to do. I'm liv-ing in a kind of day-dream, I'm hap-py as a king, and fool-ish tho' it may seem, to me that's ev-'ry-thing. The mere i-dea of you the long-ing here for you, You'll nev-er know how slow the mo-ments go 'til I'm near to you. I see your face in ev-'ry flow-er; your eyes in stars a-bove, It's just the thought of you, The Ver-y Thought Of You, my love. The Ver-y love.

Walk Don't Run

Words and Music by JOHNNY SMITH

Copyright © 1960 by Peermusic Ltd., On Board Music and Mesa Verde Music Co.
Copyright Renewed
All Rights Administered by Peermusic Ltd.

Moderately

TOO LATE NOW

Words by ALAN JAY LERNER
Music by BURTON LANE

VISA

By CHARLIE PARKER

UNLESS IT'S YOU

Lyric by MORGAN AMES
Music by JOHNNY MANDEL

Lyrically

I wonder why I've loved so few; I guess I'm shy, I'm just like you. And so I try to turn a-way, though you're the sky to me, the joy to me, the day. At times I stray and think I'm free, then in your way you reach for me. You know I'll stay, I always do, for what is love to me Unless It's You? I wonder You?

WATERMELON MAN

By HERBIE HANCOCK

Jazz-Rock

WALTZ NEW

By JAMES S. HALL

WAVE

Words and Music by
ANTONIO CARLOS JOBIM

WE'LL BE TOGETHER AGAIN

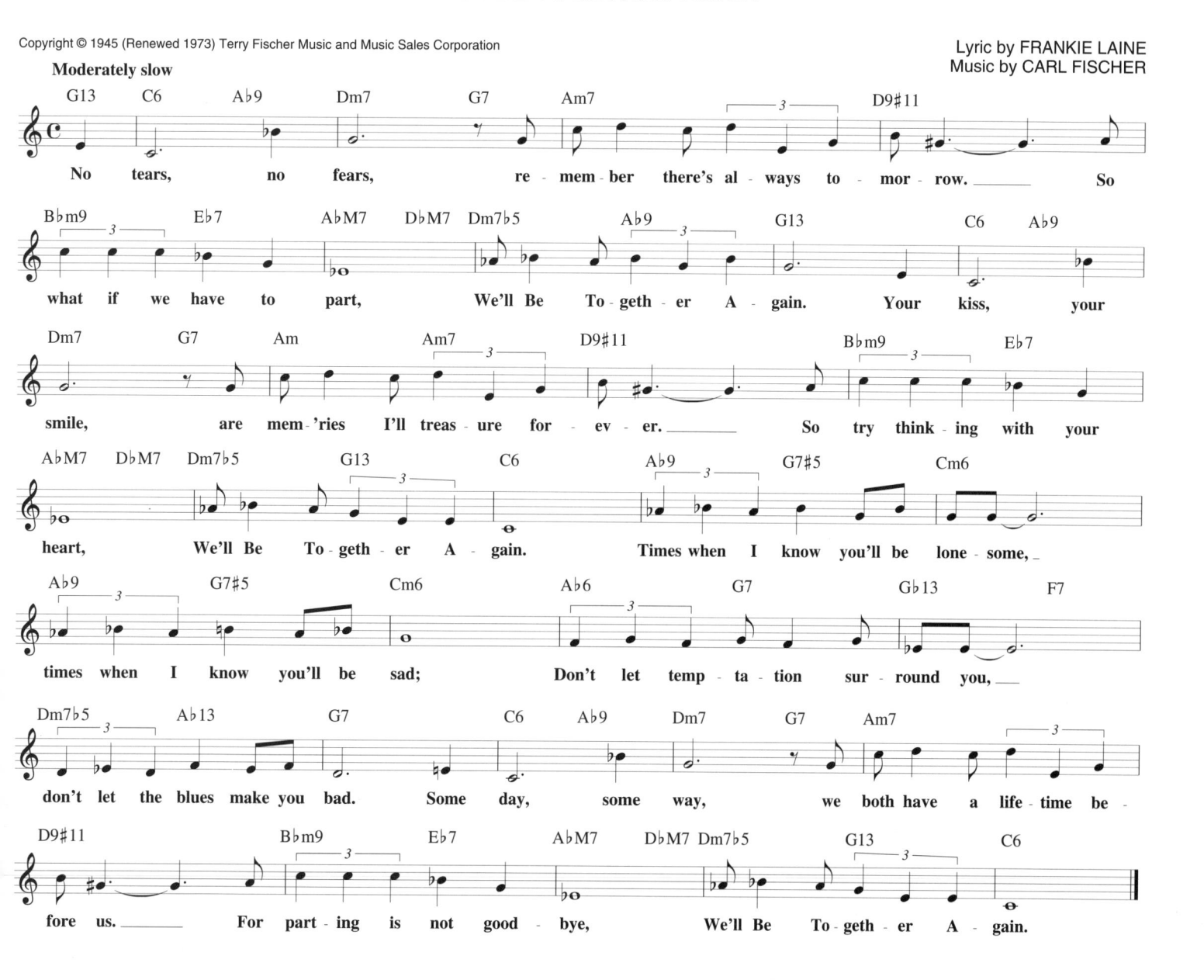

Copyright © 1945 (Renewed 1973) Terry Fischer Music and Music Sales Corporation

Lyric by FRANKIE LAINE
Music by CARL FISCHER

WENDY

WE THREE BLUES

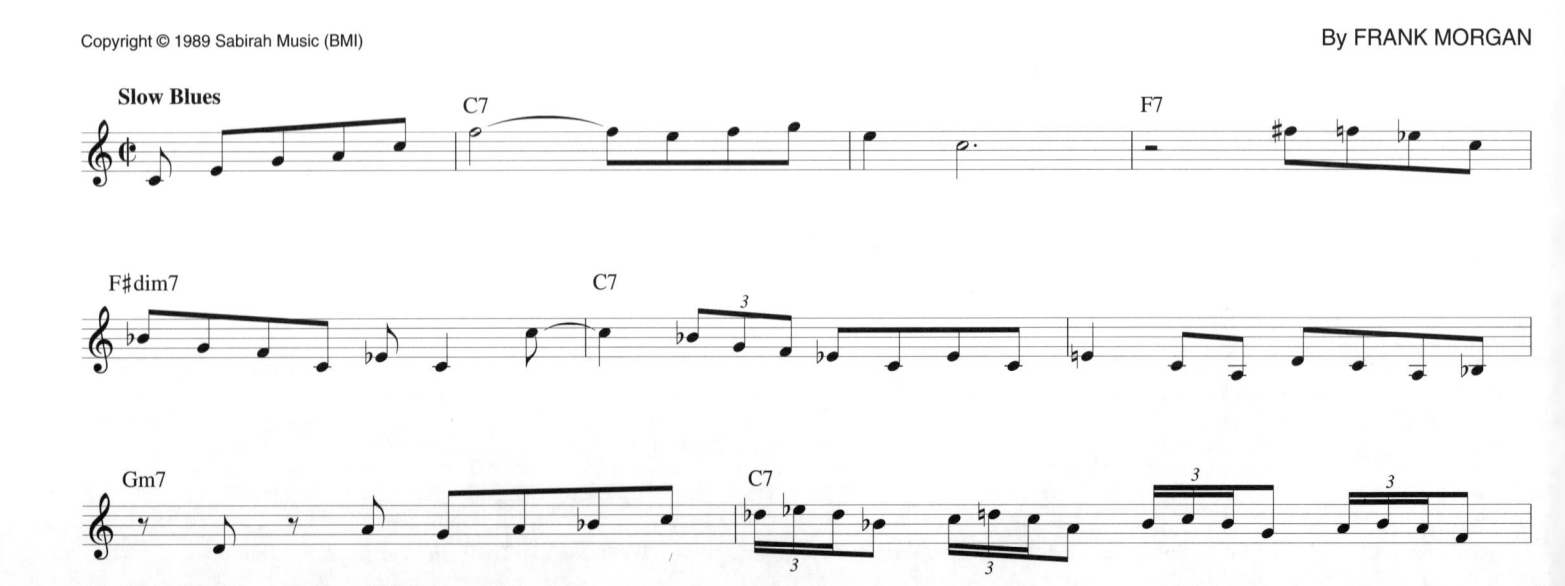

WEST COAST BLUES

By JOHN L. "WES" MONTGOMERY

Copyright © 1960 (Renewed) by TAGGIE MUSIC CO., a division of Gopam Enterprises, Inc.

TWO DEGREES EAST, THREE DEGREES WEST

By JOHN LEWIS

Copyright © 1956 (Renewed 1984) by MJQ Music, Inc.

WHAT IS THERE TO SAY
from THE ZIEGFELD FOLLIES OF 1934

Words and Music by VERNON DUKE
and E.Y. HARBURG

Copyright © 1933 PolyGram International Publishing, Inc.
Copyright Renewed

What Is There To Say and what is there to do? The dream I've been seek-ing has, prac-ti-c'lly speak-ing, come true. What Is There To Say and how will I pull through? I knew in a mo-ment, con-tent-ment and home meant just you. You are so lov-a-ble, so live-a-ble, your beau-ty is just un-for-giv-a-ble, you're made to mar-vel at and words to that ef-fect. So, What Is There To Say and what is there to do? My heart's in a dead-lock, I'd e-ven face wed-lock with you.

WHEN SUNNY GETS BLUE

365

Lyric by JACK SEGAL
Music by MARVIN FISHER

Copyright © 1956 Sony/ATV Tunes LLC
Copyright Renewed
All Rights Administered by Sony/ATV Music Publishing, 8 Music Square West, Nashville, TN 37203

Slow Blues tempo

When Sun-ny Gets Blue, her eyes get gray and cloud-y. Then the rain be-gins to fall. Pit-ter pat-ter, pit-ter pat-ter, love is gone so what can mat-ter? No sweet lov-er man comes to call. When Sun-ny Gets Blue, she breathes a sigh of sad-ness, like the wind that stirs the trees. Wind that sets the leaves to sway-in', like some vi-o-lins are play-in' weird and haunt-ing mel-o-dies. Peo-ple used to love to hear her laugh, see her smile. That's how she got her name. Since that sad af-fair, she's lost her smile, changed her style. Some-how she's not the same. But mem-'ries will fade, and pret-ty dreams will rise up where her oth-er dream fell through. Hur-ry new love, hur-ry here to kiss a-way each lone-ly tear, and hold her near When Sun-ny Gets Blue. Hold her near When Sun-ny Gets Blue.

WHAT DO YOU SEE

By ERNIE WATTS and RIQUE PANTOJA

© 1993 URBAN RENEWAL MUSIC and RIQUE PANTOJA MUSIC
All Rights for URBAN RENEWAL MUSIC Administered by BUG

Slowly

WHAT WILL I TELL MY HEART

Words and Music by IRVING GORDON, PETE TINTURIN and JACK LAWRENCE

Copyright © 1937 by Chappell & Co. and MPL Communications, Inc.
Copyright renewed; extended term of Copyright deriving from Jack Lawrence assigned and effective February 9, 1993 to Range Road Music Inc.
Extended term of Copyright deriving from Irving Gordon and Pete Tinturin Controlled by Chappell & Co.

Very slowly

I'll try to ex-plain to friends, dear, the
eas-y to say to stran-gers that
could say you'll soon be back, dear; to

rea-son we two are a-part; I know what to tell our
we played a game from the start, it's eas-y to lie to
fool the whole town may be smart. I'll tell them you'll soon be

friends, dear, but What Will I Tell My Heart? It's
stran-gers, but
back, dear, but

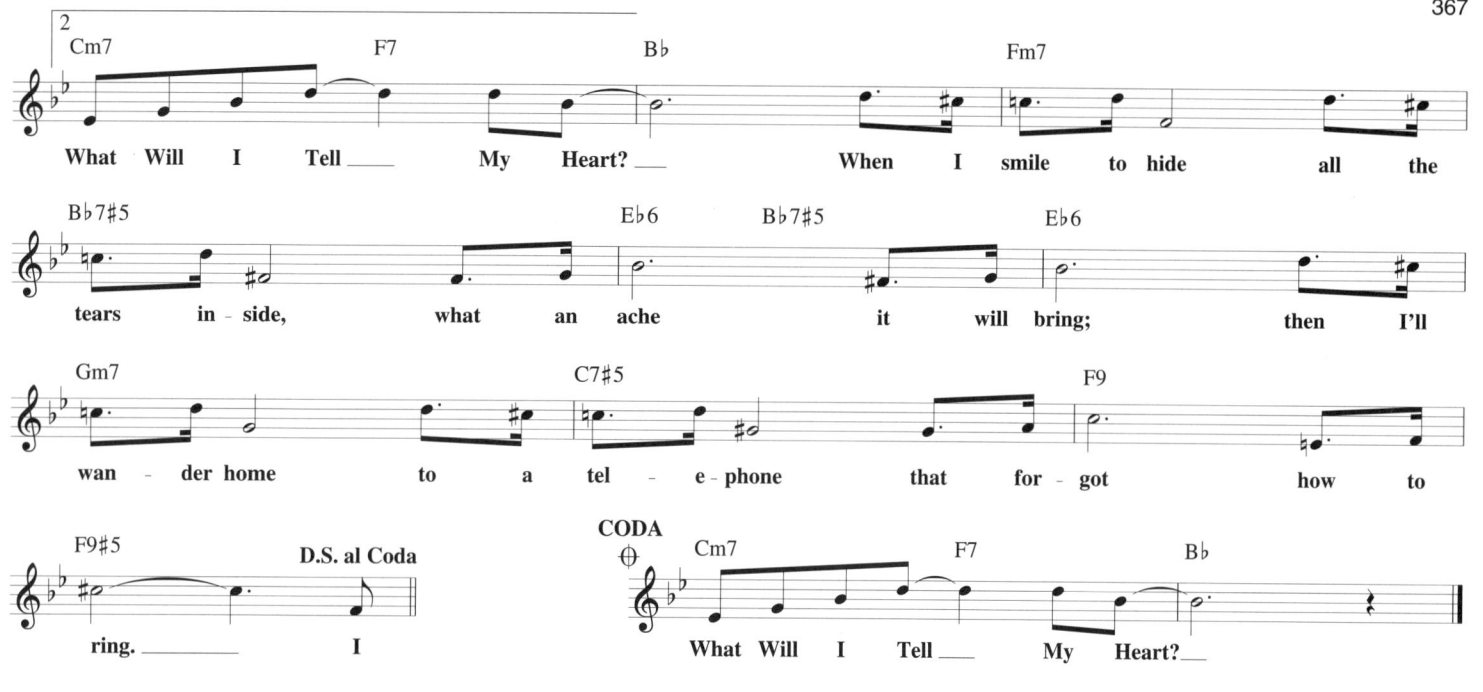

WHEN THE SUN COMES OUT

© 1941 (Renewed 1969) TED KOEHLER and S.A. MUSIC CO.
All Rights for TED KOEHLER MUSIC Administered by
FRED AHLERT MUSIC CORPORATION

Lyric by TED KOEHLER
Music by HAROLD ARLEN

WHOLEY EARTH

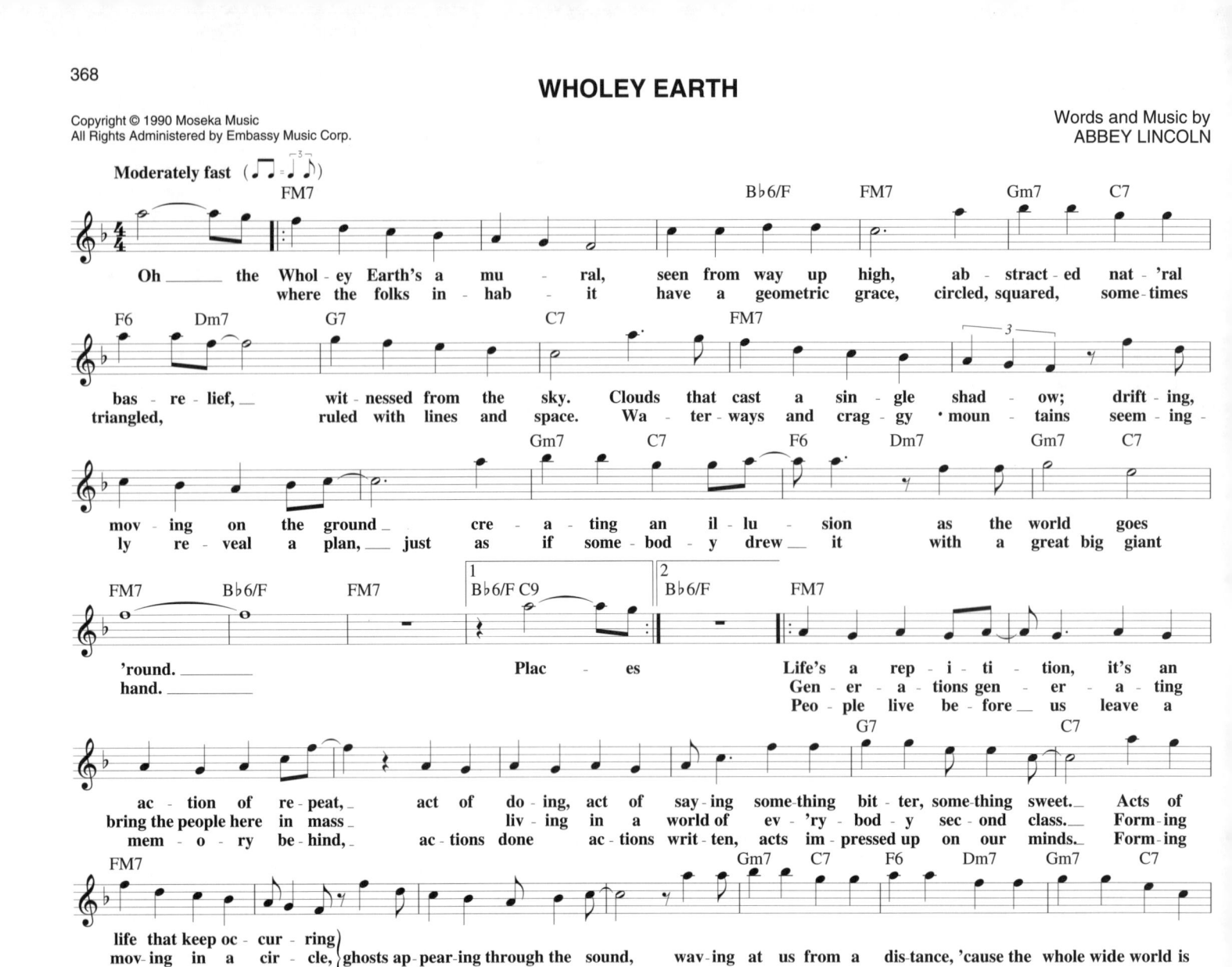

Copyright © 1990 Moseka Music
All Rights Administered by Embassy Music Corp.

Words and Music by
ABBEY LINCOLN

Oh ___ the Whol-ey Earth's a mu-ral, seen from way up high, ab-stract-ed nat-'ral
where the folks in-hab-it have a geo-met-ric grace, cir-cled, squared, some-times

bas re-lief, ___ wit-nessed from the sky. Clouds that cast a sin-gle shad-ow; drift-ing,
tri-an-gled, ruled with lines and space. Wa-ter-ways and crag-gy moun-tains seem-ing-

mov-ing on the ground ___ cre-at-ing an il-lu-sion as the world goes
ly re-veal a plan, ___ just as if some-bod-y drew ___ it with a great big giant

'round. ___ Plac-es Life's a rep-i-ti-tion, it's an
hand. ___ Gen-er-a-tions gen-er-a-ting
Peo-ple live be-fore ___ us leave a

ac-tion of re-peat, ___ act of do-ing, act of say-ing some-thing bit-ter, some-thing sweet. ___ Acts of
bring the people here in mass ___ liv-ing in a world of ev-'ry-bod-y sec-ond class. ___ Form-ing
mem-o-ry be-hind, ___ ac-tions done ac-tions writ-ten, acts im-pressed up-on our minds. ___ Form-ing

life that keep oc-cur-ring
mov-ing in a cir-cle, ghosts ap-pear-ing through the sound, wav-ing at us from a dis-tance, 'cause the whole wide world is
mov-ing in a cir-cle,

round, and round, and round, and round. ___ Yes, the whole wide world is round. ___

WHY WAS I BORN?
from SWEET ADELINE

Copyright © 1929 PolyGram International Publishing, Inc.
Copyright Renewed

Lyrics by OSCAR HAMMERSTEIN II
Music by JEROME KERN

Why Was I Born? ___ Why am I liv-ing? ___ What do I get? ___ What am I

giv-ing? Why do I want a thing I dare-n't hope for? ___ What can I hope for?

___ I wish I knew. ___ Why do I try to draw you near me?

___ Why do I cry? ___ You nev-er hear me. I'm a poor fool, but what can I

do? ___ Why Was I Born to love you? ___

(There'll Be Blue Birds Over)
THE WHITE CLIFFS OF DOVER

Words by NAT BURTON
Music by WALTER KENT

WHY DON'T YOU DO RIGHT
(Get Me Some Money, Too!)

By JOE McCOY

370

WHAT'LL I DO?
from MUSIC BOX REVUE OF 1924

© Copyright 1924 by Irving Berlin
© Arrangement Copyright 1947 by Irving Berlin
Copyright Renewed

Words and Music by
IRVING BERLIN

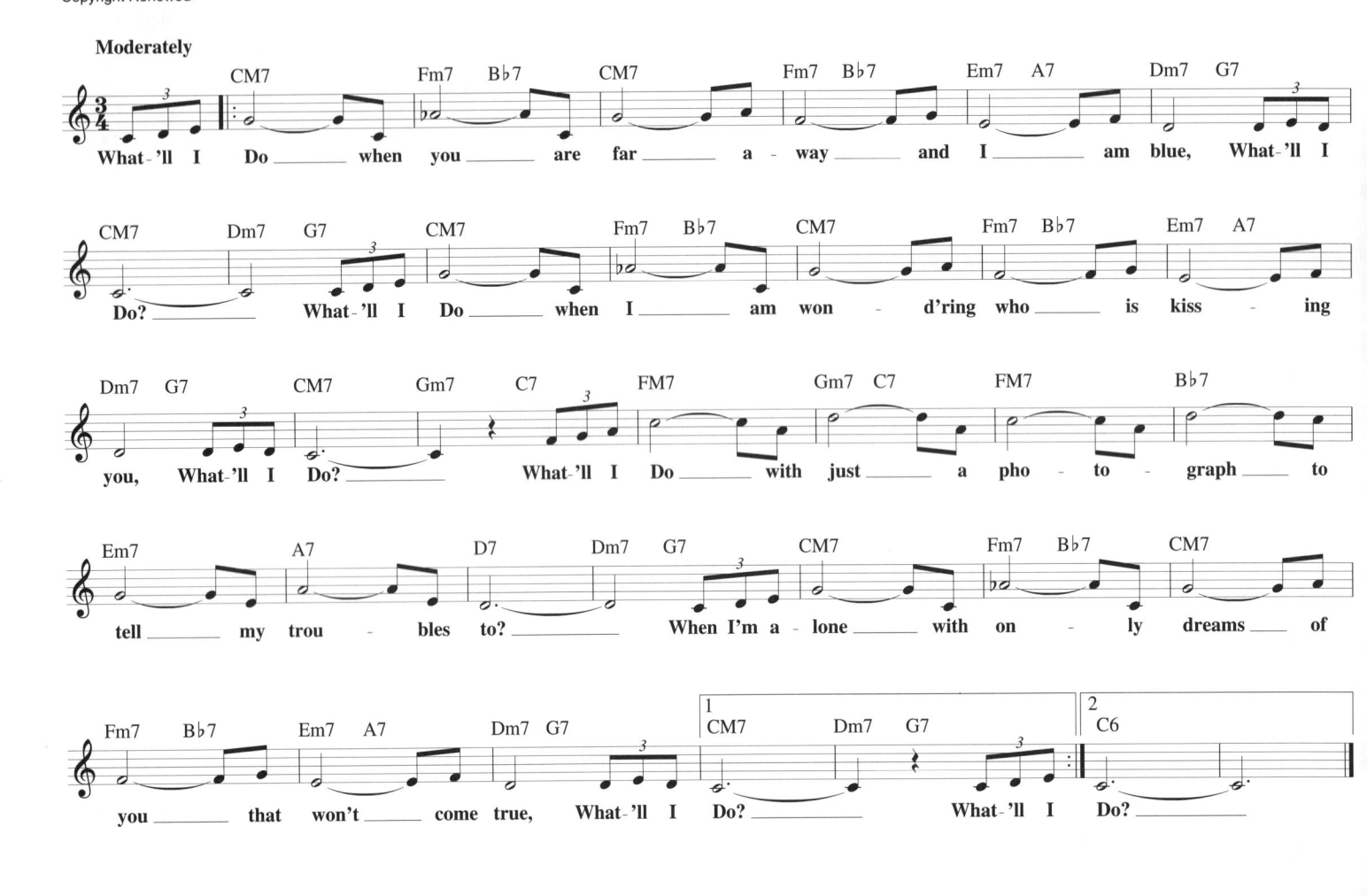

Moderately

What-'ll I Do when you are far a-way and I am blue, What-'ll I Do? What-'ll I Do when I am won-d'ring who is kiss-ing you, What-'ll I Do? What-'ll I Do with just a pho-to-graph to tell my trou-bles to? When I'm a-lone with on-ly dreams of you that won't come true, What-'ll I Do? What-'ll I Do?

THE WIND

Copyright © 1964 (Renewed 1992) Encore Music (ASCAP)

Music by RUSSELL FREEMAN
Lyrics by JERRY GLADSTONE

Slowly

The Wind is cold. I turn up my col-lar in vain. The night is still, the wind's on-ly whirl-ing in my brain. "You fool, you fool." I hear a mourn-ful sigh. "Don't you know your love has gone for-ev-er, why did you ev-er say good-bye?" And so {she's / he's} gone, a mem-'ry has tak-en {her / his} place. These emp-ty arms are hold-ing a ghost in their em-

WINDOWS

By CHICK COREA

© Copyright 1966 by MCA MUSIC PUBLISHING, A Division of UNIVERSAL STUDIOS, INC.
Copyright Renewed

WINTERSONG

By PAUL DESMOND

© 1957 (Renewed) Desmond Music Company

WITHOUT A SONG

Words by WILLIAM ROSE and EDWARD ELISCU
Music by VINCENT YOUMANS

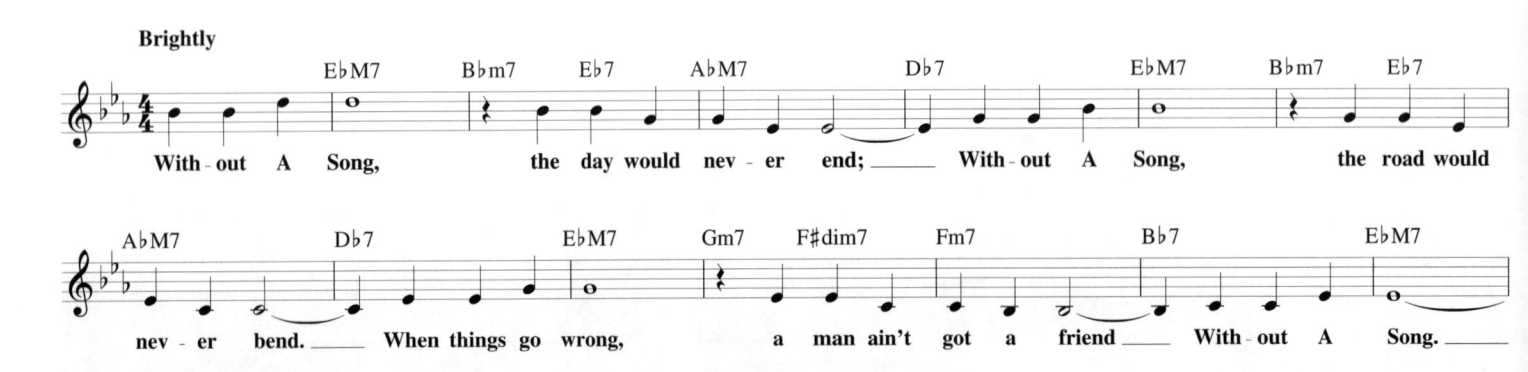

Copyright © 1929 Miller Music Corp. and Vincent Youmans, Inc.
Copyright Renewed and Assigned to Chappell & Co.,
WB Music Corp. and LSQ Music Co.

With-out A Song, the day would nev-er end; ___ With-out A Song, the road would nev-er bend. ___ When things go wrong, a man ain't got a friend ___ With-out A Song. ___

YOU'RE BLASÉ
from BOW BELLS

Copyright © 1931 by Chappell & Co. Ltd.
Copyright Renewed
Published in the USA by Chappell & Co.

Words by BRUCE SIEVIER
Music by ORD HAMILTON

YOU'RE EVERYTHING

Lyric by NEVILLE POTTER
Music by CHICK COREA

© Copyright 1973, 1978 by MCA MUSIC PUBLISHING,
A Division of UNIVERSAL STUDIOS, INC.

Medium Samba

In my life, nothing seems so right as to be with you. And when I'm with you I always sing, You're Ev-'ry-thing. And as time goes by, float-ing like a bird am I. E-ven song birds seem all to sing, You're Ev-'ry-thing. Oh, days are so much fun for those who know that in love all life's a game, and as we go, danc-ing through the sun in love. And as time goes by, float-ing like a bird am I. E-ven song birds I know all sing, You're Ev-'ry-thing.

To Coda

D.C. al Coda

CODA

Repeat ad lib.

WIVES AND LOVERS
(Hey, Little Girl)
from the Paramount Picture WIVES AND LOVERS

Words by HAL DAVID
Music by BURT BACHARACH

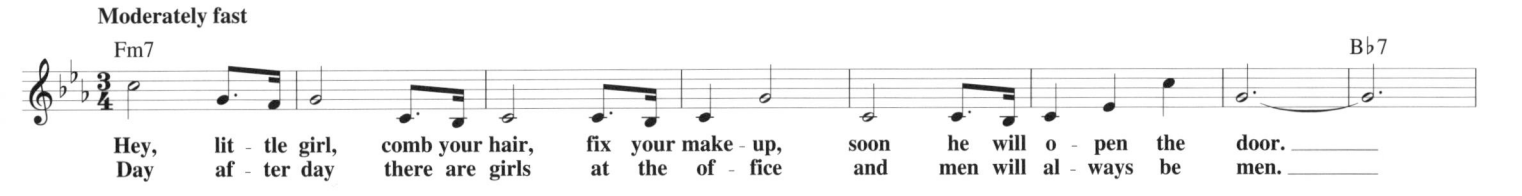

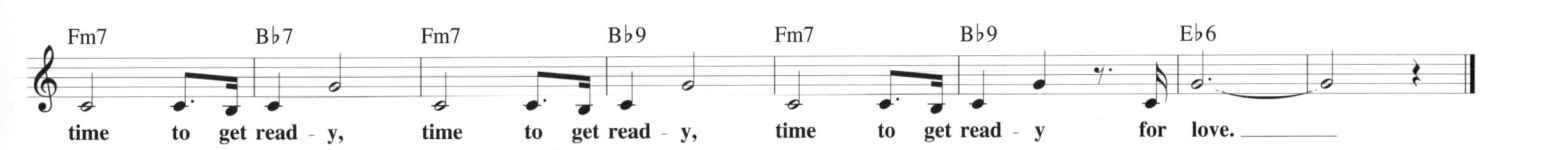

Moderately fast

Hey, lit-tle girl, comb your hair, fix your make-up, soon he will o-pen the door.
Day af-ter day there are girls at the of-fice and men will al-ways be men.

Don't think be-cause there's a ring on your fin-ger you need-n't try an-y-more. For
Don't send him off with your hair still in curl-ers, you may not see him a-gain, for

wives should al-ways be lov-ers too. Run to his arms the mo-ment
wives should al-ways be lov-ers too. Run to his arms the mo-ment

he comes home to you. I'm warn-ing you.
he comes home to you. He's al-most here.

Hey, lit-tle girl, bet-ter wear some-thing pret-ty, some-thing you'd wear to go to the cit-y. And

dim all the lights, pour the wine, start the mu-sic, time to get read-y for love. Oh,

time to get read-y, time to get read-y, time to get read-y for love.

WOODYN' YOU

By DIZZY GILLESPIE

YOU'RE NEARER
from TOO MANY GIRLS

Words by LORENZ HART
Music by RICHARD RODGERS

You're Near-er than my head is to my pil-low, near-er than the wind is to the wil-low. Dear-er than the rain is to the earth be-low, prec-ious as the sun to the things that grow. You're Near-er than the i-vy to the wall is, near-er than the win-ter to the fall is. Leave me, but when you're a-way you'll know You're Near-er for I love you so.

YOU'RE DRIVING ME CRAZY!
(What Did I Do?)

Words and Music by WALTER DONALDSON
Copyright © 1930 (Renewed) by Donaldson Publishing Co.

Slowly

You! You're Driv-ing Me Cra-zy. What did I do? What did I do?
My tears for you make ev-'ry-thing ha-zy, cloud-ing the skies
of blue. How true were the friends who were near me, to cheer me, be-lieve me, they knew.
But you were the kind who would hurt me, de-sert me, when I need-ed you! Yes!
You! You're Driv-ing Me Cra-zy! What did I do to you?

YOU'RE MINE YOU

Words by EDWARD HEYMAN
Music by JOHN W. GREEN
Copyright © 1933 (Renewed 1960) by Famous Music Corporation

Slowly

You're Mine, You! You be-long to me, you! I will nev-er free you, you're here with
me to stay. You're Mine, You. You are mine com-plete-ly, love me strong or sweet-ly,
I need you night and day. Arm in arm, hand in hand, we will be found to-geth-er.
Heart to heart, lips to lips, we're chained and bound to-geth-er. I own you,
I don't need to buy love, you're a slave to my love. In ev-'ry way, you're mine.

YOU ARE TOO BEAUTIFUL
from HALLELUJAH, I'M A BUM

Words by LORENZ HART
Music by RICHARD RODGERS

Copyright © 1932 by Williamson Music and The Estate Of Lorenz Hart in the United States
Copyright Renewed
All Rights on behalf of The Estate Of Lorenz Hart Administered by WB Music Corp.

Slowly, with expression

You Are Too Beau-ti-ful, my dear, to be true, and I am a fool for beau-ty.
You Are Too Beau-ti-ful for one man a-lone, for one luck-y fool to be with,
Fooled by a feel-ing that be-cause I had found you, I could have bound you, too.
when there are oth-er men with eyes of their own to see.
with. Love does not stand shar-ing, not if one cares. Have you been com-par-ing
my ev-'ry kiss with theirs? If on the oth-er hand I'm faith-ful to you, it's
not through a sense of du-ty. You Are Too Beau-ti-ful and I am a fool for beau-ty.

YOU COULDN'T BE CUTER
from JOY OF LIVING

Lyric by DOROTHY FIELDS
Music by JEROME KERN

Copyright © 1938 by PolyGram International Publishing, Inc.
Copyright Renewed

Moderately

You Could-n't Be Cut-er, plus that you could-n't be smart-er, plus that in-tel-li-gent face, you
have a dis-grace-ful charm for me. You could-n't be keen-er, you look so
fresh from the clean-er, you are the lit-tle grand slam I'll bring to my fam-i-ly.
My ma will show you an al-bum of me that'll bore you to tears! And

YOU BROUGHT A NEW KIND OF LOVE TO ME
from the Paramount Picture THE BIG POND

Copyright © 1930 (Renewed 1957) by Famous Music Corporation

Words and Music by SAMMY FAIN, IRVING KAHAL and PIERRE NORMAN

Moderately

If the night-in-gales could sing like you, they'd sing much sweet-er than they do, for you've brought a new kind of love to me. If the sand-man brought me dreams of you, I'd want to sleep my whole life through, for you've brought a new kind of love to me. I know that I'm the slave, you're the queen, but still you can un-der-stand that un-der-neath it all, you're a maid and I am on-ly a man. I would work and slave the whole day through if I could hur-ry home to you, for you've brought a new kind of love to me.

YOU DON'T KNOW WHAT LOVE IS

Words and Music by DON RAYE
and GENE DePAUL

YOU'VE MADE ME SO VERY HAPPY

Words and Music by BERRY GORDY, FRANK E. WILSON,
BRENDA HOLLOWAY and PATRICE HOLLOWAY

381

Am7		Bm7 Am7/D		

You treat-ed me so kind, I'm a-bout to blow my mind. You Made Me So
You al-ways showed me that lov-ing you was where it's at.

Ver-y Hap-py; I'm so glad you came in-to my life.

GM7   Bm7/E

F
I love you so much, it seems that you're e-ven in my dreams. I hear you call-ing me.

C   G

F   Em7/A   Am7/D
I'm so in love with you. All I ev-er want to do is thank you, ba-by, thank you, thank you ba-by.

Repeat and Fade

GM7   Bm7/E
You made me so ver-y hap-py, I'm so glad you came in-to my life.

YOU LEAVE ME BREATHLESS
from the Paramount Motion Picture COCONUT GROVE

Copyright © 1938 (Renewed 1967) by Famous Music Corporation

Words by RALPH FREED
Music by FREDERICK K. HOLLANDER

Moderately

Gm7b5   C7   A7b9   Dm7   G9
You Leave Me Breath-less, you heav-en-ly thing. You look so

F   F#dim7   C7   C7#5   F6   F#dim7   Gm7b5
won-der-ful, you're like a breath of spring. You have me speech-less, I'm

C7   A7b9   Dm7   G9   F   F#dim7   C7   C7b9
just like the birds, I'm filled with mel-o-dy, but at a loss for

F6   Eb9   F6   Db7   Gm7b5   C7   F6
words. That lit-tle grin of yours, that fun-ny chin of yours, does so much to my heart.

Db7   Gm7b5   Gm7
Oh! Give your lips to me, for, dar-ling, that would be the fi-nal touch to my heart.

C7   F#dim7   Gm7b5   C7   C#dim7   Dm7   G9
You Leave Me Breath-less, that's all I can say. I can't say

F   F#dim7   C7   C7b9 |1. F6   F#dim7 |2. F6   Bbm6   F6
more, be-cause you take my breath a-way. You Leave Me way.

YOU TOOK ADVANTAGE OF ME
from PRESENT ARMS

Words by LORENZ HART
Music by RICHARD RODGERS

I'm a sent-i-ment-al sap, that's all. What's the use of try-ing not to fall? I
have no will, You've made your kill 'cause You Took Ad-van-tage Of Me!

I'm just like an ap-ple on a bough and you're gon-na shake me down some-how. So
what's the use, you've cooked my goose 'cause You Took Ad-van-tage Of

Me! I'm so hot and both-ered that I don't know my el-bow from my
ear; I suf-fer some-thing aw-ful each time you go and much worse when you're
near. Here am I with all my bridg-es burned, just a babe in arms where
you're con-cerned. So lock the doors and call me yours, 'cause You Took Ad-van-tage Of Me!

YOU'VE CHANGED

Words and Music by BILL CAREY and CARL FISCHER

You've Changed, the spar-kle in your eyes is gone, your
Changed, your kis-ses now are so bla-sé, you're
Changed, you're not the an-gel I once knew, no

smile is just a care-less yawn, you're break-ing my heart, You've Changed.
bored with me in ev-'ry way, I
need to tell me that we're through, it's

You've can't un-der-stand, You've Changed. You've for-
got-ten the words "I love you," each mem-o-ry that we've shared. You ignore ev-'ry star a-bove you, I can't re-a-lize you ev-er cared.

D.C. al Coda   CODA

You've all o-ver now, You've Changed.

THE ULTIMATE JAZZ FAKE BOOK

FINALLY! THE JAZZ COLLECTION THAT EVERYONE'S BEEN WAITING FOR!

THE ULTIMATE JAZZ FAKE BOOK INCLUDES:

- More than 625 songs important to every jazz library.
- Carefully chosen chords with some common practice chord substitutions.
- Lyrics to accommodate vocalists.
- Easy-to-read music typography.
- Composer and performer indexes.

The selection of songs in *The Ultimate Jazz Fake Book* is a result of an exhaustive effort to represent the many styles of music that make up that beloved idiom we call jazz. The styles found in this collection include: traditional, swing, bebop, Latin/bossa nova, hard bop/modern jazz and Tin Pan Alley standards/show tunes.

MORE THAN 625 SONGS INCLUDING:

After You've Gone • Afternoon In Paris • Ain't Misbehavin' • Air Mail Special • All Of Me • All The Things You Are • Along Came Betty • Alright, Okay, You Win • Among My Souvenirs • And All That Jazz • Angel Eyes • Autumn Leaves • Baby, Won't You Please Come Home • Bag's Groove • Basin Street Blues • Bernie's Tune • Bewitched • Billie's Bounce • Birdland • Blue Champagne • Blues For Pablo • Bluesette • Body And Soul • Button Up Your Overcoat • Caldonia • Carolina Moon • C.C. Rider • Cherokee • Confirmation • Cry Me A River • Darn That Dream • Deed I Do • Dinah • Django • Do You Know What It Means To Miss New Orleans • Donna Lee • Don't Get Around Much Anymore • Donna Lee • Down By The Riverside • Ev'ry Time We Say Goodbye • Everybody Loves My Baby • Everything's Coming Up Roses • Falling In Love With Love • Fever • A Fine Romance • Fly Me To The Moon • A Foggy Day • (I Love You) For Sentimental Reasons • Four • Gee Baby, Ain't I Good To You • The Girl From Ipanema • The Glory Of Love • The Glow Worm • A Good Man Is Hard To Find • Groovin' High • Happy Talk • Harlem Nocturne • Haunted Heart • How High The Moon • I Can't Get Started • I Concentrate On You • I Could Write A Book • I Cover The Waterfront • I Don't Know Why (I Just Do) • I Got Plenty O' Nuttin' • I Love Paris • I Remember Duke • I'll Remember April • I'll Take Romance • I'm Old-Fashioned • If I Were A Bell • In A Little Spanish Town • In The Mood • Is You Is, Or Is You Ain't (Ma Baby) • It Might As Well Be Spring • It's Only A Paper Moon • Jelly Roll Blues • Jersey Bounce • The Joint Is Jumpin' • King Porter Stomp • The Lady Is A Tramp • Lester Left Town • Let's Call The Whole Thing Off • Let's Fall In Love • Little Boat • Little Brown Jug • Love For Sale • Love Walked In • Lullaby Of Birdland • Lush Life • Mad About The Boy • Malaguena • The Man That Got Away • Maple Leaf Rag • Misty • Moonglow • Moonlight In Vermont • More • Moten Swing • My Funny Valentine • My Melancholy Baby • My Romance • A Night In Tunisia • A Nightingale Sang In Berkeley Square • Old Devil Moon • One Note Samba • Opus One • Ornithology • Paper Doll • People Will Say We're In Love • Quiet Nights Of Quiet Stars • 'Round Midnight • Route 66 • Ruby, My Dear • Satin Doll • Sentimental Journey • Shivers • Skylark • Slightly Out Of Tune (Desafinado) • Solar • Solitude • Song For My Father • Speak Low • Stompin' At The Savoy • A String Of Pearls • Summer Samba • Take The "A" Train • There's A Small Hotel • The Thrill Is Gone • Tuxedo Junction • Undecided • Unforgettable • Waltz For Debby • 'Way Down Yonder In New Orleans • The Way You Look Tonight • We Kiss In A Shadow • When I Fall In Love • Witchcraft • Woodchopper's Ball • You Made Me Love You • You'd Be So Nice To Come Home To • You're My Everything • and many, many more!

Spanning more than nine decades of music, *The Ultimate Jazz Fake Book* fills a void for many musicians whose active repertories could not possibly include this vast collection of classic jazz compositions and durable songs.

FOR MORE INFORMATION, SEE YOUR LOCAL MUSIC DEALER, OR WRITE TO:

HAL•LEONARD® CORPORATION

7777 W. BLUEMOUND RD. P.O. BOX 13819 MILWAUKEE, WI 53213

Available in three editions:

00240079	C Edition	$39.95
00240081	E♭ Edition	$39.95
00240080	B♭ Edition	$39.95

Price, contents, and availability subject to change without notice.